KYOTO AREA STUDIES ON ASIA

CENTER FOR SOUTHEAST ASIAN STUDIES, KYOTO UNIVERSITY

VOLUME 16

East Asian Economies and New Regionalism

KYOTO AREA STUDIES ON ASIA

CENTER FOR SOUTHEAST ASIAN STUDIES, KYOTO UNIVERSITY

The Nation and Economic Growth: Korea and Thailand
YOSHIHARA Kunio

One Malay Village: A Thirty-Year Community Study
TSUBOUCHI Yoshihiro

Commodifying Marxism:
The Formation of Modern Thai Radical Culture, 1927–1958
Kasian TEJAPIRA

Gender and Modernity: Perspectives from Asia and the Pacific
HAYAMI Yoko, TANABE Akio, TOKITA-TANABE Yumiko

Practical Buddhism among the Thai-Lao:
Religion in the Making of a Region
HAYASHI Yukio

The Political Ecology of Tropical Forests in Southeast Asia:
Historical Perspectives
LYE Tuck-Po, Wil DE JONG, ABE Ken-ichi

Between Hills and Plains:
Power and Practice in Socio-Religious Dynamics among Karen
HAYAMI Yoko

Ecological Destruction, Health and Development:
Advancing Asian Paradigms
FURUKAWA Hisao, NISHIBUCHI Mitsuaki, KONO Yasuyuki, KAIDA Yoshihiro

Searching for Vietnam:
Selected Writings on Vietnamese Culture and Society
A. Terry RAMBO

Laying the Tracks: The Thai Economy and its Railways 1885–1935
KAKIZAKI Ichiro

After the Crisis:
Hegemony, Technocracy and Governance in Southeast Asia
SHIRAISHI Takashi, Patricio N. ABINALES

Dislocating Nation-States: Globalization in Asia and Africa
Patricio N. ABINALES, ISHIKAWA Noboru and TANABE Akio

People on the Move: Rural–Urban Interactions in Sarawak
SODA Ryoji

Living on the Periphery: Development and Islamization among the Orang Asli
NOBUTA Toshihiro

Myths and Realities: The Democratization of Thai Politics
TAMADA Yoshifumi

East Asian Economies and New Regionalism
ABE Shigeyuki and Bhanupong NIDHIPRABA

The Rise of Middle Classes in Southeast Asia
SHIRAISHI Takashi and Pasuk PHONGPAICHIT

KYOTO AREA STUDIES ON ASIA

CENTER FOR SOUTHEAST ASIAN STUDIES, KYOTO UNIVERSITY

VOLUME 16

East Asian Economies and New Regionalism

ABE Shigeyuki

and

Bhanupong NIDHIPRABA

Kyoto University Press

The publication of this volume was partially funded by the JSPS Global COE Program (E-04): In Search of Sustainable Humanosphere in Asia and Africa.

First published in 2008 jointly by:

Kyoto University Press
Kyodai Kaikan
15-9 Yoshida Kawara-cho
Sakyo-ku, Kyoto 606-8305, Japan
Telephone: +81-75-761-6182
Fax: +81-75-761-6190
Email: sales@kyoto-up.or.jp
Web: http://www.kyoto-up.or.jp

Trans Pacific Press
PO Box 164, Balwyn North, Melbourne
Victoria 3104, Australia
Telephone: +61 3 9859 1112
Fax: +61 3 9859 4110
Email: tpp.mail@gmail.com
Web: http://www.transpacificpress.com

Copyright © Kyoto University Press and Trans Pacific Press 2008

Figures and tables set by Kyoto University Press.

Printed in Melbourne by BPA Print Group

Distributors

Australia and New Zealand
UNIREPS
University of New South Wales
Sydney, NSW 2052
Australia
Telephone: +61(0)2-9664-0999
Fax: +61(0)2-9664-5420
Email: info.press@unsw.edu.au
Web: http://www.unireps.com.au

USA and Canada
International Specialized Book
Services (ISBS)
920 NE 58th Avenue, Suite 300
Portland, Oregon 97213-3786
USA
Telephone: (800) 944-6190
Fax: (503) 280-8832
Email: orders@isbs.com
Web: http://www.isbs.com

Asia and the Pacific
Kinokuniya Company Ltd.

Head office:
Shin-Mizonokuchi Bldg. 2F
5-7 Hisamoto 3-chome
Takatsu-ku, Kawasaki 213-8506
Japan
Telephone: +81(0)44-874-9642
Fax: +81(0)44-829-1025
Email: bkimp@kinokuniya.co.jp
Web: www.kinokuniya.co.jp

Asia-Pacific office:
Kinokuniya Book Stores of Singapore Pte., Ltd.
391B Orchard Road #13-06/07/08
Ngee Ann City Tower B
Singapore 238874
Telephone: +65 6276 5558
Fax: +65 6276 5570
Email: SSO@kinokuniya.co.jp

ISSN   1445–9663 (Kyoto Area Studies on Asia)
ISBN   978–1–920901–23–3

Contents

List of Figures   vi
List of Boxes   vi
List of Tables   vii
List of Contributors   xi

Introduction   *Shigeyuki Abe and Bhanupong Nidhipraba*   1

1   The New Development Paradigm in East Asia
    Mahani Zainal-Abidin   14
2   The Emergence and Proliferation of FTAs in East Asia
    Shujiro Urata   39
3   ASEAN's Strategy toward an Increasing Asian Integration
    Suthiphand Chirathivat   81
4   ASEAN, China and India: Are They More Competitive or
    Complementary to Each Other? *Yumiko Okamoto*   109
5   Aging and Productivity Growth for the Japanese Manufacturing
    Industries *Shandre M. Thangavelu and Shigeyuki Abe*   126
6   Productivity, Technological Progress and Factor Substitution in the
    Malaysian Manufacturing Sector *Lai Yew Wah*   141
7   Rural Economy in Myanmar at the Crossroads: With Special
    Reference to Rice Policies *Koichi Fujita*   160
8   Social Safety Nets in Southeast Asia: With Special Reference to
    Thailand *Srawooth Paitoonpong and Shigeyuki Abe*   193
9   Credit Crunch in East Asia: A Retrospective
    Masahiro Enya, Akira Kohsaka and Mervin Pobre   231
10   Contractionary Devaluation Revisited: Can Appreciation be
    Expansionary? *Bhanupong Nidhiprabha*   249
11   The Role of the Investment Climate in East Asia: What Really
    Matters? *Shoko Negishi*   275

Index   295

List of Figures

2-1	Exports of Developing East Asia and Latin America	79
2-2	FDI Inflows in Developing East Asia and Latin America	79
2-3	RTA in the World	80
3-1	Regional Integration Schemes among the Three Blocs from an ASEAN Perspective	93
4-1	Matrix of RCA Index and IIT Index	118
5-A1	Labor Force by Age in Japan in 2001	139
5-A2	Labor Force by Age Category for Singapore in 2000	139
7-1	Rice Production and Export in Myanmar	167
7-2	International versus Domestic Rice Price	168
7-3	Wholesale Price of Rice in Yangon	186
9-1	Actual Loan and Estimated Loan Demand and Supply	240
9-2	Macroeconomic Indicators	243
9-A1	Data Appendix	246
10-1	Impulse Response Functions to Change in Exchange Rate Depreciation	266
10-2	Currency Appreciation and Growth	269
10-3	Domestic Credit and Investment	269
10-4	Exchange Rate Appreciation and Current Account in 2007	271
11-1	Trends in External Finance to Developing Countries	277
11-2	Concentration of FDI	279
11-3	Regional Trends in FDI	279
11-4	FDI Flows in East Asia	280
11-5	M&A Sales in East Asia	281
11-6	FDI and Investment Climate in Developing Countries	282

List of Boxes

8-1	Thailand: Strengthening the Social Safety Net	218

List of Tables

1-1 Export and Import Growth Rates in Selected East Asian Countries 17
1-2 Growth and Inflation Rates in Selected East Asian Countries 17
1-3 Sharing the Fruits of Economic Growth: Social Indicators for Asia 18
1-4 GDP Contraction, Exchange Rate, Stock Market and Capital
 Outflow 19
1-5 Performance of Crisis Economies in 2000 25
1-A1 Growth Rates for East Asian Countries 1970–2002 35
1-A2 Fiscal Balance (% of GDP) 1990–2002 35
1-A3 Reserves (US$mn) 1990–2002 36
1-A4 FDI Inflows (US$mn) 1990–2002 37
2-1 International Trade of East Asian Economies in the 1980s and
 1990s 66
2-2 Foreign Direct Investment (FDI) Flows of East Asian Economies
 in the 1980s and 1990s 68
2-3 Intra-Regional Dependence for Trade and FDI 70
2-4 Sources of Inward Foreign Direct Investment in East Asian
 Economies 71
2-5 Sources of Inputs in Production for East Asian Economies 1985
 and 1995 72
2-6 Inter-Economy, Inter-Industry Linkages in East Asia 73
2-7 Procurements and Sales of Foreign Affiliates of Japanese Firms
 1992 and 1998 74
2-8 Intra-Firm Transactions in Procurements and Sales of Foreign
 Affiliates of Japanese Firms 1992 and 1998 76
2-9 Selected FTAs in East Asia (as of June 2004) 77
2-10 Effects of East Asia FTA on Real GDP and Equivalent Variation 77
2-11 Effects of East Asia FTA on Production by Sectors 78
3-1 Relative Importance of Intra-ASEAN Trade 84
3-2 Number of Tariff Lines in the Tentative 2003 CEPT Package 85
3-3 Number of Tariff Lines at 0–5% in the Tentative 2003 CEPT
 Package 86
3-4 FDI Inflows to ASEAN, China and Asian NIEs 87
3-5 Key Features of the AEC 90
3-6 Preferential Trade Agreement Participation in East Asia 96
3-7 Implications of Tariff Liberalization under FTAs with Different
 Trading Partners for the Total Welfare of Thailand 98

3-A1 Implications of ASEAN Agreements on Trade and FDI   102
3-A2 FDI Response to Regional Economic Integration   104
4-1   Shares of ASEAN, China and India in the World Economy   111
4-2   Export Orientated FDI Projects in Call Centers, Shared Services
      Centers (SSCs) and IT Services by Destination 2002–2003   112
4-3   Inflow of FDI in ASEAN, China and India, and their Shares in the
      World Total   113
4-4   Spearman's Rank Correlations Coefficients of the Rankings of the
      RCA Indexes between ASEAN and China, and ASEAN and India   115
4-5   IIT Indexes Between ASEAN, China and India   117
4-6   Shares of ASEAN, China and India in the Major International
      Markets   120
4-7   Spearman's Rank Correlation Coefficients of the Rankings of the
      Market Shares in the U.S. between ASEAN and China   122
4-8   Spearman's Rank Correlation Coefficients of the Ranking of the
      Market Share in Japan between ASEAN and China   123
5-1   The Growth Rate of Labor Quality by Age for Selected Japanese
      Manufacturing Industries 1990–1999   132
5-2   The Growth Rate of Labor Quality by Education for Selected
      Japanese Manufacturing Industries 1990–1999   134
5-3   The Growth Rate of Total Labor Quality and Contribution to
      Labor Productivity Growth for Selected Japanese Manufacturing
      Industries 1990–1999   135
5-4   Contribution of Labor Quality to Productivity Growth for the
      Manufacturing Sector for Japan and Singapore 1990–1999   137
5-5   Sources of Growth for Japan and Singapore 1990–1999   137
6-1   Growth Rates in Labor and Capital Productivities   145
6-2   Growth Rates in Unit Labor Cost and Capital Intensity   147
6-3   Growth Rates in Output, Inputs and TFP in the Manufacturing
      Sector 1981–2000   149
6-4   Contribution to Growth in the Manufacturing Sector 1981–2000   150
6-5   Elasticity of Substitution in the Manufacturing Sector 1981–2000   153
6-6   Rate of Technical Progress in the Manufacturing Sector 1981–2000   154
7-1   GDP Growth and Sectoral Shares in Myanmar since 1988   163
7-2   Employment Structure   163
7-3   Investment and Saving Rates   164
7-4   Investment and Saving Rates in Southeast Asia   164
7-5   Balance of Payments   164
7-6   Public Sector Budget   165
7-7   Inflation and Depreciation of the Currency   166

7-8   Distribution of Sampled Households   170
7-9   Distribution of Major Assets among Sampled Households   172
7-10 Process of Diffusion of Farm Machineries   173
7-11 Disposal of Produced Paddy   175
7-12 Cost and Return of Monsoon Paddy Production   176
7-13 Cost and Return of Summer Paddy Production   178
7-14 List of Borrowers from Informal Sources   182
8-1   Sources of Income for the Elderly (60 years and older) in Thailand
      and Selected Countries 1996   214
8-2   NGOs by Field of Service and Region   217
8-3   Budget for Grassroots Economic Policy and Social Safety Nets
      Programs   224
9-1   Parameter Estimates of the Loan Demand and Supply Functions   237
9-2   Credit Crunch Periods   242
9-3   Summary of Results on Credit Crunch in East Asia in the 1997
      Crisis Period   242
10-1 Key Macroeconomic Variables 1994–2001   252
10-2 Deviation During the Crisis from Normal Episodes   254
10-3 Correlation Coefficients among Key Macroeconomic Variables   254
10-4 Variance Decomposition of Variables from VAR   267
11-1 FDI and the Investment Climate   285
11-2 FDI and Investment Climate by Components   287
11-3 Estimated Cumulative FDI Changes from Increases in ICRG
      Indices by 1% 2003–05   288
11-A1 Categories of Country Policy and Institutional Assessment   290
11-A2 Categories of International Country Risk Guide   291
11-A3 List of Countries   292

List of Contributors

Shigeyuki Abe, Professor, Faculty of Policy Studies, Center for Contemporary Asian Studies, Doshisha University

Bhanupong Nidhipraba, Associate Professor, Thammasat University

Mahani Zainal-Abidin, Director General, Institute of Strategic and International Studies, Malaysia

Shujiro Urata, Professor of International Economics, Graduate School of Asia-Pacific Studies, Waseda University

Suthiphand Chirathivat, Chairman, Economics Research Center and Center for International Economics, Faculty of Economics, Chulalongkorn University

Yumiko Okamoto, Professor, Faculty of Policy Studies, Doshisha University

Shandre M. Thangavelu, Associate Professor, Department of Economics, National University of Singapore

Lai Yew Wah, Former Professor, Universiti Sains Malaysia

Koichi Fujita, Professor, Division of Economics and Politics, Center for Southeast Asian Studies, Kyoto University

Srawooth Paitoonpong, Senior Research Specialist, Human Resources and Social Development Program, Thailand Development Research Institute

Masahiro Enya, Associate Professor, Department of Politics, Economics, and Law, Osaka International University

Akira Kohsaka, Professor, Osaka School of International Public Policy, Osaka University

Mervin Pobre, Senior Manager, Customer Acquisition and Relationship Management Department, American Express

Shoko Negishi, Professor, Faculty of Policy Studies, Doshisha University

Introduction

Shigeyuki Abe and Bhanupong Nidhipraba

The occasion of the tenth anniversary of the Asian financial crisis has been a time for many in the international community to reflect upon its various causes, the ways in which affected countries have responded and the prospects for the wider Asian economy in the coming years. Academic conferences have been held around the world to coincide with the anniversary and a degree of consensus has now emerged among intellectuals and policy makers regarding a number of aspects of the crisis. Asia was severely damaged by the largely unexpected events of the summer of 1997. With the exception of Thailand, traditional macroeconomic imbalances were not evident beforehand and did not play a major role in what occurred. Rather, weaknesses in the financial and corporate sectors, which were not widely recognized at the time, were the primary causes. Pegged exchange rates with excessive unhedged foreign borrowing and inadequate reserve levels were also important contributing factors.

East Asian countries have made considerable progress in strengthening the systemic weaknesses that the crisis exposed and in the past ten years Asia has bounced back to become once more one of the most dynamic regions of the world economy. Asia as a whole now has the opportunity to consolidate its position and advance to a level of economic prosperity unprecedented in modern times. If anything, this prospect makes the second post-crisis decade even more important for Asian economies than the first. Making the right policy choices now will be vital and several important policy debates are at present taking place within the region and beyond. This volume contributes to these debates by grounding them firmly in the progress made in the post-crisis years. The title—East Asia and New Regionalism—may perhaps require a few words of explanation.

The 'new regionalism' characterizing the process of economic integration in Asia today began slowly in the 1990s and started to accelerate after 1997. The term 'new' captures not only the sense that it is different from past forms of regionalism in Asia, such as the post-war experience of the American umbrella, but also the fact that it is substantially a new type of regionalism in the world economy, different in kind from the EU or NAFTA, for example. New regionalism has been market-driven, rather than government-led. It derives in part from the increased fragmentation of production processes facilitated by high levels of foreign direct investment (FDI). It has no single geographical

1

center, nor yet does it have a clear leader—neither ASEAN, nor China, nor Japan, though each of these could conceivably play that role. New regionalism has benefited from pursuing trade liberalization and from the dynamic gains that have resulted from Free Trade Agreements (FTAs).

The particular nature of these FTAs is another essential feature of new regionalism. Compared to other regions, Asian FTAs tend to be bilateral, these being easier to negotiate than comprehensive regional agreements; a more integrated regional approach is meanwhile sought in such forums as APEC or ASEAN+3. In addition, the FTAs are mostly in the form of Economic Partnership Agreements (EPAs), which include measures for broader economic cooperation on top of traditional tariff-reduction agreements. Furthermore, Asian countries seek to negotiate FTAs that are consistent with WTO rules and try to make them building blocks for future cooperation beyond the region, not stumbling blocks preventing such progress.

In East Asia, economic growth has been powered by exports and supported by flows of FDI. This has led to increasingly region-wide production and distribution networks, which have in turn required greater international collaboration, both at business and state levels, on practical and on more formal issues. As part of this process of regionalization, ASEAN, which began as a loose anti-Communist alliance of five countries in Southeast Asia, has doubled in size and expanded in scope to become a major intergovernmental organization playing an important role in facilitating economic cooperation throughout Asia.

December 1997, six months after the crisis broke, saw the first meeting of ASEAN+3—ASEAN plus China, Korea and Japan—a forum that has since played and will continue to play a key role in the region. In 2000, ASEAN+3 launched the so-called Chiang Mai Initiative, an innovative network to facilitate currency swaps for countries suffering extreme pressure in the foreign exchange markets. Besides this, ASEAN+3 has expanded its horizons to discuss wider regional cooperation in fields including finance, trade, investment and security issues.

Thus we can see the nature of the development of economic integration in Asia has proceeded quite differently to the cases of Europe or North America. In Asia, *de facto* integration has come before institutional integration; this is in contrast to the *de jure* approach to integration elsewhere in which institutions have come first. The increasing complexity of interdependent relations has resulted in East Asian countries starting to erect institutions to support current arrangements and provide a solid basis for future collaboration. A first step on this path was the establishment of the ASEAN Secretariat in Jakarta; mooted future developments include a possible ASEAN+3 Secretariat in Kuala Lumpur or elsewhere. Asia as a whole, then, must now consider what institutions would be best for the further development of integration. There is clearly a risk of choosing the wrong kinds of institutions, ones that fail to foster an optimal framework for future progress. The situation is a complex one which must be properly understood if the right institutional set-up is to be found.

Already there is industrial integration in the region, and we can observe a dynamic and very extensive international division of labor taking place. A misjudged attempt at institutionalization could restrict or dissipate this advantage, but the right set of institutions could accelerate the integration process and secure the benefits of economic growth and prosperity for years to come. A salutary example is that of the Asian electrical/electronics manufacturing industry. With government help tariff rates have been reduced to levels as low as 5 percent. A multiplicity of FTAs and EPAs, each with their own rules-of-origins, have resulted in exporting companies finding the costs of providing the necessary verification documentation for these rules greater than the tariff. Consequently, companies in this industry gain less from institutionalized FTAs than might otherwise be the case. Region-wide rules-of-origin arrangements could reduce transaction costs; the current spaghetti bowl effect of agreements is not in the interests of some Asian exporters.

In this volume, we explain new regionalism in detail by looking at recent developments in the theoretical paradigm before engaging with many aspects of Economic Partnership Agreements, using both quantitative analysis and case-study methods. The book consists of eleven studies, the first drafts of which were completed in 2003 by authors who are leading academics from across Asia. Many of them played important roles in shaping post-crisis economic policy in their respective countries; others worked on the ground in international organizations gaining first-hand experience of the issues they here discuss. The authors first began working together on new regionalism in 1999 as part of a Core University Project between Kyoto University and Thammasat University, under the sponsorship of the Japan Society for the Promotion of Science.

These studies address a range of inter-related policy questions that have arisen out of the financial crisis, including: Which paradigm best explains the current trends in economic development in Asia? What will be the impact of the bilateral FTAs that have proliferated in the past ten years? How can the Asian investment climate be improved to encourage optimal inflows of FDI? What lessons are to be learned from the credit crunch experience of the past? And, what steps can be taken to maintain and maximize productivity growth, bearing in mind the social problems faced in many Asian countries? The authors draw on a broad range of examples from across the region in addressing these issues, analyzing how the economies of the region have reacted to the crisis and assessing how resilient they now are, in various respects.

In the remainder of this introduction, we reproduce the main arguments from each chapter, introduce each author and discuss how each argument is unique.

A New Development Paradigm in East Asia?

Prior to the economic crisis, East Asian countries had experienced high economic growth rates for several decades. The crisis exposed underlying structural problems in those economies and a vulnerability to external shocks. The common regional growth strategy that had been based on exports and investment was seen to be insufficient for providing sustainable economic growth. After the crisis, the East Asian countries employed a new development strategy, which placed more emphasis on the stimulation of domestic demand. Korea increased consumer spending through consumer credit expansion, while Thailand and Malaysia increased public spending and extended credit to low-income groups.

Since 1985, many East Asian countries have successfully attracted foreign investment through the liberalization of their domestic economies, by reducing restrictions in the manufacturing and financial sectors. This policy shift was motivated by the desire to reduce vulnerability to external shocks in global export markets. There has been a proliferation of bilateral FTAs between countries in the region in recent years, helping drive the movement towards broader regional integration. China, Japan and Korea have all begun closer economic cooperation with ASEAN.

These FTAs must serve as a building block for regional integration. While balancing nationalistic policies with an outward-oriented development strategy to create resilient economies that are internationally competitive, East Asian countries must be sure to maintain prudent macroeconomic policies. Lessons from the past mistakes of pursuing high growth with unsustainable current account deficits must be learned in order to avoid repeating them in future.

Mahani Zainal-Abidin analyses the paradigm shift persuasively by surveying the experiences of the crisis-affected countries in the region. As a policy maker and leading negotiator in Malaysia's FTA arrangements, Mahani observed at first hand the changing paradigms she describes in this essay. At the time of writing this chapter she was head of a globalization consultancy team in the Economic

Planning Unit of the Malaysian Prime Minister's Department. She is now director general of Institute of Strategic and International Studies (ISIS), one of the most active think tanks in Malaysia. Her other works include *Rewriting the Rules: The Malaysian Crisis Management Model* (Prentice Hall, 2002).

The Emergence of New Regionalism in East Asia

In the face of the successes of NAFTA and the EU, and slow progress in WTO talks, Asia found itself in a relative vacuum regarding economic integration. One reaction to this has been the proliferation of FTAs and EPAs. As a latecomer to the table of economic integration and with vast differences of economic status between countries in the region, Asia has encountered many problems.

As East Asian countries move toward integration, the new regionalism must avoid the trade diversion effect from discrimination against non-member countries. Multiple Free Trade Agreements might help to lessen the trade diversion impact. In addition, if member countries continue to reduce overall import barriers, the damage of trade diversion can be substantially reduced. Countries adopting a new regionalist approach can expect to benefit from learning-by-doing in negotiations as representatives develop their skills through formulating a series of FTAs. These countries must allow adequate time for negotiators to maximize the benefits of trade liberalization while minimizing the adverse impact on disadvantaged sectors.

Strict rules-of-origin can thwart trade integration but trade-oriented countries will eventually reduce stringent rules if they envisage that they are in fact trade impediments. New regionalism must encompass the elimination of all sorts of hidden barriers to trade and capital flows such as food safety standards and technical barriers.

Despite varying relative bargaining powers, both parties in FTAs can nevertheless gain from trade even though the gains might not be evenly distributed. What is important is that welfare improvements arising from the dynamic impact of trade liberalization can outweigh the static impact of welfare loss in non-competitive sectors. Since groups lobbying on behalf of disadvantaged sectors may seek to impede FTAs, citing 'national interests,' sufficient time must be given to allow negatively affected sectors to adjust to the new competitive environment.

As less competitive domestic sectors will inevitably face increased competition within the free trade area, governments should mitigate the adverse impact on affected labor while nonetheless pursuing necessary structural reforms. More highly developed countries can help lower-income countries by permitting market access for their agricultural products, in addition to offering technical assistance. Having more liberal policies on foreign workers is another way to mitigate the problem of labor adjustment in the affected sectors. Furthermore, welfare gains from new regionalism can be higher if the agreements are not limited to trade liberalization—for example, comprehensive partnership agreements that also involve trade and investment facilitation as well as labor movement. Finally, the new East Asian regionalism should be a complement to, rather than a substitute for, the movement toward multilateralism within the WTO framework. FTAs must go beyond the East Asian region.

In this section of the book, Urata makes an empirical study of the effects of new regionalism on various countries in East Asia, Suthiphand argues for ASEAN's view on Asian economic integration, and Okamoto expands the regional perspective to include India.

Shujiro Urata surveys the 'Emergence of New Regionalism in East Asia' and analyzes the effects of this development by conducting CGE model simulations. In his concluding remarks he points out that the East Asian countries should not stop their efforts after completing an East Asian FTA; rather, they should regard it as a step toward achieving global free trade under the WTO.

Professor of Waseda University and Faculty Fellow of the Research Institute of Economy, Trade and Industry (RIETI) in Tokyo, Shujiro Urata has written over two hundred articles and edited more than ten books, including *Asia: The Era of FTAs* (2004) and *Japan's New Trade Policy* (2005) (both in Japanese).

Suthiphand looks at Asian regionalism from the wider perspective of an ASEAN view. ASEAN's Bali Summit commitment to an ASEAN Economic Community (AEC) and the Comprehensive Economic Partnerships (CEPs) signed with China, Japan and India, have been two important steps in linking ASEAN to wider Asian integration. When the AEC becomes a reality, ASEAN will be in a strong position to provide leadership to the whole of Asia on the road towards economic integration. A key question is whether bilateral and sub-regional CEPs can positively promote closer economic arrangements in tandem with the APEC process and the WTO. In his chapter, Suthiphand argues that the answer lies in how CEPs are constructed and whether they are based on principles compatible with the best possible linkages for wider mutual partnerships.

Suthiphand Chirathivat has been an advisor to Thailand's Ministry of Foreign Affairs. He is Associate Professor of Chulalongkorn University.

Okamoto, on the other hand, analyzes empirically the current status of competitiveness or complementarity between ASEAN, China and India by using intra-industry indices. The further rise of China as an industrial power, especially after its entry into the WTO, is now regarded as an opportunity rather than as a threat for ASEAN. Both Singapore and Malaysia should gain both through inter- and intra-industry specialization if an FTA is formed between ASEAN and China. Thailand appears to gain significantly as well through intra-industry specialization vis-à-vis China. Indonesia and the Philippines, on the other hand, may not gain much. The promotion of economic cooperation between ASEAN and India could make sense in the long run, but its immediate impact on both sides would seem to be very limited.

Yumiko Okamoto is Professor of Doshisha University. She has been working on trade and investment related issues and has published a number of important papers in the field. Her past career has included appointments at the Institute of Development Economics, Kobe University and Nagoya University.

Human Capital, Productivity Issues and Agricultural Development

As Krugman postulated in a famous article in *Foreign Affairs*, Asia's recent growth was based upon capital and labor augmentation and not upon technology development. Economic Partnership Agreements contain arrangements for labor movements between countries. For example, the Japan-Philippines EPA promotes Japan's acceptance of Filipino nurses and the Japan-Thailand EPA its acceptance of Thai cooks and spa service workers. In addition, Thailand in particular invites 'silver workers' as a way to transfer technologies, as well as having silver settlement villages to take care of nursing retired Japanese expatriates. Singapore's aging population problem is already a serious one, while Thailand's own age demographic is beginning to resemble that of Singapore and Japan.

Shandre and Abe compare productivity and aging issues for Singapore and Japan. This chapter studies the changing age and educational composition of the labor force in selected Japanese manufacturing industries. Their results indicate that the age category made little contribution to quality improvements of the Japanese labor force in the manufacturing sector. In contrast, the contribution from education appears to have improved labor quality and sustained the contribution of labor input in the overall production of the economy. A declining contribution of education to overall labor quality is also found, and this could have serious implications for the recovery and future sustained growth of the Japanese economy. How to utilize aged workers becomes a key to economic growth, not only in Japan but also in other parts of the world. If EPAs can provide freer movements, better allocation of otherwise-unused labor force would result in higher economic growth. Also, in order to reap the full benefits of the new regional integration, East Asian countries must make sure that their labor forces are equipped with solid general education and ample specific human capital in order to allow the economy to sustain long-term economic growth when intra-East Asian regional investment has been intensified.

Shandre Thangavelu, Associate Professor of the National University of Singapore, gained first-hand knowledge of productivity issues while working at Singapore's Ministry of Manpower. Professor Shigeyuki Abe of Doshisha University in Kyoto, who provides a Japanese perspective to the study, complements this study with his expertise in the field. This chapter is, as such, a joint effort.

Productivity and Technological Progress in the Malaysian Manufacturing Sector

High growth rates of labor productivity were observed in Malaysian industries between 1981 and 2000. The manufacturing output growth was driven by capital accumulation. The electrical/electronics and textiles industries experienced the highest growth rates in labor productivity. The two industries both received substantial amounts of foreign direct investment that boosted the entire sector's labor productivity. However, despite these labor productivity improvements, there was no significant decline in unit labor cost because of excess capacity due to lack of external demand. There was also a shortage of skilled labor, which will require the government to focus future educational spending on the areas of science and technology. To maintain high labor productivity the problem of excess capacity must be solved through creating favorable external demand conditions. East Asian countries, while attracting capital-augmenting technological processes via foreign investment, must continue to expand intra-regional trade. This is why regional trade integration is a crucial factor in labor productivity enhancement.

Lai Yew Wah is former Professor of Universiti Sains Malaysia. He has done many manufacturing survey studies for international organizations in the past. This chapter is an extension of such studies and finds increasing labor productivity accompanying a decrease in capital productivity. The CES production function estimation revealed some moderate technical progress and low elasticity of substitution, thereby suggesting complementary effects between capital and labor inputs in the production structure. For future growth, Lai concludes that expansion of trade is a necessity, which in turn will be a catalyst for regional integration.

Rural Economy in Myanmar at the Crossroads

East Asian countries' development levels are diverse in terms of income and economic structure, from the high-income industrial economies of Japan and Korea to the low-income agricultural economy of Myanmar. If the volume of intra-regional trade expanded, there would be a tremendous gain from trade accrued to countries at a lower level of development. In consequence, agricultural product specialization would improve productivity and raise income in agricultural economies. If Myanmar allowed the price mechanism to work properly, productivity gains in agricultural production could be obtained. As a result, Myanmar could alleviate poverty in rural areas by adopting a more trade-oriented policy. As long as the government continues to intervene heavily in the production and market distribution system through export and price controls, the country will not benefit from trade engagement. There will be no productivity improvement in agriculture unless the government is willing to dismantle its inward-looking development policy. East Asian regional integration will be a gradual process in which more outward-oriented countries will formulate their own Free Trade Agreements, while inward-oriented countries like Myanmar might be left behind with low productivity due to the lack of competition.

Koichi Fujita is a leading expert on agricultural economic issues in Southeast and South Asia, having written numerous articles in this field in both Japanese and English. This study involved one year of fieldwork research, which gave Fujita an insight into the workings of government and the challenges of data-collection in a country like Myanmar. His other works include *Rural Development and Changing Class Structure in Bangladesh* (2005), which received the Okita Memorial Prize for International Development Research.

Economic Crisis and Social Safety Nets

In Southeast Asia, the issue of social safety nets (SSNs) emerged with the financial crisis. One condition of international organizations such as the IMF, the World Bank and the Asian Development Bank (ADB), was that crisis countries applying for assistance declare in their letters of intent a set of policies that gave due consideration to the social impacts of the crisis. Accordingly, concerns about social safety nets surfaced and studies on this issue looked into how the crisis affected countries in the region. Most studies so far have found that the social impact of the crisis showed the need for policies that specifically incorporate safety nets for vulnerable groups; that is, a country cannot rely on economic growth alone to look after its people.

In this chapter, Srawooth and Abe look at social safety nets in Southeast Asia with particular reference to Thailand. They note that not only is a review of the existence of social safety nets needed, but the concept itself also needs further examination. This chapter surveys some important literature in the field and serves as the first step for further empirical studies. Srawooth Paitoonpong is an economist at the Thailand Development Research Institute (TDRI). His early career was spent at the UN-ESCAP as a population officer. Since then, he has been working on social aspects of development for almost three decades. After the crisis, his TDRI team made a large-scale analysis of the impacts of the crisis on the poor in Thailand.

Currency Management and Credit Crunch

It is obvious that East Asian countries need to cooperate in the event of massive currency depreciation. The currency crisis of 1997 was followed by a severe output contraction. With banking systems heavily reliant on foreign borrowing to finance domestic investment, the reversal of capital inflows caused domestic firms to suffer shortages of working capital as banks became unwilling to lend.

The East Asian economies are primarily bank-based economies, relying less on financial resources raised through capital markets. Consequently, they suffered badly from financial disintermediation during the crisis. The corporate sectors of these economies depend heavily on external funds, rather than their own internal funds, to finance their investment. This high dependency on debt is the result of rapid economic growth and a stable macroeconomic environment. In these circumstances, when the environment becomes unfavorable due to high interest rates, large currency depreciations and current account deficits, domestic investment and consumption contract substantially, which in turn precipitates a further decline in bank lending. With banks already reluctant to lend, borrowers meanwhile struggle and often fail to service existing stocks of debt. During the financial crisis period, the effect of the credit crunch was to further weaken economic activities already affected by the imposition of IMF austerity programs.

Instead of relying on the IMF as a lender of last resort, East Asian countries can and should become self-reliant by jointly pursuing policies that reduce the likelihood of crises occurring. The benefits of cooperation in the financial sector have been demonstrated by the Chiang Mai initiative, which has built a network to manage currency swaps between ASEAN+3 countries to be used in the event of currency turmoil.

The move to liberalize capital controls must be accompanied by establishing prudent rules for the financial sector and by strengthening bank supervision. In the absence of capital controls, allowing the exchange rate to float during a period of capital flight can push the exchange rate below the threshold that would trigger financial instability. The degree of vulnerability for a country depends on levels of foreign leverage amongst its firms, which is in turn related to interest rate differentials and the exchange rate risk. As the East Asian economies return to pre-shock growth paths their economies will be characterized by strong export growth and high capital inflows. Their currencies will naturally appreciate and they will see booms in the equity and property markets. By reducing intervention in the foreign exchange markets, East Asian countries can reach a healthier position in which they rely less on growth stemming from undervalued exchange rates—for example, by tying them to the depreciating dollar—and more on growth that depends on domestic demand components. Management of exchange rate policies and public deficits must be conducted in line with sustainable growth. East Asian countries must also learn to cope with inflows of capital that tend to appreciate their currencies and erode their competitiveness.

Kohsaka, Enya and Pobre discuss the issue of credit crunch in East Asia over the period 1980 to 2002. They detect some episodes of credit crunch both before and after the Asian crisis; these results are different from previous studies. Their empirical results imply that the impact of the IMF austerity programs after the crisis was so severe that the credit crunch or supply retrenchment was overwhelmed by a sharp fall in credit demand because of real and expected persistent overall economic depression.

Akira Kohsaka, former Dean of Osaka School of International Public Policy, has published extensively on the Asian economy for almost twenty years. He is also coordinator of the Pacific Economic Outlook project. His most recent works include *New Development Strategies: Beyond the Washington Consensus* (Palgrave-MacMillan, 2004).

The Asian financial crises occurred because of too much dependence on short-term capital with promises of fixed baht/dollar exchange rates. Bhanupong focuses on exchange rate issues and how the market reacts to these changes.

He presents a simple VAR model that explains how a country may experience a severe contraction after devaluation, particularly in an economy where bank credit is an important source of funds for investment. If firms and banks accumulate large amounts of unhedged foreign debt, a high rate of depreciation that exceeds the threshold can trigger technical bank failure, thereby reducing bank lending.

Bhanupong Nidhipraba is a leading macro economist in Thailand and Professor of Thammasat University. He is the author of many Thai macroeconomic policy papers and is known widely for his joint World Bank book with Peter Warr, *Thailand's Macroeconomic Miracle* (1997).

Investment Climate and Foreign Investment

There is growing empirical evidence to support the view that the investment climate is an important factor in attracting FDI. Because economic risk is the most influential factor determining the investment climate, East Asian countries that desire to obtain technology transfers via foreign investment must ensure that their macroeconomic policies support high growth and price stability; they must maintain external balances and keep budget deficits manageable. Furthermore, increased political risks can aggravate foreign investment outflows. Government instability, internal conflict, ethnic tensions, corruption, declining democratic accountability and the deterioration of law and order can increase political risk. On the other hand, East Asian economies can reduce financial risk in order to attract foreign investors by strengthening monitoring systems of financial institutions. Foreign direct investment can be complementary to domestic investment through providing productivity gains in the manufacturing sector.

Negishi's study indicates a significant positive impact of an improved investment climate in attracting FDI to the host country. The author finds new evidence for the role in the investment climate in determining FDI inflows. She uses the International Country Risk Guide (ICRG) rating system as a proxy for business climate and finds an improvement in the investment climate indices by one percent can lead to a sizeable increase in FDI for some East Asian economies.

Shoko Negishi is Associate Professor of Doshisha University. Her research has focused on FDI and related fields since her time as an economist in the World Bank's Development Prospect Group.

This publication has its origins in 'State, Market, Society and Economic Cooperation in Asia,' a four-year study project made possible by the kind sponsorship of the Japan Society for the Promotion of Science (JSPS). The Center for South East Asian Studies (CSEAS) at Kyoto University has also been a source of continuing support to the project. We are grateful to Dr. Janis Kea of West Valley College for her work with the original manuscripts. Itaru Saito of Kyoto University Press and Mariko Yonezawa of CSEAS kindly helped coordinate the publication of this volume. Yuko Sato of CCAS dealt with the necessary administrative tasks with admirable efficiency. Last but not least, we would like to thank James Brady of Osaka School of International Public Policy for his help with this volume.

Shigeyuki Abe, Doshisha University
Bhanupong Nidhipraba, Thammasat University

1
The New Development Paradigm in East Asia[1]

Mahani Zainal-Abidin

Introduction

The development model used from the late 1960s to late 1990s has produced a phenomenal and unmatched growth in East Asia. This economic development model was based on the 'Washington consensus model' that enabled the East Asian economies to build a core of common factors such as high savings rate, high investment in human capital, prudent macroeconomic policy, political stability, protection of property rights and openness to world trade and investment. In other words, this development paradigm is predicated on getting the fundamentals right, including price of factors of production. However, there is another view, which believes that it was the 'developmental state' growth paradigm with significant government intervention that was largely responsible for the backward, late industrializing East Asian economies catching up so rapidly with advanced countries. State intervention, by sometimes 'getting prices wrong,' had created sectors with competitive advantage that can penetrate the global market.

The Asian crisis has dented some of the achievements and growth prospects of the affected countries and exposed some weaknesses in these economies. These were structural problems, the most serious being high non-performing loans; vulnerability to external shock; high levels of investment that led to high debt; fledging institutions not ready for a liberalized capital account; and high degrees of dependence on exports for economic growth.

Economic uncertainties since 2001 and the less than full recovery from the crisis have prompted East Asian economies to adopt a new economic strategy. The new economic development paradigm saw the return of the public sector as the engine of growth through fiscal stimulus programs. The vulnerability to changing global export market has prompted some East Asian countries to introduce a 'dual track economic development strategy' that emphasizes both the promotion of exports as well as strengthening the domestic economy. Many East Asian countries are seeking new sources of growth and the services sector has been identified as the sector that will put East Asia back on its high growth path. More liberalization has been introduced, some in protected sectors, to attract more foreign investment, as well as to increase efficiency. There is now a proliferation of bilateral free trade agreements (FTAs) in East Asia. Besides trade integration, there is a new regionalism in East Asia which is proceeding rapidly on financial issues, including developing an effective mechanism for the recycling of regional savings.

Is new direction in the East Asian development strategy a precursor of a more fundamental shift, namely the adoption of a new development paradigm?

East Asia Development Model: Late 1960s to mid-1990s

East Asia Development Paradigm

The rapid growth of the East Asian economy has generated numerous studies on the model that had produced this superior performance. The most well known description of the East Asian development experience is the flying geese model with Japan leading the economic development in East Asia from the newly industrialized economies (Korea, Taiwan, Hong Kong and Singapore) to the Asian Tigers (Malaysia, Thailand, Indonesia, the Philippines). Japanese industries that had matured and became uncompetitive due to rising labor costs were transferred firstly to the newly industrialized economies (NIEs).

The NIEs manufactured finished and intermediate products that were exported back to Japan for final consumption or further processing. In the process, the NIEs gained technological capability primarily through the transfer of technology by multinational companies. The same pattern was repeated where these industries in NIEs matured and their cost of production increased. The best examples of such industries were textiles and consumer products. The matured NIEs industries were then relocated to ASEAN countries and the same process reoccurred. The industrialization of the East Asian economies through this flying geese model had resulted in high economic growth based on exports and the acquisition of manufacturing competency and technological capability.

This ability to industrialize quickly and produce high performance economies (HPE) has received much attention. The predominant explanation of this development achievement was given by the World Bank, with the coining of the term 'East Asian Miracle' in their 1993 book.[2] This explanation linked the role of the state in economic development in general and industrial development in particular and the centrality of this relationship in producing a high performing economy. A minimalist, free-market neo-classical school of thought as represented by the so-called 'Washington Consensus model,' in the view of the World Bank, was the economic development model that enabled the HPE to build a core of common factors such as high savings rate, high investment in human capital, prudent macroeconomic policy, political stability, protection of property rights and openness to world trade and investment. In other words, this development paradigm is predicated on getting the fundamentals right, including the price of factors of production.

Beyond getting these 'fundamentals right,' this 'growth based on free market' paradigm assumes a minimal role of the state—careful government intervention in the market is kept to a minimum with its primary function being the creation of a conducive economic and business environment as well as to ensure political stability, both of which are important for the private sector to operate efficiently. The underlying assumption is that markets will emerge naturally if the state reduces its presence through liberalization and privatization. An open trade policy is also a critical component of this paradigm where countries should concentrate on producing and exporting goods and services in which they have a comparative advantage.

Although this 'getting the fundamentals right' paradigm produced the economic miracle—high economic growth, strong exports and sound macro-economic fundamentals—some economists questioned the validity of this theory. From empirical observation and micro-level studies, economists such as Amsden (1989), Wade (1990), Chen (1996) and Rodrik (1995), concluded that the East Asian experience demonstrated the need for strong state intervention to promote rapid economic development. This 'developmental state' growth paradigm believes that it was the significant government intervention that was largely responsible for these backward, late industrializing East Asian economies catching up rapidly with advanced countries. State intervention, sometimes by 'getting prices wrong,' had created sectors with competitive advantage that can penetrate the global market. The policy of 'picking winners'—the process of identifying selected sectors or industries that were targeted to lead the industrialization process—was the hallmark of this development paradigm. Normally, this policy of targeting selected sectors or industries would involve the provision of incentives, cross-subsidization between sectors, industries or business activities and protection through high import duties.

Another development school of thought was put forward by Japanese development scholars that attributed the success of the East Asian economies to the long-term vision of the state and targets set by the government (Wong and Ng 2001). In this development model, the emphasis was on the achievements of the real sector, namely output, employment and industrial structure (Ohno and Ohno 1998). Like the developmental state development paradigm, this explanation of the East Asian performance also credited active government support in promoting growth and industrialization.

Table 1-1   Export and Import Growth Rates in Selected East Asian Countries

	Export growth % (1980-90)	Export growth % (1990-2000)	Import growth % (1980-90)	Import growth % (1990-2000)
Korea	15.0	10.1	11.9	7.1
Taiwan	14.9	7.2	12.4	8.5
Singapore	9.9	9.9	8.0	7.8
Malaysia	8.6	12.2	7.7	9.5
Thailand	14.0	10.5	12.7	5.0

Source: Asian Development Bank, *Key Indicators of Developing Asian and Pacific Countries*, various issues.

Phenomenal Growth in East Asia

The development path taken by the East Asian countries produced a sustained high level of growth for nearly 30 years, which is unmatched by other regions in the world. The following indicators demonstrate this strong economic performance:

- sustained high economic growth through robust exports as shown in Table 1-A1 (see Appendix) and Table 1-1
- sound macroeconomic fundamentals achieved fiscal surpluses, as shown in Table 1-A2 (see Appendix), growth without inflation as shown in Table 1-2, and large international reserves as shown in Table 1-A3 (see Appendix)
- rapid industrialization across East Asian countries
- high savings—in 1990 the savings rate in Korea was 37.2 percent of GDP, in Singapore 43.4 percent, in Malaysia 34.4 percent, in Thailand 34.3 percent, in Hong Kong 35.4 percent and in Taiwan 28.1 percent
- large inflow of FDI as shown in Table 1-A4 (see Appendix)—ASEAN countries were heavily dependent on FDI but not Korea and Taiwan
- rapid catching-up technology
- socio-economic progress such as higher life expectancy rate, lower infant mortality rate and improved income distribution (Table 1-3)

Investment was a key factor in this growth process. Most countries had a high rate of investment, for example in Korea, Malaysia and Thailand the investment

Table 1-2   Growth and Inflation Rates in Selected East Asian Countries

	Annual growth % (1975-85)	Annual growth % (1986-96)	Annual inflation % (1975-85)	Annual inflation % (1986-96)
Korea	7.6	8.6	13.5	5.7
Taiwan	8.3	7.7	6.3	3.0
Singapore	7.2	8.4	3.4	1.9
Malaysia	6.3	7.8	4.8	2.6
Thailand	6.6	9.1	7.2	4.5

Source: Asian Development Bank, *Key Indicators of Developing Asian and Pacific Countries*, various issues.

Table 1-3   Sharing the Fruits of Economic Growth: Social
Indicators for Asia (annual average)

Life Expectancy:	1970-75	1990
Years	60.4	68

Infant mortality rate:	1970	1990
Per 1000 live births	87	34

Income inequality:	1980s	1990s
Average Gini coefficient	38.7	38.1

Source: Asian Development Bank, *Key Indicators of Developing
Asian and Pacific Countries,* various issues.

rate was around 40 percent of GDP in the 1990s. But investment efficiency
declined—for example in Korea and Thailand incremental capital-output ratio
doubled between 1990–95.

Characteristics of East Asian Economic Model
The East Asian development experience can be summarized by the following
characteristics:
- dependence on exports for mass manufacturers in key markets
- growth based on low wage and surplus labor comparative advantage
- investment flow and intra-regional trade having developed a regional
production network
- East Asia's growth was based on a high rate of factor accumulation,
namely labor and capital
- strong role played by the private sector in driving the growth process
with the public sector creating favorable conditions for the private sector
to operate
- political stability was essential to facilitate economic growth
- liberalization extended from the real sector to include the financial sector
and capital account
- 'Management' of a competitive exchange rate helping exports
- prudent macroeconomic management anchoring the growth process.

Taking into consideration and in reconciling the three schools of thought on
the performance of the East Asian countries, there are a number of common
approaches that were taken:
- HPE growth was based on manufacturing, mostly those involving low
value added and low skilled labor-intensive processes. The economies
are heavily dependent on foreign technology for their manufacturing
activities. However, there are countries such as Korea and Taiwan that

had built their own domestic technological capability and could produce higher value-added products.

* Their growth was very dependent on a favorable external environment that allowed the rapid expansion of exports.

* Some of these economies were too dependent on FDI to drive their economic and export growth and, as a result, neglected the need to nurture the domestic capacity to participate in the global market.

The emergence of China is threatening to break the chain of regional development as set out by the flying geese pattern. Unlike other emerging economies in East Asia such as Vietnam, Cambodia, Laos and Myanmar, China is not starting its industrialization process by only producing low value added and intensive-intensive manufactured goods but it is also producing high technology goods, especially electronic components. Some electronic manufacturers have relocated their factories from ASEAN countries to China to take advantage of the lower labor cost as well as the availability of skilled workers, particularly engineers and technicians. In addition, the availability of R&D capability has attracted foreign investment to set up manufacturing facilities with higher level of technology. Consequently, China is competing with many East Asian countries in export markets for both low-end and high value added products.

The Asian Crisis and its Impact on Growth

Impact of the 1997–98 Crisis and Recovery
Given that they shared many common characteristics, it was not surprising that the four economies (Indonesia, Malaysia, South Korea and Thailand) experienced a common initial impact (see Table 1-4). In 1998 all the four economies experienced, most probably, their worst ever recession—private consumption decreased substantially by about 11 percent in Malaysia and in Thailand and South Korea by 10 percent. Meanwhile in Thailand and Malaysia, private investment crashed by a third, whereas in Korea the fall was less at 21

Table 1-4   GDP Contraction, Exchange Rate, Stock Market and Capital Outflow (1998)

	Korea	Malaysia	Thailand	Indonesia
GDP %	-5.8	-7.5	-10.4	-13.2
Private consumption %	-9.6	-10.6	-10.8	-3.3
Exchange rate depreciation (1997-98) %	49.1	49.9	54.6	83.6
Stock market index (97-98) %	-30.4	-47.1	-40.8	-31.1
Private capital outflow (US$ million)	13,027	3,461	11,735	19,609

Source: Asian Development Bank, *ADB Review*, various issues.

percent. In Indonesia private consumption decreased marginally by 3 percent, while its investment contracted massively at 38 percent.

Although the recession was caused by the collapse of domestic demand and investment, weak exports also contributed to the economic decline and indeed in 1998 the exports of all four economies contracted. Uncertain external conditions and the closely integrated economic relationships had caused the intra-regional trade to fall sharply. But in 1998 the collapse of imports and steep currency depreciation, which boosted export revenue (despite a smaller total volume), had turned the current account deficits into surpluses.

In 1997, Indonesia, South Korea and Malaysia experienced massive private capital outflows led by short-term capital (see Table 1-4). For Korea and Thailand, the net flows of private portfolio remained positive in the crisis years of 1997 and 1998. Indeed, the outflows of short-term capital were mainly due to other private flows, arising from debts, trade credits and changes in non-residents accounts in the banking systems.[3] The erosion of market confidence and fear of economic collapse had triggered the massive capital outflows from the four countries in 1998. Indonesia registered the largest outflow, reaching almost US$ twenty billion.

The performance of FDI was rather mixed with FDI continuing to flow into both Malaysia and Thailand in 1997 and 1998. Korea, which had previously recorded negative FDI net flows because of residents' high investments abroad, also became a FDI recipient during the crisis period. As part of its corporate restructuring program, foreign investors were, for the first time, allowed to purchase Korean assets and businesses. The situation in Indonesia was different. The deep economic contraction turned FDI inflow into an outflow.

The collapse of the East Asian stock markets was so huge that it became one of the two most-mentioned features of the 1997–1998 upheaval—the other being the exchange rate depreciation. The South Korean and Malaysian markets were the biggest losers when their indices plummeted by more than 50 percent. Speculations on regional currencies, and outflows of capital crushed the exchange rates of all four countries. In the seven month period from 1 July 1997 to 24 January 1998, when these currencies faced their severest test, the Indonesian Rupiah depreciated by 83.6 percent, the Thai Baht by 54.6 percent, the Korean Won by 49.1 percent and the Malaysian Ringgit by 49.9 percent.

The deteriorating economy and the bearish equity market had quickly exposed the banking sector loan problems. In Indonesia the level of NPL jumped to 63 percent from 8 percent in 1997, while in Thailand it was already at a high level of 20 percent prior to the crisis. The relatively well-controlled NPL situation in 1997 helped to contain the deterioration of the banking sector in Malaysia and South Korea.

All of the crisis countries were anticipating runaway inflation from higher import prices since their currencies were sharply depreciated. This turned out to be true for Indonesia, which had 57 percent inflation in 1998. But in the other three countries the effects of imported inflation were generally subdued because of the deeply deflated economy and most prices increased by no more than 8.5 percent. Malaysia's inflation in 1998 of 5.3 percent was the lowest among the four countries.

Response Policy: IMF Assisted Economies and Malaysia

In responding to the crisis, Korea, Thailand and Indonesia (IMF-3) had followed the IMF prescribed solutions of reduction in government spending, imposition of higher interest rates, removal of subsidies, closed troubled financial institutions and floated the exchange rate. On the other hand, Malaysia, which had initially followed the IMF policy, changed response by implementing counter cyclical measures—fiscal stimulus, lowered interest rates, assistance to distressed sectors. Malaysia had also introduced capital controls and pegged the Ringgit to the US$. Korea, Thailand and Indonesia later followed counter cyclical measures.

Fiscal contraction was large in the four countries: in both Thailand and Indonesia public sector expenditures were reduced by 3 percent of GDP to yield fiscal surpluses of 1 percent of GDP in 1997 and again in 1998. The fiscal surplus target for South Korea in 1997 was 2 percent while Malaysia's was 2.7 percent. In both Thailand and South Korea, tax measures such as raising the VAT rates and widening tax bases had increased government revenues. The removal of subsidies and price adjustments, which were part of the fiscal package in Indonesia, unfortunately had wide-ranging and devastating consequences.

Besides assuring markets that the crisis economies were serious about correcting the prevailing economic imbalances, fiscal austerity was needed to raise funds for the financial restructuring programs and for improving current account positions. However, the measures aggravated the economic contractions, as were seen earlier in the IMF-3 countries, without producing the expected results, so new response directions were soon required by all the crisis-hit economies. In early 1998, the fiscal surplus policies for the IMF-3 countries were reversed. Even these reversals were insufficient to halt the economic decline. As the economic conditions deteriorated badly, the fiscal stance of the IMF-3 swung to the other extreme of large deficits to counteract recession. Thailand's public sector deficit was targeted at 3 percent of GDP for 1998 while Korea's was larger at 5 percent. In the case of Indonesia, the budget deficit was used for social expenditure to increase the supply of food, fuel and medical items; this large deficit had to be capped to 8.5 percent of GDP. Malaysia relaxed its fiscal stance in 1998 to target a deficit of 3.7 percent.

Monetary Policy
Tight monetary policy was implemented to stabilize exchange rates. Dramatic hikes in interest rates regularly occurred between mid-1997 and mid-1998. For example, Indonesia's prime lending rate, which was already high in 1996, jumped by half to 33 percent in 1997. Korea also had a big interest rate (its nominal lending rate) increase from 8.8 percent in 1996 to 11.9 percent in 1997 while the rates of increment for Thailand and Malaysia were relatively lower.

Malaysia resisted pressure to have a higher interest rate regime and together with its relatively lower pre-crisis level rates, meant its rates were the lowest among the four crisis countries throughout the crisis period. The deep recession caused by the slowdown of economic activities eventually forced the reversal of the high interest rate regime. Except for Indonesia, the other three economies began lowering their interest rates in the second half of 1998.[4]

Monetary growth slowed down in Malaysia, South Korea and Thailand during the crisis due to a sharp deceleration of credit growth and a liquidity crunch. The concern was so serious in Malaysia that the government reduced the statutory reserve requirement (SRR)[5] from 13.5 percent in January 1998 to 4 percent in September 1998 in order to boost liquidity. However, in Indonesia the money supply, instead of contracting, had doubled with its M2 growth increasing from 30 percent in 1996 to 62 percent in 1997 to cope with high inflation.

Structural Reforms
The crisis economies also implemented structural transformation programs, which were intended to extend market-based mechanisms in the economy, deepen the role of the private sector and liberalize the economy. In Indonesia, monopolies and subsidies for essential commodities were removed and restrictive market arrangements were eliminated. For example, the monopoly of the national rice marketing board was limited and domestic trade in agriculture produce was deregulated. The distribution system was overhauled to ensure adequate supplies of essential commodities, particularly food, throughout the country.

Wide ranging liberalization was introduced, in particular in South Korea. Trade-related subsidies were abolished, capital account transactions were liberalized, foreign participation was increased and labor market reforms were introduced. Foreign ownership was allowed in previously closed areas such as the financial sector. Likewise, privatization was advocated to reduce public sector economic participation. In this regard, the dismantling of non-transparent and sometimes inefficient ties between the government, banks and businesses (popularly known as crony capitalism) had been the battle cry for groups pushing for reforms. In South Korea, the relationship and structure of the *chaebols* came under close scrutiny.

Malaysia adopted a more cautious approach to structural reforms. It removed restrictions on foreign equity on investments in the manufacturing sector but, unlike other crisis economies, did not open its financial sector to foreign investors. Besides manufacturing, foreign investment limits were also relaxed in other areas, namely property, telecommunication and cement industries.

Recovery: Mixed Performance Among Crisis Countries

Beyond most people's expectations, all have recovered quickly, but inevitably some faster than others. In 1999, South Korea was the best performer with a real GDP growth of 10.7 percent. Next was Malaysia at 5.8 percent followed by Thailand at 4.2 percent and Indonesia 0.3 percent. Coming from a very deep recession (for example, GDP contraction of 13 percent for Indonesia in 1998), this performance could only be labeled as a 'V' shape recovery.

What are the sources of this dramatic rebound? A common theme is exports: in the three top performing economies merchandise exports registered strong growth. By contrast, after a collapse, the decrease in Indonesian merchandise exports was minimized. No clear pattern emerged on domestic sources of growth. The resumption of private sector activities was most prominent in South Korea where private consumption and investment recovered strongly. Thailand's private sector performance mirrored that of Korea but investment was much lower than consumption. On the other hand, in Malaysia although private consumption made a mild recovery, investment was still down in 1999.

The weak private sector contribution in Malaysia was compensated by the large expansion in public consumption. However, in both Korea and Thailand, the role of the public sector in reviving the economy was less prominent.

An expansionary monetary policy certainly helped to increase liquidity and keep the cost of funds at a reasonable rate, alleviating the corporate sector difficulties. Monetary growth has returned to pre-crisis levels, except in Thailand where it remained low. Likewise, interest rates have also been restored to the pre-crisis level or lower. Even though liquidity and interest rates have reverted to normal, their impact on loan growth is minimal (except for Korea) due to excess capacity in the economy.

Economic recovery was meaningful because inflation was under control or brought down to a low level and unemployment was tamed. The inflationary threat rising from the currency depreciation did not materialize because domestic demand collapsed massively. In addition, there was excess capacity to meet the revival of consumer demand during recovery.

The strong export performance and the massive collapse of demand for imports have turned current account deficits into surpluses. As these economies recovered, it was natural that imports should also rise. But the rate of import growth in South Korea and Thailand has outpaced that of exports. This is why their positive current account balances are smaller than Malaysia, which has a lower import growth rate. Malaysia enjoyed the strongest current account balance position (5.8 percent of GDP) in 1999.

Capital continued to flow out of Indonesia, Malaysia and Thailand in 1999. Separating the components of capital flows, Malaysia, South Korea and Thailand continued to receive FDI even during the crisis and in recovery. Unlike Malaysia and Thailand, which received less FDI in 1999 than in 1998, South Korea's liberalization approach to debt restructuring has attracted a large amount of investment, particularly through mergers and acquisition.

Private capital[6] continued to leave Indonesia, Malaysia and Thailand in the recovery period. Korea balked the trend by registering positive inflow due to the return of portfolio investments. The former three countries sought foreign financing through loans and bonds for fiscal expansion and financial sector restructuring. However, Korea made substantial loan pre-payments in 1999, indicating its improved financial position.

The nominal exchange rates of IMF-3 economies all appreciated in 1999, with Indonesia showing the largest gain. The Ringgit exchange rate remained unchanged due to the peg.

In 2000, the growth continued in the crisis economies as shown in Table 1-5. Although exports continued to be the driver for recovery, improving domestic demand, particularly the revival of private consumption, became a key factor for sustaining growth. Strong export performance had also extended the gain in trade surpluses made when the crisis began, culminating in larger current account positive balance.

Interpretation of the Rapid Recovery by the Crisis Economies

With this rapid recovery, some commentators and analysts of the East Asian economies concluded that the crisis was just a blip in these countries growth path because the economic downturn was primarily caused by a liquidity problem due to the massive outflow of capital and a domestic credit crunch. Thus, when liquidity is restored through fiscal stimulus, lower cost of funds (by lowering the level of interest rates) and increasing liquidity in the financial system, then these economies would be back on their previously high growth path. This belief was supported by these economies' strong fundamentals where the crisis did not impair their production capacity—they took advantage of the deeply depreciated currency to increase production for exports. Furthermore,

Table 1-5   Performance of Crisis Economies in 2000

2000	Korea	Malaysia	Thailand	Indonesia
GDP %	8.8	8.3	4.4	4.8
Private consumption %	7.4	12.2	4.6	3.6
Exports growth %	21.1	17	19.6	16.1
Current account balance as % of GDP	2.6	10.1	8.5	5.2
Total external debt as % to GDP (1999)	33.5	53.4	76.9	103.4

Source: Asian Development Bank, *ADB Review*, various issues.

other economic fundamentals remained robust during the crisis—savings rates had increased, inflation was relatively low and unemployment levels decreased quickly to near pre-crisis level.

However, when examined closer, the crisis also exposed some weaknesses in these economies:

- Structural problems, namely high non-performing loans, indicating a serious weakness in the financial sector; excess capacity especially in the property sector and the dependency on the banking sector and stock market as the source of financing.
- Vulnerability to external shock—as open economies, these countries are susceptible to global volatility, for example in 1995, the global electronic industry slowdown had caused a severe decline in electronics exports, a key contributor to growth and in 1997, a massive outflow of short-term capital which led to the crisis.
- The high growth strategy, based on high levels of investment, had led to high levels of debt—Korea, Thailand and Indonesia had turned to foreign sources for raising financing while Malaysia had tapped the domestic supply.
- Fledgling institutions were not ready for a liberalized capital account.
- High degree on dependence on exports for economic growth.

Post–Crisis Asian Economies

The view that the crisis economies were back on their pre-crisis growth path was changed when economic performance became weak again from 2001. East Asian economies were effected by the slowdown in the US economy that began the first quarter of 2001 and later by the devastating impact of the September 11 incident. In 2001, Indonesia's economy grew by 3.3 percent, Korea by 3.1 percent and Thailand by 1.9 percent while Malaysia barely escaped recession when its growth was only 0.4 percent. The 2002 performance was also affected by global and regional events, namely the war on Iraq and the SARS outbreak—Korea grew by 6.3 percent, Thailand by 5.2 percent, Malaysia by 4.2 and Indonesia by 3.7 percent.

This below par performance shows that the economic uncertainties, a product of global vagaries, are still prevalent and the recovery did not remove the vulnerability of these East Asian economies to external shocks. In addition to being heavily dependent on key export markets for growth East Asian economies are now susceptible to global security and political conflicts. Another concern is that those East Asian countries that received a large inflow of, and are very dependent on FDI for economic development and exports are receiving less. To compensate for this smaller FDI inflow, these countries, in particular ASEAN economies, need to generate domestic private investment. Unfortunately, domestic private investment remained weak because the impact of the crisis was so severe that many domestic firms went into liquidation.

State of the East Asian Economies

Thus, it is pertinent to analyze the state of the East Asian economies as they enter into the new millennium to gauge whether their growth path is sustainable in a more volatile global environment.

Clearly the take off stage of economic growth in these economies is over. Some of these economies have achieved a relative high level of per capita income and have reached the status of developed and middle-income developing countries. For example, Korea is a member of OECD, Singapore per capita income is second highest in Asia after Japan, while Malaysia is in the top income group of developing countries. What this means is that it would be much more difficult for these economies to generate high growth rates because of the higher level of economic base and the sophistication in the quality of growth. For an economy with a higher level of economic base, it requires a larger expansion of economic production and activities to produce a reasonable growth. In these economies, growth could not be attained by just an accumulation of labor and capital—productivity improvement is an essential component for growth.

Although the East Asian economies have industrialized, many consider that, with the exception of Korea and Taiwan, it is just a 'skin-deep industrialization' due to the low level of manufacturing. The manufacturing activities primarily involve assembling work while R&D and production of critical components are done outside East Asia. Foreign multinational companies (MNC) that came to East Asia to take advantage of the low labor costs drove the industrialization process. Notwithstanding some of the industrial development achieved, the level of technology competency is still at a low level. Many of the East Asian economies have a dichotomous industrial structure where competitive foreign multinational production is for the export markets while the local companies have weak industrial capacity in producing goods for the protected domestic market. Linkage between the foreign MNCs and the domestic sector is minimal.

The market, as evidenced by the 1997–98 crisis, has recognized East Asia as a 'single market.' The regional contagion links the region in terms of capital flows, exchange movements and stock market performance. Besides this financial link, the region has also developed a network of regional production, investment flow and intra-regional trade. This regional linkage originates from the Japanese production and investment network, but since the 1990s the Newly Industrialized Economies (Korea, Taiwan, Hong Kong and Singapore) have become the major investors in some East Asian countries. Moreover, the region is also connected through the movement of people, namely the flow of tourists. Regional tourism is now a major economic contributor in many countries.

As East Asian economies mature, they are faced with rising wages and a larger proportion of older population. With higher wages, some countries have lost their low cost labor competitiveness and hence have to move higher in the value added chain. For this to take place, enhancement of human capital is essential, which will ultimately be captured by productivity improvement. East Asia has relatively well-educated human resources with a strong work ethic. As such the cost of investment in education to upgrade the capability of the workforce would not be too burdensome.

Despite the progress made in developing domestic capacity, for example the manufacturing sector, and in increasing regional integration, East Asia is still vulnerable to changes from outside the region. Although rising intra-regional trade has somewhat diversified the East Asian export markets, demand from the U.S. remains the key factor that determine East Asia's export performance. The domestic sector could not take up the slack left by lower exports as shown by the experience in 2001 when export demand from the U.S. declined. However, since the mid-1990s, East Asia has exhibited another vulnerability—the rapid movement of international capital flows can seriously affect its capital market. The rapid rise and fall in East Asian equity markets is often attributed to foreign flows.

Economic Policies in Selected East Asian Economies Post-Crisis

Policies used by the crisis economies to respond to the crisis could be regarded as the beginning of a turning point in their development path. Initially these policies were targeted to revive the domestic economy so that it can lead the growth process while waiting for the unfavorable external environment to improve. But the dismal and uncertain global condition since 2001, has forced some of these economies to continue with the crisis response measures. Furthermore, there are signs that these economies have taken a new approach in their development strategy and these crisis response measures (often regarded as short-term in nature) have been transformed into long-term policies.

Example of policies taken after the crisis:

- Malaysia:
  - expand domestic demand through lower interest rates and giving bonuses for the public sector
  - government continued budget deficits to boost growth
  - liberalized equity requirements to attract foreign investors
  - promotion of services industries.
- Korea:
  - boost domestic demand e.g. credit card facilities
  - liberalization in most sectors e.g. foreign equity ownership in financial and auto industries
  - promotion of services activities e.g. business and logistic center for Northeast Asia.
- Thailand:
  - dual-track strategy: first track to increase export competitiveness; second track to strengthen domestic economic capability
  - low-cost mass-housing project
  - building one million houses for low-income groups
  - tax relief and financial measures to help house buyers
  - giving one million Baht each to 70,000 villages
  - encouraging entrepreneurship and assisting small and medium-scale enterprises (SMEs).

The New East Asian Development Paradigm

The approach of economic policy taken by the East Asian countries since 2000 has suggested that there may be a paradigm shift in the East Asian development path. The move towards a nationalistic and regional development policy agenda may signal the beginning of a focus on relying less on exports for growth, strengthening the resilience of the domestic economy and giving priority to regional integration. The Asian crisis has raised doubts about the infallibility of the export-oriented development model pursued by the East Asian economies since the early 1970s. The premise of this model is that outward-oriented policies would create a competitive and flexible economy, operating on a market-based system, which would in turn produce sustainable growth. However, the Asian crisis proved that such an economic system did not prevent economies from global volatility, market failures and loss of market confidence that culminate in economic recession. Thus, this new direction of reducing the heavy dependence on exports and the global economy has raised the question whether this approach is going to be the new norm for East Asia?

The new economic development paradigm has the following features:

A key policy shift is the return of the public sector as the engine of growth through fiscal stimulus programs. Since the early 1990s, the public sector has lessened its role and the private sector was promoted and encouraged to be the driver for economic growth. But the failure of the private sector, which was among the main reasons for the crisis, and its inability to lead the recovery process, has forced the public sector to resume its previous active role. The role of the public sector was not only in increasing economic activities through expanding its investment and consumption but also to take over failed privatized projects and to absorb non-performing loans accumulated by the banking sector.

The vulnerability to changing global export market has prompted some East Asian countries to introduce a 'dual track economic development strategy' that emphasizes both the promotion of exports as well as strengthening the domestic economy. The expansion of the domestic economy requires the creation of a robust domestic demand, strengthening and accelerating the development of domestic companies, especially SMEs. In this regard, interest rates have been kept at a low level to encourage consumption. Increasing the contribution of domestic companies is important, not only to reduce the over-reliance on the MNCs, but also to augment the use of domestic inputs for production. In addition, measures have been taken to increase the availability and channels of financing for the SMEs, enhancing technological capability and encouraging entrepreneurship.

Recognizing that the manufacturing sector has almost reached its maximum share in contributing to GDP with some countries having difficulties in transforming to higher value added manufacturing processes, many East Asian countries are seeking new sources of growth. The services sector has been identified as the sector that can put East Asia back on its high growth path. The choice of the services sector is a natural one considering East Asia's stage of development as it adds the largest value to production and must increase its contribution if they are to become developed economies. Moreover, East Asian economies have a comparative advantage in some services sub-sectors such as education and health services, tourism and logistics transportation.

More liberalization is introduced, some in protected sectors, to attract more foreign investment as well as to increase efficiency. With a much more competitive environment to attract FDI, East Asian countries have offered far ranging and deep liberalization to make more conducive investment conditions. Many of the restrictions for the manufacturing sector, such as equity requirements, have been removed. Liberalization policies targeted the services sector, previously considered sensitive because of a lack of capacity from domestic providers—this includes the financial sub-sector, in an effort to strengthen the banking sector, transportation sub-sectors such as ports, and the education sub-sector.

Despite the extensive market-driven intra-regional trade and investment flows, historically the East Asia economies have not been as enthusiastic about trade integration arrangements as Europe or North America. The only significant regional grouping in East Asia is the Association of Southeast Asian Nations (ASEAN). Only after 1992 did ASEAN seriously address the issue of economic integration through the ASEAN Free Trade Area (AFTA) initiatives. East Asian economies such as Japan, China and Korea until recently preferred to take the route of multilateral integration through the WTO and APEC.

Since 1998, there was a proliferation of bilateral FTAs, with Singapore being the trendsetter. Singapore has now signed five bilateral FTAs and is in negotiation with a number of other countries. This drift into bilateral trade arrangements is gathering force, and now almost every country in East Asia is party to one or more FTA arrangements. Japan no longer views FTAs as political taboo. Indeed it has abandoned the single-track policy that it has pursued ever since WWII—Japan now has a dual track policy, pursuing bilateral agreements as a complement to the WTO. It now envisages FTAs with Korea, Mexico and Chile. After signing with Singapore, Japan is now in talks about a bilateral FTA with individual ASEAN members. Thailand has signed an FTA with Bahrain and is in negotiation with many others.

While bilateral FTAs are proliferating, there are also moves to have broader regional integration. China and ASEAN are planning to form an FTA within ten years while Japan has initiated closer economic cooperation with ASEAN. Another initiative, mooted by ASEAN is an ASEAN+3 grouping.

Besides trade integration, there is a new regionalism in East Asia, which is proceeding rapidly on financial issues. As an outcome of the Asian crisis, the Manila framework was established to promote financial stability through cooperation among regional countries. East Asian countries also formed a joint surveillance mechanism to monitor short-term capital movements and to give an early warning system. Another example of financial cooperation is the Chiang Mai Initiative to build a network of currency swap arrangements between ASEAN+3 countries when their currencies are faced with unusual depreciation pressures.

East Asia is proposing to develop an effective mechanism for the recycling of regional savings, in particular their huge international reserves. Recently, the Asian bond fund was mooted with an initial injection of US$ one billion to buy

East Asian government bonds. In addition, the Asian Bond Market Initiative (ABMI) was launched to create a deep, broad and liquid bond market in Asia to efficiently recycle funds within the region.[7] This initiative is essentially to improve financial infrastructure and introduce appropriate policies in supporting the development of regional bond markets. While the ABMI aims to address the supply-side measures that are necessary to encourage active participation of both bond issuers and investors, the Asian bond fund complements the ABMI on the demand side by channeling a portion of East Asia's reserves back into the region. The Asian bond fund concept being considered would include bonds denominated in regional currencies.

New Thinking on the East Asian Development Model

This possible shift in development paradigm in East Asia is influenced by the following factors:

Uncertain External Environment
The global environment, in particular export markets, is unlikely to provide a long-term sustained expansion like those from the middle of 1985 to the late 1990s. This situation is the result of low growth prospects in major markets—although the US economy expansion was driven by productivity improvements, the long period of growth in the US that ended in 2001 is difficult to repeat due to over-investment in technology and the large twin deficits. Similarly, growth in the Euro Zone has been sluggish while the decade long recession has yet to show a sustained reversal. Of particular concern is the volatility in capital flows that has made it more arduous to achieve sustained stable and expanding global economic conditions.

The Emergence of China as an Economic Power
As a global emerging economic power, China has reshaped the competitiveness and market landscape for the region. Its large population of 1.3 billion provides a strong comparative advantage in an elastic supply of low-cost labor that resulted in a keen competition in exports of labor-intensive products between China and the other East Asian economies. The full integration of China's huge labor force into the international division of labor could cause some East Asian countries to face the possibility of de-industrialization, but this will only happen if FDI flows to the region affect these economies' domestic technological upgrading process. The FDI flow, with the technology that it brought along, is also being influenced by China because it attracts about 70 percent of the amount that comes into the region while ASEANs has been declining. Consequently, China

has become the world largest out-sourcing production center. In turn, this will attract manufacturers to relocate their activities to China from other Asian countries. China is also developing a technological capability that will allow it to produce high-technology products and exports, activities that many East Asian countries are trying to achieve in order to overcome their loss of competitiveness in labor-intensive, low value added products. In addition, more FDI will invest in China because of liberalization, improving market access for exports and a more rule-based system with the accession of China to WTO membership.

But China also offers opportunities. Because of WTO commitments, China will have to open up its market—it is likely to increase its imports of capital-intensive goods from developed countries as well as primary commodities and agriculture goods from developing countries. More over, the growing size of the middle class with a higher purchasing power will consume more imported products. Already, there is rising demand for services, especially tourism and education.

Regionalism in East Asia

The new regionalism in East Asia is influenced by concerns about the region's economic vitality, developments in bilateral trade arrangements in other parts of the world and the pace of multilateral liberalization. ASEAN's economic dynamism has not fully recovered from the Asian crisis and at one time there were concerns that AFTAs were not progressing as fast as had been expected. Thus, there was a belief that new markets could be found and economic dynamism will return through the formation of FTAs. The growing intra-Asian trade re-enforces the idea that by focusing on East Asian integration, it will internally generate higher growth for the region and begin to reduce the dependency on the U.S. market. Moreover, the WTO liberalization process is seen as difficult and slow, especially after the 1999 WTO Ministerial Meeting in Seattle. This can be overcome through bilateral initiatives, which can speed up liberalization particularly in sensitive areas such as services and the so-called 'new issues,' namely competition policy, investment rules, government procurement and trade facilitation. Services liberalization is deemed necessary to produce new sources of growth. Another reason for the bilateral FTAs is that it can be used as a way to restructure and increase the efficiency of protected industries, for example the opening up of the agriculture sector in Japan.

Financing East Asian Development

The East Asian financial model for fueling economic development is described by some analysts as an imbalanced model. While East Asia has large savings in East Asia, there is question of whether it is mobilized effectively. The East Asian financing model is regarded as a 'mild financial repression' where it subsidized domestic industries and services to ensure manufacturing exports remained competitive. The capital market is dominated by the banking system and efforts to develop the bond market were not given a high priority. Furthermore the large foreign exchange reserves were invested in instruments with low returns, namely the U.S. Treasury bonds. Another part of the imbalanced model concerns the flow of foreign and domestic capital. Although East Asia countries prefer an inflow of capital, they do not encourage outward investment of domestic capital. The trapped domestic liquidity often fuelled property and stock market bubbles. Hence, the move to restructure sources of financing development in East Asia has been receiving much support. For example, the high savings (including compulsory ones) need to be effectively invested to bring better returns to finance the aging society. Liberalization of outward investment for domestic capital has been gradually introduced for better management of risks and to balance the impact of a slowdown from a particular region or a type of investment. Part of the restructuring is to deepen the capital market by having a more active bond market to finance long-term projects. These efforts are aimed at producing a competitively priced funding to finance a sustained growth for East Asia.

Conclusion: Will East Asia Embark on a New Growth Model?

The new direction in the East Asian development strategy may be a precursor to a more fundamental shift, namely the adoption of a new development paradigm. There are compelling reasons for East Asian countries to re-examine the model that was previously used and had produced good economic performance. Perhaps some of the basis for a successful outward-oriented strategy will be restored—primarily the global economic conditions and exports demand expanding at the 1990s rate of growth. In that case, robust growth will be achieved and there will be no need for a new model.

However, considering the increasingly volatile global environment, such a scenario may be difficult to attain. If so, what will the likely new paradigm be? The new model should build on the existing one but at the same time provide flexibility and the ability for countries to cope and respond to a more uncertain global environment. The new model should have the following characteristics:

  • Balancing a nationalistic policy with an outward-looking orientation to create a resilient domestic economy that is also internationally competitive. The 1997–98 crisis exposed the trade orientated and internationally linked East Asian economies as being vulnerable to rapid global changes. Before this episode, these countries had benefited from the expanding world trade, but the massive outflow of capital and collapse in international confidence had resulted in serious economic recession and currency depreciation. Thus, these countries want to build a stronger domestic economy by strengthening and expanding domestic demand with measures such as fiscal stimulus and increasing rural sector income. At the same time, as exporters, they also have to be internationally competitive. For this purpose, they should continue to liberalize their trade, attract foreign capital and technological expertise, and adopt an exchange rate regime that can help exports. In many ways, the two sets of policies are mutually exclusive with governments having to balance the need to strengthen the domestic economy with maintaining export competitiveness.

- Measures to boost the domestic economy must be done in line with prudent macroeconomic management. For example, government revenue must be sufficient to finance measures to boost domestic economy and not increase government debt. This is very difficult to achieve because normally fiscal stimulus programs result in higher public debt. The preferable way is for the private sector to lead the growth process.
- The creation of a contestable or competitive domestic market to encourage the development of domestic companies that can export to the global market.
- FTAs must be the building blocks for regional integration.

Appendix

See Tables 1-A1, 1-A2, 1-A3, 1-A4.

Notes

1 Paper presented at the JSPS–NRCT Workshop on 'Perspectives of Roles of State, Market, Society, and Economic Co-operation in Asia,' Kyoto, November 6–7, 2003.
2 World Bank. 1993. *The East Asian Miracle: Economic Growth and Public Policy.* New York: Oxford University Press.
3 Malaysia does not desegregate its data on short-term capitals and as such it is impossible to separate the movement of portfolios from other private short-term flows.
4 The 1998 interest rate figure for Korea was average for the year. The Korean interest rate reached a peak of 17.3 percent in 1Q1998 and declined steadily

Table 1-A1   Growth Rates for East Asian Countries 1970–2002

	1970	1980	1985	1990	1995	1996	1997	1998	1999	2000	2001	2002
Cambodia	n.a.	n.a.	n.a.	1.2	6.9	5.0	6.8	3.7	10.8	7.0	5.7	5.5
China	n.a.	7.8	13.5	3.8	10.5	9.6	8.8	7.8	7.1	8.0	7.3	8.0
Hong Kong	9.2	10.2	n.a.	3.4	3.9	4.5	5.0	-5.0	3.4	10.2	0.6	2.3
Indonesia	7.6	9.8	2.5	7.2	8.2	7.8	4.7	-13.1	0.8	4.9	3.3	3.7
Japan	10.9	2.8	4.4	5.6	3.1	3.3	0.2	-0.7	1.0	3.2	-1.2	1.5
Korea	n.a.	-2.1	6.5	9.0	8.9	6.8	5.0	-6.7	10.9	8.8	3.1	6.3
Lao PDR	n.a.	n.a.	n.a.	6.7	4.0	7.0	5.8	8.1	7.0	6.9	6.9	4.0
Malaysia	n.a.	n.a.	-1.1	9.0	9.8	10.0	7.3	-7.4	6.1	8.3	0.4	4.2
Myanmar	n.a.	n.a.	2.9	2.8	6.9	6.4	5.7	5.8	10.9	13.7	n.a.	n.a.
Philippines	n.a.	n.a.	-7.3	3.0	4.7	5.9	5.2	0.4	3.7	4.8	3.5	4.6
Singapore	13.7	9.7	-1.4	8.1	8.0	7.5	8.5	-0.8	6.4	9.9	-2.4	2.2
Taiwan	11.4	7.3	5.0	5.4	6.4	6.1	6.7	4.6	5.4	5.9	-2.2	3.5
Thailand	6.9	4.6	4.7	11.2	8.9	5.9	-1.7	-10.2	4.2	4.4	1.9	5.2
Vietnam	1.9	-2.9	6.0	5.1	9.5	9.3	8.2	5.8	4.8	6.8	6.9	7.0

Source: Asian Development Bank, *Key Indicators of Developing Asian and Pacific Countries*, various issues.

Table 1-A2   Fiscal Balance (% of GDP) 1990–2002

	1990	1991	1992	1993	1994	1995	1996	1997	1998	1999	2000	2001	2002
Cambodia	-4.5	-3.4	-3.6	-4.8	-5.8	-7.3	-6.3	-0.4	-2.5	-1.3	-1.4	-2.8	n.a.
China	-0.8	-0.9	1.4	2.2	1.7	1.5	-1.4	-1.5	-2.1	-2.9	-2.8	-2.6	-3.0
Hong Kong	0.7	3.3	2.8	2.1	1.1	-0.3	2.1	6.5	-1.8	0.8	-0.6	-5.0	-5.5
Indonesia	-0.8	-0.7	-1.1	-0.5	1.0	2.2	1.0	0.5	-1.7	-2.5	-1.2	-2.8	-1.7
Japan	0.3	0.5	0.5	0.2	0.5	0.5	0.9	0.6	0.3	1.1	1.0	0.8	0.4
Korea	-0.7	-1.6	-0.5	0.6	0.3	0.3	0.3	-1.5	-4.2	-2.7	1.3	1.3	3.8
Lao PDR	-9.7	-6.1	-5.2	-2.7	-5.0	-3.9	-5.7	-5.2	-6.4	-2.5	-2.5	-4.5	n.a.
Malaysia	-2.9	-2.0	-0.8	0.2	2.3	0.8	0.7	2.4	-1.8	-3.2	-5.8	-5.5	-5.6
Myanmar	-2.8	-3.7	-2.1	-1.4	-2.5	-3.2	-2.2	-0.1	0.8	-0.2	0.7	n.a.	n.a.
Philippines	-3.5	-2.1	-1.2	-1.5	1.0	0.6	0.3	0.1	-1.9	-3.8	-4.0	-4.0	-5.2
Singapore	10.8	8.7	12.5	15.5	16.1	14.6	10.5	11.7	3.4	7.3	10.2	5.2	n.a.
Taiwan	1.9	-2.2	-5.4	-3.9	-1.7	-1.1	-1.4	-1.6	0.1	-1.3	-4.7	-6.5	n.a.
Thailand	4.8	4.3	2.6	1.9	2.7	3.0	0.9	-1.5	-2.8	-3.3	-2.2	-2.4	-1.4
Vietnam	-7.2	-2.3	-2.4	-4.6	-1.6	-0.8	-0.7	-0.8	n.a.	n.a.	n.a.	n.a.	n.a.

Source: Asian Development Bank, *Key Indicators of Developing Asian and Pacific Countries*, various issues.

to 12 percent by end-1998 (Goldman Sachs, 1999, The Asian Economic Quarterly, November, Hong Kong). Thus, even though the 1998 average interest rate level was higher than that of 1997, the monetary policy was, in reality, relaxed.

5 Statutory reserve requirements (SRR) is the minimum percentage of total assets, which banks or other financial institutions are required to hold in money balances or in some form of highly liquid assets. SRR may be used as instruments of monetary policy, or as methods of trying to ensure BIs' solvency.

6 Private capital includes portfolio investment, debt, trade credits and changes in non-resident accounts in the banking system.

7 Before the 1997–98 crisis, most of the crisis-hit economies did not give high

Table 1-A3   Reserves (US$ million) 1990–2002

	1990	1991	1992	1993	1994	1995	1996	1997	1998	1999	2000	2001	2002
Cambodia	n.a.	n.a.	n.a.	n.a.	n.a.	191.98	265.78	298.53	324.28	393.19	501.68	586.81	776.15
China	30,209	44,308	21,230	22,999	53,560	76,036	107,676	143,363	149,812	158,336	168,855	218,698	295,202
Hong Kong	488,744	532,086	542,568	561,794	664,075	711,002	672,456	693,454	590,840	572,038	558,041	516,395	506,327
Indonesia	8,520	10,250	11,394	12,354	13,199	14,787	19,281	17,396	23,517	27,257	29,268	28,018	31,577
Japan	77,053	68,980	68,685	95,589	122,845	182,820	217,867	220,792	215,949	288,080	361,638	401,959	469,728
Korea	14,825	13,733	17,153	20,261	25,673	32,712	34,073	20,405	52,041	74,054	96,198	102,821	121,414
Lao PDR	2.4	29.2	40.9	63.6	61.5	92.7	170.1	112.8	112.8	105.3	139.6	133.5	194.1
Malaysia	9,871	11,003	17,343	27,364	25,545	23,899	27,130	20,899	25,675	30,645	29,576	30,526	34,277
Myanmar	325	271	292	315	435	573	241	261	326	277	234	411	481
Philippines	2,048	4,526	5,338	5,921	7,121	7,775	11,745	8,738	10,781	15,012	15,024	15,659	16,180
Singapore	27,748	34,133	39,885	48,361	58,177	68,695	76,847	71,289	74,928	76,843	80,132	75,375	82,021
Taiwan	78,064	88,325	88,308	89,298	98,273	95,911	93,594	88,186	95,084	111,061	111,370	126,572	166,046
Thailand	14,273	18,416	21,182	25,440	30,279	36,945	38,645	26,892	29,536	34,781	32,661	33,041	38,915
Vietnam	n.a.	n.a.	n.a.	n.a.	n.a.	n.a.	n.a.	n.a.	n.a.	n.a.	n.a.	n.a.	n.a.

Source: Asian Development Bank, *ADB Review*, various issues.

Table 1-A4   FDI Inflows (US$ million) 1990–2002

	1990	1991	1992	1993	1994	1995	1996	1997	1998	1999	2000	2001	2002
Cambodia	n.a.	n.a.	33	54	69	151	294	168	243	230	149	148	54
China	3,489	4,366	11,156	27,515	33,787	35,849	40,800	44,237	43,751	40,319	40,772	46,846	52,700
Hong Kong	1,728	538	2,051	1,667	7,828	6,213	10,460	11,368	14,766	24,580	61,939	23,775	13,718
Indonesia	1,093	1,482	1,777	2,004	2,109	4,346	6,194	4,678	-356	-2,745	-4,550	-3,279	-1,523
Japan	1,753	1,730	2,756	210	912	39	200	3,225	3,192	12,742	8,323	6,243	9,326
Korea	788	1,180	727	588	991	1,357	2,308	2,844	5,412	9,333	9,283	3,528	1,972
Laos	6	8	8	30	59	88	128	86	45	52	34	24	25
Malaysia	2,333	3,998	5,183	5,006	4,581	5,816	7,296	6,323	2,714	3,895	3,788	544	3,203
Myanmar	5	0	171	149	126	227	310	879	684	304	208	192	129
Philippines	530	544	228	1,238	1,591	1,459	1,520	1,261	1,718	1,725	1,345	982	1,111
Singapore	5,575	4,879	2,204	4,686	8,550	7,206	8,984	13,533	7,594	13,245	12,464	10,949	7,655
Taiwan	1,330	1,271	879	917	1,375	1,559	1,864	2,248	222	2,926	4,928	4,109	1,445
Thailand	2,444	2,014	2,114	1,804	1,343	2,000	2,405	3,882	7,491	6,091	3,350	3,813	1,068
Vietnam	16	32	385	523	1,936	2,349	2,455	2,587	1,700	1,484	1,289	1,300	1,200

Source: UNCTAD, *World Investment Report*, various issues.

priority to developing active bond markets because of the lack of government bonds during surplus budget periods. The private debt securities markets were also small because businesses raised most of their funding through banks.

References

Amsden, A. H. 1989. *Asia's Next Giant; South Korea and Late Industrialization.* New York: Oxford University Press.

ASEAN Secretariat. 2003. *ASEAN Secretariat Database.*

Asian Development Bank (ADB). *Key Indicators of Developing Asian and Pacific Countries* (various issues). Manila: ADB.

Chen, B. L. 1996. Picking the Winners and Industrialization in Taiwan. *Journal of International Trade and Economic Development,* 5: pp. 137–159.

Goldman Sachs. 1999. *The Asian Economic Quarterly,* November.

Ohno, K. and Ohno, I. eds. 1998. *Japanese Views on Economic Development: Diverse Paths to the Market.* London: Routledge.

Rodrick, D. 1995. Getting Intervention Right: How South Korea and Taiwan Grew Rich. *Economic Policy,* pp. 55–107.

United Nations Conference on Trade and Development (UNCTAD). *World Investment Reports* (various issues). New York: United Nations

Wong, P., and Ng, C. eds. 2001. *Industrial Policy, Innovation and Economic Growth: The Experience of Japan and the Asian NIEs.* Singapore: Singapore University Press.

World Bank. 1993. *The East Asian Miracle: Economic Growth and Public Policy.* New York: Oxford University Press.

2

The Emergence and Proliferation of FTAs in East Asia

Shujiro Urata

Introduction

Globalization of economic activities has been accelerating rapidly in recent years with the remarkable expansion and cross border movements of goods, money, information and people. Although globalization has allegedly brought some negative consequences such as widening income gaps between countries as well as within countries, on the whole it has brought positive impacts such as rapid economic growth and technological progress. One factor that contributed to globalization is substantial trade liberalization, carried out under the auspices of the GATT/WTO.

Up against rapid globalization, regionalization—or regional economic integration—has emerged in recent years throughout various parts of the world. Regionalization takes two forms. One type of regionalization arises as a result of natural economic developments where the benefits of agglomeration including economies of scope, scale and speed outweigh the costs of agglomeration such as congestion. Indeed, rapidly growing economies in proximity interacting with each other through market and non-market channels accelerate their economic growth. The other type of regionalization involves institutional arrangement such as regional trade agreements (RTAs) including free trade agreements (FTAs) and customs unions. RTAs are discriminatory trade agreements, providing members with preferential treatment. The former type of regionalization may be characterized as 'market-driven,' while the latter 'institution-driven.'

Rapid economic growth in East Asia has increased its importance in the world economy in the post-WWII period. As a consequence, East Asia has become recognized as an important region that influences the world economy along with North America and Western Europe. Regional economic integration in Western Europe started in the early post-WWII period, mainly in the form of establishing regional institutions, while regional economic integration in North America was initially developed through market forces before being supplemented by regional institutions. As such regionalization in Western Europe may be characterized as

39

'institution-driven,' while regionalization in North America was 'market-driven' in the early stages and supplemented by 'institution-driven' regionalization. In light of these global and regional developments, this paper examines the patterns of regional economic integration in East Asia. From the analysis we observe a shift from 'market-driven' to 'institution-driven' regionalization in East Asia, similarly to North America.

The remainder of the paper consists of six sections. The following section examines globalization of East Asia in terms of trade and foreign direct investment (FDI) for the 1980s and 1990s. The third and fourth sections ('Increasing Intra-Regional Dependence in Trade and FDI' and 'Creation of Intra-Regional Production Systems in East Asia') investigate the patterns of regionalization in East Asia with the third section focusing on trade and FDI flows separately, and the fourth section focusing on the regional production system by taking into account trade and FDI flows jointly. Section five ('Recent Surge of FTAs in East Asia') turns to the institution-driven regionalization in East Asia. Section six ('Factors Behind the Proliferation of FTAs in East Asia') examines the factors leading to the emergence and proliferation of FTAs, while sections seven and eight ('Benefits of FTAs in East Asia' and 'Obstacles to FTAs in East Asia') examine the benefits of an East Asian FTA and the obstacles to the formation of an East Asian FTA, respectively. The final section concludes the paper by providing some suggestions to overcome the obstacles.

Rapid Expansion of Foreign Trade and FDI in East Asia

Foreign trade and FDI have played important roles in international economic activities for the world and in particular for East Asia.[1] Indeed, rapid expansion of foreign trade and FDI has been considered crucial factors contributing to rapid economic growth for East Asia. This section reviews the globalization of economic activities in East Asia by focusing on the changing patterns of foreign trade and FDI in the 1980s and 1990s, in order to set the stage for the analysis of the changing nature of regionalization from market-driven to institution-driven types toward the end of the 1990s.

Foreign Trade
Foreign trade in the East Asian economies expanded rapidly, beginning in the mid-1980s until the outbreak of the East Asian financial crisis (Table 2-1 and Figure 2-1, see Appendix). Between 1985 and 1997 exports from emerging East Asian economies expanded steadily to register an almost fivefold increase, before

declining in 1998 as a result of the crisis. The rate of expansion was particularly high from 1986 to 1988, when the annual rate of growth exceeded 20 percent. The 1990s saw fluctuations in the annual rates of growth with a peak at 22 percent in 1995 followed by a decline, resulting in negative growth in 1998. The patterns of export growth for the period of 1985 to 1999 are similar for all emerging East Asian economies, with few exceptions. Compared with the four newly industrializing economies (NIE-4, i.e., Hong Kong, Korea, Singapore and Taiwan) and the core Association of Southeast Asian Nations (ASEAN) economies (Indonesia, Malaysia, the Philippines, and Thailand), China registered a significantly higher growth rate in the 1990s. Compared with the emerging East Asian economies, Japan fared less favorably in terms of export expansion, as Japan's exports increased only 2.4-fold between 1985 and 1997.

As a result of rapid export expansion, East Asia increased its share of world exports from 9 percent in 1980–85 to 18 percent in 1997, before declining slightly in 1998. As a group, the NIE-4 expanded their share from 5 percent in 1980–85 to 10 percent in 1997. China became the largest exporter among the emerging East Asian economies in 1999, accounting for 3 percent of world exports. Although still maintaining a substantial share in world exports, Japan's share in world exports declined from 10.3 percent in 1986 to 7.2 percent in 1998 because of relatively slower growth.

One notable development was the rapid expansion of manufactured exports. Specifically, the share of manufactured products in total exports for the NIE-4 and the ASEAN-5 increased from 71 percent and 18 percent, respectively, in 1980 to 87 percent and 60 percent in 1995. For China, the corresponding share increased from 67 percent in 1990 to 79 percent in 1995.

Similar to the case of exports, imports to emerging East Asian economies increased substantially in the 1980s and 1990s before the crisis. Specifically, their imports increased 6.5 times between 1980 and 1997, before a decline in 1998 due to the crisis. Among the emerging East Asian economies, Hong Kong achieved the largest increase with an almost tenfold increase during the period of 1980 to 1997. Hong Kong was followed by China and Malaysia whose imports increased 7.3-fold. In contrast to the emerging East Asian economies, which achieved remarkable import expansion, Japan saw its imports only double in seventeen years from 1980 to 1997. Indeed, it should be noted that the magnitude of Japan's imports was comparable to that of the emerging East Asian economies in the early 1980s, but in the late 1990s it was almost one-third of the imports of the emerging East Asian economies.

The rapid expansion of imports by the emerging East Asian economies resulted in the increase of their share in world imports from 8.1 percent in 1980 to 18 percent in 1997. Contrasting this to the increased share by the emerging East Asian economies, Japan's share in world imports declined from 7.4 percent in 1980 to 5.1 percent in 1998, before a slight increase in 1999.

An examination of foreign trade by East Asian economies revealed a substantial increase in both exports and imports in the 1980s and 1990s before they were struck by the financial crisis in 1997. We also observed somewhat contrasting developments between the emerging East Asian economies on the one hand and Japan on the other hand. Emerging East Asian economies, particularly China in the 1990s, registered a remarkable growth, while Japan achieved a less spectacular performance. As a result of rapid trade expansion by East Asian economies, their share in world exports and imports increased from 15 and 15 percent in 1980, to 25 and 21 percent in 1999, respectively. A large part of the increase was achieved by the emerging East Asian economies, although Japan still has a substantial position, amounting to about one-third of trade conducted by all East Asian economies. It is worth noting that the magnitude of exports by East Asian economies was twice as large as the magnitude for the U.S. and approximately 65 percent of the value for the EU in 1999, while the corresponding values in terms of imports were 114 and 56 percent, respectively. These observations indicate that East Asia represents a significant position in world trade.

Foreign Direct Investment

FDI inflows to emerging East Asian economies grew at a remarkably high rate from the mid-1980s to 1998, significantly faster than exports. Indeed, FDI inflows increased more than 12 times in the 14 years from 1985 to 1999 (Table 2-2 and Figure 2-2, see Appendix). Unlike exports, FDI inflows continued to grow throughout the period. As result of this rapid expansion, the share of emerging East Asian economies in world FDI inflows increased from 8 percent in 1985 to 22 percent in 1994, before declining sharply to 9 percent in 1999. China increased its share in world FDI inflows from 3 percent in 1985 to 14 percent in 1994, though the share declined to 4 percent in 1999. Despite this decline, China was the largest recipient of FDI among emerging market economies and the third largest recipient in the world, behind the United States and the United Kingdom, in 1999. Compared with emerging East Asian economies, Japan received very small amount of FDI inflows throughout the period, although it has begun to register sizeable amount in recent years. East Asia increased its share in world FDI inflows in the pre-crisis period up to 1997 as the share increased from 7.6 percent in 1985 to 19 percent in 1996 before declining in 10 percent in 1999. The share of East Asia in world FDI inflows is significantly smaller when compared to the case of foreign trade. Indeed, the corresponding shares of the U.S. and the EU in world FDI inflows are much larger at 30 and 40 percent, respectively in 1999.

Two developments are important concerning recent FDI in emerging East Asia. One is its resilience, even during the period of economic crisis. Compared with other forms of international capital flows such as bank lending, which declined precipitously before and after the crisis, FDI inflows remained relatively stable in emerging East Asian economies, even in those economies that were seriously affected by the crisis. Another important development is the increase in mergers and acquisitions (M&As) as a mode of entry, particularly after the economic crisis (United Nations 1999). Historically, green-field operations used to be a preferred mode of entry for multinationals in East Asia, mainly because of restrictions on equity participation. The economic crisis changed this. Emerging East Asian economies with a keen interest in attracting FDI relaxed the restrictions. Coupled with relaxation of the FDI regime, the huge decline in the values of East Asian currencies and assets encouraged multinationals to undertake M&A.

Turning to FDI outflows from East Asia, one finds that East Asian economies, with the exceptions of Japan and Hong Kong, have not been large investors. Although Hong Kong registers sizeable FDI outflows, it may not be considered as a large investor because a substantial amount of FDI outflows from Hong Kong originates in other countries. One finds a dramatic decline in the position of Japan as an FDI supplier in the 1990s. In 1990 Japan was the world largest FDI supplier as it supplied 20 percent of world FDI outflows. However, in ten years its share declined to less than 3 percent.

Rapid Globalization of Economic Activities in East Asia
Foreign trade and FDI inflows became increasingly important in emerging East Asian economies. All of the economies, except China and Indonesia, registered a ratio of exports to GDP exceeding 30 percent, significantly higher than the average ratio of approximately 23 percent for the developing economies in 1997 (World Bank 2000). Hong Kong and Singapore had extremely high ratios, which are attributable to their engagement in entrepôt trade. Although high, the ratios for Korea and Taiwan declined from the mid-1980s to the mid-1990s because of the rapid increase in GDP. ASEAN-4 countries, consisting of Indonesia, Malaysia, Philippines, and Thailand, exhibited an increase in the ratio of exports to GDP, reflecting faster growth of exports compared with GDP. Considering that large countries tend to be less dependent on foreign trade than small countries, it is notable that the export to GDP ratios for China and Indonesia exceeded 20 percent.

Although increasing steadily for most developing East Asian economies, the ratio of FDI inflows to GDP was significantly smaller than the ratio of exports to GDP and varied widely within the region. Singapore had the highest ratio, around 10 percent, while Korea and Taiwan had the lowest, around 0.5–1.0 percent. China and Malaysia registered a rapid increase in the ratio, each reaching about 5 percent in 1997. The role of FDI in emerging East Asian economic activities is even more important because the foreign affiliates of multinationals engage actively through production, employment, purchases and sales, including foreign trade, in the FDI recipient economies.

Factors Behind the Rapid Expansion of Trade and FDI

Factors behind the significant expansion in foreign trade and FDI inflows in East Asia fall into two groups, one concerning domestic factors and the other concerning external factors. The most important domestic factor was the liberalization of both trade and FDI policies. In addition, a favorable macroeconomic environment reflected in relatively stable price levels, together with an abundant supply of well educated, low-wage labor contributed to the expansion of exports and FDI inflows. As for the external factors, the substantial realignment of exchange rates, particularly the yen-dollar exchange rate in the mid-1980s, was important in promoting exports and FDI inflows. In the 1990s the record-breaking long economic boom in the U.S. provided huge markets for East Asian exports. In addition, the remarkable technical progress achieved in information technology, which reduced the cost of communications, facilitated global operations by multinational firms. Finally, increased competition among multinational firms, which resulted partly from liberalization and deregulation in various sectors in many countries of the world, promoted their global activities, thereby expanding trade and FDI.

Emerging East Asian economies embarked on the liberalization of trade and FDI policies, and deregulation in domestic economic activities as part of more comprehensive structural reform policies. Such policy changes were due to the realization that liberalization and deregulation would promote economic growth. The liberalization of trade and FDI policies led to the expansion of exports and inward FDI because it shifted the incentives from import-substituting production to export production and increased the attractiveness of these economies to foreign investors.

Emerging East Asian economies liberalized their import regimes by lowering tariff rates and non-tariff barriers from the early 1980s through the early 1990s (PECC 1995). The notable exception was Hong Kong and Singapore, which had virtually adopted free trade regimes. China and Indonesia significantly reduced their average tariff rates. The incidence of non-tariff barriers declined in many

East Asian economies, except in China. The most remarkable is Indonesia, which reduced non-tariff barriers from 95 percent in 1984–87 to less than 3 percent in 1991–93. Korea also reduced both its tariff rates and the incidence of non-tariff barriers during the period from 1988 to 1993.

Inward FDI policies were liberalized in the mid-1980s as East Asian economies began to realize that FDI inflows would promote economic growth. Although it is difficult to quantify the restrictiveness of an FDI regime, it is clear that many emerging East Asian economies have liberalized their FDI policies since the mid-1980s (Yamazawa and Urata, 2001). Restrictions on FDI took various forms, including restrictions on market access, most-favored-nation treatment and national treatment. Many emerging East Asian economies reduced the restrictions on market access by reducing the number of sectors and industries on the negative list and by relaxing the limits on foreign equity ownership. Among the emerging East Asian economies, Indonesia, Korea, Malaysia, the Philippines, and Thailand adopted substantial FDI liberalization measures in an effort to attract foreign investors. Furthermore, recognizing the important contribution that FDI may make toward economic growth, a number of economies introduced incentives such as tax breaks to attract FDI. Indeed, there has been keen competition amongst emerging East Asian economies to attract FDI by reducing barriers and providing incentives.

Liberalization of trade and FDI also progressed under regional and global frameworks. The members of ASEAN formed the ASEAN Free Trade Area (AFTA) in 1992, the only formal regional trade arrangement in East Asia. The 1992 agreement provided for the liberalization of tariff and non-tariff measures under the Common Effective Preferential Tariffs. The target year for achieving tariff and non-tariff liberalization was originally set for 2008, but was later moved forward to 2003. FDI liberalization in ASEAN has been underway after the creation of the ASEAN Investment Area (AIA) in 1998, which provides coordinated investment cooperation and facilitation programs, market access, and national treatment of all industries. The target dates for the creation of the AFTA are 2003 for the original ASEAN members and Myanmar, and 2010 for Vietnam, Laos and Cambodia.

APEC has also contributed to the liberalization and facilitation of trade and FDI for emerging East Asian economies. This trans-regional forum includes not only East Asian economies but also countries in North and South America and Oceania. Following the Bogor declaration in 1994 calling for full liberalization of trade and FDI by 2010 for developed-country members and by 2020 for developing-country members, APEC members agreed to prepare and implement individual action plans specifying near- and medium-term liberalization measures. Peer pressure is expected to play a crucial role in implementation.

All APEC members have made significant progress toward freer trade and FDI regimes.

The Uruguay Round of multilateral trade negotiations under GATT started in 1986 and ended in 1994. Although the negotiations lasted eight years, the Uruguay Round made substantial progress toward liberalizing trade and FDI. The achievements include: a reduction in tariff rates; framework agreements on trade in services, intellectual property rights and trade-related investment measures; a timetable for phasing out all quantitative restrictions on trade; first steps toward bringing agriculture more firmly under a multilateral discipline; a stronger dispute settlement mechanism; and the establishment of the World Trade Organization. Though it is difficult to estimate the impact of these achievements individually, there is no doubt that the GATT/WTO has promoted trade and FDI liberalization in East Asia.

Increasing Intra-Regional Dependence in Trade and FDI in East Asia[2]

The preceding section reviewed the recent developments in East Asia's trade and FDI vis-à-vis the rest of the world. In other words, it focused on the globalization of East Asia. This section turns to the subject of regionalization in East Asia by reviewing trade and FDI patterns. The analysis reveals the formation of regional production systems by multinational corporations (MNCs), which appears to have contributed to regionalization in East Asia.

The Measurement of Intra-Regional Dependence

Several studies have examined the changes in intra-regional dependence in foreign trade in East Asia. Computing three sets of measures, Petri (1993) finds that intra-regional dependence in foreign trade in East Asia increased steadily in the post-World War II period, after declining in the pre-World War II period, and that intra-regional bias declined in the post-World War II period. Frankel (1993) also finds a decline in intra-regional bias in foreign trade in the 1980s by estimating the magnitude of the bias in the gravity model framework. This subsection investigates the changing patterns of intra-regional trade and FDI in East Asia from the early 1980s to the late-1990s. Following Petri (1993), the following three measures are computed for foreign trade and FDI: absolute measures, relative measures, and double-relative measures.

Absolute measure (A): $A = X_{ij} / X..$

Relative measure (B): $B = A / (X_i. / X..) = X_{ij} / X_i.$

Double-relative measure (C): $C = A / [(X_{i.} / X..) (X_{.j} / X..)] = X_{ij} * X.. / X_{i.} * X_{.j}$

where Xij represents exports (or outward FDI) from region i to region j, and '.' indicates the summation across all i or j. Therefore, $X_{i.}$ represents total exports (or outward FDI flows) of region i, $X_{.j}$ represents total imports (or inward FDI flows) of region j, and $X..$ represents world trade (or world total FDI flows).

The absolute measure compares the scale of a particular bilateral trading (or FDI) relationship to world trade (or world FDI), while the relative measure compares it to trade (or FDI) of one or the other of the two partners participating in the relationship. The double-relative measure, which is commonly called the intensity index, shows the intensity or bias of the bilateral trading (or FDI) relationship by taking into account its importance in world trade (or world FDI). The value of unity for the double-relative measure can be interpreted so that the bilateral relationship is neutral, while the relationship is more (or less) biased when the measure is greater (or less) than unity.

Foreign Trade

Table 2-3 (see Appendix) shows the estimated values of the three measures of foreign trade and FDI for several regions in the world—East Asia, the North American Free Trade Agreement (NAFTA) region, the European Union, and the MERCOSUR region. The results indicate that intra-regional trade in East Asia became more important not only in terms of world trade but also in terms of regional trade. However, intra-regional bias became smaller over time.

The importance of intra-East Asian trade in world trade increased significantly from 5 percent in 1980 to 13 percent in 1995, though it declined slightly to 11 percent in 1999. The share of intra-NAFTA trade in world trade also increased over the same period, but the share was smaller, at 10 percent in 1999. The corresponding share for the European Union was significantly higher, at 23 percent in 1999, although the share had declined sharply from 29 percent in 1990.

A significant part of intra-East Asian trade takes place between Japan and emerging East Asian economies. This can be seen from the fact that the share of intra-regional trade among emerging East Asian economies (6 percent in 1999) amounts to only slightly more than half of the level observed for East Asia as a whole (11 percent), that is, including Japan. The magnitude of intra-regional trade for the Asian NIE-4 and for the ASEAN-10 is still quite small in world trade, amounting to 1.2 percent and 1.4 percent of world trade in 1999, respectively.

Intra-East Asian trade increased its importance for East Asia's total trade (exports + imports) over time, as shown in the increase in the relative measure from 36 percent in 1980 to 50 percent in 1997, followed by a slight decline to 49 percent in 1999. The comparable figures for emerging East Asia were 22 and 39 percent in 1980 and 1999, respectively. The importance of intra-regional trade in total regional trade also increased for the members of NAFTA from 33 to 47 percent during the same period, but it declined for the European Union from 65 percent in 1990 to 61 percent in 1999, after rising between 1980 and 1990. Among the sub-groups in East Asia, intra-group trade between the NIE-4 was quite small, amounting to only 13 percent of total trade, while intra-ASEAN-10 trade was larger, at 23 percent.

An analysis of the relative measures computed for exports and imports shows that intra-East Asian trade is more important as a source of imports than as a destination for exports. This finding indicates a trading pattern in which East Asian economies procure imports within the region and sell exports outside the region. This appears to reflect the behavior of multinationals, as will be confirmed in a later section. Many multinationals use East Asia as an export platform, in which they assemble export products for regions outside of East Asia by importing parts and components from within the region. In contrast, intra-NAFTA trade is more important for NAFTA's exports than for its imports.

The results of the double-relative measure (or the trade intensity index) reveal an interesting contrast concerning the intra-regional trade bias for East Asia, on the one hand, and the NAFTA and the European Union, on the other hand. Specifically, intra-regional bias declined in East Asia from 2.6 in 1980 to 2.3 in 1999, while the corresponding values for the NAFTA and the European Union increased from 2.1 and 1.5 to 2.3 and 1.7, respectively, over the same period. Among East Asian subgroups, intra-regional trade bias is very high for ASEAN, with the double-relative measure at 4.2 in 1999, although the size of the bias has declined over time.

The estimated measures of intra-regional trade dependence reveal that the importance of intra-regional trade in East Asia increased not only in world trade but also in regional trade over time. However, extra-regional trade also expanded rapidly. Indeed, intra-regional trade bias declined in East Asia, while it increased in the NAFTA and the European Union. One may attribute these differences partly to differences in the institutional arrangements. Both NAFTA and the European Union have trade arrangements that give preferential treatment to their members, possibly leading to an increasing regional bias. In East Asia, a preferential trading arrangement has been set up only for the ASEAN members that make up a small portion of intra-East Asian trade, and other economies that do not have any discriminatory arrangements. The absence of discriminatory trade arrangements may have caused a decline in trade bias. Unilateral trade liberalization without discriminatory treatment among trading partners, even including those of ASEAN, may have contributed to a decline in regional trade bias in East Asia. Furthermore, a decline in the cost of communications and transportation services, resulting from technological progress and liberalization, contributed to the diversification of trading partners. Rapid industrialization centered on similar industries such as textiles and electric machinery, forcing many East Asian economies to look outside the region for markets for their products, diminishing the intra-regional trade bias (Petri 1993).

Foreign Direct Investment

Similar to the changing patterns of trade, intra-regional FDI in East Asia increased from 4 percent of world FDI in 1980 to 8 percent in 1994. The corresponding share for the European Union also increased from 13 to 19 percent, while it declined for NAFTA from 14 to 5 percent. Among the East Asian sub-groups, the stock of intra-regional FDI in the emerging economies registered relatively high growth, increasing from 2 to 6 percent of world FDI during the period of 1980 to 1994.

Intra-regional FDI in East Asia increased from 40 percent in 1980 to 43 percent in 1994. Among the sub-groups, intra-regional FDI became particularly important for emerging East Asian economies. Coupled with this observation, the relatively small shares of intra-regional FDI for NIEs and ASEAN indicate the importance of FDI from the former to the latter sub-group. Intra-regional FDI is particularly important because 87 percent of outward FDI has been directed to emerging East Asian economies. The share of inward FDI has increased in East Asia, which means that an increasing share of inward FDI originates inside the region. However, the share of intra-regional FDI in regional FDI is substantially smaller for emerging East Asian economies, reflecting the importance of Japan as a source of FDI.

The results of double-relative measures show an interesting contrast between East Asia and the European Union. Although the magnitude of the bias is higher for East Asia than for the European Union, the magnitude of the bias declined for East Asia, while it increased for the European Union. The extent of the bias remained more or less the same for NAFTA. These observations are consistent with those made for foreign trade, and differences in the direction of bias for East Asia and for the European Union may reflect differences in institutional arrangements, as argued in the case of foreign trade.

Patterns similar to those of trade are found for intra-regional FDI in East Asia. That is, from 1980 to 1994 the importance of intra-regional FDI in East Asia increased not only in world FDI but also in overall regional FDI in East Asia. However, a regional bias declined during the period of 1980 to 1994. These findings indicate that the increasing importance of intra-regional trade and FDI is attributable largely to the rapid expansion of overall trade and FDI in the region that is driven by market forces. This contrasts with the case in the

European Union or NAFTA, where intra-regional bias in foreign trade and FDI increased possibly because of discriminatory institutional arrangements under which regional members receive preferential treatment, worsening resource allocation.

A lack of necessary information precludes us from computing the measures for intra-regional dependence in FDI for the period after 1994. However, there appears to be some evidence that would indicate the declining intra-regional dependence in FDI for East Asia since the mid-1990s. One piece of evidence is substantial declines in the shares of East Asia in world FDI inflows and outflows for the latter half of the 1990s (Table 2-2, see Appendix). Another is the sharp decline in the importance of East Asian economies as foreign investors in East Asia. According to the figures in Table 2-4 (see Appendix), East Asia lost its share as FDI supplier in all the East Asian economies listed in the table except Indonesia. In contrast to the position of East Asia, the EU increased its shares in many East Asian economies. These findings indicate the declining importance of East Asia not only in world FDI but also as a supplier of FDI in East Asia, which in turn tends to show a decline in intra-regional dependence in FDI.

Creation of Intra-Regional Production Systems in East Asia

Increasing Intra-Regional Dependence in Production
So far the changing patterns of foreign trade and FDI in East Asia have been examined without considering their relations with the economic structures of the East Asian economies. Our earlier observation that foreign trade in the East Asian economies and, in particular, intra-regional trade in East Asia, which has expanded rapidly since the 1980s, may indicate a substantial impact on economic structures of the East Asian region as well as those of the individual economies. This section investigates intra-regional trade patterns in East Asia by explicitly relating them to procurement sources of the inputs for production by using international input-output tables. From this analysis, the changing characteristics of intra-regional, inter-industry relationships in East Asia will be discerned.

The Institute of Developing Economies in Japan constructed international input-output tables covering East Asian economies and the U.S. for 1985, 1990 and 1995. The international input-output tables are constructed by linking input-output tables of the individual economies by explicitly specifying the import sources and export destinations of the products. The international input-output table shows the sources of inputs for production, that is, inputs from domestic markets and imported inputs from other economies. Like input-output tables, the international input-output table shows destinations of outputs, that is, outputs sold in domestic market and those exported to other economies. Below we examine the sources of inputs for production by East Asian economies, as our main interest is to examine the inter-industry and intra-regional production relationships of East Asia.

Table 2-5 (see Appendix) shows the production (input) structures of East Asian economies in 1985 and 1995. Between 1985 and 1995 the importance of imported inputs in production increased for the East Asian economies except Singapore, Korea and Japan, indicating increasing dependence on foreign countries for the supply of intermediate inputs. Wide variations in the importance of imported inputs in production can be observed for East Asian economies. Malaysia, the Philippines, Singapore, Thailand and Taiwan exhibit high dependence, as the share of imported inputs in production for these economies exceeded 10 percent. Indonesia, China and Korea have low shares at around 6 percent.

To examine intra-regional dependence for production in East Asia we computed the share of imported inputs, which originated inside the region, in total inputs (total intermediate goods and value added). The results, which are shown under 'East Asia (including Japan) excluding own domestic production,' show the increase in intra-regional dependence in production for East Asian economies except Korea and Japan. Singapore and Malaysia register particularly high dependence, while dependence for China and Japan is quite low.

The foregoing analysis did not reveal 'true' intra-regional dependence in production, as it only took account of direct inputs and did not consider indirect inputs, which are required for the production of inputs. To shed light on the true intra-regional dependence, we computed the magnitude of output being induced by a unit increase in final demand in a particular economy in East Asia by using international input-output tables. The results of the computation, which incorporates not only inter-industry relationships inside the economy but also those with other East Asian economies, are presented in Table 2-6 (see Appendix). For example, in 1985 one unit increase in final demand in Indonesia increases output of Indonesia by 1.6026 units.[3] It also increases output of Korea and Taiwan by 0.0039 and 0.0030, respectively.

The figures in Table 2-6 show that intra-regional, inter-industry relationships deepened from 1985 to 1995, because for East Asia a higher level of output is obtained in 1995 (16.2102 units), compared with 1985 (16.1393 units), from a unit increase in final demand of all East Asian economies. Although a large part of induced production is realized in the economy registering an increase in final demand, the output of other economies also increases. Indeed, the induced level of output in other East Asian economies, excluding output induced in an economy having an increase in final demand, increased from 0.9762 in 1985 to 1.3591 in 1995, indicating a 'net' deepening in intra-regional, inter-industry relationships. However, the magnitude of the contribution to the deepening of intra-regional, inter-industry relationship is not uniform among East Asian economies. Concerning the 'net' contribution all East Asian economies, excluding Indonesia and Japan, contributed to a deepening of the relationship. An examination of the magnitude of output induced in East Asian economies shows more or less equal dependence on other emerging East Asian economies and Japan for the supply of intermediate inputs. It should be noted that their dependence on Japan increased significantly between 1985 and 1995, probably indicating that large amounts of FDI from Japan promoted imports of inputs from Japan. This finding also indicates the increasing importance of emerging East Asian economies for Japan's economic growth.

Multinational Firms: Promoters of Regional Economic Integration
East Asian economies have experienced rapid expansion of foreign trade and FDI in recent years. We observed increasing intra-regional dependence in foreign trade and production in East Asia. Recognizing the increasingly important role of FDI in economic activities, we investigate the behavior of multinational firms and major foreign investors to examine their role in regional integration. Specifically, we analyze the procurement and sales patterns of their affiliates in Asia. To examine this issue in a comprehensive way, we need the detailed information on trade by multinationals in East Asia. However, necessary data to carry out such an analysis is not available for foreign firms of all origins in East Asia. Below we use the information on Japanese multinationals to examine this issue. Although limited in its coverage, the data on Japanese multinationals would provide us with useful information on the trading patterns of foreign firms in East Asia because Japanese multinationals account for a large portion of multinationals operating in East Asia.

Table 2-7 (see Appendix) presents the procurement and sales patterns of Japanese manufacturing multinationals in Asia in 1992 and 1998. One observes that for the Asian affiliates of Japanese firms, the share of local procurements and sales in their total declined and the share of foreign trade increased from 1992 to 1998. Specifically, the share of imports in total procurements and the share of exports in total sales for their Asian affiliates increased from 51 and 34 percent in 1992 to 56 and 50 percent in 1998, respectively. The corresponding figures for the North American affiliates changed from 49 and 8 percent to 48 and 12 percent, while the figures for European affiliates declined from 71 and 44 percent to 59 and 40 percent (not shown in the table). This data indicates that the Asian affiliates exhibit a greater trade-orientation when compared with those in North America, but they record a lower trade-orientation than those in Europe.

An examination of the regional composition of foreign trade for the overseas affiliates of Japanese firms reveals an increasing importance of intra-regional trade in Asia. For imports by the Asian affiliates, the share of Asia (including

Japan and other Asian economies) in total procurements increased from 47 percent in 1992 to 53 percent in 1998. The corresponding shares for exports in total sales increased from 27 percent to 42 percent. It is of interest to observe that for procurements by the Asian affiliates dependence on other Asian economies increased from 1992 to 1997, while that of Japan declined, possibly reflecting a shift from Japan to other Asian economies as a source of imports. By contrast, for sales by the Asian affiliates, dependence on both Japan and other Asian economies increased at the expense of other regions' exports. Among manufacturing sub-sectors, the affiliates in the electronic machinery sub-sector exhibit high dependence on trade, especially on intra-regional trade, in their procurements and sales, reflecting the presence of regional production networks.

Rapid expansion of foreign trade in Asia by Japanese multinationals was attributable to a rapid expansion of intra-firm trade, that is, foreign trade between the Japanese parent and foreign affiliates, or between foreign affiliates. In particular, intra-firm trade accounts for a substantial share of foreign trade by Asian affiliates in their trade with Japan. For Asian affiliates in Asia in 1998 as much as 96 percent of exports to Japan were destined for their parents in Japan (Table 2-8, see Appendix). Although the dependence on intra-firm trade is less for their imports, as much as 83 percent of the imports by the Asian affiliates from Japan came from their parents. The importance of intra-firm trade is lower for the trade between the affiliates in Asia, when compared with the case for the trade between the affiliates and the parents.

Two interesting observations may be made from the findings on procurement and sales patterns of Japanese multinational firms. Firstly, Japanese multinationals have contributed to the promotion of foreign trade in Asia, in particular intra-regional trade. Secondly, Japanese multinationals have become more active in pursuing intra-regional, inter-process division of labor, probably contributing to the efficient use of factors of production in Asia.

A large number of multinationals in East Asia have been found to be of efficiency-seeking type, not market-seeking type. As such, these multinationals locate themselves in an economy where they can perform their operation most efficiently or at the least cost. Japanese multinationals in machinery sectors such as electronics, which account for a large part of Japanese multinational activity in East Asia, break up their production process into several sub-processes, and locate each sub-process in an economy where that particular sub-process may be carried out most efficiently. For example, some TV producing Japanese multinationals break up the production process into sub-processes such as parts production and assembly operation, and relocate these sub-processes in economies where the required factor inputs are relatively abundant; for example, high-skilled workers for parts production and low-wage labor for assembly operation. The TV manufacturers export parts to an economy where the final products are assembled and export the assembled TVs to other economies.

U.S. multinationals have also been active in setting up production networks in East Asia. Unlike a more or less closed production system favored by Japanese multinationals, production networks constructed by U.S. multinationals are said to be more open to firms from other nationalities such as those from Korea, Singapore and Taiwan. Indeed, the basic strategy of U.S. multinationals is to link up with the most efficient producers regardless of their nationality.[4] Like Japanese multinationals, U.S. multinationals have contributed to an increase in trade-orientation of the host East Asian economies, but they have not contributed much to the promotion of intra-regional trade, as their ties with the U.S. market are, expectedly, strong.[5]

Many firms from the Asian NIEs also set up production networks in various parts of the world, particularly in East Asia. One of the industries that have actively pursued such a globalization strategy is textiles. All these production systems and networks have clearly contributed to greater intra-regional trade interdependence in East Asia.[6]

Recent Surge of FTAs in East Asia

The analysis in the previous sections found market forces as the major driver of regional economic integration in East Asia. This pattern began to change in the late 1990s as many East Asian countries became interested in institutional regional arrangements in the form of FTAs. This section examines recent developments of FTAs in East Asia.

East Asia has in recent years been witnessing the emergence and proliferation of FTAs. One notable characteristic of FTAs in East Asia is their comprehensive coverage. As such, some of the FTAs established in East Asia are termed as an Economic Partnership Agreement (e.g. Japan–Singapore EPA, JSEPA), or Closer Economic Partnership Arrangement (e.g. China–Hong Kong CEPA). These new types of FTAs typically include facilitation of foreign trade, liberalization and facilitation of FDI, economic and technical cooperation, in addition to trade liberalization, which is included in traditional FTAs. It may be worth noting that the basic philosophy of these new types of FTAs is similar to that of the Asia Pacific Economic Cooperation (APEC) forum, whose three pillars are: liberalization; facilitation of foreign trade and foreign investment; economic and technical cooperation.

East Asia was not active until recently in the formation of regional trade agreements (RTAs), which include FTAs and customs union (Table 2-9, see Appendix).[7] Indeed, the ASEAN Free Trade Area (AFTA) was the only major

FTA until Japan and Singapore enacted JSEPA in 2002. AFTA was established in 1992 with six ASEAN member countries, Indonesia, Malaysia, the Philippines, Singapore, Thailand and Brunei. New ASEAN members Cambodia, Laos, Myanmar and Vietnam joined AFTA in the latter half of the 1990s, and currently AFTA has 10 member countries. Besides AFTA, ASEAN as a group, as well as its individual members, have become active in FTA discussions with other countries in recent years. One of the FTAs involving ASEAN that has received most attention recently is with China. ASEAN and China started FTA negotiations in January 2003 with the target of concluding the negotiations by June 2004. ASEAN is also discussing the possibility of FTAs with Japan and Korea. Some ASEAN members have become active in establishing bilateral FTAs. Singapore enacted or signed several FTAs with countries such as New Zealand, Japan, Australia, the U.S., the EFTA, and began negotiations with countries including India. Thailand has also become active in establishing FTAs, as it is currently under negotiations with the U.S. and Japan. The Philippines and Malaysia began negotiations with Japan in 2004.

Compared to ASEAN countries in Southeast Asia, the economies in Northeast Asia including China, Japan, Korea and Taiwan had not been active in FTAs until recently. Despite increasingly strong interest in FTAs by Northeast Asian countries, there is only one FTA (JSEPA) that has been enacted so far. Japan is currently negotiating an FTA with Mexico, Korea, Thailand, Malaysia and the Philippines. Furthermore, it has been studying possible FTAs with ASEAN, Indonesia and Vietnam. Korea started having an interest in FTAs before Japan. In 1998 Korea disclosed a plan to start FTA negotiations with Chile, while it also set up a joint study group (at a private level) on a possible FTA with Japan. Korea started negotiations with Chile in 1999 before signing the agreement in October 2002 after difficult negotiations on the liberalization of agricultural imports. After reaching an agreement, it took the Korean National Assembly more than a year to ratify it, because of strong opposition from the farmers. Korea then started studying the possibilities of FTAs with Singapore, New Zealand and ASEAN.

China's active FTA strategy has received a lot of attention. China joined the WTO in 2001, establishing an access to the world market and pursuing regional strategies by using FTAs. China signed a framework agreement on comprehensive economic cooperation with ASEAN in November 2002. The agreement, which was strongly proposed by China, contains not only trade liberalization but also cooperation in the areas of FDI and economic development. As noted above, China and ASEAN started negotiations on FTA in 2003. China has offered various schemes attractive to ASEAN, and particularly to its new members, such as economic cooperation for the new ASEAN members and advanced trade liberalization (early harvest) in agricultural products. In addition to ASEAN,

China has proposed the establishment of a trilateral FTA with Japan and Korea. China has also enacted an FTA (CEPA) with Hong Kong.

The idea of an FTA covering East Asian countries has emerged. At the leaders' summit meeting of ASEAN+3 (China, Japan and Korea) in 1998 the leaders decided to set up the East Asia Vision Group to study long term vision for economic cooperation. The group has presented the leaders with recommendations including the establishment of an East Asia FTA. Despite the recommendation from the Vision Group, an East Asia FTA has not yet become a concrete agenda at the leaders meeting.

Factors Behind the Proliferation of FTAs in East Asia

Various factors can be identified behind the emergence of strong interest in FTAs in East Asia. Firstly, rapid expansion of FTAs in other parts of the world has prompted East Asian economies to have an interest in establishing FTAs, in order to maintain and expand market access for their exports (Figure 2-3, see Appendix). Many East Asian economies have come to realize the benefits of trade liberalization for the promotion of economic growth, as it has brought an expected outcome of rapid economic growth. Despite the desire of many policy makers for promoting trade liberalization, it has become apparent that trade liberalization under the GATT/WTO has become increasingly difficult. As the number of GATT/WTO members increased, their views on the pace and the extent of trade liberalization have diverged. Indeed, the fact that it took the GATT members eight years, twice as long a period as initially planed, to conclude the Uruguay Round (UR) negotiations, indicates the increasing difficulty in reaching a consensus on trade liberalization. The increasing difficulty in reaching a consensus was a factor that led to a failure by the WTO members to initiate a new round of trade negotiations in Seattle in 1999. Although an agreement was reached in Doha to launch a new round, the new round has faced difficulty in starting substantive negotiation, as even the modality of the negotiations has not yet been agreed upon. Faced with the difficulty in carrying out trade liberalization on the global scale, many countries in other parts of the world have opted to form FTAs among like-minded countries to pursue trade liberalization. As a result of increasing FTAs in other parts of the world, East Asian countries started to feel that they are being discriminated against in many world markets. To overcome such disadvantage and to secure markets for their exports, East Asian countries have become active in forming FTAs.

It should also be noted that many countries in the world, including those in East Asia, began to realize that the GATT/WTO rules could not adequately deal with newly emerging international economic activities such as FDI, services trade, mobility of labor, and others. To put it differently, the rules concerning border measures such as tariffs, which are main focus of the GATT/WTO, cannot provide foreign as well as domestic companies with a level-playing field. It is necessary to go deeper, beyond the border measures, and set up rules covering domestic systems such as competition policy. Many countries share a view that GATT/WTO cannot provide such rules and thus have opted for using FTAs to deal with the problem.

It is important to note that East Asian countries recognize that the EU and NAFTA are very successful in promoting economic growth, and thus East Asian countries have become interested in forming FTAs. East Asia's interest in FTAs has intensified as the EU and the North and South Americas are expanding their FTA networks.

A second related point is that East Asian economies have become interested in using FTAs as a way to promote deregulation and structural reforms in the domestic market. Many East Asian economies pursued deregulation and structural reforms in the 1990s, which contributed to the realization of rapid economic growth. Although the need for accelerating deregulation and structural reforms to further promote economic growth is recognized, many East Asian economies are still recovering from the crisis, meaning room for further deregulation is limited as a result of earlier deregulation. Under these circumstances, external pressures such as FTAs are considered very effective in pursuing deregulation.

Third, many East Asian economies have become interested in using FTAs to promote economic and other types of cooperation in East Asia. The financial crisis in the late 1990s in East Asia increased the awareness of the need for regional cooperation such as FTAs to avoid another crisis and to promote regional economic growth because East Asian economies could not get as much assistance as they hoped from countries outside the region. Indeed, as we have repeatedly pointed out earlier, FTAs and future FTAs in East Asia include not only trade liberalization under traditional FTAs, but also trade and FDI liberalization and facilitation under the name of EPAs. It should be noted that regional cooperation in the area of finance has moved forward significantly as many East Asian economies realized the need for such cooperation to avoid another financial crisis. Specifically, selected East Asian countries instituted the Chang-Mai Initiative, consisting of bilateral currency swap arrangements.

Fourthly, it has to be emphasized that political factors have contributed to the increased interest in FTAs in East Asia. A rivalry between China and Japan to become a 'leader' in East Asia has made them interested in using FTAs to strengthen their relationships with ASEAN and the NIEs. Indeed, in November 2002 Japan proposed an economic partnership framework to ASEAN one day after China agreed to start FTA negotiations with ASEAN. It should also be noted that ASEAN and the NIEs consider FTAs a means to maintain and increase their influential position in East Asia. This is particularly notable for ASEAN as it has been seeking to establish FTAs with China, Japan and Korea separately, or three 'ASEAN+1' FTAs, to maintain and increase its influence before the establishment of an East Asia wide FTA, which will be dominated by China and Japan. ASEAN has been successful in attracting India, the U.S., the EU and other countries outside East Asia to form FTAs, mainly to maintain its influential position in East Asia. It should be noted that India, the U.S., the EU and other countries outside the region regard their relationship with ASEAN countries as important to maintaining their presence in East Asia, particularly in the light of emerging regionalization in East Asia.

Korea, one of the NIEs, which is sandwiched between China and Japan not only geographically but also economically and politically, is keen on maintaining its position as a balancer between the two countries. Indeed, Korea has been an active advocate of an FTA involving China, Japan and Korea. It should also be noted that Korea is interested in establishing a cooperation mechanism in Northeast Asia with China and Japan as a way of helping facilitate the reunification of South and North Korea.

Taiwan stepped up its efforts to establish FTAs with various countries after becoming a WTO member in 2002. Taiwan is interested in using FTAs not only to expand economic relationships but also establishing political and diplomatic relationships. Despite its desire to form FTAs with many countries, its diplomatic status in the international community has made it difficult to achieve its objectives so far.

Finally, we should point out the reasons for the emergence of EPAs rather than traditional FTAs in East Asia. One notable characteristic of East Asia is diversity in the level of economic development for the countries in the region, ranging from high-income countries such as Japan and Singapore to low-income countries such as new ASEAN members. In order for FTAs involving such diverse countries to become a success, traditional trade liberalization under FTAs should be supplemented with cooperation programs such as trade and FDI facilitation, and economic assistance under EPAs, as such programs reduce the adjustment costs of trade liberalization.

Benefits of FTAs in East Asia

The countries interested in FTAs expect various benefits from the formation of FTAs, ranging from economic to non-economic benefits. This section first discusses the benefits of FTAs in terms of trade liberalization and then turns to additional benefits from deeper integration through implementing additional features such as FDI liberalization and economic cooperation under new types of FTAs.

Let us first examine the possible impacts of an FTA on member countries through foreign trade. The trade impacts of an FTA can be classified into two types. One is the static effect and the other is the dynamic effect. In regards the static effect, trade creation, trade diversion and terms of trade effects are important. Removal of trade barriers among the members would promote trade among them (trade creation effect) sometimes at the expense of imports from non-members (trade diversion effect). If an FTA leads to a reduction in imports from non-members, FTA members are likely to experience an improvement in their terms of trade vis-à-vis non-members (terms of trade effect). Trade creation effect and terms of trade effect lead to an increase in economic welfare of the members, while trade diversion effect is likely to reduce economic welfare of the members because imports from most efficient suppliers in non-members are replaced by imports from less-efficient producers from the members. It is important to note that for non-members trade diversion effect and terms of trade effect lead to harmful impacts on their economic welfare.

The preceding discussions on the impact of FTA on foreign trade are given from the point of view of an economy as whole. From the point of the view of the business sector, which has strong influence on policy-making process, two different types of effects are expected. For competitive business, FTA will bring benefits as it enables them to increase their access to members' markets. However, for the non-competitive business sector, FTA will have a harmful effect as it introduces competitive pressure.

In addition to these static effects, dynamic effects can be expected. They include mainly scale effect and competition enhancing effect, both of which would increase economic welfare for both members and non-members. The scale effect may arise from the formation of larger markets as a result of an FTA. Faced with larger markets, companies may be able to exploit the benefits of economies of scale, giving beneficial impacts to consumers in not only member but also non-member countries. A pro-competition effect may be expected, as competition in the market of member countries is likely to intensify as a result of trade liberalization. This pro-competition effect may give rise to new products and new technology, which in turn would benefit consumers in both member and non-member countries. One may consider pro-competition as the effect that would promote domestic policy reform. Many countries can use external pressure to promote domestic reform. In the past, GATT commitments as well as threats from the U.S. and other countries were effective external pressure. However, at present, these pressures are weak. Under such circumstances, FTAs could be effective external pressure.

In addition to the impacts on foreign trade, FTAs are likely to have impacts on FDI. As to the possible impacts of FTAs on FDI, one would expect both an FDI creation effect and an FDI diversion effect. An FDI creation effect indicates an increased FDI among member countries, while an FDI diversion effect refers to a shift of FDI from non-member to member countries. Both effects have positive impacts on member countries in that FDI would be flown into member countries, as trade liberalization via an FTA would increase the attractiveness of members' market. While an FDI creation effect does not have any immediate negative impacts on non-member countries, an FDI diversion effect has negative impacts as FDI is diverted from non-member to member countries. So far the impacts of FTAs on FDI were discussed. If an agreement has FDI liberalization under a new type of FTAs, then naturally it would directly yield the kinds of impacts on FDI discussed above.

The preceding discussions indicate possible benefits for member countries and possible negative impacts on non-member countries. Having noted this, we would like to emphasize the point that the above statement is correct only if the static effects of FTAs are considered, and if both static and dynamic effects are taken into account FTAs are likely to bring benefits not only to members but also to non-members.

Let us examine the possible impacts of an East Asian FTA on East Asian economies. Urata and Kiyota (2003) conducted a simulation exercise by using a general computable equilibrium (CGE) model. Table 2-10 (see Appendix) presents their results for GDP and welfare, measured by equivalent variation (EV), for East Asian economies with a few selected countries. The results indicate that all FTA member economies gain benefits from an East Asian FTA in terms of GDP and EV. The positive impacts are very large for the ASEAN countries. Among the ASEAN countries Thailand gains substantially. Indeed, Thai GDP is estimated to increase as much as 16 percent from the East Asian FTA. A large gain for Thailand is attributable mainly to high protection imposed on the Thai economy before the formation of an East Asian FTA. Vietnam and Indonesia would also gain substantially from the East Asian FTA.

In contrast to the gains accrued to the FTA members, non-member countries experience negative impacts in the forms of declines in GDP and EV. These negative impacts are mainly attributable to the trade diversion effect from the East Asian FTA, through which non-member countries' exports to East Asia are substituted by member countries' exports as a result of preferential treatment given to trade involving the members. It should be noted that the negative impacts on the United States and the EU are quite small, while they are somewhat substantial for Australia/New Zealand and other Asian economies. Relatively large negative impacts for Australia/New Zealand and other Asian economies are attributable to the fact that East Asia is a very important region as an export destination.

Having presented the estimates based on the CGE model exercise, it is important to note that these estimates are likely to be smaller than actual impacts, because they do not fully include dynamic effects. In addition, the impacts would be greater if deeper integration including trade and FDI facilitation, and economic cooperation is adopted.

Before ending the discussions on the benefits of FTAs and EPAs on member countries, we should emphasize the non-economic benefits from these arrangements. Through EPAs the member countries expect to deepen mutual understanding, which would reduce political and social frictions to achieve social and political stability. Social and political stability would in turn contribute to economic growth.

Obstacles to FTAs in East Asia

One may classify the obstacles on the formation of FTAs in East Asia into several categories including economic, historic and political factors. Let me begin with economic factors. The formation of FTAs involving countries at different levels of economic development, as in the case of East Asia, is likely to result in sizeable economic benefits as the removal of trade barriers through FTAs enables the members to use resources efficiently by making them specialize in the production of goods with a comparative advantage. Theoretically, this point may be used as a rationale for establishing FTAs in East Asia, particularly an East Asia-wide FTA, but in reality the formation of such an FTA would encounter strong opposition from non-competitive sectors, which are pressured to go through painful structural adjustment. Indeed, it may be argued that the formation of an FTA involving countries with similar levels of development is easier because they are engaged in intra-industry trade of a horizontal type more actively and, under such circumstances, weaker opposition may be expected.

This point may be supported by the results of simulation exercises by Urata and Kiyota (2003). According to their estimates shown in Table 2-11 (see Appendix), the level of production of the non-competitive and 'sensitive' sectors is projected to decline as a result of FTA. For example, an East Asian FTA would result in the reduction in output of agriculture in Japan and Korea, transportation machinery in China, Taiwan, Malaysia, Indonesia and several other countries. Although agriculture is a declining industry for Japan and Korea, and therefore it may be better to reduce the size of agricultural production from the point of view of resource allocation, a strong opposing coalition of farmers, politicians and bureaucrats makes it difficult for these governments to pursue an East Asian FTA. Many developing East Asian countries, which are interested in developing the automobile sector, presently a non-competitive sector, would not like to see the decline of the sector.

In addition to these economic factors, several political factors are a hindrance to FTAs in East Asia. One is a security issue. East Asia has countries with different political systems. Most countries have democratic political systems but China and Myanmar have authoritarian regimes. While many countries have security alliances with the U.S., China is still considered a possible threat to these alliances. These issues may dissolve as economic development is achieved and as international exchange among these countries is enhanced, resulting in the sharing of common views towards political systems and regional security.

Another political problem in this region towards the establishment of an East Asia FTA is the absence of strong political leadership toward its formation. The experience of Europe reminds us of the crucial role that strong political leadership played in the formation of the EEC (European Economic Community). It is reasonable to assume that China and Japan should take joint leadership roles in East Asia but so far the differences in their views on various issues such as political systems and regional security, as noted above, have been obstacles.

Finally, different views on history involving the Northeast Asian countries, namely, China, Japan and Korea are obstacles to an East Asian FTA. Closer economic and social relations will contribute to reducing the gaps in their views on historic and other issues.

Conclusion: Towards the Establishment of an East Asian FTA

East Asian countries have been active in forming FTAs with other East Asian countries. Many East Asian countries consider the formation of an East Asian FTA as a tentative goal and deeper economic integration like the EU as a long-term goal. The motive behind these policies is potential economic and non-economic benefits from these arrangements. However, various obstacles do exist, as was discussed in the previous section. In this section some possible ways to overcome these obstacles will be presented.

One of the obstacles has to do with the structural adjustment that is required from the formation of FTAs. More specifically, non-competitive sectors have to face increased competitive pressure from FTA partners. One possible way to deal with the necessary structural adjustment is to implement scheduled trade liberalization in sensitive sectors as part of an FTA agreement. GATT/WTO allows the members ten years to complete the FTA. East Asian countries should use this breathing space to facilitate structural adjustment through appropriate adjustment policies. For example, impacted workers should be given financial, technical and other types of assistance so that they can improve their quality of human resources, in order to be able to obtain more productive jobs. If such a program is successful, trade liberalization through an FTA can be pursued smoothly resulting in benefits for all the countries. Indeed, the necessary assistance should be provided by members as a part of economic assistance programs under new types of FTAs. For example, in the case of educating and training workers for upgrading their skills, more developed members such as Japan, Korea, Taiwan and Singapore can provide useful assistance to other countries. In the case of developing competitive small and medium-sized enterprises (SMEs), which would ease the transition process, Japan can provide assistance to other countries. Furthermore, it is very important to analyze the economic and other issues jointly to learn important policy lessons, which may be applicable to the countries. The need for establishing new types of FTAs should be stressed.

As repeatedly noted, East Asian countries need to deepen mutual understanding at all levels, from top leaders to young people, to increase the awareness of the importance of integrated regional markets and regional political and social stability. Leaders' meetings should be held at least annually to increase their mutual understanding. Frequent television-conferences can be used to supplement face-to-face meetings. Policy makers, who are responsible for formulating policies, should establish close communication links. Bureaucrats, business people, academics, students and others should also increase their exchange. In order to facilitate such exchange, the establishment of frameworks such as student exchange programs is effective. Such programs can be set up independently but they would be more effective if they were coordinated under FTAs. Having discussed the need for deepening mutual understanding in the implementation of FTAs in East Asia, it should be emphasized that strong political leadership is a crucial factor that would realize new and drastic policies such as FTAs.

Finally, East Asian countries should not regard completing integration of regional markets in East Asia under an FTA as a goal, rather they should regard it as a step toward achieving global free trade under the WTO. This is very important not only because an East Asian FTA has negative impacts on non-members such as the U.S., the EU and other countries, but also because East Asian countries benefit most from global free trade. To avoid an East Asian FTA becoming a stumbling bloc for global free trade, East Asian countries should make every effort to promote multilateral trade negotiations under the WTO and establish FTAs with countries outside East Asia.

Appendix

See Tables 2-1 to 2-11 and Figures 2-1, 2-2 and 2-3 on the following pages.

Notes

1 An analysis of trade and FDI in sections II and III draws on Kawai and Urata (2004).

2 Urata (2001) conducted similar analyses for the earlier period.

3 The figures are computed as follows. International input-output tables with a 24-sector disaggregation and 10 economies are used in the analysis. To derive the amount of output induced by an increase in final demand, the Leontief inverse matrix is multiplied by a final demand vector consisting of unity for 24 sectors. The resulting output is divided by 24 to obtain the level of output induced by one unit increase in final demand.

4 See Borrus (1998) for the case of U.S. electronics firms in East Asia.

5 Dobson (1997).

6 Gereffi (1999) presents an interesting analysis of an apparel commodity chain developed by firms form the NIEs.

7 In the GATT/WTO, regional trade agreements (RTAs), which violate one of its basic principles of non-discrimination, are permitted under GATT Article XXIV with several conditions, which include substantial liberalization of all trade of the members, not increasing trade barriers on non-members, and completing the RTA process within ten years. For developing countries, more lenient conditions are applied under the enabling clause. An FTA is considered to be a shallow form of regional integration, because it only removes tariff and non-tariff barriers among the members, while a customs union is a deeper integration, as it adopts common external tariffs on non-members, in addition to the removal of tariff and non-tariff barriers on trade among the members.

References

Borrus, Michael. 1999. Exploiting Asia to Beat Japan. In D. Encarnation, ed. *Japanese Multinationals in Asia*. New York: Oxford University Press.
Dobson, Wendy. 1997. Crossing Borders. In Wendy Dobson and Chia Siow Yue, eds. *Multinationals and East Asian Integration*. Canada: International

Development Research Center, and Singapore: Institute of Southeast Asian Studies.

Frankel, Jefferey. A. 1993. Is Japan Creating a Yen Bloc in East Asia and the Pacific? In Jefferey A. Frankel and Miles Kahler, eds. *Regionalism and Rivalry: Japan and the United States in Pacific Asia*. Chicago: University of Chicago Press.

Gereffi, Gary. 1999. International Trade and Industrial Upgrading in the Apparel Commodity Chain. *Journal of International Economics*, 48.

Kawai, Masahiro and Shujiro Urata. 2004. Trade and Foreign Direct Investment in East Asia. In G. de Brouwer and M. Kawai, eds. *Exchange Rate Regimes and East Asia*. London: RoutledgeCurzon.

Pacific Economic Cooperation Council. 1995. *Survey of Impediments to Trade and Investment in the APEC Region*. Singapore: PECC.

Petri, Peter A. 1993. The East Asian Trading Bloc: An Analytical History. In Jefferey A. Frankel and Miles Kahler, eds. *Regionalism and Rivalry: Japan and the United States in Pacific Asia*. Chicago: University of Chicago Press.

United Nations 1999. *World Investment Report 1999*. New York and Geneva: United Nations.

United Nations. 2000. *World Investment Report 2000*. New York and Geneva: United Nations.

Urata, Shujiro. 2001. Emergence of an FDI-Trade Nexus and Economic Growth in East Asia. In Joseph Stiglitz and Shahid Yusuf, eds. *Rethinking the East Asian Miracle*. New York: Oxford University Press.

Urata, Shujiro. 2003. East Asian Economic Partnership Agreement (EPA) and Sustainable Economic Growth. Paper presented at the *International Conference on Political & Economic Security in Asia-Pacific*. Taipei (Taiwan): September 29.

Urata, Shujiro and Kozo Kiyota. 2003. The Impacts of an East Asia FTA on Foreign Trade in East Asia. Paper presented at the *Fourteen Annual East Asian Seminar on Economics*. Taipei (Taiwan): September 5–7.

World Bank. 2000. *East Asia: Recovery and Beyond*. Washington, DC: World Bank.

Yamazawa, Ippei and Shujiro Urata. 2001. Trade and Investment Liberalization and Facilitation. In Ippei Yamazawa, ed. *Asia Pacific Economic Cooperation [APEC]: Challenges and Tasks for the Twenty-first Century*. London: Routledge.

Table 2-1 International Trade of East Asian Economies in the 1980s and 1990s

(a) Value in US$ million

Regions/Countries	Exports					Imports					Total trade (exports + imports)				
	1980	1985	1990	1995	1999	1980	1985	1990	1995	1999	1980	1985	1990	1995	1999
WORLD	1,832,508	1,874,505	3,381,690	5,070,827	5,663,310	1,918,724	1,975,924	3,517,259	5,137,927	5,810,326	3,751,232	3,850,429	6,898,949	10,208,754	11,473,636
U.S.A.	220,781	213,146	393,106	583,451	690,689	256,959	361,620	517,020	770,972	1,048,435	477,740	574,767	910,126	1,354,423	1,739,124
European Union-15	751,159	708,197	1,488,365	2,018,290	2,208,491	843,944	724,609	1,538,964	1,914,173	2,143,856	1,595,103	1,432,805	3,027,329	3,932,463	4,352,347
East Asia	279,576	370,825	715,547	1,332,658	1,429,911	292,342	323,547	669,517	1,267,960	1,202,865	571,918	694,372	1,385,064	2,600,618	2,632,776
Japan	130,435	177,189	287,678	443,047	419,207	141,284	130,516	235,307	336,027	310,733	271,719	307,705	522,985	779,074	729,940
Emerging East Asia	149,141	193,636	427,869	889,611	1,010,704	151,058	193,031	434,210	931,932	892,132	300,199	386,667	862,079	1,821,544	1,902,836
NIEs-4	76,262	113,966	269,222	529,143	553,671	88,148	107,119	271,594	556,160	521,150	164,410	221,085	540,815	1,085,303	1,074,821
Hong Kong	19,720	30,182	82,144	173,556	173,793	22,399	29,701	82,482	192,764	179,650	42,119	59,883	164,626	366,321	353,443
Korea	17,439	30,289	67,812	125,588	143,647	22,063	31,058	74,405	135,352	119,740	39,502	61,347	142,217	260,940	263,387
Singapore	19,377	22,812	52,753	118,187	114,730	24,013	26,237	60,954	124,394	111,071	43,390	49,049	113,707	242,581	225,801
Taiwan	19,726	30,683	66,513	111,813	121,501	19,673	20,123	53,753	103,649	110,689	39,399	50,806	120,266	215,462	232,191
ASEAN-9	52,162	49,692	91,612	204,417	255,046	40,525	39,999	102,289	235,746	197,636	92,686	89,691	193,902	440,163	452,682
Indonesia	21,909	18,596	25,675	45,428	57,193	10,837	10,275	22,005	40,629	28,950	32,747	28,871	47,680	86,056	86,142
Malaysia	12,960	15,408	29,420	73,724	84,550	10,821	12,301	29,170	77,620	65,491	23,782	27,709	58,590	151,344	150,042
Philippines	5,787	4,614	8,194	17,371	35,474	8,295	5,351	12,993	28,282	31,368	14,082	9,965	21,186	45,653	66,842
Thailand	6,501	7,123	23,072	57,201	61,797	9,213	9,259	33,407	73,692	53,207	15,714	16,382	56,479	130,892	115,003
Vietnam	0	693	2,525	5,450	10,474	0	1,842	2,842	8,155	13,213	0	2,535	5,367	13,606	23,687
Other ASEAN-9	5,004	3,258	2,727	5,243	5,559	1,359	970	1,872	7,368	5,407	6,362	4,228	4,599	12,611	10,966
China	18,139	27,329	62,760	148,955	194,931	19,505	42,480	53,809	132,163	165,718	37,644	69,809	116,569	281,118	360,649
Other East Asia	2,577	2,648	4,275	7,096	7,056	2,880	3,433	6,517	7,863	7,628	5,458	6,081	10,792	14,959	14,685

Table 2-1 International Trade of East Asian Economies in the 1980s and 1990s

(b) Shares in world trade (%)

Regions/Countries	1980	1985	1990	1995	1999	1980	1985	1990	1995	1999	1980	1985	1990	1995	1999
WORLD	100.0	100.0	100.0	100.0	100.0	100.0	100.0	100.0	100.0	100.0	100.0	100.0	100.0	100.0	100.0
U.S.A.	12.0	11.4	11.6	11.5	12.2	13.4	18.3	14.7	15.0	18.0	12.7	14.9	13.2	13.3	15.2
European Union-15	41.0	37.8	44.0	39.8	39.0	44.0	36.7	43.8	37.3	36.9	42.5	37.2	43.9	38.5	37.9
East Asia	15.3	19.8	21.2	26.3	25.2	15.2	16.4	19.0	24.7	20.7	15.2	18.0	20.1	25.5	22.9
Japan	7.1	9.5	8.5	8.7	7.4	7.4	6.6	6.7	6.5	5.3	7.2	8.0	7.6	7.6	6.4
Emerging East Asia	8.1	10.3	12.7	17.5	17.8	7.9	9.8	12.3	18.1	15.4	8.0	10.0	12.5	17.8	16.6
NIEs-4	4.2	6.1	8.0	10.4	9.8	4.6	5.4	7.7	10.8	9.0	4.4	5.7	7.8	10.6	9.4
Hong Kong	1.1	1.6	2.4	3.4	3.1	1.2	1.5	2.3	3.8	3.1	1.1	1.6	2.4	3.6	3.1
Korea	1.0	1.6	2.0	2.5	2.5	1.1	1.6	2.1	2.6	2.1	1.1	1.6	2.1	2.6	2.3
Singapore	1.1	1.2	1.6	2.3	2.0	1.3	1.3	1.7	2.4	1.9	1.2	1.3	1.6	2.4	2.0
Taiwan	1.1	1.6	2.0	2.2	2.1	1.0	1.0	1.5	2.0	1.9	1.1	1.3	1.7	2.1	2.0
ASEAN-9	2.8	2.7	2.7	4.0	4.5	2.1	2.0	2.9	4.6	3.4	2.5	2.3	2.8	4.3	3.9
Indonesia	1.2	1.0	0.8	0.9	1.0	0.6	0.5	0.6	0.8	0.5	0.9	0.7	0.7	0.8	0.8
Malaysia	0.7	0.8	0.9	1.5	1.5	0.6	0.6	0.8	1.5	1.1	0.6	0.7	0.8	1.5	1.3
Philippines	0.3	0.2	0.2	0.3	0.6	0.4	0.3	0.4	0.6	0.5	0.4	0.3	0.3	0.4	0.6
Thailand	0.4	0.4	0.7	1.1	1.1	0.5	0.5	0.9	1.4	0.9	0.4	0.4	0.8	1.3	1.0
Vietnam	0.0	0.0	0.1	0.1	0.2	0.0	0.1	0.1	0.2	0.2	0.0	0.1	0.1	0.1	0.2
Other ASEAN-9	0.3	0.2	0.1	0.1	0.1	0.1	0.0	0.1	0.1	0.1	0.2	0.1	0.1	0.1	0.1
China	1.0	1.5	1.9	2.9	3.4	1.0	2.1	1.5	2.6	2.9	1.0	1.8	1.7	2.8	3.1
Other East Asia	0.1	0.1	0.1	0.1	0.1	0.2	0.2	0.2	0.2	0.1	0.1	0.2	0.2	0.1	0.1

Source: International Monetary Fund, IFS CD-ROM.

Table 2-2   Foreign Direct Investment (FDI) Flows of East Asian Economies in the 1980s and 1990s

(a) US$ million

Regions/Countries	Inflows					Outflows					Total FDI (inflows + outflows)				
	1980	1985	1990	1995	1999	1980	1985	1990	1995	1999	1980	1985	1990	1995	1999
WORLD	52,216	55,502	202,635	318,883	917,481	55,390	59,971	245,820	335,501	871,010	107,606	115,473	448,455	654,384	1,788,491
U.S.A.	16,930	20,010	48,497	57,776	275,535	19,230	14,060	37,184	98,750	150,900	36,160	34,070	85,681	156,526	426,435
European Union-15	21,264	15,836	96,173	115,316	371,839	27,067	25,689	130,595	160,931	592,633	48,331	41,525	226,768	276,247	964,472
East Asia	2,654	4,868	19,795	59,590	99,633	2,535	7,964	59,815	39,209	56,918	5,188	12,832	79,609	98,799	156,551
Japan	280	638	1,777	39	12,308	2,390	6,492	50,497	22,508	22,267	2,670	7,130	52,274	22,547	34,575
Emerging East Asia	2,374	4,230	18,017	59,551	87,324	145	1,472	9,318	16,701	34,652	2,518	5,702	27,335	76,252	121,976
NIEs-4	1,242	1,280	7,693	10,541	42,312	124	829	8,334	12,816	32,465	1,365	2,109	16,027	23,358	74,777
Hong Kong	0	0	0	0	23,068	0	0	0	0	19,904	0	0	0	0	42,973
Korea	6	234	788	1,776	9,333	26	591	1,052	3,552	4,198	32	825	1,840	5,328	13,531
Singapore	1,236	1,047	5,575	7,206	6,984	98	238	2,034	6,281	3,943	1,333	1,284	7,609	13,488	10,927
Taiwan			1,330	1,559	2,926			5,249	2,983	4,420	0	0	6,579	4,542	7,346
ASEAN-9	1,018	1,180	6,566	12,593	5,936	3	1	140	1,888	359	1,021	1,181	6,706	14,481	6,294
Indonesia	0	310	1,093	4,346	-2,745	0	0	0	603	72	0	310	1,093	4,949	-2,673
Malaysia	934	695	2,332	4,178	1,553	0	0	0	0	0	934	695	2,332	4,178	1,553
Philippines	-106	12	530	1,478	573	0	0	0	0	-59	-106	12	530	1,877	514
Thailand	190	163	2,444	2,068	6,213	3	1	140	399	346	193	164	2,584	2,954	6,559
Other ASEAN-9	0	0	167	523	342	0	0	0	886	0	0	0	167	523	342
China	0	1,659	3,487	35,849	38,753	0	629	830	2,000	1,775	0	2,288	4,317	37,849	40,528
Other East Asia	114	111	271	567	324	18	14	13	-3	53	132	125	285	564	377

Table 2-2 Foreign Direct Investment (FDI) Flows of East Asian Economies in the 1980s and 1990s

(b) Shares in world FDI (%)

Regions/Countries	1980	1985	1990	1995	1999	1980	1985	1990	1995	1999	1980	1985	1990	1995	1999
WORLD	100.0	100.0	100.0	100.0	100.0	100.0	100.0	100.0	100.0	100.0	100.0	100.0	100.0	100.0	100.0
U.S.A.	33.6	29.5	19.1	23.9	23.8	34.7	23.4	15.1	29.4	17.3	32.4	36.1	23.9	18.1	30.0
European Union-15	44.9	36.0	50.6	42.2	53.9	48.9	42.8	53.1	48.0	68.0	40.7	28.5	47.5	36.2	40.5
East Asia	4.8	11.1	17.8	15.1	8.8	4.6	13.3	24.3	11.7	6.5	5.1	8.8	9.8	18.7	10.9
Japan	2.5	6.2	11.7	3.4	1.9	4.3	10.8	20.5	6.7	2.6	0.5	1.1	0.9	0.0	1.3
Emerging East Asia	2.3	4.9	6.1	11.7	6.8	0.3	2.5	3.8	5.0	4.0	4.5	7.6	8.9	18.7	9.5
NIEs-4	1.3	1.8	3.6	3.6	4.2	0.2	1.4	3.4	3.8	3.7	2.4	2.3	3.8	3.3	4.6
Hong Kong	0.0	0.0	0.0	0.0	2.4	0.0	0.0	0.0	0.0	2.3	0.0	0.0	0.0	0.0	2.5
Korea	0.0	0.7	0.4	0.8	0.8	0.0	1.0	0.4	1.1	0.5	0.0	0.4	0.4	0.6	1.0
Singapore	1.2	1.1	1.7	2.1	0.6	0.2	0.4	0.8	1.9	0.5	2.4	1.9	2.8	2.3	0.8
Taiwan	0.0	0.0	1.5	0.7	0.4	0.0	0.0	2.1	0.9	0.5	0.0	0.0	0.7	0.5	0.3
ASEAN-9	0.9	1.0	1.5	2.2	0.4	0.0	0.0	0.1	0.6	0.0	1.9	2.1	3.2	3.9	0.6
Indonesia	0.0	0.3	0.2	0.8	-0.1	0.0	0.0	0.0	0.2	0.0	0.0	0.6	0.5	1.4	-0.3
Malaysia	0.9	0.6	0.5	0.6	0.1	0.0	0.0	0.0	0.0	0.0	1.8	1.3	1.2	1.3	0.2
Philippines	-0.1	0.0	0.1	0.3	0.0	0.0	0.0	0.0	0.1	0.0	-0.2	0.0	0.3	0.5	0.1
Thailand	0.2	0.1	0.6	0.5	0.4	0.0	0.0	0.1	0.3	0.0	0.4	0.3	1.2	0.6	0.7
Other ASEAN-9	0.0	0.0	0.0	0.1	0.0	0.0	0.0	0.0	0.0	0.0	0.0	0.0	0.1	0.2	0.0
China	0.0	2.0	1.0	5.8	2.3	0.0	1.0	0.3	0.6	0.2	0.0	3.0	1.7	11.2	4.2
Other East Asia	0.1	0.1	0.1	0.1	0.0	0.1	0.0	0.0	0.0	0.0	0.2	0.2	0.1	0.2	0.0

Source: International Monetary Fund, IFS CD-ROM.

Table 2-3   Intra-Regional Dependence for Trade and FDI

(a) Absolute Measure (%)

	Trade					FDI	
	1980	1985	1990	1995	1999	1980	1994
East Asia, incl. Japan	5.4	6.7	8.3	12.7	11.3	3.5	8.4
Emerging East Asia-14	1.7	2.5	3.9	6.6	6.4	1.5	5.5
NIEs-4	0.4	0.5	0.9	1.5	1.2	0.1	0.1
ASEAN-10	0.7	0.7	0.8	1.5	1.4	0.5	0.8
ASEAN-9, excl. Singapore	0.1	0.1	0.1	0.3	0.4	-	-
NAFTA	5.7	7.9	6.6	7.8	10.3	13.6	5.3
Mercosur	0.2	0.1	0.1	0.3	0.3	-	-
European Union-15	24.3	21.7	28.3	23.8	23.1	12.9	19.3

(b) Relative Measure (%)

	Exports					Outward FDI	
	1980	1985	1990	1995	1999	1980	1994
East Asia, incl. Japan	35.9	34.5	40.1	49.3	45.0	38.1	35.0
Emerging East Asia-14	23.3	26.4	32.4	39.6	37.0	86.8	86.6
NIEs-4	9.7	8.9	12.4	16.1	14.8	8.6	2.8
ASEAN-10	18.7	19.8	19.8	25.4	22.2	73.2	56.5
ASEAN-9, excl. Singapore	3.9	5.1	5.0	7.3	8.1	-	-
NAFTA	33.6	43.9	41.4	46.2	54.6	27.5	18.7
Mercosur	11.6	5.5	8.9	20.3	20.5		
European Union-15	60.8	59.2	65.9	62.4	62.8	38.6	47.9

	Imports					Inward FDI	
	1980	1985	1990	1995	1999	1980	1994
East Asia, incl. Japan	35.3	40.5	43.6	51.2	54.1	42.0	54.0
Emerging East Asia-14	21.1	24.2	30.6	34.6	40.5	19.7	38.3
NIEs-4	7.1	8.2	10.3	11.8	11.4	4.1	4.6
ASEAN-10	18.2	19.7	16.4	19.4	23.9	10.2	11.3
ASEAN-9, excl. Singapore	5.0	6.9	4.8	7.3	10.7	-	-
NAFTA	32.8	34.4	33.9	38.4	41.1	41.5	21.2
Mercosur	8.3	9.5	14.2	18.2	19.2	-	-
European Union-15	54.0	57.5	63.1	61.3	59.6	36.2	55.0

	Trade (Exports + Imports)					FDI (Out + In)	
	1980	1985	1990	1995	1999	1980	1994
East Asia, incl. Japan	35.6	37.3	41.8	50.2	49.2	40.0	42.5
Emerging East Asia-14	22.2	25.3	31.5	37.1	38.7	32.1	53.1
NIEs-4	8.3	8.6	11.3	13.9	13.2	5.6	3.5
ASEAN-10	18.4	19.7	18.0	22.2	22.9	17.9	18.8
ASEAN-9, excl. Singapore	4.3	5.9	4.9	7.3	9.2	-	-
NAFTA	33.2	38.3	37.2	42.0	46.8	33.0	19.9
Mercosur	9.7	7.0	11.0	19.2	19.8	-	-
European Union-15	57.2	58.3	64.5	61.9	61.2	37.3	51.2

(c) Double-Relative Measure (Trade Intensity Index, %)

	Trade					FDI	
	1980	1985	1990	1995	1999	1980	1994
East Asia, incl. Japan	2.56	2.28	2.27	2.14	2.25	4.59	2.25
Emerging East Asia-14	2.97	2.93	2.84	2.32	2.49	11.36	6.08
NIEs-4	2.09	1.75	1.70	1.64	1.75	4.20	0.98
ASEAN-10	5.12	6.06	4.60	3.80	4.15	14.09	7.59
ASEAN-9, excl. Singapore	1.70	2.65	1.87	1.64	2.34	-	-
NAFTA	2.05	1.96	2.15	2.39	2.27	0.84	0.74
Mercosur	6.55	4.93	9.70	13.27	14.68	-	-
European Union-15	1.48	1.60	1.51	1.66	1.66	1.08	1.37

Notes: Definitions are described in the text.
Source: Computed from the data from the following sources:
    Trade data: IMF, Direction of Trade Statistics, and FDI data: Industry Canada

Table 2-4   Sources of Inward Foreign Direct Investment in East Asian Economies (%)

	China (actualized value)			Indonesia (approved)			Korea (approved)			Malaysia (approved)			Philippines (BOP)			Singapore (committed)			Taiwan (approved)			Thailand (BOP)		
	1990	1995	1999	1990	1995	1999	1990	1995	1999	1991	1995	1999	1990	1995	1999	1990	1995	1999	1990	1995	1999	1990	1995	1999
World	100.0	100.0	100.0	100.0	100.0	100.0	100.0	100.0	100.0	100.0	100.0	100.0	100.0	100.0	100.0	100.0	100.0	100.0	100.0	100.0	100.0	100.0	100.0	100.0
U.S.A.	13.1	8.2	10.5	1.8	6.9	1.3	39.6	33.2	24.1	10.5	19.7	42.0	26.9	6.8	4.5	47.6	42.8	57.3	25.3	44.6	222.7	9.5	13.0	8.0
East Asia	69.8	77.9	64.1	55.3	20.8	30.0	31.9	29.0	17.3	65.9	58.5	18.6	46.6	70.1	26.4	31.9	23.8	18.9	50.0	27.3	25.3	75.5	54.0	46.4
Japan	14.4	8.3	7.4	25.6	9.5	5.9	29.3	21.5	11.3	21.7	22.9	8.2	27.7	30.0	16.0	31.9	23.8	18.9	36.4	19.6	12.2	43.2	27.8	12.2
Korea	0.0	2.8	3.2	8.3	1.7	2.4	0.0	0.0	0.0	10.7	6.6	0.3	3.9	1.0	0.7	0.0	0.0	0.0	0.1	0.1	0.1	0.8	0.6	0.2
Taiwan	0.0	8.4	6.4	7.1	1.4	13.7	0.5	0.5	0.2	21.1	15.8	2.2	3.9	0.9	0.8	0.0	0.0	0.0	0.0	0.0	0.0	11.1	4.8	3.9
Hong Kong	53.9	53.5	40.6	11.4	4.4	0.7	0.4	3.0	3.0	3.5	1.9	0.5	7.9	28.9	1.1	0.0	0.0	0.0	10.3	5.0	3.8	10.9	13.9	7.2
Singapore	1.4	4.9	6.6	3.0	3.7	6.7	1.7	3.4	2.7	6.5	11.0	7.3	3.2	9.3	1.9	0.0	0.0	0.0	3.2	2.6	9.2	9.5	6.8	23.0
China	0.0	0.0	0.0	0.0	0.0	0.5	0.0	0.6	0.2	2.3	0.2	0.1	0.0	0.0	5.9	0.0	0.0	0.0	0.0	0.0	0.0	0.2	0.1	-0.1
EU	3.4	5.2	10.0	8.1	21.4	6.1	20.8	17.5	35.5	4.7	5.6	10.0	7.7	12.9	22.7	17.5	30.9	17.4	8.4	10.4	9.4	5.7	12.3	41.6
Italy	0.1	0.7	0.5	0.0	0.1	0.0	0.2	0.2	0.0	0.2	0.2	0.6	0.0	0.2	0.0	0.0	0.3	1.4	0.0	0.0	0.0	0.1	-0.3	0.0
UK	0.4	2.4	2.6	0.7	15.8	4.7	5.6	4.5	3.1	3.2	2.1	1.6	4.4	6.5	0.5	4.1	15.9	1.5	3.9	6.7	3.4	1.7	2.8	5.1
Netherlands	0.5	0.3	1.3	6.5	0.9	0.4	4.5	8.8	21.4	0.0	0.6	6.3	1.7	3.7	20.3	3.3	8.1	3.0	2.2	2.6	4.6	1.0	4.3	18.1
Germany	1.8	1.0	3.4	0.2	3.4	0.8	7.8	2.3	6.2	1.1	1.6	1.5	1.1	2.0	1.3	7.5	3.8	10.1	1.6	0.8	0.7	1.0	1.9	8.2
France	0.6	0.8	2.2	0.8	1.2	0.2	2.8	1.8	4.9	0.2	1.1	0.1	0.5	0.8	0.6	2.7	2.9	1.5	0.8	0.4	0.8	1.1	3.6	10.2

Source: Country sources.

Table 2-5   Sources of Inputs in Production for East Asian Economies 1985 and 1995

		Indonesia	Malaysia	Philippines	Thailand	Singapore	Taiwan	Korea	China	Japan
Domestic inputs	1985	0.3517	0.3367	0.3843	0.4073	0.2976	0.4614	0.4435	0.5008	0.4737
	1995	0.3920	0.3371	0.3385	0.3719	0.3433	0.3869	0.4782	0.5547	0.4395
Imported inputs	1985	0.0624	0.1718	0.0797	0.0996	0.3353	0.1371	0.1290	0.0417	0.0481
	1995	0.0692	0.2396	0.1452	0.1605	0.2868	0.1621	0.0612	0.0614	0.0306
From NIEs-3	1985	0.0062	0.0298	0.0045	0.0106	0.0117	0.0022	0.0024	0.0010	0.0022
	1995	0.0079	0.0397	0.0198	0.0189	0.0260	0.0090	0.0031	0.0071	0.0022
From ASEAN-4	1985	0.0007	0.0073	0.0067	0.0112	0.0635	0.0062	0.0095	0.0011	0.0053
	1995	0.0018	0.0096	0.0084	0.0097	0.0553	0.0094	0.0060	0.0026	0.0027
China	1985	0.0012	0.0028	0.0040	0.0021	0.0350	0.0000	0.0000	0.0000	0.0019
	1995	0.0018	0.0052	0.0036	0.0042	0.0072	0.0044	0.0053	0.0000	0.0015
From Emerging East Asia	1985	0.0080	0.0399	0.0151	0.0239	0.1102	0.0083	0.0119	0.0021	0.0094
	1995	0.0115	0.0545	0.0317	0.0327	0.0884	0.0228	0.0144	0.0097	0.0064
From Japan	1985	0.0121	0.0287	0.0051	0.0150	0.0338	0.0242	0.0241	0.0095	0.0000
	1995	0.0100	0.0560	0.0191	0.0339	0.0663	0.0342	0.0196	0.0095	0.0000
From East Asia	1985	0.0201	0.0686	0.0202	0.0389	0.1440	0.0325	0.0360	0.0115	0.0094
	1995	0.0216	0.1105	0.0508	0.0666	0.1547	0.0569	0.0340	0.0193	0.0064
From Rest of the World	1985	0.0423	0.1033	0.0595	0.0607	0.1913	0.1045	0.0930	0.0302	0.0387
	1995	0.0476	0.1291	0.0944	0.0939	0.1320	0.1051	0.0271	0.0421	0.0242
Total inputs	1985	0.4141	0.5085	0.4640	0.5069	0.6329	0.5985	0.5724	0.5425	0.5218
	1995	0.4612	0.5767	0.4837	0.5324	0.6301	0.5490	0.5393	0.6160	0.4700
Value added	1985	0.5859	0.4915	0.5360	0.4931	0.3671	0.4015	0.4276	0.4575	0.4782
	1995	0.5388	0.4233	0.5163	0.4676	0.3699	0.4510	0.4607	0.3840	0.5300
Output	1985	1.0000	1.0000	1.0000	1.0000	1.0000	1.0000	1.0000	1.0000	1.0000
	1995	1.0000	1.0000	1.0000	1.0000	1.0000	1.0000	1.0000	1.0000	1.0000

Source: Institute of Developing Economies, *International Input-Output Tables*, 1985 and 1995 versions.

Table 2-6   Inter-Economy, Inter-Industry Linkages in East Asia
(An Increase in Final Demand in Percentage)

	Indonesia	Malaysia	Philippines	Thailand	Singapore	Taiwan	Korea	China	Japan	Total
Increase in production										
Domestic production										
1985	1.6026	1.4722	1.6189	1.7045	1.5308	1.7638	1.6971	1.8965	1.8768	15.1631
1995	1.5680	1.4469	1.4850	1.5685	1.5083	1.6420	1.6553	2.1608	1.8161	14.8511
1985-95	-0.0346	-0.0253	-0.1338	-0.1360	-0.0225	-0.1218	-0.0417	0.2644	-0.0607	-0.3121
NIEs-3										
1985	0.0172	0.0914	0.0141	0.0278	0.0275	0.0050	0.0060	0.0029	0.0067	0.1987
1995	0.0171	0.0728	0.0557	0.0381	0.0567	0.0222	0.0063	0.0227	0.0066	0.2981
1985-95	-0.0001	-0.0187	0.0417	0.0102	0.0292	0.0172	0.0003	0.0197	-0.0001	0.0995
ASEAN-4										
1985	0.0029	0.0186	0.0157	0.0159	0.1106	0.0119	0.0152	0.0031	0.0224	0.2163
1995	0.0040	0.1088	0.0184	0.0162	0.0979	0.0221	0.0222	0.0078	0.0099	0.3072
1985-95	0.0011	0.0901	0.0027	0.0003	-0.0128	0.0102	0.0071	0.0048	-0.0125	0.0909
China										
1985	0.0041	0.0160	0.0130	0.0091	0.0714	0.0008	0.0007	0.0000	0.0061	0.1211
1995	0.0053	0.0135	0.0135	0.0112	0.0281	0.0165	0.0153	0.0000	0.0056	0.1090
1985-95	0.0012	-0.0026	0.0006	0.0021	-0.0433	0.0157	0.0146	0.0000	-0.0005	-0.0121
Emerging East Asia excluding own domestic production										
1985	0.0242	0.1261	0.0428	0.0528	0.2096	0.0177	0.0218	0.0060	0.0352	0.5361
1995	0.0264	0.1950	0.0877	0.0655	0.1827	0.0608	0.0438	0.0305	0.0221	0.7144
1985-95	0.0022	0.0689	0.0449	0.0127	-0.0269	0.0431	0.0219	0.0245	-0.0131	0.1783
Emerging East Asia including own domestic production										
1985	1.6268	1.5983	1.6616	1.7573	1.7404	1.7815	1.7189	1.9025	1.9120	15.6992
1995	1.5944	1.6418	1.5727	1.6340	1.6910	1.7028	1.6991	2.1913	1.8382	15.5654
1985-95	-0.0324	0.0436	-0.0889	-0.1233	-0.0494	-0.0787	-0.0198	0.2889	-0.0738	-0.1338
Japan										
1985	0.0378	0.0839	0.0206	0.0488	0.0897	0.0627	0.0639	0.0327	0.0000	0.4401
1995	0.0263	0.1221	0.0657	0.0769	0.1777	0.0922	0.0479	0.0359	0.0000	0.6448
1985-95	-0.0115	0.0382	0.0451	0.0281	0.0880	0.0296	-0.0160	0.0032	0.0000	0.2047
East Asia excluding own domestic production										
1985	0.0619	0.2100	0.0634	0.1017	0.2993	0.0803	0.0857	0.0387	0.0352	0.9762
1995	0.0527	0.3170	0.1534	0.1424	0.3604	0.1530	0.0916	0.0664	0.0221	1.3591
1985-95	-0.0092	0.1071	0.0900	0.0407	0.0611	0.0727	0.0060	0.0277	-0.0131	0.3830
East Asia including own domestic production										
1985	1.6646	1.6822	1.6822	1.8062	1.8301	1.8441	1.7828	1.9352	1.9120	16.1393
1995	1.6207	1.7639	1.6384	1.7109	1.8688	1.7951	1.7470	2.2272	1.8382	16.2102
1985-95	-0.0439	0.0817	-0.0438	-0.0953	0.0386	-0.0491	-0.0358	0.2920	-0.0738	0.0709

Source: Institute of Developing Economies, *International Input-Output Tables*, 1985 and
1995 versions.

Table 2-7 Procurements and Sales of Foreign Affiliates of Japanese Firms 1992 and 1998
(Percentage of Total Procurements or Sales)

Procurements	1992 WORLD Local Procurements	1992 WORLD Imports from Japan	North America	Asia	Europe	1992 ASIA Local Procurements	1992 ASIA Imports from Japan	North America	Asia	Europe	1998 WORLD Local Procurements	1998 WORLD Imports from Japan	North America	Asia	Europe	1998 ASIA Local Procurements	1998 ASIA Imports from Japan	North America	Asia	Europe
Manufacturing Total	**46.5**	**40.9**	**1.3**	**5.2**	**5.0**	**48.5**	**37.9**	**1.8**	**8.9**	**0.5**	**46.9**	**36.6**	**3.2**	**8.1**	**4.6**	**43.9**	**34.8**	**1.6**	**18.2**	**0.6**
Food	84.8	6.1	0.1	7.0	0.2	72.0	4.5	0.3	22.9	0.1	81.7	4.1	1.8	10.0	0.3	78.8	6.6	0.4	8.0	0.5
Textiles	44.4	20.8	4.0	9.8	6.1	40.7	22.4	4.7	12.1	1.4	56.2	23.2	3.1	9.5	2.4	52.9	26.1	2.9	11.2	0.6
Wood and Pulp	89.1	7.8	1.8	0.1	1.2	83.7	13.2	0.9	0.3	1.9	94.5	2.2	0.3	1.3	1.7	76.8	12.4	1.0	7.7	2.1
Chemical Products	64.9	26.2	2.5	1.5	3.2	71.4	16.9	3.7	3.5	1.3	64.0	20.7	4.0	5.2	4.7	54.4	18.6	7.1	14.8	2.2
Iron and Steel	75.5	16.4	0.0	7.6	0.0	29.0	47.3	0.0	22.3	0.0	63.2	29.9	1.9	3.7	0.2	19.2	70.0	0.0	10.4	0.2
Nonmetallic Products	67.0	9.9	0.4	5.0	1.2	64.8	9.2	0.4	6.2	0.4	71.7	13.2	1.5	6.2	6.1	44.1	31.7	0.3	19.0	1.1
General Machinery	43.4	47.6	2.1	1.7	5.1	49.0	47.8	1.7	1.1	0.4	38.6	44.1	2.6	2.8	11.3	57.7	32.2	0.8	8.8	0.4
Electric Machinery	26.6	53.8	1.1	9.2	9.3	36.6	46.7	1.2	15.4	0.1	36.8	44.1	1.0	15.4	2.4	35.7	37.0	0.4	26.4	0.2
Transport Machinery	55.1	39.3	1.3	2.5	1.1	52.9	43.8	1.8	1.1	0.4	50.2	35.8	6.1	2.0	5.6	53.7	37.0	2.5	6.0	0.7
Precision Instruments	22.7	58.3	0.9	0.8	17.4	34.2	60.2	1.9	3.7	0.0	39.0	45.2	2.1	12.3	1.2	40.2	41.2	2.6	14.5	1.5
Coal and Petroleum Products	86.8	10.3	0.9	2.0	0.0	92.6	3.8	1.1	2.5	0.0	21.0	15.2	3.2	27.3	33.2	21.7	18.0	10.3	45.5	3.9
Other Manufacturing	61.8	24.2	1.7	6.2	5.5	58.6	27.5	4.0	6.2	2.1	49.6	32.1	2.2	8.2	7.4	52.8	29.7	1.8	14.2	0.9

Continued on next page.

Table 2-7 Procurements and Sales of Foreign Affiliates of Japanese Firms 1992 and 1998
(Percentage of Total Procurements or Sales) (continued)

Sales	WORLD					ASIA					WORLD					ASIA				
	Local Sales	Exports to				Local Sales	Exports to				Local Sales	Exports to				Local Sales	Exports to			
		Japan	North America	Asia	Europe		Japan	North America	Asia	Europe		Japan	North America	Asia	Europe		Japan	North America	Asia	Europe
Manufacturing Total	**76.7**	**6.3**	**2.7**	**3.6**	**9.9**	**66.1**	**15.8**	**3.7**	**11.2**	**2.0**	**70.0**	**9.6**	**4.7**	**5.7**	**8.8**	**49.8**	**25.1**	**4.5**	**16.6**	**2.6**
Food	63.7	20.8	2.4	2.8	3.5	46.0	26.5	3.1	4.9	2.0	76.7	11.6	1.4	2.5	7.0	69.1	16.1	3.3	6.4	3.5
Textiles	58.5	11.3	6.6	10.4	9.9	56.1	14.2	7.2	12.3	6.7	57.6	16.6	8.4	8.7	7.2	47.7	22.2	10.9	12.0	5.5
Wood and Pulp	47.7	32.5	11.1	2.4	4.1	50.2	47.2	2.4	0.3	0.0	37.7	34.4	12.1	7.9	6.4	58.9	26.7	2.1	10.9	0.0
Chemical Products	64.5	4.9	3.0	10.1	15.4	64.7	4.9	0.4	28.6	0.2	76.1	4.5	2.2	6.3	9.2	72.4	7.6	0.6	16.6	1.7
Iron and Steel	95.8	0.8	2.1	0.8	0.1	85.5	2.1	3.0	8.6	0.0	91.7	1.3	2.2	2.2	0.7	85.3	3.0	2.7	6.6	0.1
Nonmetallic Products	67.7	18.1	0.4	12.2	1.4	63.3	21.4	0.1	14.9	0.0	63.0	14.6	2.8	9.5	9.9	55.9	15.6	0.9	26.3	1.0
General Machinery	72.3	4.2	5.1	2.1	15.3	53.0	23.6	2.1	11.3	9.8	65.4	10.8	4.6	4.4	12.3	32.4	40.6	5.5	14.8	4.6
Electric Machinery	60.6	9.3	3.3	6.1	19.9	45.7	27.2	5.3	19.0	2.2	57.9	15.4	4.0	11.5	10.0	32.3	33.0	5.3	24.8	2.9
Transport Machinery	94.1	1.4	1.8	0.4	1.9	92.6	1.7	3.9	1.0	0.5	81.2	2.6	6.6	0.5	8.6	81.1	11.0	3.5	2.2	1.5
Precision Instruments	71.4	21.3	2.7	0.7	3.7	36.9	51.8	5.2	1.9	3.8	46.5	27.6	5.9	13.1	5.2	27.2	46.0	1.5	23.0	2.0
Coal and Petroleum Products	58.1	0.8	38.3	2.0	0.8	55.9	0.0	43.9	0.2	0.0	18.9	63.3	0.1	1.6	15.0	21.2	65.7	0.0	2.9	10.2
Other Manufacturing	80.7	4.4	1.7	1.8	1.1	78.6	9.4	2.6	5.6	2.8	81.3	7.2	3.0	2.3	5.0	59.8	24.9	4.1	8.9	1.8

Source: Ministry of International Trade and Industry, Kaigai Jigyo Katsudo Kihon Chosa (Comprehensive Survey of Overseas Activities of Japanese Firms), Nos. 5 and 7, 1994 and 2001.

Table 2-8 Intra-Firm Transactions in Procurements and Sales of Foreign Affiliates of Japanese Firms 1992 and 1998 (Percentage Share in Each Procurement or Sales)

	Procurements WORLD Local	Japan	N.Am	Asia	Europe	Proc ASIA Local	Japan	N.Am	Asia	Europe	Sales WORLD Local	Japan	N.Am	Asia	Europe	Sales ASIA Local	Japan	N.Am	Asia	Europe
1992																				
Manufacturing Total	9.0	84.3	52.6	58.9	68.6	4.2	78.0	47.7	50.2	35.8	17.4	78.3	47.5	43.9	37.8	6.3	84.2	62.4	44.4	47.6
Food	5.4	93.1	33.8	54.3	0.9	0.2	75.8	14.3	48.8	0.0	5.2	84.6	27.2	17.2	18.6	7.6	85.4	51.9	26.3	50.1
Textiles	15.1	37.1	3.2	31.5	2.7	19.5	34.2	3.3	31.5	14.3	3.1	40.1	1.1	20.9	21.2	4.3	36.1	1.1	23.0	0.9
Wood and Pulp	6.3	30.1	0.0	0.0	0.0	0.1	79.4	0.0	0.0	0.0	2.3	80.9	0.0	0.0	0.0	0.0	57.9	0.0	0.0	0.0
Chemical Products	13.5	81.7	31.8	4.6	50.8	18.0	57.5	7.7	4.3	17.1	9.2	50.4	52.3	9.5	30.8	2.4	49.0	11.5	3.2	17.6
Iron and Steel	0.7	2.0	0.0	0.0	0.0	5.2	1.1	0.0	0.0	0.0	0.0	16.2	3.2	0.0	0.0	0.0	29.0	23.3	0.0	0.0
Nonmetallic Products	8.4	67.6	7.3	1.0	78.3	0.0	26.0	0.0	0.0	0.0	7.8	82.6	73.5	53.0	18.9	0.8	82.6	0.0	55.1	0.0
General Machinery	28.7	90.8	32.5	78.7	60.1	4.5	93.9	80.3	84.8	23.9	18.3	91.2	61.6	52.8	75.2	3.0	96.7	54.3	55.6	93.9
Electric Machinery	16.6	76.0	69.0	62.6	77.3	2.0	84.6	86.6	59.8	98.1	17.2	86.2	49.5	52.7	34.8	8.0	90.0	82.6	53.7	58.0
Transport Machinery	3.3	98.6	72.2	90.3	19.0	0.6	81.7	76.2	34.6	86.2	24.5	49.0	67.8	75.0	42.9	7.2	73.9	71.2	57.9	28.3
Precision Instruments	9.9	74.9	93.4	15.2	98.4	17.5	85.6	0.0	100.0	0.0	7.5	95.1	39.2	74.1	42.2	32.4	96.5	51.1	77.9	50.8
Coal and Petroleum Products	0.0	100.0	100.0	10.0	0.0	0.0	100.0	100.0	10.0	0.0	0.0	100.0	0.0	90.1	100.0	0.0	67.0	0.0	0.0	0.0
Other Manufacturing	4.3	72.2	5.9	22.5	46.4	7.3	64.1	0.7	61.8	11.8	5.5	62.0	28.3	51.4	28.6	6.3	67.0	25.3	49.8	18.4
1998																				
Manufacturing Total	22.2	92.3	39.8	59.9	40.7	11.3	83.2	72.5	58.5	45.3	20.4	94.6	50.6	56.7	40.5	16.1	95.7	66.4	58.9	66.1
Food	13.6	93.3	56.1	44.0	9.1	3.9	94.4	48.8	71.7	15.1	10.7	78.6	18.6	55.8	9.5	26.1	85.7	15.9	73.3	18.0
Textiles	13.1	87.0	49.6	52.7	48.9	22.1	85.1	40.5	54.8	14.2	5.8	84.2	62.0	52.6	48.0	11.2	83.4	1.1	52.2	66.5
Wood and Pulp	37.4	60.5	20.6	0.0	0.0	3.5	53.8	20.6	0.0	0.0	4.2	87.3	35.3	20.5	0.0	16.3	76.6	30.4	42.4	0.0
Chemical Products	16.9	86.5	71.7	0.0	47.7	17.6	76.8	20.6	79.5	82.6	16.5	92.1	37.5	27.2	23.1	12.0	91.3	42.5	25.4	38.3
Iron and Steel	13.6	85.6	0.0	100.0	0.0	42.6	85.3	85.4	39.9	0.0	1.5	74.3	42.2	29.1	90.9	3.1	95.4	74.0	34.6	33.5
Nonmetallic Products	29.3	83.2	10.4	39.5	16.0	20.3	78.9	58.1	37.9	1.4	35.4	90.4	13.9	32.3	5.7	14.8	99.3	98.9	32.8	94.4
General Machinery	8.9	94.4	41.7	79.7	76.6	3.9	93.5	21.2	89.7	0.0	11.3	98.1	90.8	81.5	69.8	10.8	98.5	95.0	94.4	99.2
Electric Machinery	19.2	91.2	39.1	59.6	51.4	8.6	80.8	32.8	58.8	10.8	16.0	96.5	49.1	64.1	53.1	20.5	96.3	55.3	66.4	66.1
Transport Machinery	29.8	95.1	35.3	82.0	16.3	13.4	86.7	100.0	66.2	62.5	33.8	94.0	45.6	59.9	21.4	11.5	96.9	98.6	56.7	94.7
Precision Instruments	28.9	95.7	13.3	34.3	94.4	39.1	95.5	0.0	28.3	99.5	24.6	98.4	50.0	21.8	54.0	58.3	98.4	24.2	19.1	49.6
Coal and Petroleum Products	59.5	2.0	0.0	9.4	0.0	74.6	1.7	0.0	9.4	0.0	6.2	90.8	0.0	0.0	0.0	6.9	91.3	0.0	0.0	0.0
Other Manufacturing	13.7	90.6	38.3	35.3	77.6	6.1	81.2	48.0	57.3	34.2	10.7	92.1	41.1	31.3	46.1	8.1	94.3	62.7	32.7	29.4

Source: Ministry of International Trade and Industry, Kaigai Jigyo Katsudo Kihon Chosa (Comprehensive Survey of Overseas Activities of Japanese Firms), Nos. 5 and 7, 1994 and 2001.

Table 2-9   Selected FTAs in East Asia (as of June 2004)

Action	Negotiation	Study
Bangkok Treaty (1976)	China-ASEAN	Japan-ASEAN
AFTA (1992)	Hong Kong-New Zealand	Korea-ASEAN
Singapore-New Zealand (2001)	Japan-Mexico	Korea-Australia
Japan-Singapore (2002)	Japan-Korea	Korea-New Zealand
Singapore-EFTA (2003)	Japan-Thailand	Singapore-Chile
Singapore-Australia (2003)	Japan-Philippines	Singpore-Taiwan
China-Hong Kong (2004)	Japan-Malaysia	Thailand-Peru
Singapore-U.S.A. (2004)	Korea-Singapore	ASEAN-India
Korea-Chile (2004)	Singapore-Canada	ASEAN-U.S.A.
	Singapore-Mexico	
	Singapore-India	
	Taiwan-Panama (concluded)	
	Thailand-Baharain (concluded)	
	Thailand-India (concluded)	
	Thailand-U.S.A.	
	Thailand-Australia	

Source: Author's compilation from national sources.

Table 2-10   Effects of East Asia FTA on Real GDP and Equivalent Variation

	GDP	Equivalent Variation	
	(Changes from base data, %)	(Changes from base data, US$ million)	(Changes divided by GDP in 1997, %)
Australia/New Zealand	-0.23	-1,342	-0.29
China	1.27	5,485	0.64
Hong Kong	1.41	3,389	2.42
Japan	0.05	8,199	0.19
Korea	1.71	7,805	1.75
Taiwan	1.51	5,597	1.87
Indonesia	5.61	10,209	4.89
Malaysia	2.83	2,279	2.15
Philippines	2.02	602	0.77
Singapore	2.26	2,944	3.69
Thailand	15.90	19,790	12.54
Vietnam	8.42	1,446	6.61
Other Asia	-0.31	-1,803	-0.34
U.S.A.	-0.06	-7,059	-0.09
EU	-0.01	-1,807	-0.02

Notes: The figures indicate the changes from the base data.
Source: Urata and Kiyoto (2003)

Table 2-11 Effects of East Asia FTA on Production by Sectors (percentage change)

Sector	China	Japan	Korea	Hong Kong	Singapore	Taiwan	Indonesia	Malaysia	Philippines	Thailand	Vietnam
Agriculture	4.5	-3.9	-11.9	0.3	4.7	1.6	1.3	0.4	2.0	5.2	0.4
Forestry	-0.2	-1.8	-3.6	1.7	-7.4	3.2	8.6	2.1	2.1	16.3	11.4
Fishing	0.9	-2.8	7.6	-2.6	7.8	-1.0	3.9	2.5	1.3	12.6	6.1
Mining	-0.2	-0.7	-2.1	3.8	4.1	-0.9	1.4	1.7	4.1	19.2	-8.3
Food products and beverages	1.6	-3.4	30.1	19.3	36.7	6.9	5.3	15.3	-1.3	23.5	8.9
Textiles	-0.2	-2.3	17.4	3.2	1.9	17.1	3.7	7.7	13.9	8.4	174.8
Pulp, paper and paper products	-1.1	-0.4	1.9	3.3	3.7	1.6	8.9	4.3	0.8	16.1	16.9
Chemicals	-1.6	1.1	3.4	5.5	11.1	7.1	1.4	4.4	2.0	10.6	-2.0
Iron, steel and metal products	-1.5	2.2	-1.4	4.7	7.7	0.0	2.9	1.4	6.7	20.1	-18.3
Transportation machinery	-16.2	5.2	1.0	-7.9	-14.3	-6.9	-47.8	-24.0	29.3	-11.0	-55.1
Electronic equipment	6.9	-0.7	-1.9	0.9	1.9	-2.5	17.4	5.7	8.9	29.2	-0.9
General machinery	-1.6	2.2	-4.8	7.4	5.5	1.7	22.8	7.4	12.7	26.8	-3.7
Other manufacturing	1.6	-0.5	0.9	8.1	5.0	2.5	7.3	1.2	5.8	18.1	12.9

Notes: The figures indicate the changes from the base data.
Source: Urata and Kiyoto (2003)

Figure 2-1   Exports of Developing East Asia and Latin America

US$ million

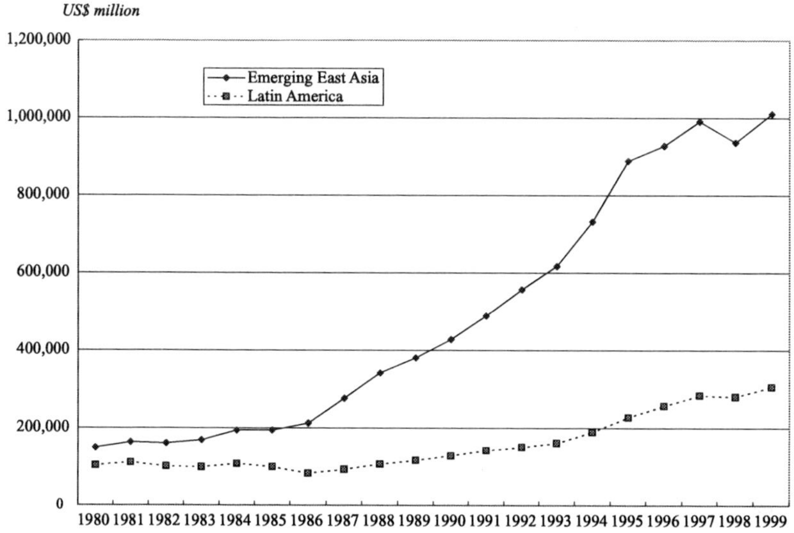

Figure 2-2   FDI Inflows in Developing East Asia and Latin America

US$ million

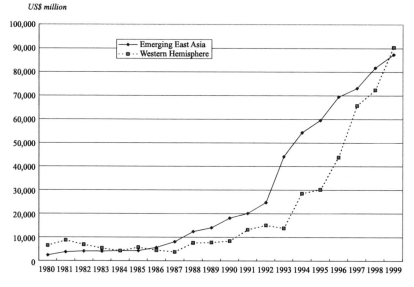

Figure 2-3   RTA in the World (Cumulative Number of RTAs Reported to GATT/WTO as of May 1, 2004)

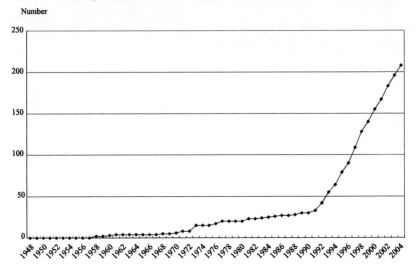

3
ASEAN's Strategy toward an Increasing Asian Integration

Suthiphand Chirathivat

Introduction

The evolution of ASEAN into the ASEAN Economic Community (AEC) by the year 2020 is a significant milestone in terms of regional arrangements for the developing world. The AEC is one of three pillars of the ASEAN community whose purpose is to ensure durable peace, stability and shared prosperity within the region.[1] With the AEC, the grouping had decided to deepen and broaden its economic integration efforts through existing and new initiatives with clear guidelines. In this sense, the AEC is therefore an important initiative aimed at reinforcing the position of Southeast Asia as a competitive place for business opportunities at a time when its larger neighbors (i.e., China and India) are becoming increasingly attractive to firms within and outside the region (especially firms from Japan, the EU, the U.S. and Australia).

These latest commitments on the part of ASEAN leaders demonstrate ASEAN's aim to reach a higher goal through a strong mix of market-driven plus institution-led integration. A tremendous amount of effort will need to be made by all people involved to help them better understand and adapt in this new phase of integration. This venture will also help ASEAN to establish a European-style single market and an important production base, characterized by the free movement of goods, services, investment and capital. There is also a need to establish mechanisms and measures to strengthen implementation of existing economic initiatives including the ASEAN Free Trade Area (AFTA), the ASEAN Framework Agreement on Services (AFAS) and the ASEAN Investment Area (AIA).[2]

With the AEC, ASEAN's strategy is consistent with the goal of overall ASEAN integration, which is to enhance regional economic competitiveness. Guided by the ASEAN Vision 2020[3] and its succeeding action plans, as well as the Initiative for ASEAN Integration (IAI) and the Roadmap for the Integration of ASEAN (RIA), the AEC is a strategy that also addresses the economic integration of Cambodia, Myanmar, Laos and Vietnam (CMLV). The ASEAN members are well aware that liberalization and cooperation measures are required to realize a fully integrated economic community in the future. In sum, ASEAN has responded to the new dynamics of economic changes that have taken place within and outside the region.

This new development is very different from the past where ASEAN used to be the only formal regional arrangement in East Asia with an outward orientation that fostered more trade and investment inside and outside the region. The recent blossoming of new bilateral, sub-regional and even East Asia-wide preferential trade arrangements (PTAs) has changed this trend. There have been numerous discussions and negotiations on PTAs; some PTAs have begun to be implemented, while many others are still in the pipeline. This trend has caused some concern over the rationale of such initiatives and the implications that would follow from such a strategy. Since the turn of the century up to the present, ASEAN is no longer the only PTA; instead, the entire East Asian region is now promoting closer economic cooperation through multiple PTAs.

Even ASEAN has had to adopt the PTAs strategy, signing agreements with countries outside the grouping. The financial crisis of 1997–98 has helped ASEAN to form an ASEAN+3 financial cooperation that has, finally, led to thoughts over the formation of an East Asian Free Trade Area (EAFTA) as well. Due to difficulties in forming an EAFTA at the moment, ASEAN has first entered into a framework agreement (since 2002) at the invitation of China to liberalize trade and cooperate on various activities. Japan followed suit in the next year with the signing of a framework agreement at the Bali summit for a comprehensive economic partnership between ASEAN and Japan. The ASEAN grouping has also signed a framework agreement with India. Meanwhile, ASEAN and Korea are also developing a comprehensive economic partnership. Thus, it looks like ASEAN, with active involvement of the large Asian powers, has rejuvenated itself amidst the rise of bilateral, sub-regional and even East Asia-wide integration.

In the next section (Impetus for ASEAN Economic Integration), this paper aims to explain the logic of ASEAN economic integration up to the present. With the rise of Asian bilateralism and regionalism, ASEAN needs a new response with the AEC and its multiple courtship; this is the focus of section three (Toward an AEC and Multiple CEPs for Further Integration). Section four (The New Emerging Regionalism in East Asia) discusses how these initiatives will turn out in terms of the rationale, further implications and outcome of these cooperation schemes. One could argue that a region-wide regionalism that is complementary to the WTO process, much like how APEC and ASEAN did for its open regionalism, should be further explored. Meanwhile, as discussed in the last section (Challenges for Conceptual Framework), ASEAN could play a role in an ASEAN-centered EAFTA.

Impetus for ASEAN Economic Integration

Beginning with the five founding members in 1967 (Indonesia, Malaysia, the Philippines, Singapore and Thailand) the objective of ASEAN has been to promote political and economic cooperation, to foster regional and economic cooperation and to foster regional stability and peace. After gaining independence from the United Kingdom, Brunei joined the grouping in 1984. But it was the end of the Cold War that helped to reunite the nations and people of the region. Thus, ASEAN's membership expanded throughout the 1990s to include Vietnam in 1995, Laos and Myanmar in 1997 and Cambodia in 1999. Through the expanded coverage of ASEAN to all countries in Southeast Asia, this regional institution achieved the objective prescribed in the Bangkok Declaration and fulfilled the initial intention of the original ASEAN leaders.

However, before any kind of regional economic cooperation could take place in ASEAN, the fact was that these countries were (and are still) at very different levels of economic development and a diverse range of political regimes. These differences could serve as stumbling blocks for any kind of regional economic initiative. Thus, there is a strong need for structural and industrial reforms in each member country in order to make them inclined to new economic development and further growth. The original five countries spent a great deal of time in removing these kinds of economic inefficiencies through domestic policy reforms in the 1970s and the 1980s in terms of industry, trade, finance, manpower and proper infrastructure. They all phased out their import substitution policies to cater to the new needs of export-oriented industrialization.

The results of their efforts paid off in the latter half of the 1980s. ASEAN economic cooperation was successful in creating a common policy framework for member countries. They are now embracing an outward economic orientation and open regionalism as a means of accelerating economic growth. They see increasing opportunities with the emergence of the trade-investment nexus and appreciate how this investment and trade can support broad-based development. From the period 1985 up to the financial crisis of 1997–98, there was a surge in FDI and trade, primarily as a result of Japanese firms (and to a certain extent from NIEs' firms) outsourcing production of parts and goods for more labor-intensive products in LDCs.[4] There was also increasing linkages to regional and global production networks especially those that revolved around the electronic and automobile industries. These FDI-led production networks have also spurred cross-intra-regional trade in the East Asia region. It is also important to note that all of this occurred in response to macroeconomic policies that were well managed by ASEAN countries.

As ASEAN realized the importance of increasing trade and investment with one another and the rest of the world, they began to adopt a regional

Table 3-1   Relative Importance of Intra-ASEAN Trade (%)

Country/group	1975	1985	1995	2001
ASEAN/world	2.7	3.6	6.0	6.3
East Asia[a]	11.3	19.0	25.6	25.7
Intra-ASEAN/world	0.3	0.6	1.3	1.2
Intra-East Asia/world	2.4	4.0	8.4	8.8
Value of trade (US$ billion)				
Intra-ASEAN exports	2.5	11.3	64.6	74.2
ASEAN exports	22.0	72.0	307.8	404.1
Intra-ASEAN/ASEAN exports	11.4	15.7	20.9	18.3

Note: a. Includes ASEAN-10 (excludes Myanmar), China, Japan, Korea, Hong Kong, Taiwan and Mongolia.
Sources: International Monetary Fund (various years).

cooperation strategy that suited these trends. From a modest regional PTA, the ASEAN members agreed to form a full-fledged ASEAN Free Trade Area (AFTA) in 10 years starting from 1993. Trade liberalization at first focused on tariff reductions on manufactured goods. Then in 1995, they agreed to expand AFTA to include non-tariff barriers, services, intellectual property rights and investment regulations. Furthermore, they signed an agreement in 1998 to form an ASEAN Investment Area (AIA) to enhance ASEAN's attractiveness and competitiveness as an investment area. As for the new members of ASEAN, in the 1990s they were allowed to first enjoy market access for their exports and to delay their obligations. For example, Vietnam has until 2006 to comply with the AFTA, while Myanmar and Laos have until 2008 and Cambodia until 2010 to reduce their tariffs below 5 percent.

Indeed, ASEAN's share of world trade has significantly increased from 2.7 percent to stand at 6.3 percent in 2001, even after the financial crisis of 1997–98 (Table 3-1). The share of intra-ASEAN trade as compared to world trade has also jumped four times from 0.3 percent in 1975 to 1.2 percent in 2001. Moreover, intra-ASEAN trade has increased at faster rates of growth compared to ASEAN's overall trade expansion between 1985–95, although this trend was decelerated by the financial crisis during the period of 1997–2000. Despite the growth, overall intra-ASEAN trade made up only one-fifth of total ASEAN exports; this suggests that ASEAN still relies too heavily on outside markets for its goods. The increase in both intra-ASEAN and extra-ASEAN trade since the 1980s has been due to the relative success of the ASEAN countries, including its ability to transform the regional market into a successful production base for multinational firms.

Thus, while AFTA may not have contributed directly to trade expansion and FDI growth in the region, it has made fair progress in implementing the ASEAN-6 (Tables 3-2 and 3-3). Some countries still have reservations in certain

Table 3-2   Number of Tariff Lines in the Tentative 2003 CEPT Package[a]

Country	Number of tariff lines					Percentage				
	IL[b]	TEL	GEL	SL/HSL	Total	IL[b]	TEL	GEL	SL	Total
ASEAN-6	44,361	218	292	29	44,900	98.80	0.49	0.65	0.06	100.00
Brunei	6,337	-	155	-	6,492	97.61	-	2.39	-	100.00
Indonesia	7,206	-	68	11	7,285	98.92	-	0.93	0.15	100.00
Malaysia	10,116	218	53	8	10,395	97.32	2.1	0.51	0.08	100.00
Philippines	5,632	-	16	10	5,658	99.54	-	0.28	0.18	100.00
Singapore	5,859	-	-	-	5,859	100.00	-	-	-	100.00
Thailand	9,211	-	-	-	9,211	100.00	-	-	-	100.00
CLMV	16,126	5,603	395	207	22,331	72.21	25.09	1.77	0.93	100.00
Cambodia	3,115	3,523	134	50	6,822	45.66	51.64	1.96	0.73	100.00
Lao PDR	2,533	856	74	88	3,551	71.33	24.11	2.08	2.48	100.00
Myanmar	4,182	1,224	48	18	5,472	76.43	22.37	0.88	0.33	100.00
Vietnam	6,296	-	139	51	6,486	97.07	-	2.14	0.79	100.00
Total ASEAN	60,487	5,821	687	236	67,231	89.97	8.66	1.02	0.35	100.00

Note: a. Data as of Feb. 28, 2003.

b. IL means Inclusion List, TEL means Temporary Exclusion List, GEL means General Exclusion List, SL/HSL means sensitive list and highly sensitive list.

Source: ASEAN Secretariat (2003).

areas—for example, motor vehicles and parts for Malaysia[5] and petrochemical products for the Philippines[6]—so special arrangements have been made for sensitive and highly sensitive products. As for CMLV, their inclusion lists are still insignificant in terms of value to total trade. But overall, the progress on trade liberalization has helped their industries be more active in terms of the proper role of industrial protection and competitiveness in regional and domestic development strategies.

Given the past experience with implementation of AFTA, there remains a great deal to be done if ASEAN desires to achieve an FTA. Real challenges remain and there is still a need to remove several obstacles such as:

- Utilization of the CEPT concession is still very low[7] mainly due to a lack of clear and transparent procedures to comply with the rules of origin, or Form D. In addition, there is an unwillingness to form mutual trust between member countries as well as other complications to gaining low margins of preference.

- Improvements in non-tariff measures are still needed. These include licensing restrictions, customs procedures, and mutual recognition of technical standards to name a few.

- Dispute settlement mechanisms have not been put in place to address problems that may arise from members who fail to comply with their obligations.

Table 3-3   Number of Tariff Lines at 0–5% in the Tentative 2003 CEPT Package[a]

Country	Number of tariff lines				Percentage			
	0-5%	>5%	Other[b]	Total	0-5%	>5%	Other[b]	Total
ASEAN-6	44,160	51	150	44,361	99.55	0.11	0.34	100.00
Brunei	6,285	28[c]	24	6,337	99.18	0.44	0.38	100.00
Indonesia	7,206	-	-	7,206	100.00	-	-	100.00
Malaysia	10,041	-	75	10,116	99.26	-	0.74	100.00
Philippines	5,565	23[d]	44	5,632	98.81	0.41	0.78	100.00
Singapore	5,859	-	-	5,859	100.00	-	-	100.00
Thailand	9,204	-	7	9,211	99.92	-	0.08	100.00
CLMV	8,977	6,412	737	16,126	55.67	39.76	4.57	100.00
Cambodia	238	2,877	-	3,115	7.64	92.36	-	100.00
Lao PDR	1,357	1,176	-	2,533	53.57	46.43	-	100.00
Myanmar	3,262	920	-	4,182	78.00	22.00	-	100.00
Vietnam	4,120	1,439	737	6,296	65.44	22.86	11.71	100.00
Total ASEAN	53,148	6,463	887	60,487	87.85	10.68	1.47	100.00

Notes: a. Data as of Feb. 28, 2003.
   b. Items with no information on CEPT rates (e.g., items that are scheduled to be phased into IL by 2003).
   c. Item that has just moved from General Exclusion List into Inclusion List.
   d. Item that has just moved from Sensitive List into Inclusion List and items of petrochemical products.
Source: ASEAN Secretariat (2003).

• CMLV may possibly delay their AFTA efforts if their industries are increasingly faced with regional competition. Thus, there are industrial adjustments and costs involved for which these countries may not be well prepared.

Overall, AFTA's strategy needs to address the mitigation of risks and demonstrate increasing opportunities for all members in order for the grouping to complete such a scheme. AFTA will lead to increasing links to the trade and investment nexus in regional markets and the world. There is no way to turn back as AFTA has to move further in an AEC. With the emergence of China and India, it is particularly important for ASEAN to define the context in which the grouping would like to remain competitive in order to attract investors. There is also the issue of taking further advantage of the expertise of each member nation and outsourcing of raw materials to maximize trade and production activities.[8]

The ASEAN Framework Agreement on Services (AFAS) signed in 1995 was aimed at enhancing ASEAN cooperation in services trade by reducing intra-ASEAN services impediments and expanding the scope of regional services trade liberalization beyond the General Agreement on Trade in Services (GATS). That is, the AFAS was meant to be GATS-plus. Negotiations were taking place

Table 3-4   FDI Inflows to ASEAN, China and Asian NIEs (US$ million)

Host region/ economy	1983-88	1990	1995	1996	1997	1998	1999	2000	2001
World	91,554	211,425	331,068	386,140	478,082	694,457	1,088,263	1,491,934	735,146
Developed economies	71,779	176,436	203,462	219,908	267,947	484,239	837,761	1,227,476	503,144
Developing economies	19,759	34,689	113,338	152,685	191,022	187,611	225,140	237,894	204,801
ASEAN-10	3,708	12,156	25,121	28,716	29,667	18,287	19,095	10,456	12,997
Brunei	n.a.	1	13	654	702	573	596	600	244
Indonesia	341	1,093	4,346	6,194	4,677	-356	-2,745	-4,550	-3,277
Malaysia	731	2,331	5,816	7,296	6,324	2,714	3,895	3,788	554
Philippines	249	530	1,459	1,520	1,249	1,752	578	1,241	1,792
Singapore	1,947	5,575	8,788	8,608	10,746	6,389	11,803	5,407	8,609
Thailand	439	2,444	2,004	2,271	3,626	5,143	3,561	2,813	3,759
Vietnam	1	16	2,336	1,803	2,587	1,700	1,484	1,289	1,300
Lao PDR	n.a.	6	95	128	86	45	52	34	24
Myanmar	n.a.	161	277	310	387	314	253	255	123
Cambodia	n.a.	n.a.	151	586	-15	230	214	179	113
NIEs Asian	2,178	3,773	9,548	14,649	16,460	20,404	36,855	76,149	30,141
Hong Kong	1,343	1,728	6,213	10,460	11,368	14,770	24,596	61,938	22,834
Korea	387	715	1,776	2,325	2,844	5,412	9,333	9,283	3,198
Taiwan	448	1,330	1,559	1,864	2,248	222	2,926	4,928	4,109
China	1,823	3,487	35,849	40,180	44,237	43,751	40,319	40,772	46,846

Source: UNCTAD (2002), Annex Table B.1.

on numerous sectors such as financial services, transport, telecommunications, tourism, professional business services and others.

The AFAS operates like GATS on a positive list approach. However, under the AFAS, regional services trade liberalization was not as bold or as far-reaching as it was under GATS (Stephenson and Nikhomborirak 2002). Some sectors continued to receive preferential treatment, and thus AFAS cannot be considered as GATS-plus.

The progress of ASEAN's integration is based on a central aegis; that is, its cross-intra-regional trade liberalization known as AFTA is aimed at engaging the market more with extra-regional trade and FDI. The AFAS and AIA are supposed to help further deepening of regional integration. From this perspective, FDI becomes increasingly important to the ASEAN countries. The longstanding determinants of FDI flows to ASEAN have recently been fairly assessed, and studies reveal that the environment for FDI in developing countries like ASEAN is undergoing significant change.[9]

FDI inflows to ASEAN were quite substantial during the period up to before the financial crisis of 1997–98 (Table 3-4). The surge in FDI, a few years after the financial crisis, was however not totally in green field areas of FDI. Since then, several ASEAN countries have struggled to remain attractive to FDI. There has been an increase in FDI to China since the end of the Cold War and, in fact, China was quickly catching up to match FDI flows to the ASEAN region in 1993. Since 1996, FDI inflows to China rose to more than US$40 billion per year, almost reaching US$50 billion in 2001 and 2002, before growing again to more than US$50 billion in 2003 and 2004. Hence, any empirical assessment of the determinants of FDI flows to these countries must take into account new developments alongside the more traditional determinants of FDI.

The complementary relationship between trade and FDI was examined following the formation of the AFTA and its implications on FDI and trade patterns in the region (Athukorala and Menon 1997; Rutngamlug 2002). The authors of the study applied the effects of economic integration on four types of investment responses as follows:

- reorganizational investment (i.e., optimum location-seeking investment)
- defensive import-substitution investment (i.e., tariff-jumping investment)
- offensive import-substitution investment (i.e., market-seeking investment)
- rationalization investment (i.e., efficiency-seeking investment).

Three major factors affecting the gains on FDI from economic integration are market size, market growth and trade openness. Athukorala and Menon (1997) look into two particular categories of FDI: market-seeking investment and efficiency-seeking investment. They concluded that the formation of AFTA seems to be relying on efficiency-seeking investment in vertically integrated production processes. The potential of AFTA is then related to cross-border production activities that would create both intra and extra-regional trade links and integration in the region.

Toward an AEC and Multiple CEPs for Further Integration

At the Bali Summit and after a decade of AFTA, ASEAN agreed to move towards deeper economic integration and agreed to form an ASEAN Economic Community (AEC). The grouping realizes the need for accelerating its own integration to match up with new developments and changes taking place regionally and globally. The Comprehensive Economic Partnerships (CEPs) signed first with China in 2002, and CEPs that were later concluded with Japan and India are important steps for linking ASEAN to wider Asian integration. With an AEC, ASEAN can work properly for deeper economic integration. On the other hand, all CEPs that ASEAN enters into can help to widen its scope for Asian integration.

In this context, ASEAN actually needs both an AEC and reliable CEPs with major markets. With East Asia's high-growth performance and dynamic production sectors, ASEAN needs to remain competitive by creating a European-style single market and a reliable production base for firms looking to do business across the region. This could also help to link ASEAN with other Asian countries like China, Japan and India in an increasingly integrated Asia and global economy. Thus, by taking further steps toward regional integration, ASEAN will be in a better position for becoming a hub. But the question remains whether ASEAN realistically can provide a hub for the region? When ASEAN organized the ASEAN+3 leaders meeting in 1997, it had no intention of institutionalizing the ASEAN+3 framework. However, judging from the results of ASEAN+3 and India at the latest summit in Bali, other Asian countries have responded by negotiating more CEPs with ASEAN.

In terms of substance, the AEC is aimed at creating a single market and production base, characterized by the free movement of goods, services, investment and capital by the year 2020.[10] It is an important initiative that is aimed at turning Southeast Asia into a competitive place to do business at a time when some Asian neighbors are becoming increasingly attractive to foreign investors (Ong Keng Yong 2003). In moving towards the AEC, ASEAN needs to strengthen its implementation of existing economic initiatives including AFTA, AFAS and AIA. It must go further along its roadmap following the key features of the AEC including trade in goods, trade in services, capital movement and other areas (Table 3-5).

According to the Secretary-General of the ASEAN Secretariat (Ong Keng Yong 2003), the AEC is important to ASEAN in several ways:

- The creation of real and wider economic space for developing economies while remaining committed to the multilateral trading system.
- The logical steps of further integration in the AEC will further enhance ASEAN's economic engagements with its major trading partners, including bilateral and collective free trade arrangements in which ASEAN enters into closer economic partnerships with such neighbors as China, Japan, India and South Korea.
- The AEC is only one of the three pillars of the ASEAN Community. The broader goals must be taken into consideration.
- The AEC is certain to carry weight towards further improvement of ASEAN mechanisms and institutions.

Hence, the AEC is another logical step toward deeper and broader ASEAN economic integration. It has put into place several new features which merit further detailed studies. However, in terms of requirements for common rules governing taxes, wages, competition and monopolies, technical harmonization

Table 3-5   Key Features of the AEC

Issues	Goals
Scope	
AEC is one of the three pillars	ASEAN Community
Deeper integration	A single market and production base
Trade in goods	
Priority sectors	Thrust to faster integration for 11 sectors, including electronics, air travel and tourism, on fast track to cut tariff and non-tariff barriers by 2010, rather than 2020
Border controls	Standardize customs costs and procedures
Non-tariff barriers	Identify and begin breaking down by 2005
Technical harmonization	Harmonization across the region by the end of 2004
Trade in services	
Movement of people	Visa procedures to be simplified, allowing ASEAN nationals to freely travel within the area without visas by 2005 and to eventually issue a single ASEAN visa for overseas visitors
Professional services and labor movement	Standardize requirements for professional services to enable free movement of professional and skilled labor within the region
Capital movement	
Free movement of capital	Removal of capital controls
	Financial services liberalization, capital market development and currency cooperation
Investment	
A network of FTAs	Must set up within ASEAN to make manufacturing more cost-competitive and to give firms greater economies of scale
Other areas	
Dispute settlement mechanisms	System needs to be overhauled with the establishment of an ASEAN legal unit and other bodies
Intellectual property rights	Cooperation beyond trademarks and patents by including cooperation in copyright information exchange and enforcement by 2004

Source: Adapted from recommendations of the high-level task force on ASEAN economic integration (ASEAN Secretariat 2003).

and national treatment on ASEAN investors, there remains a great deal of controversy that will require further consideration.

At the Bali Summit, ASEAN also made substantial progress for simultaneous relations with China, Japan and India. Both China and India have signed a nontraditional security agreement for cooperation, among others, to combat terrorism. This is apart from the ASEAN-China framework agreement on strategic economic partnership. Japan and India have also entered into a framework for comprehensive economic partnership and cooperation with ASEAN. For Japan, this is the 25ᵗʰ anniversary of the ASEAN–Japan relationship. For India, it is part of its 'Look-East Policy' developed in the early 1990s. In order to give this trend further impetus, ASEAN concluded a closer economic partnership agreement with Japan and India at the Bali Summit.[11]

Among the three partners, China has emerged as the new Asian powerhouse shaping ASEAN and beyond. Its relations with ASEAN are rapidly developing and comprehensive in most fields. Following the successful launch in 2002 to complete the ASEAN–China FTA by 2010, ASEAN has been evidently pulled to become strategic partners with China. And with China's push in several Southeast Asian capitals, each country, in some ways, was shown the way to trade liberalization with early harvest programs. The ASEAN countries came to realize the importance of common efforts among themselves after they signed with China, as seen in the protocol at Bali to amend the Framework Agreement on acceleration, rules of origin, revision of 'Early Harvest,' mutual recognition and prohibition to enter other agreements between them. The ASEAN Summit in Vientiane in November 2004 further extended plans of action to implement the joint declaration on the ASEAN–China strategic partnership for peace and prosperity, agreement on dispute settlement mechanism of the Framework Agreement on Comprehensive Economic Partnership between ASEAN and China, in addition to the agreement of trade in goods of the Framework Agreement (See Chairman's Statement of the 8th ASEAN+China Summit, Vientiane, 29 November 2004).

In response to the Chinese challenge, Japan finally adapted and promoted economic partnership agreements (EPAs) and free trade agreements (FTAs)[12] as a means of strengthening economic partnerships beyond the WTO levels. ASEAN has still to benefit from Japan's new approach towards bilateral and regional EPAs/FTAs to expand and deepen its external economic relations. Among the ASEAN countries, Singapore had extended an earlier agreement with Japan, considered as Japan's first EPA/FTA, in November 2002. Then Japan and ASEAN signed a Framework for Comprehensive Agreement at the Bali Japan-ASEAN Summit Meeting in October 2003. For Thailand, the Philippines and Malaysia, the negotiations for the respective bilateral agreements with Japan were held in early 2004 with aims to conclude the negotiations within a reasonable period of time. As such, Japan began negotiations with Malaysia in January 2004 and with both Thailand and the Philippines in February 2004, respectively. As for Indonesia, there were steps towards the negotiations for the agreement between both countries. In sum, the overall results of bilateral agreement would allow Japan and individual ASEAN countries to reach trade liberalization and facilitation to strengthen further the close relations between them.

As compared with China and Japan, latecomer India had also moved firmly in solidifying its ties with ASEAN. India entered into a framework agreement on Comprehensive Economic Cooperation (CEC) and a free trade area in 2011 with five ASEAN countries, and 2016 with Cambodia, Laos, Myanmar, the Philippines and Vietnam. India's economic structure is largely complimentary to ASEAN economics and therefore there are significant opportunities for mutual gains. For the negotiations of bilateral FTAs and CEC, Thailand was the first among the ASEAN countries to reach such an agreement with an 'Early Harvest' trade liberalization of 82 product items since September 2004. Subsequently, in June 2005 India and Singapore signed the Comprehensive Economic Cooperation Agreement (CECA) opening up opportunities for both sides for greater trade, investment and freer movement of people. India is also negotiating with Malaysia and Indonesia to have similar deals as part of India's policy to see ASEAN as an economically important region. The progress in economic cooperation is steadily moving towards a new direction which requires a change in the mindset among ASEAN policy makers and business communities before potential for mutual gains can be effectively enhanced (Sen, Ascher and Rajan 2004, 1).

The New Emerging Regionalism in East Asia

East Asia was slow to start its own regionalism and, with the exception of ASEAN, there were no formal regional PTAs up to the late 1990s. Up until that time, the region was still divided by the Cold War and adhered to multilateralism in trade negotiations. The outward orientation of these economies with the rest of world was successful as shown by their trade patterns, investment orientation, technology transfer and further development (Langhammer 1995; Petri 1995; Urata 2003). There are welfare implications of continental trading blocs that could lower welfare for each continent (Frankel 1997) and this has been widely discussed in East Asia.

The emergence of East Asian economies, the collapse of the mid-term review of multilateralism and the formation of trade blocs in Europe and the Americas has been the force behind the concept of East Asian regionalism (Figure 1). The first in favor of this regional arrangement initiative was then Malaysian Prime

Figure 3-1 Regional Integration Schemes among the Three Blocs from an ASEAN Perspective

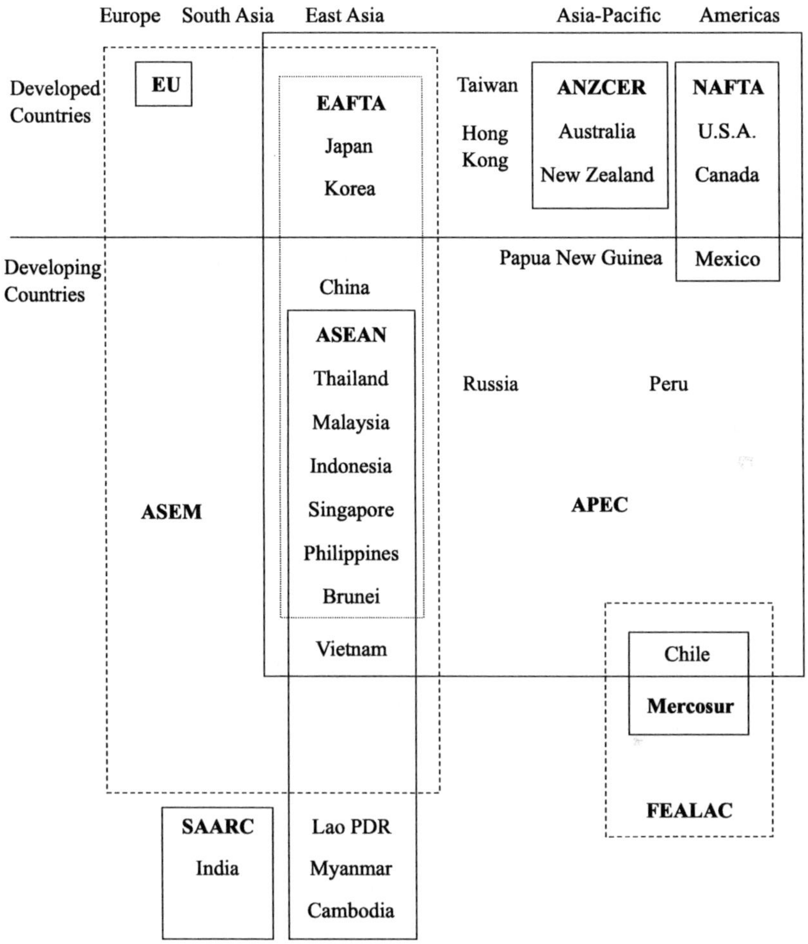

	Europe	South Asia	East Asia		Asia-Pacific	Americas
Developed Countries	EU		EAFTA Japan Korea	Taiwan Hong Kong	ANZCER Australia New Zealand	NAFTA U.S.A. Canada
Developing Countries	ASEM		China ASEAN Thailand Malaysia Indonesia Singapore Philippines Brunei Vietnam	Russia	Papua New Guinea Peru APEC	Mexico
		SAARC India	Lao PDR Myanmar Cambodia		Chile Mercosur FEALAC	

Minister Mahathir Mohamed. However, the U.S. shot down the proposal for an East Asian Economic Grouping (EAEG),[13] while Japan threatened to not join the grouping; this caused some additional thought on the part of other East Asian countries. China was viewed as being too preoccupied with its own transition to a market economy to give serious thought to such an initiative. APEC then advanced very quickly in the late 1980s to promote a multilateralism that encompassed the Asia–Pacific region. Since then, APEC has been used as a vehicle for further regional trade liberalization à la WTO-plus (Yamazawa 1992).

The region's only preferential trade grouping was ASEAN, which was upgraded to the ASEAN Free Trade Area (or AFTA) in response to increasing regionalism in the beginning of the 1990s. In 1995 Vietnam joined this grouping, followed by Laos and Myanmar in 1997, and Cambodia in 1999, and today ASEAN is made up of the 10 countries of Southeast Asia. ASEAN governments aim to push regional trade liberalization as a step toward global free trade. In this sense, regional integration of ASEAN seems to be in line with global free trade; this is very different from the usual version of the regional integration framework that has been used (Chirathivat 1996; Ariff 2001).

ASEAN looks at AFTA not as inward looking trade liberalization, but rather as an investment-driven integration framework that would serve as a 'training ground' for global competition. Precisely speaking, ASEAN's extra-regional trade links are much stronger and far more meaningful than intra-regional trade patterns. AFTA is meant to give each country a greater potential and edge towards an investment-driven area in an expanded ASEAN. Hence, the main objective of AFTA is not to increase intra-ASEAN trade per se, but rather to attract attention to the ASEAN region as an area to invest, produce and compete efficiently within the global economy. As an outward-looking regionalism framework, ASEAN sets clear objectives to establish linkages with other countries and regional groupings that would create more opportunities and new challenges for the region.

As for the Asia-Europe Meeting (or ASEM), this inter-regional grouping was formed in response to completing the linkages between East Asia and the European Union. Because East Asia is strongly involved with the Asia-Pacific region through APEC, the EU felt it important not to miss any opportunities. The ASEM dialogue has had to rethink its future orientation following the crisis. Still, the once-every-two-years Leaders Meeting seems to serve them well and allows them to air their concerns with respect to recent changes and to offer thoughtful direction for policy and future partnerships.

With the financial crisis of 1997–98, the East Asian region felt the need to promote closer economic cooperation. Although regionalism is regarded as a second-best policy, many countries have begun to explore this path. It is gaining acceptance because policymakers see advantages in regionalism itself. These advantages are interpreted as 'competitive liberalization,' which means an opening up of markets and easing of regulations within the group (which could mean unfavorable treatment of goods from an outsider country). The effects of competitive liberalization partly contributed to a rise in regionalism worldwide and also in East Asia.

To date, most Northeast and Southeast Asian countries have concluded one or more bilateral or sub-regional PTAs. Only in the past few years have various kinds of trade arrangements been proposed or put under negotiation with some agreed upon and being implemented (Table 3-6). Indeed, Japan and China have, for the first time, either signed or are negotiating PTAs. There is also a proposal to create the East Asian Free Trade Area (EAFTA) or ASEAN+3 grouping that covers the entire East Asia. Many of these new initiatives pose strong challenges to participants, outsiders of the region, and even the multilateral trading system.

With these trends, bilateral agreements represent the new dynamics toward regional and global free trade. Although it is difficult to know its short-term effects, the long-run effects seem to be positive (Lloyd 2002). Japan, Korea and Singapore have begun to sign several bilateral agreements and some are being implemented. China and several Southeast Asian countries like Thailand, Malaysia and the Philippines have followed quickly as well. Currently, the entire East Asian region now seems busy with bilateral FTAs in one way or another.

Among the ASEAN members, Singapore embraced bilateral FTAs early on. The Singapore option is aimed at being 'WTO-plus' rather than a 'WTO-substitute' (Rajan et al. 2001). Unsatisfied with the ASEAN and APEC process of regional and unilateral liberalization, recent initiatives by Singapore reflect this spirit.[14] Singapore's interest in free trade with Japan and the U.S. reflects its close de facto trade and investment links with and dependence on the two markets. Thailand is the second ASEAN country to go in this direction and is catching up very quickly with its 'competitive liberalization' policy. Although the country must still conclude a number of bilateral arrangements, it needs to pay increasing attention to overlapping areas that are opened through this involvement.

These various proposals for regional integration, such as bilateral and multilateral FTAs, are significant new features of East Asia. How can we place an ASEAN–Japan CEP in this context? The effect of an ASEAN–Japan CEP in the new regionalism of East Asia is now regarded as an important issue in terms of its significance among the multi-level FTAs, as well as agreements on a bilateral, sub-regional and region-wide basis. Taking the case of Thailand and its possible implications of various proposals, it turns out that an ASEAN–Japan could lead to the most significant impacts in terms of tariff liberalization (Table 3-7). It also shows that a Thailand–USA and ASEAN+3 FTA could also be meaningful for Thailand.

Challenges for Conceptual Framework

Regional trade liberalization is an important and complex issue in an increasingly globalized economy and it is now an important issue for East Asia as well (Abe 1996; Okamoto 2003; Yusuf 2003). Dealing with this issue requires difficult

Table 3-6   Preferential Trade Agreement Participation in East Asia

Country/grouping	Partners	Status of agreement, 2003
ASEAN	China	Agreement signed
	India	Agreement signed
	Japan	Agreement signed
	U.S. (TIFA)	Under negotiation
	CER	Under study
	ASEAN+3	Under study
	EU (Treaty)	Proposed
China	ASEAN	Agreement signed
	Australia	Proposed
	Hong Kong	Agreement signed
	Macau	Proposed
	Malaysia	Under negotiation
	New Zealand	Proposed
	Philippines	Under negotiation
	Thailand	Agreement signed
Hong Kong	China	Agreement signed
	Macau	Agreement signed
	New Zealand	Under negotiation
Japan	ASEAN	Agreement signed
	Canada	Proposed
	Chile	Under study
	Korea	Under study
	Malaysia	Under negotiation
	Mexico	Under negotiation
	Philippines	Under negotiation
	Singapore	Agreement signed
	Thailand	Under negotiation
Korea	Australia	Under study
	China	Under study
	Chile	Agreement signed
	Japan	Under study
	Mexico	Under negotiation
	New Zealand	Under study
	Peru	Proposed
	Singapore	Under study
	Thailand	Under study
	U.S.A.	Under negotiation

Continued on next page.

Table 3-6   Preferential Trade Agreement Participation in East Asia (continued)

Country/grouping	Partners	Status of agreement, 2003
Malaysia	China	Under negotiation
	Japan	Under negotiation
	U.S.A.	Proposed
Philippines	China	Under negotiation
	Japan	Under negotiation
	U.S.A.	Proposed
Singapore	Australia	Agreement signed
	Canada	Under negotiation
	EFTA	Agreement signed
	EU	Proposed (rejected by EU)
	India	Under negotiation
	Japan	Agreement signed
	Korea	Under study
	Mexico	Under negotiation
	New Zealand	Agreement signed
	Taiwan	Proposed
	U.S.A.	Agreement signed
Taiwan	Costa Rica	Proposed
	Japan	Proposed
	New Zealand	NZ withdrew from negotiations
	Panama	Under negotiation
	Singapore	Proposed
	U.S.A.	Proposed
Thailand	Australia	Under negotiation
	Bahrain	Agreement signed
	China	Agreement signed
	India	Agreement signed
	Japan	Under negotiation
	Korea	Under study
	Mexico	Under study
	New Zealand	Under study
	Peru	Under negotiation
	South Africa	Under study
	U.S.A.	Under study
	BIMSTEC	Under study

Note: a. 'Proposed' refers to the situation where an agreement has been officially proposed with varying degrees of formality by one government to another. (Numerous other proposals have been made, primarily by business groups.) Most proposals are then referred for study to either national think tanks or consultants and/or joint working parties established by the partners. Negotiations usually do not begin until governments have received these studies.

Source: Adapted from Ravenhill, John (2003), East West Center.

Table 3-7   Implications of Tariff Liberalization under Ftas with Different Trading
Partners for the Total Welfare of Thailand (US$ million)

	Overall impact[c]	Internal impact	External impact
1. ASEAN-Japan	6,848.54	5,219.35	1,568.45
2. Thailand-U.S.A.	6,661.89	1,158.71	5,382.27
3. ASEAN+3[a, b]	6,119.53	6,023.04	2,235.62
Thailand-China	1,058.28	368.39	2,235.62
Thailand-India	545.21	7.63	690.94
ASEAN-China	422.33	254.20	555.05
Thailand-Australia	349.04	70.75	274.49
ASEAN-Korea	340.19	186.39	149.66
Thailand-New Zealand	16.48	-1.41	17.82

Note: a. We need to add as well a regional impact of -1,596.03 US$ million.
b. ASEAN+3 includes ASEAN and three countries; China, Korea and Japan.
c. Internal impact derives from a country's own tariff liberalization, external impact
from trading partner's tariff liberalization. Overall impact is the sum of the two.
Source: This research makes use of the GTAP (1997) model developed by Purdue
University (for more information, see https://www.gtap.agecon.purdue.edu/
products/models/defaults.asp) as adapted in the Chulalongkorn and Monash
General Equilibrium (CAMGEM) Project of Chulalongkorn University,
Thailand. The GTAP model in the version applied here contains 45 countries and
50 production sectors, see Mallikamas (2002).

answers about whether certain arrangements should be pursued.[15] To make such
an assessment requires one to focus on some important questions that need to
be answered. The issue of costs and benefits come to mind first and whether the
formation of these PTAs will help to raise or lower welfare (Viner 1950). Then,
there is also the debate on the virtues and dangers of PTAs and whether these
arrangements can reinforce or hinder multilateral trade liberalization. In the case
of East Asia, this renewed regionalism in the form of bilateral arrangements is
very complex, and answers to these questions are not easy.

These new significant features in East Asia, however, require one to look
closely at these developments. Understanding the reasons behind these trends
is also the key to focus rightly or wrongly on further policy thought. The issue
of market access or the 'fear of exclusion from major markets' (Lloyd 2002,
7) has been advanced as one of the major factors that led to the formation of
new bilateral RTAs.[16] This argument can explain in large part the pattern of
bilateral agreements as much as the move towards bilateral arrangements in the
region. The effect of this new regionalism in East Asia is now regarded to be an
important issue in terms of the multi-level PTAs as well as bilateral, sub-regional
and region-wide initiatives.

There is cause for concern in this new regionalism in East Asia. These issues
include:

- Discrimination against nonmembers, or the trade diversion effect. In this case, competitive suppliers are unable to participate as they are not part of bilateral PTAs, and thus global welfare could suffer. For instance, the lowest-income ASEAN countries are excluded from this new regionalism.
- Coverage of existing and proposed PTAs in East Asia is far from uniform. This issue involves overlapping systems of bilateral and sub-regional trade liberalization. For example, an ASEAN–China FTA means China must deal with 10 different liberalization schemes (Chirathivat 2002).
- The outcome of liberalization schemes depends largely on negotiations and political decisions. Negotiations in the presence of a limited number of countries could lead to the more-powerful countries dictating the terms of the agreement (Ravenhill 2003, 4). In its negotiations with Singapore and Thailand, for example, the Japanese government was able to exclude trade liberalization in sectors that it considers politically sensitive.
- Multiple PTAs could lead to hubs and spokes (Wonnacott 1996). In the longer run, the new regionalism in East Asia could lead to a new trading environment of 'give and take' where the spokes run to the hubs in order to get something out it needs. Japan and China, for instance, could potentially be further hubs for these new RTAs. ASEAN is also driving fast with its new concluded arrangements, aspiring to be one of the future hubs in the region.
- Negotiating and applying multiple bilateral arrangements are known to consume a great deal of negotiation resources at the national level. Smaller countries may not be adequately prepared to deal with the negotiations and may not have an adequate number of skilled people for the negotiations. At the practical level, strict rules of origin that are intended to prevent transshipment of products will mean cumbersome routine work for custom officials and could lead to nowhere in truly expanding trade between partners.

Some of these concerns should be included in the scope and framework for future collaboration. At the moment, effects to pursue bilateral and sub-regional PTAs are often expressed as being part of FTAs. If this is the case, these countries need to look carefully at the economic effects of these arrangements. This paper offers the following suggestions on key issues to forming multiple FTAs in East Asia:

- In terms of trade creation and trade diversion, this often represents the costs and benefits involved in bilateral or regional trade liberalization. In an FTA, tariff and non-tariff barriers among member states are supposed to be eliminated while they are maintained against outsiders. It seems the East Asian nations' efforts toward bilateral FTAs are being pursued as a comprehensive FTA that would also mutually recognize member countries' systems and rules such as intellectual property right protection and FDI liberalization. The Japan-Singapore economic partnership is a good example of this comprehensive kind of FTA.

• If transactions costs among prospective members of a bloc are low, trade creation is likely to be great and trade diversion small. Transactions costs, broadly defined, are introduced in the cost function of the regional trading partners. In this sense, transactions costs involved in the process of exchange would include those of transportation, communications, bureaucratic red tape, and transshipping because of customs and border regulations, all of which are significant for the East Asian region.[17]

• The impact of transactions costs can foster market widening. Through increased access for regional partners, there is the case of increasing returns to scale. East Asia is well placed to gain 'external economies of scale.' Under favorable conditions with increasing returns, RTAs can be trade-creating since they may push labor costs towards internationally competitive price levels (Bhagwati and Panagariya 1996).

• There are also issues in which strict FTAs, in many ways, might differ from a customs union. Rules of origin can serve as additional trade barriers in an FTA in ways that cannot be under a customs union (Krueger 1997a). Thus, an understanding of differences between FTAs and customs union become important, especially for issues such as overlapping FTAs, which several East Asian countries are now running into. From a welfare point of view 'an FTA cannot lead to any more trade creation than a customs union and when rules of origin export any protection, an FTA leads to more trade diversion than does a customs union' (Krueger 1997b, 1999).

Overall, efforts toward bilateral and sub-regional or even region-wide arrangements are being pursued, not as FTAs per se, but rather as a means of Comprehensive Economic Partnership (CEPs) based on Preferential Trade Arrangements (PTAs), some being sub-regional but mostly bilateral. This new type of FTA looks like a new comprehensive framework to foster East Asian integration, and the challenges associated with these new arrangements will need to be addressed properly (Scollay 2003).

Indeed, the CEPs that have been concluded recently, as well as those currently under negotiation among the East Asian countries, deal with a number of issues beyond a traditional FTA (Elek 2003).[18] It is more likely that CEPs will become important principles toward wider cooperation in East Asia. CEPs could represent significant policy options available to the East Asian region in pursuit of wider trade liberalization at the regional and multilateral level. Thus, it is possible for East Asian economies to proceed with border liberalization alongside non-border barriers' trade and investment facilitation. In addition, these CEPs could help East Asia to implement region-wide cooperation arrangements to reduce risks and vulnerabilities related to an unstable international economic environment.[19]

In essence, CEPs 'contain a PTA for liberalizing border barriers together with a set of cooperative arrangements for reducing various costs and risks of trade and investment among the partners' (Elek 2003). Many CEPs in East Asia are likely to pursue innovative arrangements to deal with these new aspects of trade liberalization and facilitation. The EU has applied such an all-or-nothing concept known as 'acquis communautaire.'[20] Such an approach appears to be inappropriate for East Asia as the region includes a more diverse group of economies. It is likely that the region should seek cooperative arrangements with its own approach to liberalize and facilitate trade and investment.

The key issue for East Asia is whether and how bilateral and sub-regional CEPs can play constructive roles in promoting closer economic arrangements, ranging from unilateral to multilateral, alongside the APEC and WTO processes. The answer lies in the construction of CEPs being based on principles that fit the best possible linkages for wider mutual partnerships. In his paper Elek (2003) offers some possibilities for the next steps:

- Adoption of WTO-plus PTAs for any CEPs, then sensitive sectors could be avoided, but still exposed to wider competition within a well-defined timeframe.
- PTAs avoiding sensitive issues can be expected to proliferate if unchecked in East Asia. If these relative PTAs are concluded, the resistance to consider WTO-plus PTAs can be an obstacle to region-wide economic liberalization and facilitation.
- Progress toward region-wide arrangements to facilitate trade and investment need not be prevented if bilateral and sub-regional PTAs are difficult to link with an East Asia-wide zone of free and open trade and investment.

Appendix

See Tables 3-A1 and 3-A2.

Notes

1 The other two pillars are the ASEAN Security Community (ASC) and the ASEAN Socio-Cultural Community (ASCC). The ASC aims to bring about political and security cooperation to ensure peace and stability in the region and

Table 3-A1   Implications of ASEAN Agreements on Trade and FDI

Objectives	Key elements	Effects on types of FDI (the regional instrument may lead to an increase in the following types of FDI) on intraregional and from outside the region	Effects on corporate strategies
ASEAN Free Trade Area (AFTA)[a]			
• Increase ASEAN's competitiveness as a production base • Increase intra-regional trade • Promote FDI • Deepen regional economic cooperation and regional integration	• Elimination of tariff and non-tariff barriers • Trade facilitation measures: - harmonization of customs procedures, expeditious customs clearance (AFTA green lane) - products standard and conformance - mutual recognition arrangement • Rules of origin of 40% regional content	• Market seeking (trade-led investment and regional market-oriented) • Efficiency seeking (cost reduction and export-oriented) • Resource seeking (due to opening up of resource sectors)	• Better utilization of regional location complementation that facilitates regional production network and division of labor • Greater market access and market enlargement leading to opportunities for exploitation of economies of scale in production and synergies • Consolidation and rationalization of production functions in the region • Improve corporate competitiveness • Localization of production, influenced by the 40% rules of origin and greater involvement in the regional integration process

Continued on next page.

Table 3-A1   Implications of ASEAN Agreements on Trade and FDI (continued)

Objectives	Key elements	Effects on types of FDI (the regional instrument may lead to an increase in the following types of FDI) on intraregional and from outside the region	Effects on corporate strategies
ASEAN Investment Area (AIA)[b]			
• To realize a competitive and attractive area for FDI • Increase FDI • Support regional integration process	• Grant national treatment • Open up industries/ liberalization • Sectors covered: manufacturing, agriculture, forestry, fishery, mining, and services incidental of these five sectors • Transparency • Investment facilitation and promotion of the region for FDI • Investment protection • Reduce or eliminate investment impediments • Joint promotion of ASEAN as an investment region • Establish an FTA by 2010	• Resource seeking (through opening up of resource sectors for FDI) • Market seeking (regional production networks and investment) • Efficiency seeking	• Liberalization program and opening of sectors to foreign investment could influence TNCs to establish specific production activity in specific host location • More corporate investment in services incidental to the manufacturing, agriculture, forestry, fishery and mining sectors can be expected • TNCs may invest in efficient location to manufacture to service the regional market • Lower transaction cost could influence TNCs investment decision in favor of the region. Greater information provisions, transparency and investment facilitation measures could contribute to this • Greater certainty from binding liberalization schedules investment in the region

Notes: a. Agreement signed in 1992 and established on Jan. 1, 2002. The Agreement was supported by further trade facilitation arrangements such as mutual recognition, standards and conformance.
   b. Agreement signed in 1998 and established (for the manufacturing sector first) on Jan. 1, 2003.
Source: UNCTAD (2003), 227–228.

Table 3-A2   FDI Response to Regional Economic Integration

Regional integration	Investment response
External tariff realignment - Generates locational advantages for free movement of goods and services - Leads to trade diversion - Intraregional trade more attractive than extraregional trade	*Defensive import-substituting investment (tariff-jumping investment)* - Replaces exports with FDI (substitutes trade) - Needs to maintain market share and profitability by avoiding external tariffs
Internal tariff and non-tariff realignment - New configuration of locational advantages among members of the region - Leads to trade creation	*Reorganizational investment (optimum location-seeking investment)* - Complementary to trade - Adjusts existing investments in region to reflect intraregional trade - Locates investment in accordance with comparative advantage of member countries
Internal tariff and non-tariff realignment - Reduces transaction costs (cost reduction) *Market expansion* - Introduces scale economies and hence efficiency gains	*Rationalization investment (efficiency-seeking investment)* - Complementary to trade - Increases value-added activities within region - Reduces physical number of investments and replaces them with fewer but larger and more efficient investments
Internal tariff and non-tariff realignment *Market expansion* *Demand growth* *Technical progress* - Encouraging innovation and competition	*Offensive import-substituting investment (market-seeking investment)* - Replaces export with FDI (substitute trade) - Increases market share if operating in region - Enters market if not operating in region

Source: Bende-Nabende (1999), 54–55.

with the world. The ASCC aims to promote human development and establish a community of caring societies. For more on this see ASEAN Secretariat (2003).

2 This could also involve the movement of business persons, skilled labor and talents, and the strengthening of ASEAN institutional mechanisms including the improvement of the existing ASEAN Dispute Settlement Mechanism. For more on this, see ASEAN Secretariat (2003).

3 The Hanoi Action Plan (1999–2004).

4 This model of development has been called the flying geese model.

5 To be liberalized by January 2006.

6 There remain some concessions for certain petrochemical products until the end of 2004.

7 According to a recent survey by the ASEAN Secretariat, the CEPT concessions accounted for only 5 percent of intra-ASEAN trade at the turn of the century.

8 One example of this would be in corn where investment in corn could be

made in Laos to supply animal feed plants in Thailand, while Singapore could handle the logistics and supply chain management.

9 See, for example, Bartels and Freeman (2000), Heinrich and Konan (2001), and UNCTAD (2003).

10 This has now been accelerated with 2015 set as the year for completion.

11 See the Framework for Comprehensive Economic Partnership between ASEAN and Japan and the Framework Agreement on Comprehensive Economic Cooperation between ASEAN and the Republic of India.

12 Free Trade Agreements (FTAs) are generally agreements aimed at liberalizing trade in goods and services among designated countries and regions. Economic Partnership Agreements (EPAs) are generally based on the content of FTAs, but aim to further harmonize various economic systems and reinforce economic relations in a broader range of fields by promoting investment and movement of persons, rules-making in government procurement, competition policy, IPR, etc.

13 Later to be known as the East Asian Economic Caucus (EAEC).

14 Indeed, it has been said 'those who can run faster should run faster and ought not to be held back by those who choose not to run or do so at a snail's pace' (Rajan et al. 2001, 8).

15 See, for example, Bhagwati, Krisna and Panagariya (1999), Dutta (1999), and Winters (2001).

16 In this context, exclusion does not mean total denial of market access; instead, total exclusion means market access with less favorable terms than some other country or countries.

17 These costs can represent 10 or more percentage points in terms of total value-added (Reynolds 1995, 11).

18 CEPs usually consist of a PTA to liberalize border barriers to trade complemented by a number of arrangements to address new issues in order to facilitate trade and investment among the participants of the CEP. Thus, these partnerships are more than traditional trading arrangements.

19 Implementation of East Asia-wide liberalization like ASEAN+3 could be more difficult to realize.

20 Along with several hundred arrangements, known as directives issued from the EU Commission in Brussels.

References

Abe, S. 1996. Prospects for Asian Economic Integration. In S. Nishijima and P.H. Smith eds. *Cooperation or Rivalry? Regional Integration in the Americas and the Pacific Rim.* Boulder: Westview Press.

Ariff, M. 2001. Regional Integration and Global Free Trade: Working at Cross Purposes? In Akio Hosono ed. *Regional Integration and Development Policy: A Comparative Study of East Asia and the Americas*. Mimeograph.

ASEAN Secretariat. 2003. *The Declaration of ASEAN Concord II (Bali Concord II)*. Jakarta: ASEAN Secretariat. http://www.aseansec.org

Athukorala, Prema-Chandra and Jayant Menon. 1997. AFTA and the Investment-Trade Nexus in ASEAN. *The World Economy*, 20: pp. 159–174.

Bartels, F.L. and N.J. Freeman. 2002. Multinational Firms and FDI in Southeast Asia. *ASEAN Economic Bulletin*, 17(3): pp. 324–341.

Bende-Nabende, A. 1999. A Static Structural Model Analysis. In A. Bende-Nabende ed. *FDI, Regionalism, Government Policy and Endogenous Growth: A Comparative Study of the ASEAN-5 Economies, with Development Policy Implications for the Least Developed Countries*. England: Ashgate Publishing Company.

Bhagwati, J., P. Krisna and A. Panagariya eds. 1999. *Trading Blocs: Alternative Approaches to Analyzing Preferential Trade Agreements*. Cambridge: MIT Press.

Bhagwati, J. and A. Panagariya eds. 1996. *The Economics of Preferential Trade Agreements*. Washington D.C.: American Enterprise Institute.

Chirathivat, S. 1996. ASEAN Economic Integration with the World through AFTA. In J. Tan ed. *AFTA in the Changing International Economy*. Singapore: Institute of Southeast Asian Studies.

Chirathivat, S. 2001. Interdependence between China and Southeast Asian Economies on the Eve of the Accession of China into the WTO. In I. Yamazawa and K. Imai. eds. *China Enters WTO: Pursuing the Symbiosis with the Global Economy*. Tokyo: Institute of Developing Economies.

Chirathivat, S. 2002a. ASEAN-China Free Trade Area: Background Implications and Future Development. *Journal of Asian Economics*, 13: pp. 671–686.

Chirathivat. S. 2002b. Global and Regional Regulatory Changes of FDI: Challenges and Opportunities for ASEAN in the Wake of the Recent Turmoil. In F. Snyder. ed. *Regional and Global Regulation of International Trade*. Oxford: Hart Publishing.

Chirathivat. S. 2003. Towards a New ASEAN-Japan Economic Partnership: Opportunities and Modalities. Paper presented at the *International Conference on Reassessing Japan-ASEAN Relations: Between Expectations and Realities*.Organized by the Institute of Southeast Asian Studies, Singapore: September 30–October 1.

Dutta, M. 1999. *Economic Regionalization in the Asia-Pacific: Challenges to Economic Cooperation*. Cheltenham: Edward Elgar.

Dutta, M. 2002. Asian Economic Community: Intra-community Macro- and Micro-economic Parameters. Paper presented at the *Conference on Asian Economic Cooperation in the New Millennium: China's Economic Presence*. Organized by ACAES and Peking University: May 27–29.

East Asia Vision Group Report. 2001. *Towards an East Asian Community: Region of Peace, Prosperity and Progress*. Mimeograph.

East West Center. 1993. *AsiaPacific Issues*, 6 (June). Honolulu: East West Center.

Elek, A. 2003. East Asian Economic Integration: Critical Policy Choices. Paper presented at the *APEC Study Center Consortium Conference*. Phuket (Thailand): May 25–28.

Frenkel, J. 1997. *Regional Trading Blocs in the World Economics System*. Institute for International Economics: Washington D.C.

Heinrich, J. and D.E. Konan. 2001. Prospects for FDI in AFTA. *ASEAN Economic Bulletin*, 18(2): pp. 141–160.

International Monetary Fund (IMF). Various years. *Direction of Trade Statistics*. Various issues. Washington, D.C.: IMF.

Krueger, A.O. 1997a. Free Trade Agreement Versus Customs Unions. *Journal of Development Economics*, 54: pp. 169–187.

Krueger, A. 1997b. Problems in Overlapping Free Trade Areas. In T. Ito and A. Krueger eds. *Regionalism and Multilateral Trade Arrangements*. Chicago: University of Chicago Press.

Krueger, A.O. 1999. Are Preferential Trading Arrangement Trade-Liberating Or Protectionists? *Journal of Economic Perspectives*, 4: pp. 105–124.

Langhammer, R. 1995. Regional Integration in East Asia: Institutionalized Regionalism? *Welwirtschaftliches Archiv*, Band 13: pp. 167–201.

Lloyd, P.J. 2002. New Bilateralism in the Asia-Pacific. *The World Economy*, 25: pp.1279–1296.

Okamoto, J. ed. 2003. *Whither Free Trade Agreements? Proliferation, Evaluation and Multilateralization*. Tokyo: IDE.

Ong Keng Yong. 2003. ASEAN Moves Towards Building A Single Market. *The Asian Wall Street Journal*, October 9, p. A11.

Mallikamas, S. 2002. *A Study of Thailand's Readiness to Establish Free Trade Areas*. CAMGEM Development project, Faculty of Economics, Chulalongkorn University: Thailand.

Petri, P. 1995. Interdependence of Trade and Investment in the Pacific. In E.K.Y. Chen and P. Drysdale eds. *Corporate Link and Foreign Direct Investment in Asia and the Pacific*. Australia: Harper International.

Rajan, R.S., R. Sen and R. Siregar. 2001. *Singapore and Free Trade Agreements*. Singapore: Institute of Southern Anan Studies.

Ravenhill, J. 2003. The Move to Preferential Trade in the Western Pacific Rim. *Asia-Pacific Issues*, 69(June).

Reynolds, C.W. 1995. Open Regionalism: Lessons from Latin America for East Asia. Paper presented at the workshop on *The Political Economy of Regional Development and Cooperation in the Pacific Basin, with special reference to APEC*; University of Notre Dame: October 12–14.

Rutngamlug Unchalee. 2002. *ASEAN Economic Integration and its Impact on Foreign Direct Investment*. Master Thesis, Faculty of Economics, Chulalongkorn University.

Scollay, R. 2003. The Proliferation of RTAs and the Future of Asia-Pacific Economic Integration. Paper presented at the *APEC Study Consortium Conference*; Phuket (Thailand): May 25–28.

Sen R., M.G.Ascher and R.Rajan 2004. ASEAN-India Economic Relations: Current Status and Future Prospects. In *RIS Discussion Papers*, 73: New Delhi.

Stone, S. F. and Bang Nam Jeong. 2000. FDI and Trade in the Asia-Pacific Region: Complementarity, Distance and Regional Economic Integration. *Journal of Economic Integration*, 15(3): pp. 460–485.

United Nations Conference on Trade and Development (UNCTAD). 2002. *World Investment Report 2002: Transition Corporations and Export Competitiveness*. New York: UNCTAD.

United Nations Conference on Trade and Development (UNCTAD). 2003. *World Investment Report*. New York and Geneva: UNCTAD.

Urata, S. 2003. A Shift from Market-Led to Institution-Led Regional Economic Integration in East Asia. Paper presented at *JSPS-NRCT Workshop on Perspectives on Flows, Middle Class, State and Market for Asia*; Bangkok: January 14–15.

Viner, J. 1950. *The Customs Union Issue*. New York: Carnegie Endowment for International Peace.

Winters. L. Alan. 2001. Regionalism for Developing Countries: Assessing Costs and Benefits. In Sajal Lahiri ed. *Regionalism and Globalization: Theory and Practice*. London and New York: Routledge.

Wonnacott, R.I. 1996. Canadian Trade Policy: The GATT's 1995 Review. *The World Economy*, Supplement, pp. 67–80.

Yamazawa, I. 1992. On Pacific Economic Cooperation. *Economic Journal*, 102(November): pp. 1519–1529.

Yusuf, S., et al. 2003. *Innovative East Asia: The Future of Growth*. Washington, D.C.: World Bank.

4
ASEAN, China and India: Are They More Competitive or Complementary to Each Other?[1]

Yumiko Okamoto

Introduction

Beginning in the 1990s, China accelerated its economic growth with an annual average rate of as high as 10 percent (Okamoto 2005a, 48). The 1997–98 Asian Crisis, which disrupted many economies in East Asia and especially the ASEAN members, did not affect China as severely. On the contrary, the Chinese economy continued to grow at around 7 percent annually in subsequent years.

Initially the rise of China as an industrial power was regarded as a threat to the ASEAN economies. Because of its almost inexhaustible supply of unskilled labor and its absorption of a huge amount of Foreign Direct Investment (FDI), China was considered a great challenge to the ASEAN countries in their home and third-country markets (Wang 2005, 35).

Whereas China's rise in the 1990s caused a great deal of concern among the ASEAN countries, China's further expansion during the first decade of the 21st century seems to have instead generated confidence (Wang 2005, 17). The cornerstone of this shift is a framework agreement on comprehensive economic cooperation between ASEAN and China, including the establishment of an ASEAN–China Free Trade Agreement (FTA) by 2010 for the original ASEAN members, and 2015 for the new members.[2] As such, China's expanding economy is now regarded more as an opportunity than as a threat.

ASEAN also concluded a framework agreement on comprehensive economic cooperation with India in Bali in October 2003.[3] Ever since India unveiled its 'Look-East Policy' in the early 1990s (Ambatkar 2001, 85), its economy has continued to grow steadily, although not quite as fast as China. In particular, the development of IT-related industries, especially software development, has been remarkable in India. ASEAN also seems to regard India as an opportunity rather than a threat to the business of its members. An interesting question is to ask whether the rapid shift in the policy stance of ASEAN vis-à-vis China and India is consistent with underlying economic forces.

According to Langhammer and Hiemenz (1990, 59), regional integration among developing countries often fails to materialize expected benefits. This is partly because there is little scope either for inter-industry or intra-industry specialization among countries in the scheme, as they tend to possess comparative advantage in the same products (Langhammer and Hiemenz 1990, 68). Exactly for this reason, the swift shift in the policy stance of ASEAN presents an intellectual puzzle and a policy question (Wang 2005, 17).

The objective of this chapter is, therefore, to compare trade structures among ASEAN, China and India, and to investigate whether ASEAN–China and ASEAN–India are more competitive or complementary to each other. If they are more or less complementary to each other, there may be room for them to gain through trade, either through inter-industry trade or intra-industry trade, or both. If they are competitive with each other, on the other hand, there may not be much room for gain through specialization and trade.

In section two this chapter briefly compares the economic performance of ASEAN, China and India in the world economy. The third section then calculates the indexes of revealed comparative advantage (RCA) for ASEAN, China and India, respectively, and observes whether there is room for gain through inter-industry specialization. In section four, the indexes of intra-industry trade between ASEAN–China and between ASEAN–India, respectively, are calculated to investigate whether there is room for ASEAN to gain through intra-industry specialization vis-à-vis China and India. The fifth section conducts market share analyses and observes whether ASEAN and China compete or complement each other in third markets such as the U.S. and Japan, while the final section summarizes the findings.

ASEAN, China and India in the Global Economy

International Trade and Production

The term 'BRICs' is often heard in the center stage of international politics these days and refers to the countries of Brazil, Russia, India and China. The latter two countries are considered to be particularly promising and influential countries in the world, both economically and politically, in the 21st century. It is thus interesting to examine to what extent China and India are gaining in importance in the global economy relative to ASEAN?

Table 4-1 provides data that compares ASEAN, China and India in terms of production and trade. The data in the table exhibits the remarkable rise of China as an economic power in all aspects. Because of the rapid growth in China over the past decade, the share of China (including Hong Kong) will soon reach 5

Table 4-1   Shares of ASEAN, China, and India in the World Economy (%)

		1990	1995	2000	2003
GDP	China	1.6	2.4	3.4	3.9
(current US$)	(+Hong Kong)	2.0	2.9	3.9	4.3
	India	1.5	1.2	1.4	1.6
	ASEAN	1.5	2.1	1.7	1.7
Merchandise exports	China	1.8	2.9	3.8	5.8
(current US$)	(+Hong Kong)	4.1	6.2	6.9	8.8
	India	0.5	0.6	0.7	0.7
	ASEAN	4.0	6.0	6.3	5.6
Merchandise imports	China	1.5	2.5	3.4	5.3
(current US$)	(+Hong Kong)	3.9	6.2	6.5	8.3
	India	0.7	0.7	0.8	0.9
	ASEAN	4.4	6.5	5.2	4.6
Commercial service exports	China	0.8	1.6	2.0	2.7
(current US$)	India	0.6	0.6	1.2	1.4
	ASEAN	3.8	6.0	4.4	3.9
Commercial service imports	China	0.5	2.1	2.5	3.3
(current US$)	India	0.8	0.9	1.3	1.3
	ASEAN	3.6	6.3	5.5	5.1

Source: Author's calculation using World Bank, *World Development Indicators Online*.

percent of global GDP at the current exchange rate vis-à-vis the U.S. dollar (if the Chinese currency is revalued, this share increases sharply).

The actual economic power of China may be better reflected in the trade data, since the real economic value of non-tradable goods included in GDP are difficult to measure. According to the data, the share of China (including Hong Kong) in merchandise trade will reach around 9 percent both in terms of exports and imports, almost doubling the share from the past decade. China's share of services trade has also increased rapidly. Although China continues to run trade deficits in services, its share of global services exports (including Hong Kong) increased from 1 to 4 percent.

Moreover, the steady rise of India is also very clear, although the rate of growth is much slower than that of China. What is most striking in India is the rapid growth of the services sector. Unlike China, services exports of India grew much more rapidly than its merchandise exports, increasing from 0.6 percent in 1990 to 1.4 percent in 2003. In contrast, merchandise exports increased from only 0.5 percent to 0.7 percent over the same period.

Table 4-2 illustrates the characteristics of the growth pattern of FDI in the three country groups. The data shows that India has been the most successful in attracting export-oriented FDI in IT and IT-related services in Asia. This is one of the important factors that explain why services trade has been growing much faster than merchandise trade in India.

Table 4-2   Export-oriented FDI Projects in Call Centers, Shared Services
Centers (SSCs), and IT Services by Destination 2002–2003.

	Call centers		SSCs		IT services	
	No. of projects	Share of total (%)	No. of projects	Share of total (%)	No. of projects	Share of total (%)
China	30	21.7	4	6.3	60	23.9
(+Hong Kong)	32	23.2	4	6.3	74	29.5
India	60	43.5	43	67.2	118	47.0
ASEAN	46	33.3	17	26.6	59	23.5

Source: UNCTAD, *World Investment Report 2004*, p. 163.

Contrary to China and India, the dynamism of ASEAN as a whole seems to have faltered following the 1997–98 crisis. As shown in Table 4-1, the share of ASEAN in the global economy both in terms of production and trade declined during the first decade of the 21st century. The decline of ASEAN in terms of merchandise imports is particularly significant, as it indicates the fact that after the crisis, ASEAN was constrained by its capacity to borrow from abroad in order to purchase goods and services. Although the situation varies from country to country, ASEAN as a whole does not seem to have fully recovered from the crisis.

Inflow of FDI

The loss of dynamism of ASEAN can also be observed in Table 4-3, which shows the inflow of FDI in ASEAN, China and India in absolute terms, and as a share of the world total. FDI continues to flow into China and India in an increasing manner. The combined share of FDI going to China and Hong Kong exceeded more than 10 percent of global FDI flow in 2003, while India has also been increasingly successful in attracting FDI, especially after 2000. In fact, except for Singapore, the total inflow of FDI into India is larger than that of any other ASEAN country in 2003.

In contrast, the absolute amount of FDI inflow has generally declined in most of the ASEAN countries after the 1997–98 Asian crisis. This loss in dynamism is most obvious in Indonesia, from which foreign firms seem to continue to withdraw. In 2003, the inflow of FDI in the Philippines dropped significantly as well, and although the situation is not as bad as in Indonesia and the Philippines, neither Malaysia nor Thailand has regained its strength in attracting FDI following the crisis. Consequently, the share of ASEAN in world FDI flow as a whole declined from around 7 percent in 1992–97 to 2 percent after the crisis. Singapore is the only exception: the amount of FDI inflow in Singapore in the 2000s exceeds the level of the pre-crisis period.

These trends in FDI indicate that ASEAN, as a region, lost its economic attractiveness after the crisis, while China and India are viewed as an

Table 4-3   Inflow of Foreign Direct Investment in ASEAN, China and
India, and their Shares in the World Total

(a) US$ million	1992-1997 (Annual average)	2000	2003
China	32,799	40,715	53,505
Hong Kong, China	7,781	61,939	13,561
India	1,676	2,319	4,269
ASEAN	21,241	21,150	154,071
Indonesia	3,518	-4,550	-597
Malaysia	5,816	3,788	2,474
Philippines	1,343	1,345	319
Singapore	8,295	17,217	11,409
Thailand	2,269	3,350	1,802
World	310,879	1387,953	559,576

(b) %	1992-1997 (Annual average)	2000	2003
China	10.6	2.9	9.6
(+Hong Kong)	13.1	7.4	12.0
India	0.5	0.2	0.8
ASEAN	6.8	1.5	2.8

Source: UNCTAD, *World Investment Report 2004.*

increasingly appealing global partner. Does the closer economic cooperation between ASEAN and these two future economic superpowers provide a way for ASEAN to revitalize their economies and to regain its pre-crisis economic strength vis-à-vis China and India? The answer to this question partly depends on the trade structure of these economies.

The Revealed Comparative Advantage (RCA) Approach

The RCA Index and Spearman's Rank Correlation
Balassa (1989) was the first to develop an empirical approach to investigating the changing pattern of comparative advantage in goods and services, or what we refer to today as an index of revealed comparative advantage (RCA).[4] The index is calculated as follows:

$$RCA_{ij} = (X_{ij} / \Sigma X_{ij}) / (X_{iw} / \Sigma X_{iw}) \qquad (1)$$

where X_{ij} is the export value of product group i of country j, ΣX_{ij} is the total export value of country j, X_{iw} is the world export value of product group i, and ΣX_{iw} is the total world export value. An RCA_{ij} exceeding 1 indicates that country j has a comparative advantage in the production of product i in the global economy, whereas an RCA_{ij} of less than 1 indicates the opposite. The RCA indexes are calculated for each ASEAN member (Indonesia, Malaysia, the Philippines,

Singapore and Thailand) as well as for China and India at the two-digit level of SITC R1.

The indexes are then ranked for each country respectively and Spearman's rank correlation coefficients between the rankings of RCA indexes are calculated between ASEAN–China, and between ASEAN–India, respectively. If the coefficient is positive and statistically significant, the trade structures of the two country groups are very similar and they are competitive with one another. This implies that there may not be much room for ASEAN–China or ASEAN–India to gain through inter-industry specialization. On the other hand, if the coefficient is negative and statistically significant, their trade structures are very different and complementary to one another. In the latter case, the formation of a FTA could bring about substantial gains through inter-industry specialization.

Findings

Table 4-4 presents the results of the above exercise. Firstly, both Thailand and the Philippines possess high Spearman's rank correlation coefficients with both China and India, and in most years the coefficients are statistically significant. This means that both Thailand and the Philippines have trade structures that are quite similar to that of China and India. These statistical results imply that inter-industry specialization may not develop between the former (the Philippines and Thailand) and the latter (China and India), even if closer economic cooperation is promoted between the two.

Spearman's rank correlation coefficients are, on the other hand, low or even negative between China and India, and the other three ASEAN countries of Indonesia, Malaysia and Singapore. Moreover, none of the coefficients are statistically significant. This suggests it is indeterminate as to whether both groups are more competitive or complementary to each other. In other words, in some respects their trade structures may be very similar and competitive, and in other respects, they may be very dissimilar and complementary to one another.

An Intra-Industry Trade (IIT) Approach

Importance of Intra-Industry Trade in the Modern World

The opening up of the Chinese and Indian economies to the world could serve as a tremendous opportunity for ASEAN if there are strong prospects for intra-industry trade brought about by rising income, product differentiation and economies of scale (Suthiphand and Sothitorn 2005, 102–103). This is true even if the overall trade structure is very similar between the two countries.

Table 4-4   Spearman's Rank Correlations Coefficients of the Rankings of the RCA
Indexes between ASEAN and China, and ASEAN and India

ASEAN	Year	China	India	ASEAN	Year	China	India
Indonesia	1990	-0.11	0.19	Singapore	1990	0.02	0.05
	1991	-0.15	0.18		1991	-0.02	0.06
	1992	-0.06	0.22		1992	0.00	0.05
	1993	0.02	0.33**		1993	0.00	-0.01
	1994	0.03	0.29**		1994	0.04	0.05
	1995	0.01	0.23*		1995	0.06	0.06
	1996	0.00	0.10		1996	0.11	0.05
	1997	0.00	0.03		1997	0.14	0.10
	1998	-0.08	0.08		1998	-0.04	0.04
	1999	-0.07	0.07		1999	-0.08	0.07
	2000	-0.02	0.09		2000	-0.06	0.01
	2001	0.01	0.06		2001	-0.05	0.02
	2002	-0.04	0.09		2002	-0.03	0.16
	2003	-0.06	0.13		2003	-0.06	0.11
Malaysia	1990	-0.12	-0.04	Thailand	1990	0.38***	0.42***
	1991	-0.19	-0.05		1991	0.45***	0.46***
	1992	-0.12	-0.03		1992	0.53***	0.49***
	1993	-0.08	0.00		1993	0.51***	0.48***
	1994	-0.11	-0.04		1994	0.41***	0.40***
	1995	-0.08	-0.05		1995	0.33**	0.44***
	1996	-0.04	-0.07		1996	0.37***	0.37***
	1997	0.06	-0.10		1997	0.41***	0.33**
	1998	0.05	-0.07		1998	0.37***	0.34**
	1999	-0.02	-0.12		1999	0.35***	0.33**
	2000	-0.06	-0.09		2000	0.32**	0.28**
	2001	-0.03	-0.09		2001	0.29**	0.31**
	2002	-0.05	-0.06		2002	n.a.	n.a.
	2003	-0.07	-0.09		2003	0.24*	0.38***
Philippines	1990	0.17	0.21				
	1991	0.12	0.26*				
	1992	0.15	0.20				
	1993	0.18	0.21				
	1994	0.25*	0.25*				
	1995	0.23*	0.28**				
	1996	0.23*	0.23*				
	1997	0.31**	0.21				
	1998	0.30**	0.19				
	1999	0.28**	0.19				
	2000	0.31**	0.15				
	2001	0.30**	0.23*				
	2002	0.27**	0.10				
	2003	0.23*	0.06				

Source: Author's calculation using UN COMTRADE.
Note: *** represents statistical significance at the 1% level.
      ** represents statistical significance at the 5% level.
      * represents statistical significance at the 10% level.

Earlier models—such as those of Helpman and Krugman (1985), which focused on product differentiation and the horizontal division of labor in final products—argued that countries could gain through intra-industry specialization. More recent models show a gain through trade in intermediate inputs (Jones 2000). Okamoto (2005b) showed empirically the rise of intra-industry trade in intermediate inputs in the Asia–Pacific region during the 1990s and their potential impacts on industrial productivity growth of the countries in the region.

The IIT Index

The IIT index is calculated as follows:

$$IIT_{ijk} = [1 - (|X_{ijk} - M_{ijk}|/(X_{ijk} + M_{ijk})]$$ (2)

where X_{ijk} is the value of product group i that country j exports to country k, and M_{ijk} is the import value of the same product group i that country j imports from country k. The index takes a value between 0 and 1. The higher the index, the more the two countries are engaged in intra-industry trade.

In this study, the IIT index is first calculated at the four-digit level of SITC R1. Then the IIT index is aggregated at the one-digit level using the value of trade (summing up the values of exports and imports at the four-digit level of SITC R1) between the two countries as a weight.

Findings

Table 4-5 shows the IIT indexes calculated between the individual ASEAN countries (Indonesia, Malaysia, the Philippines, Singapore and Thailand) and China, and between individual ASEAN countries and India, respectively. Firstly, we find that the values of the IIT index in the product category ranging from 5 to 8 of SITC R1 are much higher than those of product category 0 to 4. This indicates that, as trade theory suggests, there is greater room for gain through intra-industry specialization between the two groups in manufactured rather than in non-manufactured goods.

Secondly, the ASEAN countries tend to have higher IIT values vis-à-vis China than India, except for product category 5 of SITC R1. Two reasons can explain this. The first reason is that India's goods market is still highly protected, meaning that there is not much room for these two groups of countries to engage in intra-industry trade. According to the trade policy review of India, as summarized by the Secretariat of the World Trade Organization (WTO) in 2002, India's applied Most Favored Nation (MFN) tariff rate is still relatively high at around 32 percent. Although there are no comparable data, the average tariff rate of China seems to be much lower than that of India.[5] The second reason is

Table 4-5   IIT Indexes between ASEAN, China and India

SITC	YEAR	IDN	MYA	PHI	SIN	THA	IDN	MYA	PHI	SIN	THA
		China					India				
0	1990	3.1	0.3	0.1	2.3	3.7	0.4	0.6	0.0	30.6	0.1
0	1995	2.2	4.0	4.1	7.4	2.6	0.6	1.4	1.5	18.7	0.4
0	2000	3.0	2.9	3.4	18.4	8.5	5.6	4.6	2.9	35.5	3.0
0	2003	4.1	11.0	4.2	9.3	18.9	4.9	3.2	2.9	19.4	5.3
1	1990	0.0	4.9	0.0	2.7	0.0	0.0	0.5	0.0	0.0	0.0
1	1995	0.1	13.5	5.0	51.3	20.8	0.0	18.8	0.0	0.3	0.0
1	2000	0.8	7.9	0.0	17.2	49.8	0.0	5.3	5.9	2.3	1.6
1	2003	0.3	28.6	0.6	8.4	33.6	0.1	23.1	0.0	9.2	0.2
2	1990	0.0	0.1	1.4	2.4	0.6	6.9	0.1	0.3	2.8	0.8
2	1995	2.6	2.4	0.3	8.8	2.4	11.2	1.8	1.3	9.1	3.0
2	2000	6.0	2.9	2.4	9.3	3.4	8.8	1.5	1.1	9.7	3.2
2	2003	5.1	3.1	6.9	7.4	2.7	5.5	7.3	13.6	7.0	5.0
3	1990	2.7	0.0	0.0	10.6	0.1	0.0	8.5	0.0	1.8	0.0
3	1995	13.8	0.3	10.9	8.7	3.0	0.0	0.0	42.6	14.6	0.4
3	2000	31.2	2.4	19.4	4.2	25.1	0.3	0.1	1.0	29.2	27.7
3	2003	46.7	24.0	43.2	0.7	0.5	0.8	0.5	34.8	4.1	2.7
4	1990	0.8	0.1	0.0	0.5	0.4	0.0	0.0	0.0	0.6	0.0
4	1995	0.3	0.1	0.1	3.0	0.0	0.0	0.0	0.0	2.0	0.9
4	2000	0.1	1.3	0.0	15.9	1.0	0.1	0.3	0.0	12.2	2.1
4	2003	0.1	0.2	0.8	15.4	20.8	0.0	0.1	12.9	22.6	0.2
5	1990	3.0	10.8	5.4	28.5	13.7	2.5	18.3	14.4	22.6	6.4
5	1995	25.1	17.5	7.1	28.7	17.3	39.1	25.4	4.6	38.8	15.2
5	2000	14.8	17.9	18.3	30.1	17.6	44.0	38.1	12.5	31.0	30.3
5	2003	23.6	19.0	22.2	21.5	26.7	28.4	41.4	7.7	33.3	27.0
6	1990	1.0	5.8	0.6	8.7	2.9	1.8	3.8	0.8	24.0	3.7
6	1995	9.8	7.0	2.0	38.4	11.2	8.3	10.5	15.5	20.6	10.3
6	2000	15.0	23.3	6.6	24.2	21.7	10.8	12.8	4.1	21.8	16.7
6	2003	20.9	32.9	5.5	40.7	27.1	13.4	15.7	3.2	24.5	17.2
7	1990	0.0	24.4	2.2	51.8	8.5	0.1	21.3	1.4	35.1	11.3
7	1995	8.0	40.3	17.3	49.0	33.8	2.4	21.4	17.5	42.3	35.1
7	2000	24.9	59.2	36.1	62.2	63.5	18.4	60.2	22.7	33.7	17.5
7	2003	36.9	55.2	39.6	57.2	74.7	21.7	23.3	15.7	14.9	38.6
8	1990	0.2	12.0	12.2	20.7	15.1	1.2	4.1	1.4	11.8	21.8
8	1995	12.2	25.1	6.2	28.7	26.5	6.9	14.4	14.1	12.5	19.2
8	2000	30.5	31.3	20.6	23.2	29.4	17.5	27.0	22.2	22.6	38.2
8	2003	25.4	43.7	14.2	24.3	33.7	19.4	34.2	14.7	13.9	36.9

Source: the author's calculation using UN COMTRADE.
Note: (1) IDN: Indonesia, MYA: Malaysia, PHI: Philippines,
          SIN: Singapore, THA: Thailand.
       (2) SITC R10: Food and live animals
          SITC R11: Beverages and tobacco
          SITC R12: Crude materials, inedible
          SITC R13: Mineral fuels
          SITC R14: Animal and vegetable oils and fats
          SITC R15: Chemicals
          SITC R16: Basic manufacturers
          SITC R17: Machinery
          SITC R18: Miscellaneous manufactured goods
       (3) IIT indexes were originally calculated at the four-digit level of SITC
          R1. The author aggregated them into the one-digit level IIT index
          using the trade share as a weight.

that multinational corporations (MNCs) have been active in direct investment activities both in China and ASEAN since the latter half of the 1980s, so that the intra-firm activities have developed fast between China and ASEAN.

Thirdly, the degree of development of intra-industry trade is different among the individual ASEAN members. Malaysia, Singapore and Thailand tend to show higher values of IIT index than Indonesia and the Philippines, especially in such product categories as 6, 7 and 8 at the one-digit level of SITC R1. This implies that a country such as Thailand tends to have more room for gain through intra-industry specialization with China, although there may not be much room to gain through inter-industry specialization as observed in the previous section on the RCA index and Spearman's Rank Correlation. A country such as the Philippines may not, on the contrary, gain much through a China–ASEAN FTA, since not only is the overall trade structure very similar between the Philippines and China, but also because the intra-industry trade between these two countries has not been very well developed thus far.

Malaysia and Singapore may, on the other hand, gain a great deal through a China–ASEAN FTA. This is partly because the overall trade structure of both countries is dissimilar to that of China, so that there is some room for them to gain through inter-industry trade. Moreover, they tend to show high values of IIT index in trade with China, especially for machinery (product category 7 at the one-digit level of SITC R1). This means that closer economic cooperation between Malaysia, Singapore and China may lead to significant gain both through inter- and intra-industry trade.

Indonesia shows a trade structure that is dissimilar to that of China, suggesting that a China–ASEAN FTA may generate some gain for Indonesia through the enhancement of inter-industry trade. There may not be much room to gain, however, through intra-industry trade in manufactured goods, since the IIT indexes in this category are still low between Indonesia and China.

Figure 4-1   Matrix of RCA Index and IIT Index

Spearman's Rank Correlations Coefficient of the
Rankings of the RCA Indexes between ASEAN and China
Low or minus ←   → High

		Low or minus	High
IIT Indexes between ASEAN and China	High ↑	Malaysia Singapore	Thailand
	↓ Low	Indonesia	Philippines

Source: Author's construction.

Figure 4-1, which summarizes the trade relationship between ASEAN and China, clarifies the fact that the trade relationship between the individual ASEAN member and China varies from country to country. Therefore, the magnitude and the source of gain or loss through closer economic relation may be quite different among the ASEAN members. Unlike the case of Europe, flexibility will be necessary when it comes to the implementation of closer economic cooperation between ASEAN and China.

Market Share Analysis in the Major International Markets

ASEAN, China and India

The formation of a FTA with China and India may also affect ASEAN through its impact on the flow of FDI. Without any doubt, FDI, especially export-oriented FDI, has played an important role in the economic development of China and ASEAN.[6] The FTA may affect ASEAN greatly if ASEAN and China or ASEAN and India compete in the same type of products in third markets such as the U.S. and Japan. In this case, the formation of a FTA between the two country groups may give MNCs an incentive to consolidate those export-oriented production sites that currently exist in different countries. ASEAN may gain or lose through the formation of a FTA depending on whether the FTA enhances the cost advantage of ASEAN more than China, India or vice versa.

If ASEAN and China or India do not, however, compete in the same category of products in the international major markets in the first place, both parties may gain through the formation of a FTA or both parties may not be affected by it at all.

Market Share Analysis

The overall competitiveness of ASEAN, China and India is initially examined in the major international markets. Table 4-6 shows the market shares of ASEAN, China and India, respectively, between 1993 and 2003 in three major international markets: Japan, the U.S. and the EU. First, India's share is growing, but its relative position in the international goods market is still considerably low. Second, the market share of ASEAN, China and India are all small in Europe, although that of China seems to be expanding rapidly even at the low level of penetration. Third, there seems to be severe competition between ASEAN and China in the U.S. market, since the share of China has expanded to reach from 7.3 percent in 1993 to 13.2 percent in 2003. On the other hand, ASEAN's share declined from 7.3 to 6.6 percent over the same period, and, as a result, ASEAN seems to be losing its competitiveness in the U.S. vis-à-vis China.

Table 4-6   Shares of ASEAN, China and India in the Major International
Markets (%)

	Japan			EU			US		
	ASEAN	China	India	ASEAN	China	India	ASEAN	China	India
1993	14.7	9.4	1.0	7.3	7.3	0.8	2.5	2.5	0.5
1994	14.4	10.9	1.0	7.9	7.5	0.8	2.5	2.5	0.6
1995	14.5	11.6	0.9	8.4	7.7	0.8	2.5	2.5	0.6
1996	15.1	12.4	0.8	8.4	7.9	0.8	2.8	2.6	0.6
1997	14.8	13.1	0.8	8.2	8.5	0.9	3.0	2.8	0.6
1998	14.2	13.9	0.8	8.1	9.1	0.9	2.9	3.0	0.6
1999	14.9	14.4	0.7	7.7	9.4	0.9	2.9	3.2	0.5
2000	15.7	15.0	0.7	7.3	9.5	0.9	3.0	3.6	0.6
2001	15.6	17.0	0.6	6.8	10.1	0.9	2.8	3.8	0.6
2002	15.3	18.8	0.6	6.8	11.9	1.0	2.7	4.1	0.6
2003	15.3	20.1	0.6	6.6	13.2	1.1	2.8	4.6	0.6

Source: Table 4-5.
Note: EU includes the following European countries: Belgium, France,
Germany, Italy, Luxemburg, Holland, Denmark, Ireland, Britain, Greek,
Portugal, and Spain.

Interestingly, while the share of China increased dramatically in the Japanese market (from 9.4 to 20.1 percent between 1993 and 2003), that of ASEAN also increased slightly from 14.7 to 15.3 percent during the same period. The rapid penetration of Chinese products in the Japanese market is clear and without question, but the competitiveness of ASEAN has not been eroded in Japan in spite of it.

Spearman's Rank Correlation Coefficients between ASEAN and China

The above difference between the Japanese and the U.S. markets seems to be confirmed by the data in Tables 4-7 and 4-8. Table 4-7 shows Spearman's rank correlation coefficients of the rankings of the market shares in the U.S. market between China and each ASEAN member. Their market shares are, first, calculated at the four-digit level of SITC R1. Then, rank correlation coefficients are calculated for each of the broader product categories.[7] High rank correlation coefficients imply that the kind of product China and each ASEAN member export to the U.S. is quite similar. In other words, ASEAN and China compete with one another in exports to the U.S. markets. Low or negative rank correlation coefficients mean that they export more or less different types of products to the U.S. Table 4-8 shows the results for the Japanese market.

According to Table 4-7, ASEAN and China show relatively high rank correlation coefficients, which are also statistically significant in product categories such as food (0), basic manufactures (6), machinery (7) and miscellaneous manufactured goods (8). This means that ASEAN may further lose its market share to China unless ASEAN makes an effort to sell differentiated and higher value-added products in the U.S. market, given the fact that China has a cost advantage over many of the ASEAN countries due to the ample availability of low-cost labor.

Table 4-8 shows the results between ASEAN and China in Japan. The Spearman's rank correlation coefficients of the rankings of their market shares in the Japanese market are much lower than those of the U.S. Moreover, many of the coefficients are not statistically significant. This implies that ASEAN and China do not necessarily compete with one another in the Japanese market. It is possible that MNCs in ASEAN and China already differentiate between the types of product exported to Japan.

Conclusion

The further rise of China as an industrial power, especially after its entry into the WTO, is now regarded as an opportunity rather than as a threat for ASEAN. The above results show that whether this view is consistent with the underlying economic force or not depends on the country in question. Both Singapore and Malaysia seem to gain both through inter- and intra-industry specialization if a FTA is formed between ASEAN and China. Thailand seems to gain significantly also through intra-industry specialization vis-à-vis China.

Indonesia and the Philippines, on the other hand, may not gain much. As yet there is not much intra-industry trade between China and these two ASEAN countries. Moreover, China and the Philippines have a very similar overall trade structures. This implies that the Philippines may not gain much through closer economic cooperation with China or India.

Substantial efforts are necessary in order to promote industrial development of Indonesia and the Philippines. Otherwise, the formation of a China–ASEAN FTA may speed up the force of divergence that seems to have set in among ASEAN countries since the 1997–98 crisis.[8]

The promotion of economic cooperation between ASEAN and India, on the other hand, may make sense in the long run, but its immediate impact on both sides still seems to be very limited. First, the success of India continues to depend on the services sector. Second, there is still very little intra-industry specialization between ASEAN and India. The announcement of the formation of a FTA between India and ASEAN may make economic sense in the long run, but substantial benefits may not be expected at least in the short run.

Table 4-7   Spearman's Rank Correlation Coefficients of the Ranking of Market Shares in the U.S. between ASEAN and China

SITC	YEAR	IDN	MYA	PHI	SIN	THA	IDN	MYA	PHI	SIN	THA
		Rank Correlation Coefficients					Statistical Significance				
0	1990	0.37	0.25	0.06	0.21	0.22	***	*			*
0	1995	0.53	0.45	0.25	0.44	0.24	***	***	*	***	***
0	2000	0.43	0.50	0.21	0.30	0.43	***	***	*	**	***
0	2003	0.47	0.35	0.23	0.23	0.52	***	***	*	*	***
1	1990	-0.27	-0.31	0.03	-0.11	0.20					
1	1995	-0.30	-0.37	0.00	-0.08	0.13					
1	2000	0.37	-0.19	0.14	-0.19	0.32					
1	2003	0.15	0.67	-0.24	0.30	-0.24					
2	1990	-0.21	-0.33	-0.12	-0.09	-0.01		**			
2	1995	-0.13	-0.10	0.00	-0.05	-0.11					
2	2000	0.06	-0.02	0.10	-0.05	-0.11					
2	2003	0.06	-0.07	0.18	-0.02	-0.06					
3	1990	-0.54	-0.28	-0.65	-0.95	-0.34				***	
3	1995	-0.50	-0.51	n.a.	-0.74	-0.69		*		***	**
3	2000	-0.19	-0.20	0.66	-0.44	-0.05			**		
3	2003	-0.33	-0.09	n.a.	-0.48	-0.24					
4	1990	-0.69	-0.55	-0.78	-0.40	0.41	*		**		
4	1995	-0.78	-0.14	-0.87	-0.54	0.52	***		***		
4	2000	-0.29	-0.57	-0.38	0.03	0.29		**			
4	2003	-0.51	-0.21	-0.34	-0.04	-0.02	*				
5	1990	-0.01	-0.14	-0.01	-0.03	-0.10					
5	1995	0.20	-0.14	0.07	0.03	0.13					
5	2000	0.23	-0.05	0.11	0.17	0.09	*				
5	2003	0.11	0.12	0.11	-0.27	0.11				**	
6	1990	0.26	0.28	0.34	0.10	0.39	***	***	***		***
6	1995	0.34	0.23	0.43	0.19	0.46	***	***	***	***	***
6	2000	0.28	0.21	0.35	0.20	0.37	***	***	***	***	***
6	2003	0.39	0.27	0.44	0.14	0.42	***	***	***	*	***
7	1990	0.21	0.47	0.23	0.36	0.53		***	*	***	***
7	1995	0.55	0.54	0.45	0.41	0.59	***	***	***	***	***
7	2000	0.52	0.52	0.36	0.40	0.48	***	***	***	***	***
7	2003	0.54	0.54	0.40	0.31	0.55	***	***	***	***	***
8	1990	0.49	0.46	0.56	-0.07	0.59	***	***	***		***
8	1995	0.51	0.38	0.38	-0.15	0.47	***	***	***		***
8	2000	0.52	0.10	0.26	-0.17	0.45	***		*		***
8	2003	0.46	0.00	0.19	-0.32	0.37	***			**	***

Source: See Table 4-5.
Note: See Table 4-5.

Table 4-8   Spearman's Rank Correlation Coefficients of the Ranking of the Market Shares in Japan between ASEAN and China

SITC	YEAR	IDN	MYA	PHI	SIN	THA	IDN	MYA	PHI	SIN	THA
		Rank Correlation Coefficients					Statistical Significance				
0	1990	-0.03	-0.05	-0.08	-0.18	0.19					
0	1995	0.12	0.08	0.00	0.08	0.30				**	
0	2000	0.16	-0.01	0.16	0.04	0.35				***	
0	2003	0.13	0.03	0.04	0.07	0.29				**	
1	1990	0.34	0.51	-0.31	-0.23	0.59					
1	1995	-0.41	0.25	-0.44	-0.18	0.29					
1	2000	-0.41	-0.46	0.03	0.14	0.04					
1	2003	-0.22	0.11	0.45	-0.06	0.36					
2	1990	-0.16	-0.30	-0.14	-0.24	-0.18	***		**		
2	1995	0.10	-0.05	0.01	0.03	0.07					
2	2000	-0.12	0.10	-0.03	0.01	0.07					
2	2003	-0.13	0.02	-0.07	0.00	-0.12					
3	1990	-0.17	-0.14	0.04	-0.37	-0.39					
3	1995	-0.48	-0.58	-0.51	-0.85	-0.63	*	**	**	***	**
3	2000	-0.78	-0.40	-0.45	-0.45	-0.70	***				***
3	2003	-0.66	-0.82	-0.68	-0.62	-0.42	**	***	**	*	
4	1990	-0.45	-0.67	-0.85	-0.50	-0.28		**	***		
4	1995	-0.26	-0.52	-0.60	0.13	0.24		*	**		
4	2000	-0.12	-0.49	-0.88	-0.14	0.09		*	*		
4	2003	0.03	-0.64	-0.51	-0.12	0.04		**			
5	1990	-0.02	-0.16	-0.02	-0.19	-0.06					
5	1995	-0.17	-0.14	-0.10	-0.29	-0.09				**	
5	2000	0.10	-0.10	-0.17	-0.26	0.12				**	
5	2003	0.10	0.03	-0.27	-0.36	0.11			**	***	
6	1990	0.11	0.09	0.16	-0.09	0.11		**			
6	1995	0.14	0.03	0.18	-0.02	0.04	*	**			
6	2000	0.07	0.02	0.13	0.00	0.09					
6	2003	0.03	0.02	0.15	-0.08	0.06			*		
7	1990	0.13	0.34	0.18	0.31	0.50		**		**	***
7	1995	0.39	0.54	0.51	0.41	0.41	***	***	***	***	***
7	2000	0.15	0.31	0.22	0.02	0.21		**	*		*
7	2003	0.26	0.44	0.38	0.19	0.29	**	***	***		**
8	1990	0.50	0.29	0.67	-0.06	0.54	***	**	***		***
8	1995	0.47	0.25	0.44	-0.18	0.37	***	*	***		***
8	2000	0.34	0.15	0.26	-0.32	0.36	**		*	**	***
8	2003	0.37	0.22	0.32	-0.22	0.35	***	*	**	*	***

Source: See Table 4-5.
Note: See Table 4-5.

Notes

1 This is a shortened version of a paper published in *The Philippines Review of Economics 2006* tilted 'China and India: Challenges and Opportunities for ASEAN from Japanese Perspectives.'
2 For details of the framework agreement on comprehensive economic cooperation between ASEAN and China, see www.aseansec.org.
3 For details of the framework agreement on comprehensive economic cooperation between ASEAN and India, see www.aseansec.org.
4 See Balassa (1989) for more detail with respect to the RCA index.
5 According to Suthiphand and Sothitorn (2005, 84), the import-weighted average tariff rate of China is around 9.4 percent.
6 See Okamoto (1994), for instance, for more on the role of FDI in the economic development of Malaysia.
7 The product category ranges from 0 to 8 at the one-digit level of SITC R1.
8 See, Okamoto (2005a), 50–52.

References

Ambatkar, Sanjay. 2001. Trade-led Strategy of India in ASEAN, *Margin* **33**(4): pp. 85–97.
Balassa, Bela. 1989. *Comparative Advantage, Trade Policy and Economic Development*. New York: Harvester Wheatsheaf.
Helpman, Elhanan and Paul Krugman. 1985. *Market Structure and Foreign Trade: Increasing Returns, Imperfect Competition, and the International Economy.*
Jones, Ronald W. 2000. *Globalization and the Theory of Input Trade.* Cambridge, MA: MIT Press.
Langhammer, R. J. and Ulrich Hiemenz. 1990. Regional Integration among Developing Countries: Opportunities, Obstacles and Options, *Kieler Studien*, 232.
Okamoto, Yumiko. 1994. Impact of Trade and FDI Liberalization Policies on the Malaysian Economy, *The Developing Economies*, 32(4/99): pp. 460–478.
Okamoto, Yumiko. 2005a. Toward the Formation of an East Asian Regional Arrangement. In Simon S.C. Tay, ed. *Pacific Asia 2022: Sketching Futures of a Region*, pp. 47–65. Japan and New York: Japan Center for International Exchange.

Okamoto, Yumiko. 2005b. Emergence of the "Intra-mediate Trade:" Implications for the Asia-Pacific Region. Paper presented at *Section 2: Does Trade Deliver What it Promises?* PAFTAD 30, Hilton Hawaiian Village Hotel, Honolulu (Hawaii): February 19–21.
Chirathvat, Suthiphand and Sothitorn Mallikamas. 2005. The Potential Outcomes of China—ASEAN FTA: Politico-Economic Implications for Participating Countries. In Ho Khai Leong and Samuel C. Y. Ku, eds. *China and Southeast Asia: Global Changes and Regional Challenges*, pp. 80–107.
UNCTAD. 2004. *World Investment Report 2004: The Shift Towards Services.* New York and Geneva: United Nations.
Wang, Vincent Wei-cheng. 2005. The Logic of China–ASEAN FTA: Economic Stagecraft of Peaceful Ascendancy. In Ho Khai Leong and Samuel C. Y. Ku, eds. *China and Southeast Asia: Global Changes and Regional Challenges*, pp. 17–41.

5
Aging and Productivity Growth for the Japanese Manufacturing Industries

Shandre M. Thangavelu and Shigeyuki Abe

This chapter studies the changing age and educational composition of the labor force in selected Japanese manufacturing industries. A quality index for the labor force is derived at 2-digit manufacturing industries by age, education and gender to reflect the contribution of different components of the workforce towards manufacturing productivity growth from 1990–1999. The results of the paper suggest that the decomposition of labor quality by age and education reveals that the age category had little contribution to the quality improvements of the Japanese labor force in the manufacturing sector. In contrast, the quality contribution from education appears to have improved labor quality and sustained the contribution of labor input in the overall production of the economy. However, the results also suggest that the contribution from education is declining over the years due to the prolonged recession in the Japanese economy. The declining contribution of education to the overall labor quality could have serious implications for the recovery and sustained growth of the Japanese economy.

Introduction

The Japanese population and its labor force are aging at a rapid rate and this aging will have important implications for the long-term growth of the economy. As the age composition of the labor force shifts towards older workers, the productive performance of the aging labor force will have an important impact on the future sustainable growth of the economy. Empirical evidence on adoption and implementation of new technologies suggests that the younger workers, who are better educated, are more able to implement new technologies as compared to older workers (Clark and Spengler 1980; Bartel and Lichtenberg 1987). Thus, the aging labor force raises important questions on the ability of the Japanese economy to sustain the level of innovation and diffusion of new technologies in the domestic economy. However, the human capital model also suggests that the productivity of workers increases with age due to their experience and technology specific training (Becker 1962). In this case, the contribution of the workforce to productivity growth depends on the age composition of the workforce, educational level, training and re-training of the workers.

The ability of older workers to retain their acquired skills depends on the stable economic structure of the economy. For instance, in a recession, the high turnover rate of employment and downsizing of the companies to adjust to newer methods of production will have significant negative impact on the technology specific skills of workers. In the case of Japan, the prolonged recession of more than 10 years will have a significant impact on the aging labor force and the productive performance of the economy. For example, the rise in the unemployment rate since 1998, from 3 percent to almost 6 percent, raises important questions on the ability of the labor force to retain its previously acquired skills. It is also highly likely that the quality of the workforce would decline with structural shifts in the economy, which could dampen the productive contribution of the workforce. This decline in the quality of the workers could have important short- and long-run implications for the economic growth of the Japanese economy. In fact, the economic recovery of the Japanese economy critically depends on the productive performance of the labor force to provide the impetus for supply side competitiveness of the economy. In addition, the ability of the economy to sustain long-term growth depends on the quality of the labor force to complement the new production structure of the economy. With a significant decline in government expenditure on education, a more pronounced decline in the quality of the labor force is expected with significant long-term implications for the growth of the Japanese economy.

This chapter studies the changing composition of the labor force in selected Japanese manufacturing industries at 2-digit industries before undertaking a comparative study with the Singaporean manufacturing industries. A quality index for labor is derived by age, education and gender to reflect the contribution of different components of the workforce towards the growth of the labor force. In particular, we study the quality contributions of age and education towards the growth of the labor force in manufacturing industries during the recession years of 1990 to 1999.

Several studies have highlighted the impact of education and age on the productive performance of workers. As compared to an educational component of workers, Chinloy (1986) reports that the age component of workers has an insignificant impact on labor productivity growth for the Canadian economy. However, Medoff and Ibrahim (1980) found positive effects of age on productivity growth but found that the age contributions increases to a certain age, normally between 55 to 60 years, and then declines thereafter. Based on the production structure of the economy, Lazear (1990) suggests that the impact of aging on average productivity depends on complementary effects between factors of production in production functions. In a more recent study on the U.S. economy, Ho and Jorgenson (2001) reports that the quality improvements in terms of age and education contributed nearly 40 percent to the growth of the total labor input. In fact, most of the contributions accrue to improvements in education as opposed to the age contribution to productivity growth.

For the Japanese economy, Imamura (1990) measured the quality change of the labor force from 1970 to 1979 and found the age contribution significantly larger than the education contribution to productivity growth. The studies by Koike (1988), Hashimoto and Raisan (1985) and Mincer and Higuchi (1988) highlight the importance of on-the-job training and the development of firm specific skills for male Japanese workers. However, Ohtake (1998) re-examined the above impact on older workers and reported that the return to tenure in the Japanese labor force is smaller than was reported earlier.

The results suggest that there are only marginal improvements in quality effects across the 2-digit manufacturing industries, and most of the improvements are in the education levels of the workers. The results also suggest that older workers in the Japanese manufacturing industries are making productive contributions to the labor productivity growth as compared to younger workers. However, we also observed a significant decline in the age components of the quality effects as compared to the educational components of the workers.

The chapter is organized as follows. The next section will discuss the methodology. In section three we will provide the results for the quality effects across industries. In section four we compare the Japanese manufacturing industries with Singapore. The concluding section is given in section five.

The Methodology

The study utilizes a growth accounting framework proposed by Chinloy (1989) and Ho and Jorgenson (2002) to study the effects of aging and education on labor productivity growth in Japan.

The production function is defined as:

$$Y = f(D, X_{L+1}, \ldots, X_N, A) \tag{1}$$

where Y is the quantity of outputs, X is non-labor inputs, and A is the technology parameter. The labor input index is defined by $D = D(X_1, X_2 \ldots X_L)$.

Total employment in the economy is defined as:

$$E = \sum X_i \tag{2}$$

and total compensation is: $C = \sum X_i W_i$, where W_i is the unit wage for the ith labor input. The labor compensation share (s_i) is given as: $s_i = \dfrac{X_i W_i}{C}$, with a sum to one and a constant returns to scale assumption.

Assuming a competitive market where the labor input index is linearly homogenous, the elasticity of D with respect to X_i equates to the labor compensation share s_i . In this case the growth rate of the labor input index (d) is given as: $d = \sum s_i x_i$, where x_i is the growth rate of labor input i. Since the input index is assumed to be linearly homogenous, it could be expressed as:

$$D = ED^*(\frac{X_i}{E}, \frac{X_2}{E},...., \frac{X_L}{E}) = ED^*(b_1.... b_L), \tag{3}$$

where D* is the index of labor quality and b_i is the employment share. As in the compensation share, the employment share will sum to one as well. The interpretation of the quality index is that if D* equals to one, the total labor inputs is equal to total employment and there is no difference in labor quality.

The total employment could also be expressed in growth rates: $e = \sum b_i x_i$. The labor quality growth rate (d*) is the difference between the growth rate of the labor quality index (d) and the employment growth rate:

$$d^* = \sum (s_i - b_i) x_i = q_i x_i . \tag{4}$$

The quality weights are given by ($s_i - b_i$) for input i. The quality weights will be positive when the unit wage of the ith unit of labor exceeds the average wage for all workers. The contribution to labor quality by the ith labor input is given by the product of quality weights and employment growth rate for the ith labor input.

Applying the growth accounting framework, output growth (Y) could be expressed as:

$$y = s_L(e + \sum q_i x_i) + \sum v_i(x_i - e) + a , \tag{5}$$

where s_l is the labor share, v_i is the share of other non-labor inputs and a is total factor productivity growth. This framework allows one to decompose the effects of aging and education on the labor force. The effects of education and age on labor productivity growth could be observed if we construct separate quality effects for age and education.

The growth of labor quality by age could be constructed in the following manner. Let j represents characteristics of employment by age and h represent characteristics of employment by education. The total employment by age is given by summing over the educational groups:

$$X_j = \sum_{h}^{H} X_{jh}, \qquad j = 1,...,J \tag{6}$$

and total employment by education is given by summing over the age groups:

$$X_h = \sum_{j}^{J} X_{jh}, \qquad h = 1,...,H \tag{7}$$

The contribution of a given age group to labor quality is given as:

$$z_j = q_j x_j, \qquad j = 1,...,J \tag{8}$$

and the contribution of a given educational group to labor quality is given as:

$$n_h = q_h x_h, \qquad h = 1,...,H \tag{9}$$

where the labor quality weights, q_j and q_h is constructed as in equation (4). We will define the growth rate of labor quality by age as d_A^* and the growth rate of labor quality by education as d_E^*. In this case, the growth in labor quality is given as the sum of the contribution of education and age:

$$d^* = \sum_{j} z_j + \sum_{h} n_h = d_A^* + d_E^*. \tag{10}$$

and the labor productivity growth is expressed analogous to equation (5):

$$y - e = s_L \left[\sum_{j=1}^{J} z_j + \sum_{h=1}^{H} n_h \right] + \sum_{i=L+1}^{N} v_i(x_i - e) + a. \tag{11}$$

Data Requirements

Annual data from 1989 to 1999 is used in our study. The labor force data by age, education and gender in terms of hours worked, wages and number of workers for the 2-digit manufacturing industries are collected from the *Japanese Statistical Yearbook*. The classification of labor input is as follows:

Sex	Age (years)	Education
1. Male	1. 17–24	1. Elementary
2. Female	2. 24–29	2. Former Junior High
	3. 30–34	3. College
	4. 35–39	4. Management and Technical Education
	5. 40–44	5. University
	6. 45–49	
	7. 50–54	
	8. 55–59	
	9. 60–64	
	7. 65–above	

As indicated by Fosgerau et al. (2002), a higher level of disaggregation does not provide much information as to the construction of the quality indices. In our analysis, we reduced the number of age categories to 17 to 39 years, 40–54 years and 55 and over years to represent the changing age composition in the labor force. We also adjusted the educational categories. For most years the data on university education for women is not available. Hence, we reduced the number of educational categories by adding elementary school with former junior high as one category, and the management and technical education with university education as the other category. Data on value-added, gross capital investment and gross capital stock data is available from the *Japanese Statistical Yearbook*. Value-added output and capital stock data is based to 1995 prices.

Results: Quality of the Japanese Labor Force in Selected Manufacturing Industries

Quality Effects from Age

The results of the quality decompositions by age and education are given in Tables 5-1 and 5-2 respectively. The labor quality by age decomposition shows an upward trend for 2 out of 8 industries under study. In particular, there are positive improvements in precision, publishing, food, chemical and electrical industries. The overall results show that only food, machinery, and chemical industries have experienced positive improvements in labor quality through age decompositions. The quality improvements are significant for machinery and chemical industries, which shows an upward trend from 1990–94 to 1995–99.

Comparing the quality contributions over time suggest that the age contribution to labor productivity is showing a declining trend. The age

Table 5-1   The Growth Rate of Labor Quality by Age (d_A^*) for Selected Japanese
Manufacturing Industries (%) 1990–1999

	17-39 years old	40-54 years old	55 and over years old	Total
Machinery Industry				
1990-1994	0.00065	0.00120	-0.00063	0.00122
1995-1999	-0.00111	-0.00191	0.00698	0.00396
1990-1999	-0.00023	-0.00036	0.00317	0.00259
Steel Industry				
1990-1994	-0.00306	0.00614	-0.00014	0.00294
1995-1999	-0.00551	0.00433	-0.00270	-0.00387
1990-1999	-0.00428	0.00524	-0.00142	-0.00046
Precision Industry				
1990-1994	0.00547	-0.00153	-0.00065	0.00329
1995-1999	0.00134	0.00087	-0.00109	0.00111
1990-1999	0.00341	-0.00033	-0.00087	0.00221
Publishing Industry				
1990-1994	-0.00067	-0.00108	0.00391	0.00216
1995-1999	-0.00238	0.00349	0.00086	0.00198
1990-1999	-0.00152	0.00121	0.00239	0.00207
Paper Industry				
1990-1994	-0.00278	0.00085	-0.00013	-0.00206
1995-1999	0.00032	-0.00200	-0.00048	-0.00216
1990-1999	-0.00123	-0.00058	-0.00030	-0.00211
Food Industry				
1990-1994	-0.00214	-0.00095	0.00082	-0.00227
1995-1999	-0.00005	0.00181	-0.00010	0.00076
1990-1999	-0.00109	0.00043	-0.00008	-0.00076
Chemical Industry				
1990-1994	-0.00152	0.00025	0.00376	0.00249
1995-1999	-0.00091	0.00151	0.00481	0.00541
1990-1999	-0.00122	0.00088	0.00429	0.00395
Electrical Industry				
1990-1994	0.00327	-0.00202	0.00267	0.00392
1995-1999	0.00161	-0.00101	0.00194	0.00254
1990-1999	0.00244	-0.00151	0.00230	0.00323

decomposition reveals that older workers at 55 years and over have not
experienced any quality improvements except for machinery and chemical
industries. Only in these two industries does the age quality effects of the
workers at 55 years and over show a rising trend from 1990–94 to 1995–99. As
compared to older workers, younger workers only show a marginal improvement
in paper, food and chemical industries, however there are significant declines
in their quality in most of the other industries.

However, taking the average of the entire period under study, the results show that the older workers of 55 years and over did contribute to quality improvements in key industries. The results in 1990–1999 shows that older workers above the age of 55 years and over have made more quality contributions in the key industries as compared to the workers below the age of 54 years. The contribution of older workers is quite significant in chemical, electrical, machinery and publishing industries. In contrast, younger workers below 39 years have only contributed to quality improvements in precision and electrical industries in the period under study.

Quality Effects of Education

The quality improvements from education are significant as compared to the quality improvements from age. In Table 5-2, the results by education decomposition of the labor quality are shown.

Among the three categories of education, tertiary and technical education has contributed most significantly to the productive improvements of all industries under study. Workers with only college or high school education have contributed the least among the three categories of education. In fact, workers with college education have been significantly affected by the prolonged recession, showing the most significant decline in their quality in the 1995–99 sub-period. As compared to workers with college education, tertiary educated workers appeared to show a positive trend. They tend to perform better over the recession as compared to the other educational categories, as they show higher quality contributions to the overall productivity growth in 1995–1999. Workers with elementary and high school education also showed some positive trends in food and chemical industries, but the contribution is not as significant as compared to tertiary education.

The overall quality improvements of workers in 1990–1999 in the above table tend to suggest that tertiary education contributes significantly as compared to other educational categories. The overall average contribution of tertiary education to labor quality is highly significant in chemical, electrical, food, machinery, paper and publishing industries. In fact, in some industries, such as food, paper and publishing industries, the contribution to the educational component of the labor quality for tertiary education contributed twice that of the other educational categories. The contribution of workers with elementary and high school education is higher in steel and precision industries.

Comparing the quality improvements between age and education, the contribution from education to labor quality improvements is highly significant. In all the industries, the quality contribution from education to the overall improvement of the labor force is at least twice that of the quality contribution

Table 5-2   The Growth Rate of Labor Quality by Education (d_E^*) for Selected
Japanese Manufacturing Industries (%) 1990–1999

	Elementary & Former Junior High	College	Management, Technical and University	Total
Machinery Industry				
1990-1994	0.01093	0.00240	0.00633	0.01966
1995-1999	0.00338	-0.00002	0.00945	0.01280
1990-1999	0.00716	0.00119	0.00789	0.01623
Steel Industry				
1990-1994	0.01474	0.00233	-0.00084	0.01623
1995-1999	0.01051	0.00206	0.00873	0.02130
1990-1999	0.01265	0.00220	0.00394	0.01878
Precision Industry				
1990-1994	0.00799	0.00252	0.00241	0.01292
1995-1999	0.00413	0.00120	0.00696	0.01229
1990-1999	0.00606	0.00186	0.00469	0.01261
Publishing Industry				
1990-1994	0.00292	0.00123	0.01061	0.01476
1995-1999	0.00171	0.00069	0.01695	0.01934
1990-1999	0.00231	0.00096	0.01378	0.01705
Paper Industry				
1990-1994	0.00950	0.00137	0.02123	0.02161
1995-1999	0.00189	-0.00120	0.01024	0.01093
1990-1999	0.00570	0.00008	0.01049	0.01627
Food Industry				
1990-1994	0.00036	-0.00017	0.02116	0.02134
1995-1999	0.00572	-0.00072	0.01022	0.01522
1990-1999	0.00304	-0.00044	0.01569	0.01828
Chemical Industry				
1990-1994	0.00172	-0.00043	0.01680	0.01812
1995-1999	0.00581	0.00299	-0.00978	0.00100
1990-1999	0.00376	0.00128	0.00353	0.00857
Electrical Industry				
1990-1994	0.00864	0.00187	0.03146	0.04198
1995-1999	0.00241	0.00083	0.00927	0.01251
1990-1999	0.00553	0.00135	0.00606	0.01294

from age. In fact, most of the quality improvements in the labor force are from
the contributions of workers with the tertiary education.

The overall growth rate of labor quality and its contribution to labor
productivity is given in Table 5-3. The overall labor quality shows a positive
contribution to the labor productivity growth. In fact, the improvements in
labor quality form an important buffer for the declining labor input during the

Table 5-3   The Growth Rate of Total Labor Quality (d^*) and
Contribution to Labor Productivity Growth for Selected
Japanese Manufacturing Industries (%) 1990–1999

	Total Labor Quality (d^*)	Contribution to Labor Productivity (d^*)(S_l)
Machinery Industry		
1990-1994	0.02088	0.0067
1995-1999	0.01710	0.0089
1990-1999	0.01882	0.0084
Steel Industry		
1990-1994	0.02369	0.0077
1995-1999	0.01336	0.0069
1990-1999	0.01806	0.0080
Precision Industry		
1990-1994	0.01563	0.0050
1995-1999	0.01426	0.0074
1990-1999	0.01481	0.0066
Publishing Industry		
1990-1994	0.01692	0.0054
1995-1999	0.02095	0.0109
1990-1999	0.01912	0.0085
Paper Industry		
1990-1994	0.01955	0.0063
1995-1999	0.00967	0.0050
1990-1999	0.01416	0.0063
Food Industry		
1990-1994	0.04589	0.0148
1995-1999	0.01762	0.0091
1990-1999	0.03047	0.0135
Chemical Industry		
1990-1994	0.02061	0.0067
1995-1999	0.00576	0.0030
1990-1999	0.01251	0.0056
Electrical Industry		
1990-1994	0.02700	0.0080
1995-1999	0.00714	0.0037
1990-1999	0.01617	0.0072

recession years. In particular, the quality improvements from education acts as the major component of this buffer, which suggests that education is an important component of the labor force to maintain its competitiveness and employability during the recession and recovery periods. However, our results show that this important buffer is narrowing over the years due to the prolonged recession in the Japanese economy.

Overall Manufacturing Productivity Growth:
A Comparative Study with Singapore

Analyses of the decomposition by age and education were also undertaken on the overall manufacturing sector and the results were compared to the manufacturing sector in Singapore. The age and educational quality components for the manufacturing sector in the Singapore economy is gathered from Thangavelu and Abe (2003). For comparative analysis, the overall manufacturing sector for the Japanese economy is used in the decomposition analysis so as to be consistent with the study for the Singapore economy. Thus, it must be highlighted that the results from the selected manufacturing industries are completely different as compared to the overall manufacturing industries.

The general distribution of workers by age is given in Figure 5-A1 and Figure 5-A2 for Japan and Singapore respectively (see Appendix). Observation of the Japanese labor force shows that the large proportion of workers is in the 45 years and above age category. The median age of the Japanese worker is around 50 to 55 years of age, which suggests the important impact of older workers on the Japanese labor market. In contrast, the large proportion of workers in Singapore is in the 35 to 40 years of age category. This suggests that the labor force in Japan is aging faster than Singapore. With a larger population and a faster aging population, the impact of aging in the Japanese economy might be more pronounced than in Singapore.

In addition to the differences in the rate of aging in the population and labor force between the two countries, there are several key differences between the manufacturing sectors in Japan and Singapore. The Japanese manufacturing sector is mainly operating at higher value-added activities as compared to Singapore, although key industries in Singapore are moving to higher value-added activities in recent years. For example, recently there has been a strong emphasis on the development of biotechnology industries in Singapore.

The results of the quality decomposition by age and education (Table 5-4) support the conjecture that aging has a more pronounced effect on the Japanese manufacturing sector as compared to the manufacturing sector in Singapore. As indicated with the industry level study, the older workers in Japan are contributing more significantly to the productivity growth as compared to the younger workers. This is a direct contrast to the Singapore economy where the younger workers are providing greater contribution to labor productivity growth. The results might be indicative of the degree of aging in both economies.

As with the U.S. economy, education is the key component in the labor force that is driving productivity in both the Japanese and Singapore economy. This

Table 5-4   Contribution of Labor Quality to Productivity Growth for the Manufacturing Sector for Japan and Singapore 1990–1999

Age (%)					
Age	15-29	30-39	40-49	50 and over	Total
Japan	-0.002	-0.001	0.003	0.005	0.006
Singapore	0.192	0.026	0.109	-0.038	0.290

Education (%)				
Education	Elementary & Former Junior High	College	Management, Technical and University	Total
Japan	0.024	0.006	0.036	0.065
Singapore	0.228	0.145	0.545	0.809

Table 5-5   Sources of Growth for Japan and Singapore 1990–1999

	(Real) Growth Rate of Output	Growth Rate of Labor Productivity $(y-e)$	Growth Rate of Capital Stock	Labor Share (S_i)	Contribution from Growth Rate of Capital per Worker $(x-e)(1-S_i)$	Contribution from Labor Quality $(d*S_i)$	TFP
Japan	-2.84	-3.37	3.04	51.79	1.21	0.07	-4.65
Singapore	9.46	7.11	7.16	33.40	4.85	1.10	1.16

suggests that education tends to be more resilient to long-term structural changes and provides a strong buffer for workers to effectively adjust to the structural changes in the economy. Comparing the quality components between the two countries, the contribution of education to overall productivity growth and the contribution of education to labor quality are much higher in Singapore than in Japan. This is an indication of the prolonged recession experienced by Japan that accelerated the depreciation of human capital and is clearly visible in the low quality contribution from the age component of the workers. Also, the contribution from education to productivity growth is much higher in Singapore as compared to Japan. In both the economies, workers with university education tend to contribute significantly to overall productivity growth.

In Table 5-5, the sources of labor productivity growth for both Japan and Singapore are given. The negative output growth and labor productivity growth for Japan indicates the decade long recession experienced in the economy. The labor quality contribution to overall labor productivity growth is positive but quite insignificant. Singapore tends to have experienced higher output growth and with positive contribution from labor quality. The total factor productivity growth (TFP) for Japan is negative as compared to a positive TFP for Singapore.

Conclusion

The importance of skills and education for the productive performance of the workforce is reflected by the current study. As workers get older, they acquire technology-specific skills and job based-experience, which are not easily transferable across industries or sectors. On the other hand, general education is the other component of human capital that allows for mobility and transferability of human skills across industries. In fact, there is evidence that general education tends to increase the returns on new technologies and increase the technology adoption in the domestic economy.

The results of our chapter suggests the labor quality effects from age has little contribution to the quality improvements of the Japanese labor force and hence to labor productivity growth in the manufacturing sector. In contrast, the contribution from education appears to improve the labor quality and sustain the contribution of labor input in the overall production and productivity of the economy. However, the results also suggest that the contribution from education is declining over the years due to the prolonged recession in the Japanese economy.

The declining contribution of the education component to labor quality has serious implications for the Japanese economy. The ability of the Japanese economy to sustain long-term growth depends on the ability of labor to complement the new economic structure the domestic economy adopts during its recovery period. If the labor force is fragile with little general education and technological-specific human capital, the ability of the economy to recover and sustain the long-term growth is still not very clear.

Due to significant downsizing and high labor turnover during this recession period, the educational quality effects are indicating a declining trend. This indicates a serious issue of sustaining the educational component of the labor force. Given the large budget deficits during recessions, the expenditure on education will be an important consideration to sustain the competitiveness of both younger and older workers in the labor market. This will become an important component for long-term sustainable growth if the Japanese economy recovers from the current recession. The other important issue is the training and re-training of the older workers who are already in the current work force.

Appendix

See Figures 5-A1 and 5-A2.

Figure 5-A1   Labor Force by Age in Japan in 2001 (thousand)

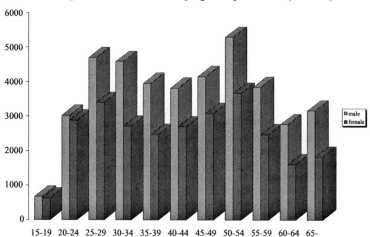

Figure 5-A2   Labor Force by Age Category for Singapore in 2001 (thousand)

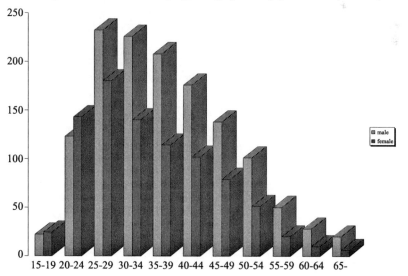

References

Bartel, Ann and Frank Lichtenberg. 1987. The Comparative Advantage of Educated Workers in Implementing New Technologies. *Review of Economics and Statistics,* 69 (1): pp. 1–11.

Clark, R. and Splengler J. 1980. *The Economics of Individual and Aging Population.* Cambridge, Mass.: Cambridge University Press.

Chinloy, Peter. 1989. The Effects of Shifts in the Composition of Employment on Labour Productivity Growth: Canada 1971–1979. In A Dogavmaci and R. Rare. ed. *Applications of Modern Production Theory.* Kluwer Academic Publishers.

Fosgerau, M., S.E. Hougaard Jensen, and A. Sorensen, 2002. Measuring Educational Heterogeneity and Labor Quality: A Note. *Review of Income and Wealth,* 48(2): pp. 261–269.

Hashimoto, Masanori. 1993. Aspects of Labor Market Adjustments in Japan. *Journal of Labour Economics,* 11(1): pp. 136–161.

Ho, M.S. and D.W. Jorgenson. 2001. *The Quality of the U.S. Workforce.* Unpublished manuscript: Harvard University.

Imamura, Hajime, 1990. Compositional Change of Heterogeneous Labor Input and Economic Growth in Japan. In Charles Hulten ed. *Productivity Growth in Japan and United States.* Chicago: University of Chicago Press.

Lazaear E. 1990. Adjusting to an Aging Workforce. In David Wise. ed. *Issues in the Economics of Aging.* Chicago: University of Chicago Press.

Owyong, David and Bhanoji Rao. 1998. Total Factor Productivity Growth in the Singapore Economy: Some Econometric Estimates. *Singapore Economic Review,* 43(1): pp. 74–81.

Rao, Bhanoji and C. Lee. 1995. Sources of Growth in Singapore Economy and its Manufacturing and Service Sectors. *The Singapore Economic Review,* 38(2): pp. 231–251.

Tan, Lin Yeok and Suchin Virabhak. 1998. Total Factor Productivity Growth in Singapore's Service Sector. *Journal of Economic Studies,* 25(5): pp. 392–409.

Thangavelu, S.M. and Bhanoji Rao. 1999. TFP Growth in the Electronic Industry. *Singapore Economic Review,* 44(2): pp. 56–68.

Thangavelu, S.M. and Shigeyuki Abe. 2003. *The Changing Age & Educational Composition of the Labor Force in Singapore: Impact on Productivity.* Unpublished manuscript, Department of Economics, National University of Singapore.

6

Productivity, Technological Progress and Factor Substitution in the Malaysian Manufacturing Sector[1]

Lai Yew Wah

Introduction

The most prominent feature of the Malaysian economy since independence is its remarkable transformation from an agro-based economy exporting primary commodities to one based on industries exporting a wide range of manufactured goods. The success of this transformation is largely due to the industrialization program vigorously pursued since the implementation of the Investment Incentives Act 1968.

The contribution of the manufacturing sector in terms of its share of GDP grew from 13.4 percent in 1970 to 26.9 percent in 1990 (Department of Statistics 2001). By 2002 its contribution increased to 31.7 percent. In terms of exports, the share of manufactured exports in total exports grew from 11.9 percent in 1970 to 58.8 percent in 1990. By 2002 it increased to 58.8 percent. In particular, the electrical and electronics sector is the most important industry, contributing 70 percent of total manufactured exports in 2000. Malaysia is currently one of the largest producers and exporters of semiconductor components in the world. In terms of employment, the contribution of manufacturing to total employment increased significantly from 9.0 percent in 1970 to 19.9 percent in 1990. By 2002, its share reached 22.7 percent. It is therefore evident that the performance of the export-oriented manufacturing sector is central to the country's economic development. Any drastic decline in its growth would have a disastrous effect on the economy.

The major challenges for the manufacturing sector today are to sustain its growth and maintain its export competitiveness in the face of increasing competition from emerging low-cost economies. A vital step towards attaining sustained growth and export competitiveness is increased productivity and technological progress. The impressive growth in the past, which was input-driven, cannot be sustained. Mere increases in inputs, without an increase in the efficiency with which these inputs are used would run into diminishing returns (Krugman

141

1994). Thus, input-driven growth is inevitably limited and is not sustainable in the long run. It is therefore important to reexamine productivity growth and the state of technological progress in the manufacturing sector with a view to assessing the growth sustainability of the sector.

The earliest analysis of productivity growth was based on partial factor productivity used by Solow (1957). The weakness of this approach is that it does not identify the factors determining productivity growth. Another measure of productivity is total factor productivity (TFP), which is computed as the difference between the rate of output growth and the weighted average of growth of inputs. A popular method used is the Gollop-Jorgenson translog method (Jorgenson et al 1987).

There have been a number of empirical studies that are related to productivity growth in the Malaysian manufacturing sector. Tham (1995), for example, analyzed the contribution of productivity to growth in the Malaysian economy and its manufacturing sector. Oguchi et al (2002) compared the productivity growth of foreign and local firms for the period 1994–96. Wong (2003) studied the TFP growth in Sarawak's manufacturing sector.

Among the earliest studies on factor substitution elasticity and technical progress were Arrow, Chenery, Minhas and Solow (1961), Solow (1962) and Brown (1968). The first study uses the CES production function to measure the substitution possibilities between factors of production and the last two studies are on measurement and sources of technical change.

The main objectives of this chapter are: to analyze the productivity growth in the Malaysian manufacturing sector by using various productivity measures such as labor productivity, capital productivity, unit labor cost, capital intensity and total factor productivity; measure the contribution of various inputs and total factor productivity to manufacturing growth; and measure the rate of technical progress and factor substitution in the Malaysian manufacturing industries.

Productivity Measures

Productivity growth is measured both in terms of productivity indicators and TFP as derived from the standard growth accounting model. Productivity indicators include labor productivity, capital productivity, labor competitiveness and capital intensity. Labor productivity is commonly measured by the value added per employee. High labor productivity indicates favorable wealth creation from the use of labor. Capital productivity indicates the extent and efficiency of the utilization of capital assets. A measure that is commonly used is the value added-fixed assets ratio. Unit labor cost (labor cost per unit of output) is a measure of labor competitiveness. A high ratio is associated with labor problems such as skilled labor shortage, high labor turnover and the like. Capital intensity is measured by the capital-labor ratio. A low ratio implies that there is a reliance on labor-intensive methods of production with low technology utilization.

The estimation of TFP is derived from the familiar neo-classical production function, using the usual assumptions of linear homogeneity, perfect competition in both product and input markets and constant output elasticity with respect to inputs. After total differentiation of the production function, output growth can be expressed as the sum total of the product of respective output elasticity with their input growth and total factor productivity. In other words, the following equation holds:

$$dhQ = d\lambda + \frac{\partial hQ}{\partial hK} dhK + \frac{\partial hQ}{\partial hL} dhL + \frac{\partial hQ}{\partial hI} dhI \qquad (1)$$

where Q, K, L and I are output, capital, labor and other inputs respectively; and $d\lambda$ is TFP growth.

Using discrete points in time and the usual assumptions listed above, which imply that income shares of the respective inputs are equal to the respective output elasticity, equation (1) can be expressed as follows (Jorgenson et al. 1987):

$$TFP\ growth\ = (lnQ_t - lnQ_{t-1}) - KS(lnK_t - lnK_{t-1}) - LS(lnL_t - lnL_{t-1})$$
$$- IS(lnI_t - lnI_{t-1}) \qquad (2)$$

where KS = average share of capital = $0.5(KS_t + KS_{t-1})$
       LS = average share of labor = $0.5(LS_t + LS_{t-1})$
       IS = average share of other inputs = $0.5(IS_t + IS_{t-1})$.

The CES production function is used to derive the estimation of factor substitution elasticity and technical progress. This particular function is popularly used in empirical work on production. Although it assumes the degree of substitution between inputs is constant, regardless of the level of output and input proportions, it does not assume *a priori* a particular value for the elasticity. In contrast, the Cobb-Douglas-type of production function assumes unitary elasticity of substitution between inputs. The elasticity of substitution is determined by the underlying technology in production and thus the value can be used to characterize the level and efficiency of technology used. Assuming constant returns to scale and perfect competition in product and input markets, the CES production function is:

$$V = \gamma\,[\delta K^{-\rho} + (1 - \delta)\,L^{-\rho}]^{-1/\rho} \qquad (3)$$

where V, K and L are value added, capital and labor inputs.

γ = efficiency parameter
ρ = substitution parameter
δ = distribution parameter

After linearisation and logarithmic transformation of the above CES production function, the following equation can be derived (Hoffman and Tan 1980):

$$\ln v = \sigma \ln [\gamma^\rho (1-\delta)^{-1}] + \sigma \ln w \qquad (4)$$

where v = value added per worker
w = wages per worker
σ = the elasticity of factor substitution.
Equation (4) can be reduced:

$$\ln v = - \sigma \ln (1-\delta) + \sigma \ln w + \sigma\rho \ln \gamma \qquad (5)$$

To show the technology change, the efficiency parameter can be represented by (Khor and Maisom 2000):

$\gamma = e^{\lambda t}$ where λ is the rate of technical progress.

Thus equation (5) can be expressed in the estimation form:

$$\ln v = \beta_1 + \beta_2 \ln w + \beta_3 t + \varepsilon \qquad (6)$$

where β_1 = - σ ln (1-δ); β_2 = σ; and β_3 = $\sigma\rho\lambda$. Since σ = 1/(1+ρ), it follows that

$$\lambda = \frac{\beta_3}{(1 - \beta_2)} \ .$$

The advantage of using this method over other approaches (Diwan 1965; Kmenta 1967; Lu and Fletscher 1968) is that it does not require capital stock data that are always very difficult to obtain.

Data Sources and Measurement of Variables

Data classified by the 3-digit Malaysia Industrial Code are obtained from the Annual Survey of Manufacturing Industries published by the Department of Statistics. The Producer Price Index (1989 = 100) is used to deflate all value data series. The study covers the period 1981–2000 and includes 17 major industry groups (out of 28 groups in the survey). Value added is computed as the difference between gross output value and cost of inputs. Labor consists of all full time paid workers. Ideally, the flow of capital services should be used rather than capital stock but no such data are available for the Malaysian manufacturing industries. Value of fixed assets is used as a proxy for capital stock, given that there are no other better measures.

Results

Productivity Indicators
Value Added Per Employee

As shown in Table 6-1, the average annual growth rate of labor productivity was 5.4 percent over the period under study. Negative growth rates were recorded in 1985–86 and 1997–98 due to adverse economic conditions. The steady rise in labor productivity was due to improved labor and management efficiency, work attitude and technical progress aside from favorable market conditions. Positive growth rates were registered in all the seventeen sub-sectors. In particular, the two most important export-oriented industries of electrical and electronic (EE), and textiles sub-sectors experienced much higher average growth rates of 7 and 8 percent respectively. Within the EE sector, the semiconductor and electronic components industries, which form the bulk of the sector in terms of value added, exports and employment, recorded an 8 percent growth.

Over the two sub-periods, labor productivity in the manufacturing sector grew from 4.7 percent to 6 percent. However the majority of industries

Table 6-1   Growth Rates in Labor and Capital Productivities (%)

Industries	Labor Productivity			Capital Productivity		
	1981-2000	1981-1990	1991-2000	1981-2000	1981-1990	1991-2000
Manufacturing	5.4	4.7	6.0	-1.4	-2.2	-0.6
Food	3.8	2.9	4.7	0.6	0.5	0.8
Beverage	3.3	9.8	-2.5	-1.0	5.2	-6.5
Tobacco	2.5	8.1	-2.6	-3.1	2.5	-8.2
Textile	7.9	8.4	7.5	-0.7	3.7	-4.5
Wearing Apparel	4.8	5.9	3.8	0.2	2.7	-2.0
Leather	4.3	0.3	7.8	1.4	-2.8	5.2
Wood	4.3	4.4	4.2	0.2	5.0	-4.1
Paper	6.4	8.0	5.1	0.3	-4.2	4.3
Ind. Chemical	15.4	2.9	2.9	4.3	12.8	-3.3
Rubber	3.4	2.3	4.5	0.4	-2.2	2.9
Plastic	6.0	6.7	5.4	0.2	1.6	-1.1
Glass	8.8	8.4	9.2	1.4	-2.6	4.9
Iron/Steel	6.7	12.7	1.4	-1.6	-0.8	-2.2
Non-ferrous Iron	5.6	0.4	10.2	-1.0	-6.1	3.6
Metal	5.9	7.2	4.7	-0.7	-1.5	-0.1
EE	6.9	4.4	9.1	-1.2	-4.1	1.3
Transport	5.7	10.1	1.6	2.9	9.5	2.0
Semicond/components	7.9	4.8	10.6	-1.5	-6.5	2.9

experienced a decline. Part of this is attributed to the dramatic increase in the use of foreign labor in the nineties, who are, in general, less productive than local workers. A recent unpublished report[2] indicates that foreign workers contribute negatively to labor productivity. For every increase of 1 percent of the number of foreign workers in the manufacturing sector, labor productivity declines by 0.09 percent. The relative contribution to output growth in manufacturing by foreign workers is also lower.

The performance of the semiconductor and components industries is an exception. Labor productivity increased from 4.8 percent to 10.6 percent over the two periods. The intense market competition and rapid change in technological requirement necessitate constant skill upgrading of workers, foreign and local, leading to increases in labor productivity. This occurred despite a decreasing growth rate in capital intensity in the sector.

Capital Productivity
Capital productivity is measured by the ratio of value added to fixed assets. As Table 6-1 indicates, capital productivity declined at an annual rate 1.4 percent. Although there was a slight improvement over the two sub-periods, this still does not augur well on the competitiveness of the manufacturing sector as it implies there is substantial excess capacity. The average rate of assets utilization was 65 percent during 1981–2000. On a sub-sectoral level, nine out of the seventeen industries showed a deteriorating rate of capital productivity growth over the two sub-periods. In particular, the growth rate in capital productivity in the semiconductor and components industry improved over the two sub-periods. This reflects the capacity of the industry to rationalize regularly to remain competitive. Nevertheless, capital productivity in this industry especially is affected by external demand conditions. In a number of years when there was sluggish demand, including the recession years in 1985–86, excess capacity deteriorated and labor productivity dipped. In some other industries such as wood-based industries, the increase in downstream activities has not been matched by a corresponding increase in the supply of raw materials resulting in excess capacity.

Unit Labor Cost
Unit labor cost, as measured by the labor cost-output ratio, has improved marginally by 0.2 percent (Table 6-2). While it grew at an average of 0.3 percent in the eighties, it declined significantly by 0.7 percent in the nineties as during this period the labor productivity growth of 6 percent more than offset the real wage growth of 3.1 percent. More recent data indicates rising unit labor costs largely due to lower capacity utilization, lower external demand and sluggish

Table 6-2   Growth Rates in Unit Labor Cost and Capital Intensity (%)

Industries	Unit Labor Cost			Capital Intensity		
	1981-2000	1981-1990	1991-2000	1981-2000	1981-1990	1991-2000
Manufacturing	-0.2	0.3	-0.7	7.7	8.7	6.8
Food	2.1	1.1	3.0	3.7	3.2	4.2
Beverage	0.1	-1.9	1.9	5.9	5.4	6.2
Tobacco	1.9	4.0	0.1	4.7	2.1	6.9
Textile	-1.7	-3.1	-0.4	9.9	5.5	13.9
Wearing Apparel	0.4	-0.2	0.9	5.0	3.5	6.4
Leather	2.3	1.6	3.0	3.8	4.5	3.2
Wood	-2.0	-2.4	-1.7	6.8	3.7	9.6
Paper	0.1	1.0	-0.7	18.8	38.3	1.2
Ind. Chemical	-0.5	-2.8	1.6	16.7	24.6	8.7
Rubber	2.9	4.2	1.8	3.5	5.2	1.9
Plastic	0.3	-0.4	0.9	6.3	5.5	7.0
Glass	-1.1	2.7	-4.6	11.2	17.3	5.7
Iron/Steel	-2.3	-7.5	2.3	14.5	23.6	6.3
Non-ferrous Iron	9.5	17.3	2.6	14.1	18.2	10.3
Metal	-0.6	-2.1	0.7	7.3	9.6	5.2
EE	-2.4	-2.5	-2.4	8.9	9.7	8.2
Transport	-2.2	-6.9	2.0	8.2	9.3	7.2
Semicond/components	-2.2	-0.5	-3.8	10.4	12.7	8.3

sales. The insignificant improvement in unit labor costs is a cause for concern as it reflects stagnation in labor cost competitiveness.

On a sectoral basis, the results are mixed. Nine of the seventeen industries under study suffered declining labor cost competitiveness. Over the two sub-periods, there was an increase in unit labor cost in eleven of the industries. The EE sector is not spared although the growth rates remained negative in both the periods. In 2001, there was a further increase in unit labor costs of almost 10 percent. This is particularly alarming in view of the increased competition from low-cost producing countries. The problem might be due to a skilled labor shortage, high worker turnover, poor labor mix and the like. If it is left unchecked, it may lead to further shutdowns and relocation of MNCs to other countries with comparatively lower labor cost.

Capital Intensity

Capital intensity is measured here by the amount of fixed assets allocated to each unit of labor or simply the capital-labor ratio. Higher capital intensity provides the advantage of technology, quality and volume to increase productivity. Table 6-2 indicates that in the manufacturing sector and its industries, capital intensity registered positive growth rates in 1981–2000. However, this does not mean there was strong capital outlay and investment continuously throughout the period. The majority of industries (10 of the 17 industries) suffered a decline in the growth rate of capital intensity over the two sub-periods. Capital outlay is influenced by market conditions, capacity utilization and new investments including FDI. In particular, growth in capital intensity declined in all industries (except two) in 1998, a direct result of adverse market conditions.

The prospect does not look encouraging either. With the bulk of FDI to this region going to China, there would be relatively less new capital investment in technology-embodied machinery and equipment. Moreover, in an environment of excess capacity, firms are cautious and reluctant to commit new capital outlay. This would inevitably lead to relatively more labor-intensive methods of production. This is evident from more recent data that showed capital intensity continuing to decline (NPC 2003).

Total Factor Productivity

Since the early nineties, there have been various estimates of TFP growth for the Malaysian economy. However, these estimates are not strictly comparable due to differences in methodology (which include growth accounting and estimations of production functions), data and sample period. This difficulty is compounded by the fact that insufficient information was provided as to the measurement of the key variables, for example, measure of capital and input share. Regardless of these differences, however, most of the estimation on TFP growth for the Malaysian economy ranged from 0.5 percent to 3 percent depending on the periods under study (World Bank 1993, Kawai 1994, Thomas and Wang 1992 as reported in Tham 1995). A few studies estimated the TFP growth to be negative. For example, Tham (1995), using the growth accounting method, concluded that TFP growth was -1.4 percent for 1971 to 1987. Consequently, its contribution to GDP growth was negative 23 percent. A general conclusion from these studies is that the Malaysian economic growth is highly dependent on investment in capital accumulation. Tham (1995) estimated that capital growth contributed 104 percent to the growth process. Recent estimates are more encouraging. The National Productivity Corporation (2001), for example, estimated that for 1996–2001, TFP grew at an average of 0.43 percent compared to 2.3 percent for capital and 1.4 percent for labor. Consequently, the contribution of TFP to economic growth was 10.4 percent while capital and labor contributed 55.7 percent and 33.9 percent respectively.

The focus of this chapter is on the manufacturing sector. The choice is based on its crucial role in the development process and data availability at the sub-sectoral level. Estimates of TFP growth were computed at the 3-digit level[3] covering the period 1981 to 2000. The results of the TFP growth estimates are shown in Table 6-3.

It is evident from Table 6-3 that the manufacturing sector experienced rapid growth with an average of 11.3 percent for the period under study. None of the

Table 6-3   Growth Rates in Output, Inputs and TFP in the Manufacturing
Sector 1981–2000 (%)

Industries	Output	Capital	Labor	Other Inputs	TFP
Manufacturing	11.32	12.95	6.12	11.36	0.45
Food	6.90	7.10	3.69	6.90	0.07
Beverage	4.36	4.85	-0.44	6.26	-0.64
Tobacco	2.46	7.09	3.20	3.70	-2.11
Textile	7.28	9.56	0.98	7.09	-0.63
Wearing Apparel	11.00	10.86	6.27	11.13	0.77
Leather	9.62	9.16	6.43	9.71	0.59
Wood	7.47	8.33	3.31	7.71	0.01
Paper	14.72	19.28	9.27	14.60	-0.74
Ind. Chemical	15.34	22.25	7.59	14.65	-8.27
Rubber	5.63	7.54	4.47	4.98	-0.21
Plastic	14.82	15.21	9.59	14.67	0.48
Glass	14.77	16.73	8.35	14.03	-2.06
Iron/Steel	10.24	14.75	4.10	10.83	-3.31
Non-ferrous Iron	3.55	16.00	7.37	2.51	-3.82
Metal	10.81	11.99	5.68	10.87	0.01
EE	16.51	16.69	8.59	16.99	0.20
Semicond/components	16.42	18.32	8.93	16.55	0.05
Transport	12.32	11.35	5.43	13.29	0.58
Manufacturing 1981–1990	9.96	13.30	6.00	9.81	-0.37
Manufacturing 1991–2000	12.55	12.63	6.23	12.75	1.14

industries registered any negative growth rates. This rapid growth was driven by capital and other inputs growth that reached 12.9 and 11.4 percent respectively. Labor grew at the relatively slower rate of 6.1 percent. The disparity in capital and labor growth may imply sub-optimal capital utilization with firms operating with excess capacity.

The good performance of the EE sector and the semiconductor and component industries was encouraging. The high growth rate of 16 percent in this sector is not unexpected given the almost dominance of the sector in manufacturing. There was an increase of above 3 percent over the two sub-periods.

TFP growth was 0.45 percent for the period. In comparison, Tham (1995) obtained 0.3 percent for the period 1986–91 while Okamoto (1994) also obtained 0.3 percent for 1986–90. Oguchi et al. (2002) obtained 0.95 percent for domestic manufacturing firms for 1992–96. This is remarkably close to our estimate of 1.1 percent for the sub-period 1991–2000. The similarity in the various estimates is somewhat surprising, considering that different methodologies, data sets and sample periods were used.

The relatively low rate of TFP growth is due to the fact that more than half of the sub-sectors (9 of 17) experienced negative TFP growth. Nevertheless, the positive TFP growth is encouraging as it indicates improved utilization

Table 6-4   Contribution to Growth in the Manufacturing Sector
1981–2000 (%)

Industries	Capital	Labor	Other Inputs	TFP
Manufacturing	45.2	11.4	39.5	3.9
Food	22.5	1.9	74.5	1.1
Beverage	58.4	-0.8	57.1	-14.7
Tobacco	77.1	7.4	31.3	-15.8
Textile	78.2	1.4	29.0	-8.7
Wearing Apparel	21.3	9.9	61.8	7.0
Leather	36.1	9.4	4.8	6.1
Wood	54.8	5.6	39.4	0.2
Paper	60.3	3.6	35.2	0.9
Ind. Chemical	76.0	1.8	23.9	-1.7
Rubber	47.3	6.3	50.2	-3.8
Plastic	53.9	7.9	34.9	3.3
Glass	74.5	6.4	33.0	-13.9
Iron/Steel	113.7	2.2	16.4	-32.3
Non-ferrous Iron	55.6	8.6	43.1	-7.3
Metal	48.3	5.6	46.0	0.1
EE	23.6	3.8	71.3	1.2
Semicond/components	26.0	4.2	69.5	0.3
Transport	41.3	3.8	50.2	4.7
Manufacturing 1981–1990	52.7	13.6	37.3	-3.7
Manufacturing 1991–2000	39.7	9.8	41.3	9.1

and management of resources and inputs in the manufacturing process. Comparing the 2 sub-periods, it is evident that there is a dramatic improvement in TFP growth (from a negative growth in 1981–90 to a positive 1.1 percent in 1991–2000). This is despite the sector suffering a demoralizing negative growth rate of -12.7 percent in 1997–98. The TFP growth in the second sub-period also corresponded with a declining growth rate of capital. This may indicate that excess capacities of previous periods are substantially reduced, resulting in increased TFP growth (Wong 2003).

It is apparent from Table 6-4 that capital and other inputs were the main sources of growth in the manufacturing sector during the period 1981–2000. Capital contributed 45 percent while other inputs contributed 39 percent. The relatively low contribution of labor to growth points to the need to improve on labor skills and the formation of human capital. The contribution of TFP growth was 3.9 percent. Although it is evident that the manufacturing sector is highly dependent on input growth, the significant improvement in the contribution of TFP is a good sign for it reflects an improvement in labor quality, technical progress, increased investment in technology-embodied machinery and research capabilities.

Of the eight industries where TFP contributed positively to growth, only two industries have contributions exceeding 5 percent. Over the two sub-periods, there was improvement in TFP contributions in 6 of the industries. In the EE sector, the contribution of TFP was negative in the eighties but turned positive in the nineties. This is not surprising as the sector has made steady progress moving up the value-chain of production evolving from simple assembly, packaging and testing activities in the eighties to sophisticated higher-end production including silicon wafer making, wafer fabrication and chip designing in the nineties. A striking feature on sources of growth in the EE sector is that the contribution of other inputs far exceeded that of capital. This reflects the relatively low value added content in the industry and the dependence on imported intermediate inputs. This problem should be addressed urgently, for example, by taking steps to accelerate growth of import substitution industries producing these intermediate inputs.

Technical Progress and Factor Substitution

As discussed earlier, the model used for the estimation of technical progress and factor substitution is:

$$ln\ v = \beta_1 + \beta_2 \ln w + \beta_3 t + \varepsilon$$

for which σ, the estimated elasticity of substitution is the estimated coefficient $\hat{\beta}_2$ and λ, the estimated rate of technical progress can be derived as

$$\hat{\lambda} = \frac{\hat{\beta}_3}{(1 - \hat{\beta}_2)}\ .$$

As the data are time series data, they have to be tested for stationarity before estimations of the model could proceed. Using the Augmented Dickey-Fuller unit root tests (Dickey and Fuller 1981), the variables used in the estimation, that is, v (real value added per worker) and w (real wages per worker) in the manufacturing sector and all the sub-industries are shown to be I (1) variables. Subsequently the Engle-Granger procedure (Engle and Granger 1987) was used to test for co-integration of the two variables. It was also shown that there is co-integration between v and w in all the cases. This implies the existence of a long run relationship between the two and it validates the estimation of the regression model.

The estimated equations were tested for normality of the residuals using Jarque-Bera statistics. The null hypothesis of normally distributed errors was not rejected at the 5 percent level of significance in all (except one) of the industries. The Breusch-Godfrey LM test was used to test for serial correlation. Serial correlation up to order two was present in the regressions in only four of the industry groups. These four equations were re-estimated by using the Newey-West procedure for correcting the OLS standard errors.[4]

The equations were also tested for structural break due to the Asian crisis. It is possible that the production structure of the manufacturing industries may have changed after the crisis. If that is the case, factor substitution and technology utilization in production may be fundamentally different between the pre-crisis and post-crisis periods. Chow's forecast test is used to test for the possibility of this structural change. Compared to Chow's breakpoint test, this test is more appropriate since it is not restricted by the condition that each sub-sample must have at least as many observations as the number of estimation parameters. In our sample, there are only three observations after the crisis.

The results of the test showed that, in all except for two of the industries, the null hypothesis of parameter stability or no structural change is not rejected. This indicates that the Asian crisis did not cause a fundamental change in the production structure in the manufacturing industries. This result is not unexpected since the Malaysian economy recovered from the crisis in a relatively short time.

The estimated results are shown in Table 6-5. Of the 17 industries covered in the study, 15 showed positive elasticity of substitution. The results obtained are similar to those of Khor and Maisom (2000). Twelve of these elasticity values are less than one[5] while three others are greater than one. Five of the elasticity values are not significantly different from zero implying that during the period under study the production functions in these five industries are close to fixed-proportion Leontief-type of functions.

In another eight of the industries, the null hypothesis of unitary elasticity could not be rejected, indicating the possibility of Cobb-Douglas production in these industries. In two other industries, the form of the production function is unclear as the estimated coefficients are significantly different from either zero or one.

In particular, the elasticity of substitution is greater than one in the industrial chemical, iron and steel industries. These industries are highly capital-intensive industries[6] and have high growth rates in capital intensity (see Table 6-2). In fact there is a correlation between capital intensity and substitution elasticity. Substitution elasticity is likely to increase with increasing capital intensity (Hoffman and Tan 1980). In the present study, the correlation coefficient between the two is 0.45 and is significantly different from zero.[7] It is possible for industries that have high substitution elasticity and capital intensity, to reduce capital intensity by substituting labor for capital with the use of capital-

Table 6-5   Elasticity of Substitution in the Manufacturing Sector: 1981-2000

Industries	$\hat{\beta}_1$	$\hat{\beta}_2=\sigma$	$\hat{\beta}_3$	$H_o: \sigma=0$	$H_o: \sigma=1$
Manufacturing	2.32	0.72	0.02	reject	accept
Food	7.14	-0.38	0.05	accept	reject
Beverage	4.67	0.33	0.03	accept	reject
Tobacco	2.45	0.88	-0.01	reject	accept
Textile	1.14	0.90	0.03	reject	accept
Wearing Apparel	3.55	0.18	0.04	accept	reject
Leather	0.36	1.11	-0.02	reject	accept
Wood	2.82	0.47	0.03	accept	reject
Paper	2.25	0.67	0.03	reject	accept
Ind. Chemical	-3.83	2.25	-0.04	reject	reject
Rubber	2.03	0.77	0.01	reject	accept
Plastic	3.62	0.28	0.05	accept	reject
Glass	5.08	0.08	0.08	accept	reject
Iron/Steel	-3.51	2.08	-0.04	reject	reject
Non-ferrous Iron	1.62	0.90	0.01	reject	accept
Metal	2.33	0.63	0.03	reject	accept
EE	1.64	0.84	0.03	reject	accept
Semicond/components	2.61	0.61	0.04	reject	accept
Transport	10.9	-1.18	0.08	reject	reject
Manufacturing 1981–1990[6]	2.43	0.69	0.02	reject	accept
Manufacturing 1991–2000[7]	2.42	0.67	0.03	reject	accept

augmenting technological progress. On the other hand, for those industries which have substitution elasticity less than one, and low capital intensities (and low growth rates, see Table 6-2), capital-augmenting technical progress may cause substitution of capital for labor thereby raising capital intensity. In the current situation where skilled labor is in short supply, the lack of substitution possibilities of labor for capital in these industries presents an opportunity for technical change that is capital augmenting.

The rates of technical progress in the manufacturing sector are shown in Table 6-6. As the rates were computed from the same equation, they depend on the estimates of the elasticities of substitution.

The rate of technical progress is positive in fifteen of the seventeen industries. A common characteristic of the two industries (tobacco and leather) that experienced negative rates of technical progress is that they have low capital intensities and the substitution elasticities are relatively high. As indicated by the growth in capital intensities (Table 6-1), the levels of reinvestments in these industries are also low. Given the relatively high substitution possibility, it is expected that these two industries would continue to use labor-intensive methods of production. Industries that have low rates of technical progress ($\lambda < 0.04$) include the food, textiles and transport industries. These industries use low levels

Table 6-6   Rate of Technical Progress in the Manufacturing
Sector 1981–2000

Industries	λ
Manufacturing	0.072
Food	0.033
Beverage	0.041
Tobacco	-0.007
Textile	0.035
Wearing Apparel	0.049
Leather	-0.018
Wood	0.064
Paper	0.088
Ind. Chemical	0.064
Rubber	0.042
Plastic	0.063
Glass	0.083
Iron/Steel	0.040
Non-ferrous Iron	0.140
Metal Prod.	0.079
EE	0.163
Semicond/components	0.098
Transport	0.037
Manufacturing 1981–1990	0.074
Manufacturing 1991–2000	0.088

of technology in their production processes and rely on relatively cheaper foreign labor. The continual reliance on labor-intensive production would not only slow down the rate of technological innovation but also conflicts with government efforts in promoting laborsaving production technologies in industries.

The majority of industries have moderate rates of technical progress ranging from 4 to 8 percent. These industries have moderate growth rates of productivity and capital intensity (Table 6-1). Except for the iron and steel, and industrial chemical industries, the substitution elasticity is low in these industries. This presents opportunities for increased capital intensity and productivity by the use of newer technology. On the other hand, the industries that experienced high rates of technical progress, namely, the EE, non-ferrous metal and paper products industries,[8] are also among the industries with the highest growth rates in capital intensity. Comparatively, these are the technologically advanced industries that offer scope for further expansion. The EE industries especially have to constantly upgrade technology to remain competitive. At a rate of technical progress of 16.3 percent, it appears that the EE sub-sector in Malaysia is keeping pace with rapid technological advancement prevalent in the industry. Other studies have shown that the sub-sector utilizes a relatively high level of technology in its production processes and that considerable technology transfer has taken place (UNDP 1994; Lai and Narayanan 1997; Hobday 1999).

Conclusion

The study has found that if labor productivity is measured by value added per worker, all the sub-sectors have registered positive growth rates. In particular, the two most important export-oriented industries of electrical and electronics, and textiles experienced high growth rates in productivity. Overall, productivity in the manufacturing sector grew at annual rate of 5.37 percent between 1981 and 2000. The increase in labor productivity occurred despite the environment of decreasing capital productivity and excess capacity. The steady rise in labor productivity is attributed to increased efficiency in management and labor, improved work attitude of workers, technological progress and demand conditions.

There is a marginal decrease in unit labor cost during the period as labor productivity increases managed to offset the increase in real wages. However the insignificant decline in unit labor cost is a cause for concern since it reflects stagnation in labor competitiveness. Part of the reason for this is the excess capacity mentioned earlier. However there are other factors beyond the control of the manufacturing firms, such as lower external demand and sluggish sales.

Although capital intensity registered positive growth rates in 1981–2000, there are indications that growth is diminishing in many of the industries in the second sub-period. Apart from adverse market condition in the period immediately after the economic crisis, excess capacity is a determining factor in investors' reluctance to commit additional capital outlay for new machinery and equipment.

TFP growth was 0.45 percent during the period under study. This estimate together with estimates for the two sub-periods, 1981–1990 and 1991–2000, are remarkably similar to various studies although differing in terms of methodology, data and sub-periods used. Although the TFP growth is relatively low, it is nevertheless encouraging as it reflects improved utilization and management of resources in the production process.

From the analysis of the sources of growth, it is evident that the manufacturing output growth is capital-driven. Capital contributed 45 percent towards growth while other inputs contributed 39 percent. The increased contribution of TFP towards growth in the second sub-period is encouraging as it signifies technical progress, which in fact, has increased from 7.4 percent to 8.8 percent over the two sub-periods (Table 6-6).

The indicators on productivity give mixed results. In terms of either labor productivity or TFP, signs are encouraging but the optimism is dampened by lingering excess capacity, stagnation in labor cost competitiveness and an overall decline in capital intensity growth. Unless these problems are addressed, labor productivity and TFP growth may well reverse in the years ahead.

In terms of substitution elasticity and rates of technical progress, the study showed that most of the industries have low levels of substitution elasticity and low to moderate rates of technical progress. The findings on substitution elasticity are similar to an earlier cross-sectional study (Hoffman and Tan 1980) and a more recent time series study (Khor and Maisom 2000). In the current state of technology, the low level of elasticity of substitution would mean that capital-augmenting technical progress reduces labor intensity and consequently the demand for labor. It is appropriate to use capital-intensive production processes that embody capital-augmenting technical progress to reduce the reliance on labor and thus alleviate the current problem of skilled labor shortage.

The industries that have either negative or low rates of technical progress are characterized by labor-intensive production processes, which are still possible due to the use of foreign labor. This retards the shift to higher-technology, higher value added production even for cases where capital-augmenting technical progress could be introduced. The majority of the industries have moderate rates of technical progress as well as low elasticity of factor substitution. This gives scope for increased use of capital-augmenting production processes and capital intensity. As expected, the export-oriented EE industry has the highest rate of technical progress. This industry has to upgrade technology regularly to sustain competitiveness in the market.

As indicated earlier, the growth of capital is more rapid compared to labor growth (Table 6-3). This would lead to an increase in capital intensity growth, which averaged 7.7 percent for 1981–2000 (see Table 6-2).

Increases in capital intensity, use of capital-augmenting technology, technology transfers and TFP growth are crucial issues. Evidently technological upgrading is the most critical since it embodies all the others. It is therefore important to develop a more mature indigenous technological base since it can accelerate both product and production technology. In this regard, the promotion of R&D activities is essential. The overall level of R&D functions in the manufacturing sector is far from satisfactory and the pace of such activities is dictated by the MNCs that dominate the technology-intensive industries. Clearly such R&D activities can only succeed in the presence of a pool of highly skillful manpower, which Malaysia lacks. The shortage of skilled human resources is a challenge and the problem cannot be solved in the short run. The education system should be reviewed and geared towards the teaching of science and technology. This is an essential step to improving the formation of human capital. An incentive system of subsidies, grants and soft loans should be devised aimed at encouraging science education in institutions, harnessing and upgrading existing science and training centers and fostering collaboration between industries and educational institutions. The government is well aware of these issues that are productivity-related as is evident in the various planning documents, which identified many of these problems. How these issues are addressed would determine the direction of further growth of the manufacturing industries.

Notes

1 Paper presented at *JSPS-NRCT Workshop: Perspectives of Roles of State, Market, Society, and Economic Cooperation in Asia*: November 6–7, 2003, Center for Southeast Asian Studies, Kyoto University, Japan.
2 An ongoing project in which the writer is currently involved.
3 The 3-digit code for 1981–1999 was based on the Malaysia Industrial Classification (MIC) code. The classification system was subsequently changed to the Malaysia Standard Industrial Classification (MSIC) from year 2000. Some adjustments were made to ensure data compatibility.
4 Strictly speaking, the Newey-West procedure is valid only for large samples (Gujarati 2003).
5 The estimated elasticity could be biased upwards due to the fact that the perfect competition assumption used in the CES production function is not realistic. Wages are generally lower than the marginal product of labor and the computed elasticities should actually be lower (Hoffman and Tan 1980).
7 For comparison, Hoffman and Tan (1980) estimated the correlation coefficient between the two to be 0.33 and also significantly different from zero.
8 Khor and Maisom (2000) obtained similar results.

References

Arrow, K.J., H. Chenery, B. Minhas and R. Solow. 1961. Capital-Labor Substitution and Economic Efficiency. *Review of Economics and Statistics*, 43: pp. 225–250.
Brown, M. 1968. *Theory and Measurement of Technological Change*. Cambridge University Press: UK.
Department of Statistics. *Annual Survey of Manufacturing Industries* (various issues). Department of Statistics: Malaysia, Kuala Lumpur.
——— . 2001. *Malaysia Economic Statistics—Time Series 2000*. Department of Statistics: Malaysia, Kuala Lumpur.

Dickey, D.A., and W.A. Fuller. 1981. Likelihood Ratio Statistics for Autoregressive Time Series with a Unit Root. *Econometrica*, 49: pp. 1057–1072.

Diwan, R.K. 1965. An Empirical Estimate of the Elasticity of Substitution Production Function. *Indian Economic Journal*, 12: pp. 347–366.

Engle, R.F. and C.W. Granger. 1987. Cointegration and Error Correction: Representation, Estimation and Testing. *Econometrica*, 55: pp. 251–276.

Gujarati, D. 2003. *Basic Econometrics* (4th edition). McGraw Hill: New York.

Hobday, M. 1999. Understanding Innovation in Electronics in Malaysia. In Jomo, K.S., G. Felker and R. Rasiah. eds. *Industrial Technology Development in Malaysia*. Routledge: London.

Hoffman L. and Tan, S.E. 1980. *Industrial Growth, Employment and Foreign Investment in Peninsular Malaysia*. Oxford University Press: UK.

Jorgenson, D.W., F. Gollop and B. Fraumeni. 1987. *Productivity and the U.S. Economic Growth*. North Holland: Amsterdam.

Kawai, H. 1994. International Comparative Analysis of Economic Growth: Trade Liberalization and Productivity. *The Developing Economies*, 32: pp. 373–397.

Khor, T.L. and Maisom Abdullah, 2000, *Technological Progress and Factor Substitution in the Malaysian Manufacturing Industry 1978–1994*. Working Paper 17, Faculty of Economics and Management, Universiti Putra Malaysia: Kuala Lumpur.

Kmenta, J. 1967. On Estimation of the CES Production Function. *International Economic Review*, 8: pp. 180–189.

Krugman, P. 1994. The Myth of Asia's Miracle. *Foreign Affairs*, 73: pp. 62–78.

Lai Y.W. and S. Narayanan. 1997. The Quest for Technological Competence via MNCs: A Malaysian Case Study. *Asian Economic Journal*, 11: pp. 407–422.

Lu, Y.C. and Fletscher, L.B. 1968. A Generalization of the CES Production Function. *Review of Economics and Statistics*, 50: pp. 449–452.

NPC. 2003. *Productivity Report 2002*. National Productivity Corporation: Malaysia, Petaling Jaya.

Oguchi, N., Nor Aini M.A., Zainon B., Rauzah Z.A. and Mazlina S. 2002. Productivity of Foreign and Domestic Firms in the Malaysian Manufacturing Industry. *Asian Economic Journal*, 16: pp. 215–228.

Solow, R. 1957. Technical Change and the Aggregate Production Function. *Review of Economics and Statistics*, 39: pp. 312–320.

——— . 1962. Technical Progress, Capital Formation and Economic Growth. *American Economic Review*, 52: pp. 76–86.

Tham, S.Y. 1995. Productivity, Growth and Development in Malaysia. *Singapore Economic Review*, 40: pp. 41–63.

Thomas, V. and Wang, Y. 1992. Government Policies and Productivity Growth: Is East Asia an Exception? Paper presented at the *World Bank Workshop on the Role of Government and East Asian Success*: Honolulu.

UNDP. 1994. *Technology Transfer in Malaysia: The Electronics and Electrical Goods Sector and the Supporting Industries in Penang*. United Nations Development Program: Kuala Lumpur.

Wong, M.N. 2003. The Productivity Performance of the Manufacturing Sector in Malaysia: the Case of Sarawak. Paper presented at the *Hawaii International Conference on Social Science*: 12–15 June, Honolulu.

World Bank. 1993. *The East Asian Miracle: Economic Growth and Public Policy*. Oxford University Press: UK.

7

Rural Economy in Myanmar at the Crossroads: With Special Reference to Rice Policies

Koichi Fujita

Introduction

Along with Thailand and Vietnam, Myanmar (Burma) was one of the major rice-exporting countries in the world before World War II. Much of this was due to the vast alluvial delta, formed by three big rivers in mainland Southeast Asia (the Chao Phraya, Ayeyarwaddy and Mekong), being rapidly reclaimed for rice production and export beginning in the mid-19th century with a large-scale migration of people from the upper part of the river basin. Thailand still remains the largest rice exporter in the world today and Vietnam has also recovered its status after the adoption of the Doi Moi policy in 1986. In recent years, exports of rice exceeded 6 million tons from Thailand and 3–4 million tons from Vietnam. However, rice exports from Myanmar, about 1.5 million tons until the mid-1960s, declined sharply thereafter and have continued to be a negligible amount for the last three decades.

The inward looking and state-controlled economic policies adopted under the 'Burmese Way to Socialism' program during 1962–1988 accounts for a large part of the disappointing performance of Myanmar's rice sector. In particular, government procurement of rice at low prices and its monopolistic exports by the state were the major obstacles. In the socialist period, most major crops were also controlled by the state in the same manner leading to a serious stagnation of the agricultural sector.

However, in 1987, just before the collapse of the socialist regime, the agricultural market was finally liberalized. It had a huge impact on the agricultural sector and the production of some crops increased remarkably after the liberalization. A notable example is pulses and beans for export, mainly to India. This export, only 17,000 tons in 1988–89, increased rapidly to 449,000 tons in 1992–93 and 742,000 tons in 1997–98, reaching more than 80 percent of total agricultural exports in Myanmar. It indicates a high development potential of Myanmar agriculture once institutional barriers are removed. From another point of view, Myanmar succeeded in taking advantage of India's loss in comparative advantage in pulses production after the 'Green Revolution.'

On the other hand, the liberalization of the agricultural market in 1987 caused a surge in the prices of agricultural products including rice, which in turn triggered the 1988 democratic movement. As a result, after the movement was suppressed, controls over the rice market were revived; i.e., the government procurement system was reintroduced despite a drastic reduction in the quota (from 25–30 baskets to 10–12 baskets[1] per acre of paddy field) and the monopoly of rice exports by the state was continued. These policies, along with the nationalized agricultural land tenure system and the heavy intervention by the state on crop choices of farmers, remain major institutional constraints that hamper agricultural development in Myanmar. Needless to say, the major difference between pulses and rice lies in its importance in the diet. Rice is the staple food for Myanmar people, meaning that price hikes can easily impact consumers adversely; this makes it difficult for policymakers to liberalize the rice market as compared to other agricultural commodities, including pulses and beans. In other words, there is a serious dilemma in the Myanmar's rice sector between producers' benefit and consumers' (thereby the present military regime's) benefit.

The purpose of this chapter is to analyze Myanmar's rice sector post 1988 to show how the issue is critical for the Myanmar economy as a whole to develop. In the following section this chapter first briefly reviews macroeconomic development in Myanmar since 1988. In section three, the development of the rice sector during the same period is reviewed, centering on the 'success' of the double cropping of rice under the Summer Paddy Program since 1992–93. However, this development was soon constrained in the mid-1990s due to the worsening terms of trade for rice production under the current policy framework, as well as problems in the rural credit market. Such issues are discussed in detail in the fourth section, based on a case study of a typical rice double-cropping village conducted in Ayeyarwaddy Division in 2001.[2] Section five explains recent movements in Myanmar's rice policy, which are considered to be epoch-making. At the same time several problems concerning the new policy are also discussed here. In the final section, the summary and conclusions of the chapter are presented.

Macroeconomic Development of Myanmar Since 1988

In Myanmar, the new military regime of SLORC (State Law and Order Restoration Council)/SPDC (State Peace and Development Council)[3] remains in power more than 15 years after the rise of the democratization movement in

1988. As mentioned above, the contradictions of the socialist policy framework had deepened by 1987, when the bold decision to liberalize the agricultural marketing system was finally made and implemented. Under the SLORC/SPDC regime, substantial efforts have continuously been made to shift toward a market economy and to open up Myanmar's economy to foreign countries. Nevertheless, many areas remain under state control and this, in turn, retards sustainable economic development. The problems of the dual exchange rate system, the delay of reform of the state economic enterprises (SEEs), the arbitrary and inconsistent policies and regulations in industry and trade, state ownership of land and control over the land tenure system, the planned (compulsory) cropping system, the rice procurement system and the ban for private rice export are the most important areas among others. The chronic macroeconomic imbalances such as the balance-of-payments deficit, the fiscal deficit, foreign reserve shortage, high inflation etc., are tightly connected to such problems. Before discussing the rice sector, let us briefly review the performance of Myanmar's macroeconomic change since 1988, based on available official statistics.[4]

Table 7-1 shows the growth rate of GDP and its sector share since 1988 until the end of the 1990s. The quick recovery and the favorably high growth rate of GDP after the sharp drop during the end of the Newin regime are evident. The liberalization policies that were adopted by the SLORC/SPDC government to enhance a market economy were quite successful, at least until the mid-1990s. Firstly, however, it should be noted that it was not until 1993–94 that the economy recovered to the same level it had been in 1986–87 or 1987–88. Secondly, the very slow structural changes of the economy are impressive; i.e., the agricultural sector still occupies about 43 percent of total output even at the end of the 1990s.

Table 7-2 indicates the economic structure in terms of labor force. The agricultural sector absorbs approximately two-thirds of the labor force. In addition, in spite of the seriousness of the problem of SEEs, which causes the fiscal deficit (as argued later), the contribution of the public sector in terms of employment is rather small. It is not clear from the data in Table 7-1, but there is a tendency of decelerated growth in the Myanmar economy since the mid-1990s, and especially after 1997 when the serious economic crisis impacted many Southeast Asian countries. The new flow of FDI (foreign direct investment), which was an important engine of growth during the first half of the 1990s in Myanmar, largely stopped after 1997, especially from Thailand, Singapore and Malaysia.

Table 7-3 illustrates the investment and saving rates at an aggregate level. The low and stagnant rates (well below 15 percent) are notable, and the low rates are even more apparent when compared to other Southeast Asian countries (Table

Table 7-1 GDP Growth and Sectoral Shares in Myanmar since 1988 (%)

	GDP growth	GDP share: Agriculture	Industry	Services
1988/89	-11.4	47.9	11.5	40.6
1989/90	3.7	48.3	12.8	39.0
1990/91	2.8	47.8	13.1	39.1
1991/92	-0.6	47.0	13.4	39.7
1992/93	9.7	47.3	13.8	38.9
1993/94	6.0	46.7	14.4	38.9
1994/95	7.5	46.0	14.8	39.3
1995/96	6.9	45.1	15.6	39.4
1996/97	6.4	44.4	16.2	39.4
1997/98	5.7	43.6	16.7	39.7
1998/99	5.8	43.0	16.8	40.2
1999/2000	10.9	43.2	17.2	39.6

Source: World Bank (1999) for the years from 1988/89 to 1997/98; ADB (2001) for the years 1998/99 and 1999/2000.
Note: At constant 1985/86 prices.

Table 7-2 Employment Structure

	1989/90 Number ('000)	Share (%)	1997/98 Number ('000)	Share (%)
Sector				
Agriculture	10,608	69.7	12,093	65.9
Industry	1,400	9.2	2,213	12.1
Services	2,740	18.0	3,761	20.5
Unclassified	472	3.1	292	1.6
Employment in:				
Public	1,324	8.7	1,411	7.7
Private and cooperatives	13,897	91.3	16,948	92.3
Labor force				
Urban	n.a.	n.a.	4,418	22.4
Rural	n.a.	n.a.	15,325	77.6

Note: n.a.: Not available.
Source: World Bank (1999).

7-4).[5] Although a sector breakdown is not available in the case of saving rates, the tendency of a rapidly decreasing contribution of the public sector since 1998–99 is worthy of attention. This may indicate a crisis of the economy, especially in terms of the government budget deficit and foreign exchange reserves in the hands of the government.[6]

Table 7-5 provides data on the balance of payments. It is evident that there is a chronic trade deficit (the import value is more or less double the export value)

Table 7-3   Investment and Saving Rates (%)

	1988/89	1990/91	1992/93	1994/95	1995/96	1996/97	1997/98	1998/99	1999/2000
Gross investment	12.8	13.4	13.5	12.4	14.3	13.4	12.4	12.3	13.2
Public	5.8	6.8	5.4	5.5	6.8	6.7	6.1	4.9	3.7
Private	3.8	7.9	7.0	6.1	6.9	7.0	7.3	7.9	7.3
Stock changes	3.2	-1.3	1.0	0.8	0.6	-0.3	-0.9	-0.5	2.2
Savings	12.8	13.4	13.4	12.3	14.3	13.4	12.2	12.2	13.1
Public	-8.3	-3.2	-1.5						
Private	19.5	14.4	14.2	11.6	13.2	12.5			
Other	-0.1	0.2	0.2	0.3	0.3	0.3	11.9	12.0	13.0
Foreign	1.7	2.0	0.5	0.4	0.8	0.6	0.3	0.2	0.1

Source: ADB (2001).

Table 7-4   Investment and Saving Rates in Southeast Asia (%)

	Investment rate			Saving rate (domestic)		
	1980	1990	1997	1980	1990	1997
Myanmar	21.5	13.4	11.1	17.7	11.7	10.4
Malaysia	30.4	31.2	42.8	32.9	33.4	44.4
Thailand	29.1	41.4	35.0	22.3	34.0	34.9
Indonesia	20.9	30.7	31.6	29.2	32.3	31.0
Philippines	29.1	24.2	25.0	26.6	18.7	15.5
Vietnam	n.a.	12.6	29.0	n.a.	12.9	20.1

Note: n.a.: Not available.
Source: ADB (1998).

Table 7-5   Balance of Payments (US$ million)

	1988/89	1992/93	1995/96	1996/97	1997/98	1998/99	1999/2000
Trade balance	-225	-419	-897	-958	-1,149	-1,318	-1,228
Exports	320	591	934	930	1,011	1,113	1,138
Imports	-545	-1,010	-1,831	-1,888	-2,160	-2,431	-2,366
Service balance	148	23	-10	87	25	158	136
Private transfers (net)	79	122	460	457	465	490	488
Current account balance	2	-274	-447	-414	-659	-670	-604
As a % of GDP	0.2	-21.3	-16.2	-13.2	-20.9	-25.1	-21.7
Nonmonetary capital movements	58	35	413	309	767	908	336
Errors and omissions	-177	-40	14	-88	-64	-174	217
Overall balance	-117	-279	-20	-193	44	64	-51
Accumulation of arrears	176	294	-1	136	242	196	n.a.
External arrears	201	754	1,480	1,461	1,636	1,975	2,309
Gross reserves (end of period)	120.7	285.5	381.1	287.8	331.3	395.1	343.4
In month of imports	2.7	3.4	2.5	1.8	1.8	1.9	1.7

Note: n.a.: Not available.
Source: ADB (2001).

Table 7-6   Public Sector Budget (million kyats)

	1992/93	1995/96	1996/97	1997/98	1998/99	1999/2000
Union government	-6,328	-21,001	-19,636	-2,318	4,546	-20,152
Revenues and grants	20,536	39,007	54,284	87,243	116,306	106,835
Expenditure and net						
lending	26,864	60,008	73,920	89,561	111,760	126,987
SEE	-4,596	-12,964	-25,366	-47,494	-85,919	-71,356
Receipts	43,092	87,221	108,608	185,004	242,197	315,554
Expenditure	47,688	100,185	133,974	232,498	328,116	386,910
Public debt account	-1,589	-5,537	-7,090	-8,489	-12,495	-19,018
Public sector total	-12,513	-39,502	-52,092	-58,301	-93,868	-110,526
Financing	12,509	39,494	52,090	58,307	93,877	110,532
Foreign loans	486	675	351	1,066	2,001	807
TB issued	12,023	38,819	51,739	57,241	91,876	109,725
Fiscal deficit						
(as a % of GDP)	-5.0	-6.5	-6.6	-5.2	-5.8	-5.3
Revenue						
(as a % of GDP)	8.3	6.5	6.9	7.8	7.2	5.1
Expenditure						
(as a % of GDP)	13.3	13.0	13.5	13.0	13.1	10.4

Source: ADB (2001).

and the service balance and private transfers do not compensate for this deficit. As a result, there is a chronic deficit in the current account with the share of the current account deficit to GDP exceeding 20 percent by the end of the 1990s. As a result, external arrears accumulated and the foreign exchange reserves declined to less than a two-month-import level, which is highly critical.

The performance of fiscal balances is summarized in Table 7-6. The large and chronic fiscal deficit, and the contribution of SEEs to it, is notable in the table; i.e., the share of SEEs deficit to the total fiscal deficit is 81.5 percent in 1997–98, 91.5 percent in 1998–99 and 64.6 percent in 1999–2000. Moreover, the most problematic issue is the financing of the fiscal deficit through the issuing of treasury bills (TB), which were finally taken up by the central bank. Naturally, this resulted in serious inflation and depreciation of the currency: kyat. In addition, it should be noted that the ratio of government revenue to GDP is only 5–8 percent, indicating the extremely low capacity of the government in the areas of taxation.

Table 7-7 shows data on inflation and the exchange rate in recent years. The high (more than 20 percent per year) inflation and, in particular, the continuous price hikes in food and beverages had serious impacts on the livelihood of people. The purchasing power of the salary of government employees decreased rapidly and by the end of the 1990s, their real wage had fallen to below 30 percent of what it was in 1988–89. The weakened kyat is the result of both the chronic

Table 7-7   Inflation and Depreciation of the Currency

	1988/89	1992/93	1995/96	1996/97	1997/98	1998/99	1999/2000
CPI growth rate (%)	22.5	22.3	21.8	20.0	33.9	49.1	11.4
Food and beverages[a]	27.0	22.9	23.8	22.8	33.6	50.3	12.3
Nonfood[a]	14.2	21.2	18.1	14.8	34.5	46.9	9.7
Exchange rate							
Official	6.46	6.08	5.62	5.91	6.22	6.25	6.24
Market	46.94	103.42	115.00	147.00	209.00	318.00	344.00
Annual wage and pension per employee in public sector	4,690	12,359	13,929	13,832	13,994	14,293	16,345
Index of real wages	100.0	110.7	62.6	51.8	39.1	26.8	27.5
Annual wages (US$)	99.9	119.5	121.1	94.1	67.0	45.0	47.5

Note: a. Weight for food and beverages = 64.9; for nonfood = 35.1.
Source: ADB (2001).

balance-of-payments deficit and the fiscal deficit–caused inflation. The U.S. dollar continued to appreciate against the kyat and was equivalent to nearly 1,000 kyat in 2003, compared to the official rate of about 6 kyat. Depreciation of the kyat could theoretically promote rice production for export through price mechanisms. Instead, it was hampered by the price hike of imported inputs like chemical fertilizers and diesel oil under a policy environment in which private rice export was banned and the volume of rice exported by the government was strictly restricted.

Performance of the Rice Sector During the 1990s

As already noted, the rice sector in Myanmar has basically been stagnant since World War II. However, if we look at the performance of the sector more closely in Figure 7-1, several points can be noted. First, after the rapid reclamation process in the Ayeyarwaddy delta since the mid-19th century, rice production reached a plateau by the 1930s.[7] Since then, the sown area of rice stagnated for a long period until the 1990s when progress was made with the double cropping of rice under the Summer Paddy Program.

Second, rice yields also stagnated for a long period at about 1.5–1.6 tons per hectare (of paddy), but it began to rise in the mid-1970s, especially during 1978–83, reaching a level slightly lower than 3 tons per hectare.[8] The main factor that contributed to this increase in yield was the introduction of high yielding varieties (HYVs) along with the dissemination of chemical fertilizers under

Figure 7-1   Rice Production and Export in Myanmar[a]

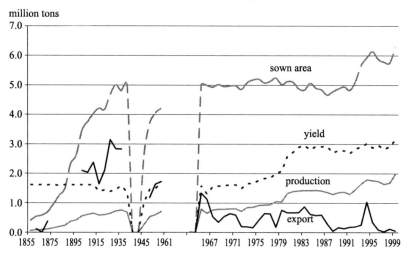

Note: a. Paddy in 10 million tons; sown area in million ha; yield in tons per ha; export in
      million tons.
Source: 1855-1970: U Khin Win (1991); 1971-1987: Tin Soe and Fisher (1990); 1988-:
      Central Statistical Organization and Ministry of Agriculture and Irrigation, Myanmar.

the Whole Township Special Rice Production Program.[9] Imported chemical
fertilizers, mainly through Japanese ODA (2 KR), also played an important role.
However, the yield of rice started to stagnate again thereafter where it remains
at this level today.

Keeping these points in mind, we can now discuss the increase in rice
production during the 1990s. The SLORC/SPDC government announced a new
policy for increased production of rice, called the Summer Paddy Program, in
1992–93. The government accelerated construction of dams and reservoirs in
order to expand canal-irrigated areas by investing a huge amount of its budget,
but the area expanded by these endeavors was actually much smaller than the
area that was expanded by pump irrigation, especially in the flat areas in the
Ayeyarwaddy delta. It was not difficult to expand pump-irrigated area in the
flat plains if field channels for both drainage purposes in the monsoon season
and irrigation purposes in the summer (dry) season are constructed. Such field
channels were in fact constructed by mobilizing voluntary manual labor of
residents in many deltaic villages under the Summer Paddy Program. Based
on this land improvement investment at the community level,[10] individual
farmers, in turn, invested in small-scale diesel pumps for irrigation, which
enabled progress of the double cropping of rice. In the deltaic areas, the land is

(deeply) flooded in the monsoon season so that the yield of monsoon paddy is usually low. However, if irrigation water is available, summer paddy production becomes possible in the dry season and its yield is much higher than monsoon paddy, by introducing HYVs with chemical fertilizers. Since the summer paddy is broadcasted in wet field conditions (instead of being transplanted), it is not only labor saving but also obtains a much higher yield.

However, as is shown in Figure 7-1, the expansion in irrigated area for rice double cropping had ceased by the mid-1990s. It seems that this was due to the exhaustion (technically) of easily irrigated areas by pumps. However, another plausible factor may be the worsened terms of trade for rice production. The price of chemical fertilizers and diesel oil, major imported inputs for pump-irrigated summer paddy production, increased rapidly under the depreciated currency, while the rice price did not rise to the same extent under its restricted export policy environment, as already mentioned.

This fundamental contradiction became very serious when the rice price collapsed in 2000, which continued for about one-and-a-half years. Figure 7-2 illustrates the movement in the rice price during the period in terms of the U.S. dollar per ton for milled rice. Some selected international FOB prices are compared with the domestic wholesale market price in Yangon, which is converted to the U.S. dollar by the market exchange rate. It is evident from the figure that the domestic rice price in Myanmar declined substantially from

Figure 7-2   International versus Domestic Rice Price

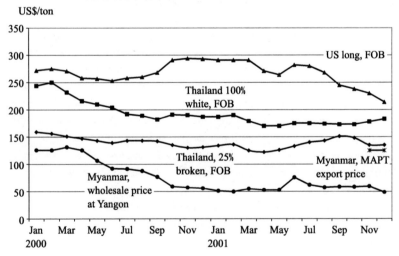

Source: Prepared by the author based on data from FAO, FAOSTAT and the Ministry of Agriculture and Irrigation, Myanmar.

about US$130 per ton in November 1999 to about US$50 by October 2000 and continued at such an extremely low level for more than one year (the farm gate price of paddy at this period was about 400 kyat per basket in lower Myanmar). On the other hand, the price of chemical fertilizers and diesel oil continued to surge under the depreciating currency. The worsened terms of trade for paddy production, especially for the summer paddy production, hit farmers very badly with the impact almost equivalent to the Great Depression of the late 1920s and the early 1930s.

The major problem was that the government did not prepare any counter-measures to reduce the effect of this serious crisis. On the contrary, the government stuck to the planned (compulsory) cropping system; i.e., farmers continued to have to meet obligations to grow monsoon paddy in farm land that was categorized as paddy field (*le*) as well as having to grow summer paddy in paddy field where irrigation water was available. The result was that many farmers, even while understanding that if they grow paddy they would lose out, were obliged to grow paddy in line with strong pressure from the government. When we conducted a study in Ayeyarwaddy Division in June 2001, the farmers were already hurting badly from the extremely low rice price at harvesting season of the last summer paddy, but they were being forced to grow monsoon paddy without sufficient working capital in hand. To make matters worse, the government had already launched a rice self-sufficiency policy at each state/ divisions level and did not change this policy initiative even in this low rice price period. This policy had the effect of increasing rice production in areas with less of a comparative advantage in rice production (such as the Shan State and Taninthayi Division), further dampening the domestic rice price in Myanmar.

In the next section, these problems are investigated more concretely by examining the situation of a pump-irrigated village in Ayeyarwaddy Division where the author conducted a survey in June 2001.

Case Study: Perspectives from a Pump-Irrigated Village in the Ayeyarwaddy Division

Outline of the Study Village and Sample Households
The study village belongs to the Myaungmya Township in Myaungmya District, Ayeyarwaddy Division and is about a one-hour journey by vehicle to the northwest of Myaungmya town where the district headquarters is located. The village is located on the newly formed portions of the Ayeyarwaddy delta and so forms a totally flat topography. The village tract (the lowest administrative unit in rural Myanmar; hereafter referred to as the village) consists of eight

Table 7-8   Distribution of Sampled Households

	Number of Households	Households with possibility of inheriting farmland in future	Number of household members	Average members per household
Nonfarm households	33	6	157	4.76
Agricultural labor households[a]	18	1	88	4.89
Other landless households	15	5	69	4.60
Farm households	67	4	353	5.27
-2.50 acres	8	1	41	5.13
2.51-5.00 acres	13	0	57	4.38
5.01-10.00 acres	25	2	134	5.36
10.01-15.00 acres	12	1	68	5.67
15.01acres+	9	0	53	5.89

Note: a. Agricultural labor households are defined as households with more than 50% of
their income coming from agricultural wages.
Source: Survey by author conducted June 22–27, 2001.

hamlets with a total 515 households and 2,452 persons in 2001. The total area of
the village is 2,871 acres, among which farmland comprises 2,327 acres. Paddy
field (*le*) is the largest, occupying 2,254 acres, followed by 42 acres of palm land
(*dani hcan*) and 31 acres of garden (*uyin hcan*). According to 2000–01 crop
production statistics collected by the Myanmar Agricultural Service (MAS), the
sown area was 2,225 acres of monsoon paddy and 2,184 acres of summer paddy.
The average yield for the entire village was 69.4 baskets and 93.8 baskets per
acre, respectively (if converted to tons per hectare, 3.58 tons and 4.84 tons).[11]

Out of the total 515 households, 283 households (55.0 percent) are landless
while the remaining 232 households are farmers.[12] Except for a few cases, under
its legal framework, there are no tenant households in rural Myanmar. The study
village is not an exception and the average farm size of farm households is about
10 acres. According to the record of the village tract secretary, there were 430
cattle and buffalo in total, which means that one farm household has slightly
less than two cattle and/or buffalo on average. Diffusion of farm machineries
began in the village in the 1990s. The number of machinery at the time of the
survey was 76 power tillers, 267 irrigation pumps, 65 excel flow pumps, 10
binders, 30 threshers and 30 fans for winnowing. In addition, there were four
small rice mills (hullers) in the village. There were no post offices, banks, rural
health centers or middle schools.[13] Five primary schools, four pagodas and two
monasteries were located in eight hamlets.

A detailed household-level survey was conducted by selecting 100 households
from three hamlets. Based on a list of all households in the three hamlets, two-

thirds (67) were selected from farm households and the remaining (33) was selected from landless households. Sampling of farm households was conducted proportionately from the different farm size groups. Table 7-8 indicates the distribution of the sample households by farm size. As the table shows, the share of farm households with 5–10 acres is the largest, followed by those with 2.5–5 acres and 10–15 acres. The smallest and largest farm size among our sample was 1.15 acres and 26.45 acres, respectively. It can be said that the distribution of farmland among farm households is not very unequal, although it should not be forgotten that there is a large number of landless households. After compiling the survey data, we classified landless households into two categories according to major income sources—agricultural labor households (where more than 50 percent of their income came from agricultural wages) and other landless households. The result was that out of a total of 33 landless households, 18 households were agricultural labor households whose livelihood highly depended on agricultural wages. Taking into consideration the fact that 55 percent of total households are landless in the village, the high dependency of such landless households on agricultural wage income indicates the high labor-absorptive power of Myanmar rice farming.[14]

Table 7-9 shows the distribution of various assets among the sample households. Draft animals, indispensable for cultivation, are distributed such that there was one head on farms less than 2.5 acres, three heads for farms of more than 15 acres and two heads for remaining farms. The distribution of farm machinery such as power tillers, irrigation pumps and others is skewed in favor of larger farms. However, it should be noted that capital goods for fisheries are held more among small farmers and landless households. The distribution of cheaper fishery instruments such as those for catching eels in the paddy field, which are not shown in the table, are more highly skewed among poorer peoples including agricultural labor households. Inland fishery, thus, is one of the most important sources of off-farm employment and income among the poor in the deltaic areas.

Process of the Rice Double Cropping in the 1990s

Until the beginning of the 1990s, the village was basically a mono-crop area of monsoon paddy and during the summer (dry) season, most of the land remained fallow. However, triggered by the digging of a network of field channels for both drainage and irrigation purposes which began in 1992 (and completed by 1995), agriculture of the study village changed drastically to the double cropping of rice in a very short period. The digging of the field channels was carried out by the voluntary labor contribution from all eligible households in the village. It should be noted that before 1992 when the main road was widened and heightened, the major transport method to Myaungmya town for the villagers was by boat.[15]

Table 7-9 Distribution of Major Assets among Sampled Households

	Number of Households	Farmland (acres)	Average farmland per Households (acres)	Bullock/ Buffalo	Cow	Adult pig	Plow	Harrow	Power tiller	Irriga-tion pump	Excel flow pump	Spra-yer	Thresher	Bullock cart	Bicycle	Motor-boat	Boat	Fishing net
Total	100	587.32	5.87	117	24	55	63	56	21	46	3	32	4	12	22	9	47	15
Nonfarm	33	0	0	0	0	6	0	0	1	0	0	0	0	0	2	1	13	5
Agr. labor	18	0	0	0	0	2	0	0	0	0	0	0	0	0	0	0	4	0
Other landless	15	0	0	0	0	4	0	0	1	0	0	0	0	0	2	1	9	5
Farm	67	587.32	8.77	117	24	49	63	56	20	46	3	32	4	12	20	8	34	10
-2.50	8	15.89	1.99	4	4	2	6	5	0	0	0	1	0	1	0	0	5	3
2.51-5.00	13	50.90	3.92	16	6	3	10	9	0	3	0	4	0	0	4	1	4	2
5.01-10.00	25	191.32	7.65	47	13	19	23	21	9	20	0	14	1	3	5	4	11	5
10.01-15.00	12	153.42	12.79	26	0	10	13	12	2	11	0	5	0	3	6	0	7	0
15.01+	9	175.79	19.53	24	1	15	11	9	9	12	3	8	3	5	5	3	7	0

Source: Survey by author conducted June 22-27, 2001.

Table 7-10   Process of Diffusion of Farm Machineries

	Irrigation pump	Excel flow pump	Power tiller	Sprayer	Thresher	Motorboat
1971	1					
1978				1		
1988				1		
1989	1					
1990						
1991	1					
1992	4			1		
1993	7		2			
1994	6		2	3		
1995	8	1	2	1		1
1996	4		4	2		
1997	4		3	4	1	1
1998	6	1	4	7	1	1
1999	3		3	5		2
2000	1	1	1	3	1	4
2001				2	1	
Unknown				2		
Total	46	3	21	32	4	9

Source: Survey by author conducted June 22–27, 2001.

Table 7-10 illustrates the diffusion process of major farm machineries, based on the data collected from the sample households. It is found that dissemination of the irrigation pump, which is critical for double cropping of rice, has accelerated since 1992 and this is consistent with the above-mentioned process of digging field channels. Moreover, power tillers were diffused a few years following the irrigation pumps, followed by sprayers and threshers. Motorboats also began to be diffused since the mid-1990s.

It is important to note that the digging of field channels was a critical communal investment for the successive agricultural intensification of the village, encouraged by the government's Summer Paddy Program. At the same time, however, it was individual farmers, not the government, that invested in farm machineries that were, in turn, indispensable for the progress of the double cropping of rice. The price hike of paddy, influenced by the liberalization of the agricultural market in 1987, gave strong incentives for farmers to increase rice production. In this context, the communal investment in land through digging field channels can be regarded as a very successful strategy for increased rice production with minimum expenditure on the part of government.

However, although the rise in the rice price was rapid since 1987, the increase was largely due to the extremely low rice price that prevailed during the socialist regime. As already discussed earlier, the domestic rice price in Myanmar remained at a substantially low level compared to international prices. On the other hand, the government subsidy to imported chemical fertilizers was almost withdrawn by the mid-1990s. The price of diesel oil also continued to rise rapidly under the depreciating currency. The result was worsening terms of trade for rice production, especially for capital-intensive summer paddy. This contradiction became more serious in mid-2000 when the domestic rice price collapsed to about US$50 per ton. We have conducted a survey in the study village in this worst period for farmers.

Analysis of Cost and Return for Rice Production

Table 7-11 shows the production of rice for the sample farmers and its disposal for various purposes such as seed for the next season, home consumption, sales to the government (procurement), sales to the private market, stock, etc. It is clear that rice production in the study village is highly market-oriented and the share of marketed to total production reached 78.7 percent on average and 62.1 percent even in the case of the smallest farms (those with less than 2.5 acres). Moreover, responses by households on the volume of home consumption are clearly overstated and, if we take this into account, the share of marketed rice will be even larger, especially in the case of large farmers. Therefore, if scarcity of off-farm employment opportunities in the village is also taken into account, the damage from the collapse in the rice price must have been tremendous.

In order to obtain reliable cost and return data, we must be cautious about many factors, which cannot be discussed here.[16] Only the results are shown in Tables 7-12 and 7-13 for the production of monsoon paddy and summer paddy, respectively. These tables can be read as follows. First, gross revenue per acre is obtained by multiplying the yield of paddy with the sales price. By deducting the costs of current input (seeds, fertilizers, chemicals and diesel oil) from gross revenue the value added per acre is derived. Next, income per acre can be calculated by deducting all costs except family labor cost from value added. Finally surplus per acre can be obtained if (imputed) family labor cost is deducted from income. Theoretically, the surplus obtained here consists of land rent for owned land and interest for the self-supplied working capital. Income is obtained by multiplying the income per acre with the total acreage of sown area per farm. In the case of monsoon paddy, since some part of the production (usually 12 baskets per acre in the study village) was procured by the government (Myanmar Agricultural Produce Trading; hereinafter referred to as MAPT) at the fixed price of 320 kyat per basket, well below the market price, total income is adjusted and shown in the adjusted income column.[17]

It is evident from the two tables that the surplus that remained in the hands of farmers was very small. In fact, its share to gross revenue was 12.4 percent

Table 7-11   Disposal of Produced Paddy

	< 2.5 acres	2.51- 5.0 acres	5.01- 10.0 acres	10.01- 15.0 acres	15.01+ acres	Average
Sampled households	8	13	25	12	9	67
Average household members	5.13	4.38	5.36	5.67	5.89	5.16
Average farm size (acres)	1.99	3.92	7.65	12.81	19.53	8.77
Average cropped area of monsoon paddy (acres)	1.92	3.70	7.53	12.60	19.36	8.62
Yield (basket/acre)	43.0	45.6	45.9	45.0	44.9	45.2
Average cropped area of summer paddy (acres)	1.86	2.87	6.25	9.05	12.93	6.47
Yield (basket/acre)	64.7	70.0	66.6	66.3	70.9	67.6
Production (baskets)						
Monsoon paddy	83	167	343	564	859	393
Summer paddy	115	198	416	604	904	437
Total	198	365	759	1168	1763	830
Disposals (basket)						
Seed	7	16	30	61	69	36
Home consumption	66	91	104	188	266	136
Government procurement	31	55	117	196	297	135
Private sales	81	166	408	583	514	369
Stock	9	33	100	130	608	150
Others	3	4	2	8	4	4
Total	197	365	761	1166	1758	830
Ratio of marketed (%)	61.4	69.6	82.1	78.0	80.7	78.8
Ratio of procurement in total marketed (%)	25.6	21.7	18.7	21.6	20.9	20.6
Procurement per acre (basket)	16.1	14.9	15.5	15.6	15.3	15.7
Per capita rice consumption (kg)	161	261	243	416	566	331
Employment of seasonal laborers	0.0	0.2	0.3	0.6	1.6	0.5

Source: Survey by author conducted June 22–27, 2001.

in the case of monsoon paddy and -0.4 percent in the case of summer paddy on average. The major part of the surplus is land rent for owned land. The small surplus is nothing but a serious effect of the collapse in the rice price, because such an adverse effect is absorbed by the production factor that has the least opportunity for other production purposes; i.e., land. Two cases of simulation were conducted for the rice price; the first is 600 kyat per basket and the second is 800 kyat per basket (if converted to U.S. dollar per ton of rice, approximately US$75 and US$100 per ton, respectively) instead of the actual 404–419 kyat. As these simulations show, even in the moderate case (600 kyat per basket), the share of the surplus rises to 38.8 percent in the case of monsoon paddy and 32.4 percent in the case of summer paddy, which are quite reasonable figures. Moreover, the average income per average sized farm (10 acres) obtained from the double cropping of rice rises from the actual

Table 7-12 Cost and Return of Monsoon Paddy Production

	-2.5 acres	2.51-5.0 acres	5.01-10.0 acres	10.01-15.0 acres	15.01+ acres	Ave-rage	Case 1 (600 kyat/basket)	Case 2 (800 kyat/basket)
Sampled households	8	13	25	12	9	67		
Farm size (acres)	1.99	3.92	7.65	12.81	19.53	8.77	8.77	8.77
Cropped area of monsoon paddy (acres)	1.92	3.70	7.53	12.60	19.36	8.62	8.62	8.62
Cropped ratio of monsoon paddy	96.5	94.4	98.4	98.4	99.1	98.3	98.3	98.3
Procurement (basket)	31	55	117	196	297	133	133	133
Yield (basket/acre)	43.0	45.6	45.9	45.0	44.9	45.2	45.2	45.2
Sales price (kyat/basket)	405	398	429	433	413	419	600	800
Gross revenue (kyat/acre)	17,415	18,149	19,691	19,485	18,554	18,939	27,120	36,160
Current input (kyat/acre)	3,654	4,997	4,366	5,102	5,857	4,736	4,736	4,736
Seed	1,359	1,831	1,547	1,620	1,291	1,558	1,558	1,558
Fertilizers	1,753	2,941	2,450	2,943	3,581	2,702	2,702	2,702
Manure	154	147	69	188	278	144	144	144
Chemicals	86	7	33	9	98	39	39	39
Diesel oil	302	71	267	342	609	293	293	293
Value added (kyat/acre)	13,761	13,152	15,325	14,383	12,687	14,203	22,384	31,424

Continued on next page.

Table 7-12 Cost and Return of Monsoon Paddy Production (continued)

	-2.5 acres	2.51-5.0 acres	5.01-10.0 acres	10.01-15.0 acres	15.01+ acres	Average	Case 1 (600 kyat/basket)	Case 2 (800 kyat/basket)
Cost (kyat/acre)	5,439	8,488	10,118	8,908	9,870	8,996	8,996	8,996
Farm machineries (rented)	871	0	293	230	0	255	255	255
Farm machineries (owned)	0	239	579	728	2,566	738	738	738
Bullock (rented)	64	230	25	0	0	62	62	62
Bullock (owned)	2,160	3,343	2,913	2,021	1,087	2,502	2,502	2,502
Daily laborers	2,167	3,365	4,825	4,400	4,418	4,094	4,094	4,094
Seasonal laborers	0	983	742	1,299	1,701	929	929	929
Paid land rent	0	0	0	0	0	0	0	0
Interest for MADB loan	77	103	64	56	42	69	69	69
Interest for informal loan	100	225	677	174	56	347	347	347
Income (kyat/acre)	8,322	4,664	5,207	5,475	2,817	5,207	13,388	22,428
Family labor	5,196	3,845	2,580	1,907	1,414	2,861	2,861	2,861
Surplus (kyat/acre)	3,126	819	2,627	3,568	1,403	2,346	10,527	19,567
Share to gross revenue (%)	18.0	4.5	13.3	18.3	7.6	12.4	38.8	54.1
Total income (kyat)	15,978	17,256	39,209	68,985	54,531	44,883	115,405	193,329
Adjusted income (kyat)	13,343	12,966	26,456	46,837	26,910	31,716	78,165	129,489
Production cost per basket (kyat)	332	380	372	354	382	367		

Source: Survey by author conducted June 22-27, 2001.

Table 7-13　Cost and Return of Summer Paddy Production

	-2.5 acres	2.51-5.0 acres	5.01-10.0 acres	10.01-15.0 acres	15.01+ acres	Average	Case 1 (600 kyat/basket)	Case 2 (800 kyat/basket)
Sampled households	8	13	24	12	9	66		
Farm size (acres)	1.99	3.92	7.64	12.81	19.53	8.77	8.77	8.77
Cropped area of summer paddy (acres)	1.86	2.87	6.25	9.05	12.93	6.47	6.47	6.47
Cropped ratio of summer paddy	93.0	75.0	82.0	69.0	68.0	73.8	73.8	73.8
Yield (basket/acre)	64.7	70.0	66.6	66.3	70.9	67.6	67.6	67.6
Sales price (kyat/basket)	395	386	405	428	404	404	600	800
Gross revenue (kyat/acre)	25,557	27,020	26,973	28,376	28,644	27,310	40,560	54,080
Current input (kyat/acre)	10,397	12,507	14,478	15,220	14,733	13,765	13,765	13,765
Seed	1,944	2,449	2,314	2,468	2,686	2,375	2,375	2,375
Fertilizers	6,155	7,654	9,238	9,643	9,043	8,599	8,599	8,599
Manure	20	34	52	60	0	39	39	39
Chemicals	120	186	206	92	229	174	174	174
Diesel oil	2,158	2,184	2,668	2,957	2,775	2,578	2,578	2,578
Value added (kyat/acre)	15,160	14,513	12,495	13,156	13,911	13,545	26,795	40,315

Continued on next page.

Table 7-13   Cost and Return of Summer Paddy Production (continued)

	-2.5 acres	2.51-5.0 acres	5.01-10.0 acres	10.01-15.0 acres	15.01+acres	Average	Case 1 (600 kyat/basket)	Case 2 (800 kyat/basket)
Cost (kyat/acre)	5,710	9,244	11,185	10,555	11,947	10,129	10,129	10,129
Farm machineries (rented)	2,837	1,782	1,216	800	0	1,282	1,282	1,282
Farm machineries (owned)	592	1,748	4,305	4,215	6,894	3,688	3,688	3,688
Bullock (rented)	128	248	4	0	0	66	66	66
Bullock (owned)	1,236	2,696	1,779	1,712	630	1,725	1,725	1,725
Daily laborers	708	1,485	2,444	2,050	2,121	1,929	1,929	1,929
Seasonal laborers	0	821	619	1,556	2,078	953	953	953
Paid land rent	0	0	59	0	0	22	22	22
Interest for MADB loan	0	25	10	0	0	9	9	9
Interest for informal loan	209	439	749	222	224	455	455	455
Income (kyat/acre)	9,450	5,269	1,310	2,601	1,964	3,416	16,666	30,186
Family labor	6,163	5,140	2,931	2,259	2,079	3,519	3,519	3,519
Surplus (kyat/acre)	3,287	129	-1,621	342	-115	-103	13,147	26,667
Share to gross revenue (%)	12.9	0.5	-6.0	1.2	-0.4	-0.4	32.4	49.3
Total income (kyat)	17,576	15,122	8,187	23,543	25,389	22,104	107,829	195,303
Production cost per basket (kyat)	344	384	429	423	406	406		

Source: Survey by author conducted June 22-27, 2001.

86,230 kyat to 300,540 kyat; this indicates how large the damage was from
the low rice price.

Problems in the Credit Market

If we compare the two tables, it is clear that the production of summer paddy
is much more capital-intensive than monsoon paddy. The share of current input
costs to gross revenue was 25.0 percent and 50.4 percent for monsoon and
summer paddy, respectively. On the other hand, the share of capital costs (sum
of the cost for draft animals, farm machineries and paid interest for borrowed
money) to gross revenue reached 21.0 percent and 26.5 percent for monsoon and
summer paddy, respectively. If these two items are added, the share to capital
cost comes to 46.0 and 76.9 percent, respectively, for each paddy production.
For reference, if we look at the case of 600 kyat per basket of paddy price, these
figures declined to 32.1 percent and 51.7 percent, respectively, which, especially
in the latter case, is still very high and represents a large burden for farmers.

One of the major factors that caused the high share to capital cost in the case
of summer paddy production is the high cost for pump irrigation. The rental
charge of irrigation pumps in the village was usually 10 baskets of paddy per
acre of irrigation. Furthermore, the cost of diesel oil for operating the pumps
should be borne by the borrower farmers. If the total cost necessary to irrigate
one acre of land (including the cost of diesel oil) is estimated, it varies between
920–8,696 kyat with an average of 7,018 kyat per acre, which represents 25.7
percent of gross revenue. The more than one-fourth share for irrigation costs
is exorbitantly high compared to the case of shallow tubewell irrigation in
Bangladesh and West Bengal (11–13 percent).[18]

Why is the cost so high in Myanmar? Table 7-14, which lists all the cases
of informal borrowing for the sample households in the village, provides us
with an important hint. The data shows that households, including farmers,
who borrowed money for rice production, did so at a high interest rate of 3–5
percent per month. Farmers had access to an institutional crop loan from the
Myanmar Agricultural Development Bank (MADB), but as is well known, the
amount that can be borrowed is only about 1,000 kyat per acre and is negligible
compared to the amount of working capital needed. It is easy to imagine that the
prolonged low rice price accelerated the shortage of working capital for farmers,
which resulted in a high dependency on the informal credit market. In sum, the
opportunity cost for self-supplied capital is very high in rural Myanmar and such
interest is included in the expensive irrigation cost, in the form of high rental
charge of the pumps, as mentioned above. If so, it should be additionally noted
that the earlier estimates of cost and return to paddy production were conducted
assuming that the interest for self-supplied working capital was zero, but this was

not appropriate. As a result, the share of capital costs to gross revenue of rice production in the study village will be even larger than the earlier estimate.

In conclusion, the problems that prevailed when the Summer Paddy Program was implemented included not only the low rice price, but the rural credit market as well, where the institutional credit supply was too small and the very high interest rates dominated the informal credit. How to improve on such a credit market situation is a very important policy issue when further expansion of summer paddy is promoted.

Recent Movements After the Announcement of the New Rice Marketing Policy

As we have investigated in detail through a case study in the Ayeyarwaddy Division, faced with a serious economic crisis for farmers due to the collapse in the rice price for about one-and-a-half years in 2000 and 2001, the government did not take any effective countermeasures such as purchasing more paddy for forming a buffer stock,[19] or allowing private traders to export rice, etc. On the contrary, the government continued the policy of planned (compulsory) cropping of paddy in the paddy field (*le*), which exacerbated the economic hardship of rice farmers. Problems in the rural credit market also retarded capital-intensive summer paddy production. The wholesale price of rice in Yangon, after stagnating at the extremely low level, however, began to surge rapidly in February 2002 and by the end of 2002 it reached about four times the lowest price recorded during November 2000–March 2001 (Figure 7-3). It is important to note as well that the general inflation rate was 21.2 percent and 57.0 percent in 2001 and 2002 respectively, thereby only less than double in the case of general prices.

In April 2003 the government suddenly announced a new rice marketing policy comprised of the following two components: the 40-year-old government procurement system of rice was to be abolished; and the private sectors would be allowed to export rice under certain conditions. These reforms seemed to be really epoch-making and it was expected that if fully implemented, they could thoroughly affect the rice economy in Myanmar.

The actual institutional settings of the reform and its implementation would be decided by the newly established Myanmar Rice Trading Leading Committee (MRTLC) led by the Secretary-2 of SPDC as chair. Other members include: the Minister for Agriculture and Irrigation, the Minister for Industry-1, the Minister for Commerce, the Minister for Energy, and two representatives each from the Union of Myanmar Federation of Chambers of Commerce and Industry

Table 7-14   List of Borrowers from Informal Sources

Household number	Farm size (acres)	Lender	Amount (kyat)	Borrowing time	Borrowing period	Interest rate (per month)	Actual usages	Outstanding (kyat)	Collateral
2	0	Fish wholesaler	50,000	3 years ago		0%	on-lending to fishermen	50,000	
3	4	N&F	5,000-10,000	Jun-97	6 months	5%		0	
9	0	N&F	1,500	May-01		0%	HC	1,500	
10	0	Employer (relative)	500	Dec-00	1 month	0%		0	
12	11.32	Pawnshop	60,000	Apr-01		4%	Medical expenses	70,000	Necklace
21	0	Pawnshop	5,000	Jun-00		4%	MP	5,000	Gold
22	5	Relative	20,000	Apr-00	7 months	0%	Medical expenses	0	
23	1.95	N&F	10,000	May-98	6 months	6.7%	MP	0	
24	4	N&F	5,000	May-00	7 months	8.6%	Land purchase, HC	0	
26	9.93	N&F	50,000	May-00	2-3 months	10%	HC, education, MP	0	
27	8	Relative	50,000	Aug-00	5 months	10%	MP	0	
31	8	Moneylender	80,000	Nov-00	6 months	12.5%	SP	0	
35	0	Employer	1,000	May-00	1.5 months	0%	HC	0	
	7	Relative	20,000	Jul-00	5 months	10%	MP	0	
	7	Relative	40,000	Jan-01	3 months	10%	SP	0	
38	5.8	N&F	10,000	Jul-00	4 months	8%	MP	0	
39	8	Relative	15,000	Jul-00	4 months	3%	MP	0	
41	0	Relative	400-500	Dec-00	10 days	0%	HC	0	
	0	Relative	300-400	Feb-01	20 days	0%	HC	0	

Continued on next page.

Table 7-14 List of Borrowers from Informal Sources (continued)

Household number	Farm size (acres)	Lender	Amount (kyat)	Borrowing time	Borrowing period	Interest rate (per month)	Actual usages	Outstanding (kyat)	Note
42	2.5	Pawnshop	10,000	Aug-00	5 months	4%	HC	0	Gold
43	8.82	Relative	10,000	Oct-00	3 months	4%	SP	0	
47	0	N&F	1000	May-00	2-3 days	0%	Medical expenses	0	
50	6.41	Grocery shop	50,000	Jan-00	3 months	4%	SP	0	Gold
52	12.64	Moneylender	20,000	Feb-00	3 months	5%	SP	0	
	12.64	Moneylender	20,000	Apr-00	2 months	5%	SP	0	
53	3.46	Pawnshop	40,000	Feb-01		4%	SP	40,000	Gold
54	14.9	Relative	30,000	Jun-00	6 months	6%	MP	0	
56	6.21	N&F	15,000	Jun-00	8 months	8%	MP	0	
58	19.98	Grocery shop	9,500	Mar-00		4%	MP/SP	9,500	Gold
61	3	Moneylender	5,000	Jul-00	5 months	4%	MP, HC	0	
66	0	Pawnshop	5,000	Mar-00		4%	HC	5,000+	Gold
70	6.67	Pawnshop	10,000	Apr-03	3 months	4%	SP	0	
71	5	Relative	10,000	Dec-00	4.5 months	10%	Repayment	0	
78	8.39	Relative	5,000	Aug-98	3 months	0%	MP	0	
79	0	Relative	4,000	Jun-01				4,000	Paid in agr. labor
81	14	Pawnshop	50,000	Jul-00	7 months	3%	MP	0	Gold
	14	Pawnshop	30,000	Nov-00	5 months	3%	SP	0	Gold
82	8	Moneylender	30,000	Jun-00	6 months	10%	MP	0	
	8	Moneylender	130,000	Jan-01	3 months	10%	SP	0	

Continued on next page.

Table 7-14   List of Borrowers from Informal Sources (continued)

Household number	Farm size (acres)	Lender	Amount (Kyat)	Borrowing time	Borrowing period	Interest rate (per month)	Actual usages	Outstanding (kyat)	Note
83	1.15	Relative	40,000	Feb-01		0%	Medical expenses	26,000	
87	11.56	Pawnshop	35,000	Oct-00		4%	SP, HC, medical expenses	35,000	Gold
	11.56	Pawnshop	12,000	Nov-00		4%	SP, HC, medical expenses	12,000	Gold
	11.56	Pawnshop	6,500	Jan-01		4%	SP, HC, medical expenses	6,500	Gold
88	0	Pawnshop	3,000	May-00	3 months	3%	Purchase of sickles	0	Gold
	0	Relative	6,000	May-01	5 months	0%	Catching eels	6,000	
89	0	Relative	3,000	May-00		0%	HC	0	
	0	Relative	3,000	Oct-00		0%	HC	0	
91	4.35	Relative	20,000	Jul-00	8 months	10%	MP	0	
92	2.15	Pawnshop	15,000	Nov-00		4%	SP	15,000	Gold
94	19.77	Pawnshop	30,000	May-99	5 months	4%	MP	0	Gold
	19.77	Pawnshop	50,000	May-00	5 months	4%	MP	0	Gold
	19.77	Moneylender	60,000	Dec-00	5 months	4%	SP	0	Gold
95	9.33	Grocery shop	40,000	Jul-00	9 months	10%	MP	0	
96	14.79	Moneylender	50,000	Jul-00	6 months	3%	MP	0	Necklace
	14.79	Moneylender	50,000	Dec-00	5 months	3%	SP	0	Necklace
97	26.45	Pawnshop	40,000	May-01		5%	MP	40,000	Gold

Note: N&F: Neighbors and friends; HC: Home consumption; MP: Monsoon paddy production; SP: Summer paddy production.

(UMFCCI), the Myanmar Rice Traders Association and the Myanmar Rice Millers Association. The total number of representatives from the private sector was six, which itself was very unusual in Myanmar.

Discussions were made in MRTLC as follows. First, the direct procurement of paddy by the government would be abolished, but purchase itself would be maintained in order to meet the ration demand for the target group. The committee examined the possibility of purchasing paddy (or rice) through traders and/or rice mills at the prevailing 'market price.'[20] However, it was finally decided that the rice ration system would be abolished for government employees and they would be compensated with a 5000 kyat increase of their monthly salary.[21] Thus the abolition of the procurement system was fully implemented from the harvesting season of monsoon paddy in 2003–04.

The second issue was rice exports by private traders. It was discussed that the volume of rice exported would be the 'surplus' after total domestic consumption has been met from production with the 'surplus' to be determined by the MRTLC. Another important issue was that the government would charge a 10 percent export tax, the same as the other commodities, but will receive another 45 percent foreign exchange in exchange for payment of the actual cost (FOB price) in kyat to the private sector. The private exporter can only keep the remaining 45 percent of foreign exchange. Although these systems involved apparent problems, the private sector responded positively and prepared for the export. For instance, they tried to organize a joint export company and went to Bangladesh to seek an export market. They also imported chemical fertilizers to boost rice production. However, in January 2004, the government suddenly announced the suspension of the export liberalization.

Behind the decision by the government to suspend rice exports was an unfavorable market condition. As is already shown in Figure 7-3, rice prices in 2003 were very high and even the low quality rice (Emata and Ngasein) reached about 6,000 kyat per 50 kg bag, which is equivalent to about US$120 per ton, only slightly lower than the international price. It is evident that the government was very afraid of the high domestic rice price, which could cause social and political instability. And after the announcement of the suspension, rice prices again collapsed (Figure 7-3). In other words, the government succeeded in reducing the rice price, at the sacrifice of private traders (including rice millers) and rice farmers.

Another notable fact is that even after the abolition of the rice procurement system, the government continued to maintain the planned (compulsory) cropping system. Farmers have to plant monsoon paddy in the paddy field (*le*) and also have to grow summer paddy where irrigation water is available, regardless of the situation of the rice market. The major purpose of the policy is no longer

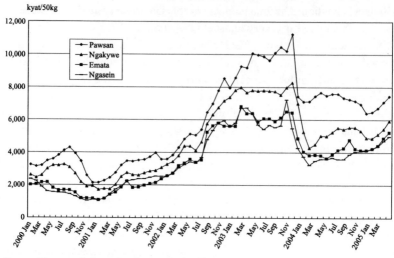

Figure 7-3   Wholesale Price of Rice in Yangon

Source: Myanmar Information System Project Data.

to secure rice for the procurement, but to increase supply to the domestic rice market and thus to lower its price for consumers.

Concluding Remarks

This chapter addressed key issues for the Myanmar rural economy, through an investigation of rice policies and the performance of the rice sector since the end of the 1980s up to the present day. After reviewing Myanmar's macroeconomic performance over the last decade or so, the development and changes in the rice sector were reviewed, centering on the Summer Paddy Program since 1992–93, with detailed information and data collected from a pump-irrigated study village in the Ayeyarwaddy Division in 2001. Finally, the recent policy changes for rice marketing system were explained, with some comments.

Finally, several conclusions of this chapter are summarized. First, the progress of the double cropping of rice (mainly by the introduction of irrigation pumps in the first half of the 1990s through the Summer Paddy Program) was induced by the rice price hike after the liberalization of agricultural marketing in 1987. Such a development in the rice sector contributed to economic growth in rural areas in Myanmar, especially in the newly formed portions of the Ayeyarwaddy delta. The construction of field channels by the voluntary manual labor of rural residents, which was a prerequisite for the later introduction of irrigation pumps, should be evaluated as a strategically essential communal investment.

Secondly, however, the price hike of rice since 1987 was rapid only when compared to the extremely low price during the socialist period, with the rice price in Myanmar remaining substantially lower than international prices. The basic reason for this is that the government (MAPT) continued to monopolize rice exports, prohibiting exports by the private sector. The rice price in Myanmar has been determined by domestic supply and demand, almost independently from movements in the international price. On the other hand, the major current inputs for rice production, such as chemical fertilizers and diesel oil, as well as farm machinery, are imported. The depreciated currency (kyat) due to the worsened macroeconomic performance caused a surge in the prices of such imported commodities but rice farmers could not benefit from the depreciated currency through rice export. Thus since the mid-1990s, the worsened terms of trade for rice production became a serious constraint for increased production of rice through double cropping. Such a fundamental contradiction for rice production became very serious after mid-2000 when the domestic rice price in Myanmar collapsed to about US$50 per ton, compared to international prices of US$140–150 per ton (in the case of 25 percent broken rice exported from Thailand). The slump in the rice market continued for about one-and-a-half years until the rice price began to rise in February 2002.

Third, in spite of such a serious situation for rice farmers, the government did not take any effective countermeasures such as the purchase of rice to accumulate stock or to export, or to allow the private sector to export rice. On the contrary, the government continued the planned (compulsory) cropping system under which farmers were obliged to grow monsoon paddy in the paddy field (le) and summer paddy in the irrigated paddy field. The strong policy directions for maximizing the self-sufficiency rate in each state/division also continued, which resulted in providing further pressure to lower the rice price. The lack of appropriate policies, which actually became adverse policy directions, impacted the rice farmers very badly and exacerbated the adverse effects of the worsened terms of trade. The price simulations based on the survey data collected showed that if the domestic price was US$75 per ton (instead of the actual US$50) farmers would have been able to obtain a reasonable profit, leaving 30–40 percent of gross revenue accruing to the key production factor, land. Such a price level could have been attained if some appropriate policy measures were taken given the fact that the international rice price during the same period was at least US$120–130 per ton for Myanmar rice.

Fourth, at the time the Summer Paddy Program was implemented, there were problems with the trade regime (whereby rice export was not allowed by the private sector) as well as the rural credit market where the institutional credit supply was too small and very high interest rates (3–5 percent per month) dominated the informal market.

Fifth, the government finally made a bold decision to liberalize the 40-year-old rice marketing system in April 2003. The abolition of the government procurement system of rice was an epoch-making reform. Rice farmers now attained total freedom to sell their products at any market (except export). MAPT (Myanmar Agricultural Produce Trading) has lost most of its economic role and a large scale restructuring is inevitable. However, other restrictions imposed on rice farmers remain as before, such as the planned (compulsory) cropping system, under which farmers must plant monsoon paddy in the paddy field (*le*) and also summer paddy in the irrigated paddy field. Also, land ownership remains in the hand of the government and its rental and/or mortgage are prohibited. On the other hand, as pointed out above, institutional credit for farmers continues to play only a marginal role,[22] which hampers the increased production of rice.

Sixth, the liberalization of rice exports, once declared, was finally suspended. Rice prices in Myanmar dropped sharply after the announcement of the suspension and remains well below its international market price. Furthermore, there is no more input subsidy from the government. Rice farmers face international prices for chemical fertilizers and diesel oil. As before, they are forced to grow rice under such unfavorable terms of trade.

Seventh, the fact that the government has no policy instruments to intervene in the rice market in order to stabilize its price should finally be pointed out. The volatility of the rice market in Myanmar is evident if we look at the movement of rice prices during the last five years in Figure 7-3, which hurts both producers and consumers. Stabilization of the rice price is one of the most urgent policy agendas in Myanmar. However, even when the government announced the liberalization of rice exports, they did not consider stabilization of the domestic rice price. They only considered how they could benefit from the foreign exchange earned by the private sector. Alternatively, the attempt to stabilize the price by controlling the 'surplus' volume to be exported, if implemented, would have involved serious technical problems. The rice premium system, once adopted in Thailand during the 1950s to 1980s, for example, can be considered as an alternative since it has a built-in price stabilization function at a very low administration cost.[23] It should be emphasized here that the establishment of a more transparent, decentralized and flexible system for any decision-making is, above all, required for the economic policy in general. Another example in this sense is that the government tried to make the MRTLC, comprised of only 10 or so persons, decide everything concerning such an important issue. Whatever the name or title used, a kind of secretariat that involves several key officials of related ministries for supporting the decision making of the MRTLC was indispensable for successful planning and implementation of the new policy.

Notes

1 The basket is the unit of capacity widely used in Myanmar. One basket is equivalent to approximately 20.9 kilograms of paddy.

2 The information and data in the study village in Ayeyarwaddy Division was collected jointly with Ms. Ikuko Okamoto (Researcher, Institute of Developing Economies, Chiba, Japan), Dr. Takashi Kurosaki (Associate Professor, Institute of Economics, Hitotsubashi University), and Mr. Kyosuke Kurita (Graduate Student, Graduate School of Economics, Hitotsubashi University). The author would like to thank these collaborative researchers.

3 The SLORC was reshuffled and renamed SPDC in November 1997.

4 See, Study Group on the Myanmar Economy (1999) for more detailed discussions.

5 The figures between Table 7-3 and 7-4 are quite different, depending on the source of information.

6 Since 1998–99, the government ceased disclosure of macroeconomic indicators through the annual publication *Review of the Financial, Economic and Social Conditions*.

7 See, for example, Adas (1974) for details on the socioeconomic changes during the process.

8 However, the statistics that show the rapid increase in rice yield in this period and the maintenance of such a high level thereafter are rather doubtful. According to recent data collected by the author in several villages in Myanmar, the average yield of paddy may not have exceeded 40–45 baskets per acre, which is equivalent to only 2.1–2.3 tons per hectare. There is a possibility that rice production data in Myanmar has been over-reported to a large extent since the early 1980s until today. The author plans to argue this point more thoroughly in the near future, by showing evidence of this in another paper.

9 This is discussed in greater detail by U Khin Win (1991), and Mya Than and Nishizawa (1990).

10 Landless households residing in the villages also participated in the construction work of such field channels.

11 However, the yield (and also the sown area of summer paddy) data are very questionable as argued later in the chapter.

12 The very high proportion of the landless is widely observed in rural Myanmar, probably except for the mountainous regions. There are no statistics on the number of landless households, but their proportion to total rural households can be estimated to be at least 30–40 percent.

13 There is a relatively small stream along the western border of the village and there is a town on the other side of the riverbank, which performs various urban functions for the surrounding villages. Many shops including fertilizer shops, farm machinery shops, pawnshops and grocery shops are located there. Several large-scale rice mills are located along the stream and also in the town.

14 The relative scarcity of off-farm job opportunities in rural Myanmar, especially compared to other South and Southeast Asian countries, should be paid some attention. Migration from rural to urban areas is also surprisingly small, if the fact that a large number of landless people reside in rural areas is considered.

15 There are no bridges crossing over the western-side stream from the village to the town, and thus the transport method to go to town is also by boat.

16 How to evaluate the self-supplied production factors (such as farm machineries, draft animals and family labor), how to evaluate in-kind portions of payment (such as meals to hired laborers), and how to evaluate the output price are major questions that need to be cautiously addressed with appropriate assumptions and imputations.

17 However, the advance payment is conducted for the procured paddy by MAPT, which is about four months before harvesting. If the interest involved in this system is taken into account, the adjusted income from monsoon paddy by this simple method has a certain bias toward underestimation of (real) income.

18 This has been investigated and estimated by Fujita (2004).

19 MAPT has many warehouses to stock paddy. However, these are not for buffer stocks used to intervene and stabilize the rice market, but are only for maintaining the ration system for the target group.

20 The committee once decided that the areas from which paddy is to be purchased are all the states/divisions except for Chin State. However, given the large regional differences in rice price in Myanmar, which reflect the differences in transportation cost, rice purchase from almost the entire country is irrational.

21 Military is the exception.

22 Since the payment under the former rice procurement system had been completed at the time of the transplanting of monsoon paddy, farmers could obtain cash about four months before harvesting for a part of their production cost. In this sense, the procurement system functioned as a supplementary source of credit (besides MADB crop loan) for rice farmers. The abolition of the procurement system, therefore, means that such a supplementary credit system was also abolished. The government needs to

strengthen the present agricultural credit system, especially if the serious market situation in rural Myanmar as presented in this chapter is taken into consideration.

23 The rice premium system adopted in Thailand is, in short, a variable taxation system under which the difference between the actual international price and the predetermined ceiling price is absorbed by the government as a tax.

References

Ambatkar, Sanjay. 2001. Trade-led Strategy of India in ASEAN, *Margin*, 33(4): pp. 85–97.

Balassa, Bela. 1989. *Comparative Advantage, Trade Policy and Economic Development*. New York: Harvester Wheatsheaf.

Helpman, Elhanan and Paul Krugman. 1985. *Market Structure and Foreign Trade: Increasing Returns, Imperfect Competition, and the International Economy*.

Jones, Ronald W. 2000. *Globalization and the Theory of Input Trade*. Cambridge, MA: MIT Press.

Langhammer, R. J. and Ulrich Hiemenz. 1990. Regional Integration among Developing Countries: Opportunities, Obstacles and Options, *Kieler Studien*, 232.

Okamoto, Yumiko. 1994. Impact of Trade and FDI Liberalization Policies on the Malaysian Economy, *The Developing Economies*, 32(4/99): pp. 460–478.

Okamoto, Yumiko. 2005a. Toward the Formation of an East Asian Regional Arrangement. In Simon S.C. Tay, ed. *Pacific Asia 2022: Sketching Futures of a Region*, pp. 47–65. Japan and New York: Japan Center for International Exchange.

Okamoto, Yumiko. 2005b. Emergence of the 'Intra-mediate Trade:' Implications for the Asia-Pacific Region, paper presented at *Section 2: Does Trade Deliver What it Promises?* PAFTAD 30, Hilton Hawaiian Village Hotel, Honolulu (Hawaii): February 19–21.

Chirathvat, Suthiphand and Sothitorn Mallikamas. 2005. The Potential Outcomes of China—ASEAN FTA: Politico-Economic Implications for Participating Countries. In Ho Khai Leong and Samuel C. Y. Ku, eds. *China and Southeast Asia: Global Changes and Regional Challenges*, pp. 80–107.

UNCTAD. 2004. *World Investment Report 2004: The Shift Towards Services*. New York and Geneva: United Nations.

Wang, Vincent Wei-cheng. 2005. The Logic of China—ASEAN FTA: Economic Stagecraft of Peaceful Ascendancy. In Ho Khai Leong and Samuel C. Y. Ku, eds. *China and Southeast Asia: Global Changes and Regional Challenges*, pp. 17–41.

8
Social Safety Nets in Southeast Asia:
With Special Reference to Thailand

Srawooth Paitoonpong and Shigeyuki Abe

Introduction

In Southeast Asia, the issue of social safety nets (SSNs) emerged with the financial crisis in mid-1997.[1] One conditionality of international organizations such as the IMF, the World Bank and the Asian Development Bank, was that the crisis countries declare in its letter of intent a set of policies that gave due consideration to the social impacts of the crisis.[2] Accordingly, concerns of social safety nets surfaced and studies on this issue looked into how the crisis affected countries in the region. Most studies indicate that the social impact of the crisis has shown the need for policies that specifically incorporate safety nets for vulnerable groups; that is, an economy cannot rely on growth alone.

Thanks to multinational and international agencies, the issue of social safety nets now receives the attention of the public and policymakers. The crisis is a good time for countries to review their policies and reform. 'Turning the crisis into opportunities,' a popular phrase during the onset of the crisis, is quite applicable on this issue. Actually, crisis or no crisis, it is necessary to provide adequate social safety nets for all, particularly the vulnerable and the poor (Cook, Kabeer and Suwannarat 2003, 17). The crisis, of course, makes the need more pronounced and more urgent.

The impact of the financial crisis may have varied among the Asian countries, but the social impact intensified existing social problems. Formal social protection and social safety net measures provided by governments cover only around 10 percent of the population in Asia, at a time when changes are challenging even this limited protection (Cook, Kabeer and Suwannarat 2003, 14). To adequately and effectively respond to social problems, social safety nets require constant review and monitoring.

The purpose of this chapter is to provide an overview of the social safety net concept and the situation in Southeast Asia with an emphasis on Thailand. The chapter has been prepared in response to the need to create an awareness of the social dimension of economic cooperation as well as the roles of the state and the private sectors in this area. Because of time constraints, the primary emphasis of the review is on discussion of the conceptual framework of social safety nets and enumeration of systems rather than detailed assessment of their strengths and weaknesses.

Definitions and Conceptual Framework

Background

The safety net analogy is drawn from high-wire walkers who, if they fall, are protected by a safety net. A study by Vivian (1994) maintained that the term 'social safety nets' has been increasingly used since the early 1990s, especially by Bretton Woods' institutions in connection with structural adjustment programs related to their lending programs. Such measures were initially introduced to mitigate the social impact of structural adjustment measures on specific sections of society. In the beginning, these social safety nets generally served three objectives: poverty alleviation, making adjustment programs more politically acceptable, and institutional reform (Vivian 1994; Wickramasekara 1999, 3). However, we find that the term was actually used by the ILO in its book *Introduction to Social Security* (ILO 1984),[3] and by the World Bank since 1990. In its *World Development Report 1990* the World Bank defined SSNs as 'a system of income insurance to help people through short-term stress and calamities' (World Bank 1990, 90).

At present, there remains some confusion about its true meaning and the consequent identification of programs. Agencies such as the World Bank (in its latest development of the term) define SSNs very broadly and even include social insurance as a part of SSNs. Jimanez (1999) distinguishes between formal and informal safety nets. ESCAP (1999) also adopts a similar view, but has reservations that safety nets should not include anti-poverty programs.

On the other hand, ILO uses a narrower definition. Social insurance systems financed by contributions from employers and workers do not strictly fall within SSNs. To the ILO, a social safety net providing basic protection such as primary health care and subsistence level income security would ordinarily come from the state and taxes. As such, SSNs are basically cash transfers or part of social assistance. Unlike ESCAP's definition, ILO maintains 'the social safety nets is a government-provided anti-poverty benefit' (Gillion et al. 2000, 465).[4]

In fact, when the World Bank initially used the term SSNs in its *World Development Report 1990*, it adopted an even narrower definition emphasizing the 'irregularity' of economic difficulties faced by individuals. As mentioned above, the World Bank's earlier definition of SSNs was 'a system of income insurance to help people through short-term stress and calamities.' This system of income insurance is targeted at those who are potentially able to support themselves through individual productive effort or through the assets that they own but are temporarily unable to do so at the relevant minimal acceptable level. In this sense, the *WDR 1990* definition distinguishes 'safety nets' from 'income or cash transfers.' The SSN is meant to assist those who are (temporarily) exposed to shocks (such as the unemployed), while income transfers are meant to assist those who are (relatively permanently) incapable of participating in the productive process (such as the elderly, the disabled or those who are otherwise incapable). However, the distinction has been removed from the definition of SSNs in the World Bank's *Poverty Reduction Handbook* (World Bank 1993).

This broader definition was also adopted in a World Bank discussion paper in 1996 which refers to SSNs as 'encompassing all informal family-based arrangements, all social security programs...and poverty-targeted interventions.' Other documents of the World Bank and UNCTAD during this period also define SSNs to include 'social action programs,' 'social investment funds' and 'emergency social funds' (Reddy 1998, 3).

Definition

Since the inception of the concept, the World Bank has continually elaborated on its definition of SSNs. Admitting that safety nets exist in a complex political and economic context and viewpoints on them may differ even within the same organizations and groups, the World Bank presently defines SSNs as follows:

> Safety nets are basically income maintenance programs that protect a person or household against two adverse outcomes: a chronic incapacity to work and earn, and a decline in this capacity caused by imperfectly predictable life-cycle events (such as the sudden death of a bread winner), sharp shortfalls in aggregate demand or expenditure shocks (through economic recession or transition), or very bad harvests. Safety net programs serve two important roles: *redistribution* (such as transfers to disadvantaged groups) and *insurance* (such as drought relief) (World Bank 2003a).

Another aspect of SSNs is clearly the redistributive role of SSNs in poverty reduction. According to the World Bank, the term 'safety nets' encompasses various transfer programs designed to play both a redistributive and risk reduction role in poverty reduction. The Bank argues that the redistributive role is intended to reduce the impact of poverty and the risk reduction role is intended to protect individuals, households and communities against uninsured income and consumption risks. Risks can be household-specific (e.g., death in a family, unemployment of the wage earner), community or regionally based (e.g., drought, famine, epidemics) or nationwide (e.g., drought, global financial risks, shifts in terms of trade, etc.). The linkage of SSNs and poverty is based on the assumption that the poor are more vulnerable than the non-poor to these risks. Thus, SSN programs should be designed to address the needs and characteristics of various categories of the poor.

SSN programs can be classified into formal (public) and informal safety nets. Formal and informal safety nets are, generally, distinguished from one another by law enforcement: that is, formal safety nets legally guarantee individuals access to economic or social support, whereas informal safety nets provide the likelihood of support to individuals to assure them of attaining or remaining above the designated minimum standard of living but with no legal guarantee (Reddy 1998, 1).

Examples of formal SSNs according to the World Bank include food subsidies, feeding programs, public works and other employment programs, credit-based self-employment programs, social funds and related interventions, and child allowances (World Bank 2003a).

It is noted that this latest World Bank definition of SSNs does not directly mention social insurance systems, employment guarantee schemes, severance payments and unemployment insurance which were included in a UNESCO study (Reddy 1998, 1).[5] According to the Bank, safety net transfers may take the form of cash or income transfers (such as pensions, child allowances, etc.) and in-kind transfers (i.e., food subsidies, housing subsidies, energy subsidies and feeding programs), or they may provide income support to the vulnerable by providing jobs in an emergency situation (say through a public works program). Specifically, the World Bank defines these as follows:

- Cash transfers: Common cash transfer programs include social assistance programs and family assistance programs. Social assistance refers to a range of benefits given in cash or in-kind intended to protect the most needy persons in society. Family assistance refers to all benefits given in cash or in-kind targeted directly to children or families with children.
- In-kind transfers: Although cash transfers are preferred to in-kind transfers for minimizing distortions in the economy, the choice may tilt in favor of in-kind transfers if the objective is to encourage consumption of a particular commodity, to encourage the modification of behavior, or if there are political objectives that are better served through in-kind transfers.
- Public works: Unlike cash and in-kind transfers, income generation programs obligate the recipient to exchange labor time for income transfer.

Public works can be used as a temporary measure for consumption smoothing during economic or natural shocks (such as drought) or as year-long poverty reduction programs (World Bank 2003b). In addition to public or formal safety nets, most societies have informal community-based arrangements (private safety nets) that help mitigate against deprivation and temporary income shortfalls. There are examples in Gambia and Pakistan where transfers to the needy are within the Islamic context of 'zakat' (an earmarked tax on the wealthy provided by the mosque). In sub-Saharan countries, there is a system of labor transfers within communities. Informal transfers on private accounts are considerable in the Philippines. The structural features of the rural economy in China (i.e., access to land, either individually or collectively) are a form of informal safety nets that guarantees economic security.

Informal SSNs could be categorized into private and public ones. Examples of private informal SSNs include transfers from family members, friends, neighbors and community members as well as institutions, including NGOs. Public informal SSNs refer to the support which individuals can hope for from the government, through programs which generate assets or employment, transfer income, or provide basic social services, as a means of helping affected individuals from falling below the designated minimum standard of living. The difference between formal and public informal SSNs is whether there exists a formal legal support of the assistance (Reddy 1998, 3).

An ESCAP study implicitly maintains that social safety nets are programs intended to assist people who have been adversely affected by shocks and other kinds of emergencies, not necessarily the poor. It draws a line between social safety nets and other related concepts such as social protection, social security and anti-poverty programs. It distinguishes between formal and informal safety nets. Moreover, ESCAP's view is that social safety nets should not include anti-poverty programs. It argues that

this is a mistake since anti-poverty programs are intended to ameliorate the living conditions of people living in poverty, i.e., not necessarily those affected by crises, while social safety nets are intended to assist people who have been adversely affected by shocks and other kinds of emergencies, not necessarily the poor. Social safety nets and anti-poverty programs have overlap. That is, the targets of social safety nets are those people adversely affected by crises or sudden shocks who mostly are poor people. They are the same people who are the targets of anti-poverty programs. Nevertheless, some of the targets of social safety nets may be non-poor, so long as they were adversely affected by shocks (Jurado 2001, 2).

Social protection has been referred to the panoply of institutions in society that provide 'security' for citizens in the widest sense of the term, that is, in terms of personal and collective security. It is not simply a term that has been co-opted by political and military interest groups, but it relates to such issues as consumer protection, crime prevention, environment protection, disaster prevention and relief, and it is social security in the sense of social insurance in one form or another (Jurado 2001, 1). ESCAP views social protection to be encompassing, covering all members of society, without exception. In comparison, social security is a part of social protection covering only employed individuals and households. Social safety nets are similarly a component of social protection, providing coverage to people adversely affected by crises, whether these are employed or not.[6] Finally, in contrast, anti-poverty programs cannot be regarded as parts of the social protection system except only in the broadest sense of providing assistance to people who lack security altogether. In their true sense, anti-poverty programs are special measures intended to extend succor to people in a state of want, regardless of whether these persons are employed or unemployed, or are adversely affected by crises or not (Jurado 2001, 2). We find that this view may be incorrect, particularly in terms of its definition of social security. The ILO definition of social security includes three major components: social insurance, social assistance and universal benefits. Only social insurance covers employed individuals while the latter two are poverty alleviation measures covering a broader range of beneficiaries. The paper also notes that, unlike most social services or assistance, social safety nets have nontransferable components.

The ILO has a rather narrow definition of social safety nets. The social safety net is considered to be cash transfers or part of social assistance because a social safety net providing basic protection such as primary health care and subsistence level income security would ordinarily come from the state and taxes. To the ILO, a social safety net is only one part of social assistance, while social assistance is a part of social security and social security is a part of social protection.

A digression on the social security system may provide a better understanding of the social safety net concept. To begin with, the ILO definition of social protection includes not only public social security schemes but also private or non-statutory schemes with a similar objective, such as mutual benefit societies and occupational pension schemes. Social protection includes all sorts of non-statutory schemes, formal or informal, provided that the contributions to these schemes are not wholly determined by market forces (ILO 2000, 29).

Social security, a term long used by the ILO, is defined as the protection which society provides for its members, through a series of public measures: to offset the absence or substantial reduction of income from work resulting from various contingencies (notably sickness, maternity, employment injury, unemployment, invalidity, old age and death of the breadwinner); to provide people with health care; and to provide benefits for families with children (ILO 2000, 29).

This definition of social security corresponds to the ILO Social Security Standard (Minimum Standards) Convention, 1952 (no. 102). The contingencies identified (except unemployment) affect individuals rather than communities. However, collective risks such as drought, bad harvests, natural disasters and war, also affect people's income security, especially in developing countries. Generally, existing social security systems do not specifically address these risks but cover them only through general 'social assistance.' The ILO definition of social security includes: social insurance (i.e., contributory schemes), social assistance (i.e., tax-financed benefits provided only to those with low income through a means test or income test), and universal benefits (i.e., tax-financed benefits provided without being income or means tested)[7] (ILO 2000, 29).

Social insurance is insurance for wage earners. The principle elements of social insurance are as follows:
• Participation is compulsory, with few exceptions;
• It is financed by contributions which are normally shared between employers and workers, with, perhaps, state participation in the form of a supplementary contribution or other subsidy from the general revenue;[8]
• Contributions are accumulated in special funds out of which benefits are paid;
• Surplus funds are invested to earn further income;
• A person's right to benefits is secured by his contribution record without any test of need or mean;
• Contribution and benefit rates are usually related to what the person is or has been earning (ILO 1984, 4).

Social assistance is the assistance provided by the government to the general public who are in need, particularly the elderly, the sick, invalids, survivors and the unemployed. Social assistance may be considered a social service to guarantee that more people can be helped in addition to social insurance. The main characteristics of social assistance include:
• A person does not have to join the program (by paying contributions) prior to receiving benefits. Benefits are paid as a legal right in prescribed categories of need;
• The whole cost of the program is met by the government;
• A person's other income and resources determine their eligibility. The benefit grant is designed to bring the person's total income up to a community-determined minimum, taking into account other factors such

as family size and unavoidable fixed obligations such as rent. Grants are
not related to the applicant's previous earnings or customary standard of
living;

• Social assistance is more or less the same as social welfare or social work.
It is problem-oriented and gives a certain amount of scope for discretion
in determining awards, within the framework of the rights established
under the law (ILO 1984, 5).

Social assistance, according to the ILO, is poverty alleviation measures or anti-
poverty programs.[9] The ILO admits that this is a much broader definition than
those used in certain countries.[10] In many other countries, a sharp distinction is
drawn between social security and poverty alleviation measures, notably social
assistance (ILO 2000, 29). Social assistance is considered a 'safety net' when
social insurance fails (ILO 1984, 6).

The ILO also expressed the view that the definition of social safety nets
should not include social insurance systems since social insurance is financed
from employers and workers. It also urges that social safety nets are a selective
and residual form of social policy, i.e., a gap-filling measure, and that too much
emphasis on social assistance and safety nets naturally erodes the role of social
insurance as a major pillar of social protection (Wickramasekara 1999, 3).

Other routes to social security include the direct provision by the government,
wholly or largely from general revenue, of standard benefits to each resident in a
specified category. These benefits may include a pension to every elderly, invalids,
orphaned or widowed residents. Some countries, including Thailand, operate a
national health service providing medical care for all without a contribution or
means test; the cost may be met wholly or mainly from public funds, although
there may be partial charges for dental, ophthalmic or the specialist services;
family benefits, provident funds and provision are made by employers.

To conclude this section, we take note of the ILO's comment that 'terminology
in this area has been very heavily influenced by institutions, no doubt because the
characteristics of the different institutions concerned are quite distinctive' (ILO
2000, 29). The World Bank has also accepted that 'safety nets exist in a complex
political and economic context, and viewpoints on them may differ, even within
the same organizations and groups' (World Bank 2003a). It can be noted that
the World Bank's discussion of safety net programs touches only cash transfers,
in-kind transfers and public works whereas discussion of social insurance, labor
and vocational training programs, and social funds are under the purview of the
Social Protection group. In this chapter, the World Bank's definition is mostly
used for simplicity of reference and because of the Bank's direct involvement on
the issue of social safety nets both in terms of concept and implementation.

Social Safety Nets and Economic Integration

A World Bank study (2002a) documents four stylized facts about economies that are in the process of economic integration (i.e., opening to foreign trade and investment). First, open economies tend to have more competition and higher firm turnover ('churning'). Liberalization leads to the exit of many firms and to a higher entry rate as well. Second, the presence of imports leads to a more competitive market and lower price-cost markups. Third, there is some evidence of spillovers from foreign trade and of investment raising productivity of domestic firms. Fourth, there can be learning and threshold effects of exporting that create a better environment for productivity growth.

As such, besides the adverse effects of the economic crisis, one of the most controversial aspects of economic integration, particularly in the context of safety nets, is that greater churning of firms results in higher labor market turnover. Although it has been argued that in the long run, integrating with the world economy benefits workers on average, the average result disguises the fact that some workers are likely to lose rents that they were sharing from import protection and may suffer permanent income loss.

Further, economic integration can adversely affect the real wages of formal workers, especially in the short run. It has been argued that the short-run effects of liberalization are quite different from the longer-run effects. In the short run, real wages of the formal sector worker are reduced by trade openness and increased by FDI. Thus, if an economy liberalizes trade but gets little FDI (perhaps due to a weak investment climate or a lagged response from investors), then opening of the economy can lead to temporary declines in formal sector wages.

In addition, openness seems to increase the skill premium (the higher wage that educated workers receive). Integration with the global economy increases the return to education. In the context of safety nets, a sound education system that provides opportunities for all is therefore critical.

Finally, there can be a mismatch in the timing of job contraction and job creation so that unemployment remains high for some period after the initiation of economic integration.

If these arguments hold, economic integration has certain implications on social protection and safety nets. For example, in the formal sector, workers' compensation programs, severance pay schemes and unemployment insurance are needed for those workers who lose their jobs. A good education system is needed to ensure more equal opportunities for all in the event of an increasing skill premium. But these schemes benefit only formal sector workers. In the case of Thailand, as already shown, the number of workers under the social security scheme and workers' compensation were relatively small; in 2000, they represented only 12 percent of the country's labor force. Besides, the unemployment insurance program is only in the very early stage of development. Thus, the informal sector or self-employed who do not benefit from such schemes need to be attended to. To a large extent, public works programs that provide pay or food for work reach this sector more effectively. That is to say, the nature of safety nets will have a large effect on the benefits of integration.

As economic integration can create losers as well as winners, it is important to learn and identify what can be done to reduce and mitigate its adverse impacts.

Overview of Social Safety Nets in Southeast Asia

There have been at least four major studies that touch upon social safety nets in Southeast Asia.

- A study by Knowles, Pernia and Racelis (1999), *Social Consequences of the Financial Crisis in Asia* for the Asian Development Bank;
- A study by Gonzales M. Jurado (2001), *An Integrated Study of Selected Social Safety Net Policies and Program in Asia and the Pacific* for ESCAP;
- A study by TDRI (2000), *Social Impacts of the Asian Economic Crisis in Thailand, Indonesia, Malaysia and the Philippines*; and
- A study by Cook, Kabeer and Suwannarat (2003), *Social Protection in Asia*.

ADB Study

In the last quarter of 1998, the Asian Development Bank (ADB) initiated a project to assess the social consequences of the financial and economic crisis, under regional technical assistance. Under the project, six case studies were undertaken for Indonesia, Korea, Lao PDR, Malaysia, the Philippines and Thailand. Because the primary aim of the project was to assess the social impact of the Asian financial crisis, there was no comprehensive review of social safety nets; rather, social safety nets were looked into in terms of responses to the crisis. Although the ADB study does not clearly define the concept of social safety nets, another ADB report mentions that formal safety net programs include unemployment insurance, old-age pension and social assistance, public works and social funds, health insurance and crop insurance, and other agricultural stabilization measures (ADB 2000, 220).

In general, it was found that most of the six countries have only limited social safety nets. For example, only Korea has a functioning unemployment insurance program that provided benefits of limited magnitude and duration only to employees of enterprises with 30 or more employees. Existing social safety nets of these countries include a very wide range of measures, some of which are questionable in terms of efficiency and equity (Knowles, Pernia and Racelis 1999, 61).

In this study, the family is counted as a safety net. To cope with the crisis, households had to adjust in terms of spending, consumption, labor allocation, etc. As for public social safety nets, governments of these countries arranged a wide range of interventions including; employment regulations; unemployment insurance and other forms of assistance to the unemployed; job training and job creation; pensions and provident funds; public works and other forms of income maintenance; price controls and subsidies; maintaining access to social services.

During the crisis, some governments also borrowed money from the ADB and the World Bank to support their safety net programs and have made key policy reforms, both to improve the effectiveness of their social safety nets (e.g., extended coverage, shift to more targeted forms of support) and to strengthen the financing and provision of social services (Knowles, Pernia and Racelis 1999, 53).

In brief, the ADB study found that the Republic of Korea has relatively sophisticated social safety nets compared to the other five countries. The programs include public assistance programs such as medical aid, veteran relief and disaster relief. However, Korea's social protection levels are limited and provide only partial protection to workers in the formal sectors. Since 1995, Korea has had an unemployment benefit scheme. However, by April 1998, it only covered an estimated 22 percent of people who lost their jobs. Since the onset of the crisis, Korea has expanded its unemployment benefits, raising the benefit level gradually from 50 to 70 percent of the minimum wage and extending the minimum duration of the benefits to two months. Also in 1998, the government increased its allocation for social welfare assistance and support by 13 percent to people with no income.

In Indonesia, through a provident fund system, lump-sum payments are provided for old age, disability and survivor benefits. These benefits are limited to firms with more than 10 employees or with a payroll above Rs 1 million (US$140) per month. Coverage is gradually being extended to smaller firms and seasonal workers. Indonesia also has a social insurance system that provides medical benefits and work-related injury benefits. In 1998, the government provided an across-the-board subsidy on food items such as rice, corn, sugar, soybean, wheat flour, soybean meal and fishmeal at a cost of 0.5–0.7 percent of GDP. Subsidies for petroleum products (kerosene and diesel) and electricity were also maintained at more than 10 percent of GDP. Other public programs include providing scholarships for needy students, financing essential drugs for rural and urban health centers, providing subsidies for low-cost housing, and expanding credit schemes to cover small and medium-sized enterprises and rural cooperatives.

According to the study, Malaysia has two types of social safety net programs: a dual provident fund that provides both lump-sum and periodic payments for old age, disability, death and medical benefits; and a social insurance system that covers disability and work-related injury benefits. The government of Malaysia later increased public expenditure on major anti-poverty programs to protect the real spending per beneficiary. The programs include the Fund-for-Food program, which provides small-scale loans to the poorest rural areas for income-generating activities, improving water supply and strengthening welfare programs. The government also expanded safety net programs such as urban micro credit for hawkers, traders and entrepreneurs; a fund for small and medium-sized industries to increase their competitiveness and viability; skill training for retrenched workers; and preserving priority long-term development investments in education and health.

The main social safety net program of the Philippines is a social insurance system that covers benefits for old age, disability, death and medical care. Participation and contributions are compulsory for all private employees who are not more than 60 years old. Government employees are covered under a separate system (the Government Service Insurance System). The government also began to promote food security by subsidizing essential staples—such as rice and oil—for the poorest households in the poorest villages. The country also introduced two types of public works schemes: the Food-for-Work scheme, established in 1987, and the Cash-for-Work scheme, established in 1990. For the latter, the wage rate was set about 25 percent higher than agricultural market wages.

In 1999, Thailand also had a social insurance system providing old age, disability, death and medical benefits for a limited number of workers in firms with 10 or more employees. Government employees were under a different system. The ADB study indicates that the safety nets during the time of the financial crisis included temporary labor-intensive civil works programs in construction and infrastructure and the Social Investment Fund. The government also strengthened its social spending programs by expanding its scholarship and loan programs to minimize student dropouts, protecting operational budgets for teacher training and instructional materials, relocating resources toward health programs for the poor and redeploying health staff to rural areas. To protect urban low-income workers, a subsidy for urban bus and rail fares would be maintained (ADB 2000, 205).

ESCAP Study

In 1999, the UN ESCAP Secretariat implemented a project aimed at strengthening policies and programs on social safety nets in the ESCAP region, through case studies of the countries that were severely affected by the 1997 Asian economic crisis and through regional seminars (including a seminar on the development of conceptualization and planning to help find ways for strengthening social safety nets). The case studies were conducted in four countries: Indonesia, the Philippines, the Republic of Korea and Thailand. As a follow-up, ESCAP convened a regional seminar to discuss the experience found by these studies.[11] An integrated report of the country studies was prepared by Gonzales M. Jurado and used as a background paper for the seminar.[12]

The ESCAP integrated report, after defining the concept, classified social safety nets in the four countries based on the following issues: food security, employment and income generation, health and welfare, education, and people's empowerment through community development.

The report noted that, based on this simple enumeration, these countries had not sacrificed long-term considerations of social development in favor of strictly short-term crisis-directed projects. For example, while food security and employment and income-generation projects were short-term in the sense that their effects addressed immediate needs, the programs relating to health, education and people's empowerment can only be considered long-term, since their impact enhanced not only the people's immediate welfare but also their overall capacity for long-term growth and development (Jurado 2001, 7).

The paper then assessed the strengths and weaknesses of these social safety nets in terms of: policy basis, program design, targeting, method of administration, monitoring and evaluation, dissemination and database. The findings for Thailand were that most programs were new; however, they benefited from detailed prior preparations as required by the external loans that underpinned them. The program design at large was overlapping and there was no clearinghouse to ensure program compatibility. Evaluation on the matter of targeting was nonexistent. Yet, while no praise was heaped on the targeting of social safety nets, no criticism was directed at it either. On the issue of program administration, no serious question has been raised related to planning, coordination and transparency or corruption.[13] With regard to the monitoring and evaluation of social safety nets, Thailand paid little attention to the qualitative aspects of the results such as the extent of beneficiary satisfaction, degree of goal achievement and so forth. Information dissemination in Thailand was found to be intermittent, spotty and half-hearted. The assessment of the database in Thailand was not clear. It was mentioned that the gathering of data for social safety nets continues at the central, provincial and community levels, but there is no discussion on the problem of the database.

For all four countries, the report indicates that they expanded their existing poverty reduction or social welfare programs, or established new social safety nets in order to lessen the social impact of the 1997 crisis. The four countries mounted social safety net programs to ensure food security, continuity of education and health services, new employment opportunities and wider participation of people in the administration of social safety net programs. The paper noted that the programs were said to have reached many thousands of people throughout the countries and ameliorated their living conditions. Nevertheless, the programs suffered from a number of defects and shortcomings in the areas of policy basis, program design, targeting, program administration, as well as monitoring and evaluation of the programs. The policy basis of most programs was uneven; it was strong in some instances but weak in others. The design of some programs was faulty and gave rise to consequences that tended to neutralize beneficial program effects. Targeting was less than outstanding, not least because the programs had no solid databases and had not benefited from maximum consultation with relevant constituents. Program administration suffered from many mistakes. Some implementers considered the social safety nets to be extraneous to their terms of reference and consequently felt imposed upon. Moreover, monitoring and evaluation (which was typically done by separate internal and external auditors) were spotty, often coming to conflicting conclusions.

TDRI Study

During 1999–2000, the Thailand Development Research Institute (TDRI) coordinated a collaborative research project among research institutes in Indonesia, Malaysia, the Philippines and Thailand with financial support from the Ford Foundation. The research focused on the social impacts of the Asian economic crisis in these four countries. In this study, social safety nets are not clearly defined and most country studies apply the concept in the sense of social security and social welfare, except in the case of Indonesia where the term safety nets tends to be more limited, referring to emergency social funds that serve to protect individuals from falling below a defined minimum standard of living.

It was found that, in general, the four Asian countries have not adequately developed formal social safety nets. Similar to what was found in the ADB study, in most countries, there was a limited mandatory compensation in the form of severance pay or other benefits for those who were laid off, there was no unemployment insurance while other social security benefits for the unemployed were very limited. Furthermore, most of the social security benefits are not available to the self-employed or workers in the informal sector, who comprise the majority of the workforce in these countries. Thus the vulnerable groups in these countries tended to rely primarily on informal and traditional safety nets provided through the family and/or community.

The Indonesian case study notes that the social safety net programs in this country have not been effective. Implementation of the programs was not only slow, but the programs were also in disarray and full of controversy. The bureaucracy lacked the capacity to manage the programs. It not only lacked experience in designing and implementing the programs, but staff were demoralized during the rapid deterioration of the crisis and political turmoil. In the case of Indonesia, the social safety net programs were spelled out explicitly in the IMF reform package in June 1998 almost a full year after the crisis began in August 1997. The social safety net programs were developed through BAPPENAS (the national planning agency) in September 1998. The programs consisted of four elements: food security program, public works program, social protection program (on health and education) and promotion of small and medium enterprises.

The safety net programs were criticized as a total failure; they did not reach the poor and the programs were tainted by corruption. The World Bank had to delay disbursement of its loan to Indonesia, partly because of some concern that the fund was not being properly used. BAPPENAS admitted, in early 1999, that disbursement of the social safety net fund had been very slow, and that the program did not function smoothly. It was also reported that only 30–34 percent of the fund was actually used (Paitoonpong 2000, 16).

The reasons behind the failure include: poor program design due to an uncoordinated collection of programs submitted by various government departments; and BAPPENAS's lack of full control and authority to channel the fund, as well as poor implementation. In fact, several NGOs were against foreign donors' assistance to social safety net programs.

The Indonesian study makes an important point: because of the failure of formal social safety nets, informal safety nets were imperative. First, the extended family is the most important source of safety nets. Second, the agricultural sector and the informal sector also provided other forms of natural safety nets. Third, female family members played an important role in providing natural safety nets.

Malaysia was in a different position, compared to Indonesia and Thailand, in facing the social impacts of the crisis. First, the impacts were less serious, and second, there already was a social protection system in place that widely provided for those in need, especially for lower-income people. In response to the crisis, specific programs and funds were designated for certain sectors or needy groups. Examples include rural social infrastructure facilities; Fund for Food program through provision of low-interest loans to small farmers and the Farmers' Association; Hardcore-Poverty Development Program to provide loans to the hard-core poor for income-earning activities through Amanah Ikhtier Malaysia (AIM); Small-Scale Entrepreneur Fund and the Economic Business Group Fund to provide assistance to petty traders, hawkers and small entrepreneurs in urban areas; Small and Medium-Scale Industry (SMI) Fund to assist small and medium-scale businesses in expanding production; and National Higher Education Fund to provide financial assistance to students in local universities and colleges.

However, program implementation was disappointing. The Fund for Food Program, for example, lent out only RM199 million out of an allocated RM 700 million. The Special Scheme for Low Cost Housing approved only RM 241 million out of the available RM 2,000 million, while the Small-Scale Entrepreneur Fund could loan out only RM 882 million out of RM 1,500 million available.

The Philippine case study, like the ADB study, indicated that there were two major formal safety nets. One is the Social Security System (SSS) for the private sector and the other is the Government Service System (GSIS) for the public sector. The author noted that both systems had limited coverage for retirement. As such, only a small portion of the system would directly benefit people affected by the crisis. Benefits such as sickness, disability and hospitalization should not be considered as direct consequences of the crisis. For the crisis-affected people, safety nets came in the form of loans; funding for displaced workers; educational, calamity and housing loans; and emergency loans. In addition, the government tapped the SSS for other types of loans such as the Guarantee Fund for Small and Medium Enterprises (GFSME), which provided funds for the Enterprise Stabilization Guarantee Fund (ESGF). The use of SSS funds was not a good idea mainly because the fund itself was not sufficient for the benefits of its direct beneficiaries.

In the Philippines, a safety net that was considered to be efficient in helping the crisis-affected people was the Public Employment Service Office (PESO) under the Department of Labor and Employment. This agency was set up to monitor laid-off workers at the local level, to provide job placements, to distribute information on job vacancies and available programs for retraining and entrepreneurship, and to provide credit/livelihood assistance. In 1998, PESO conducted job and livelihood fairs nationwide, placing 114,302 job applicants and assisting 141,122 students through its career guidance programs.[14] Other formal measures include: the National Economic Summit (NES) established in February 1998 to coordinate intersectoral cooperative responses to the crisis (two out of four of the programs involve protecting jobs and enhancing productivity, and protecting vulnerable groups); rice assistance, a form of food subsidy programs, provided in drought-affected areas; training for 1,229 displaced workers; and 10,774 scholarships in technical programs for a maximum of three years. These forms of government assistance were, however, small-scale.

In Thailand, formal safety nets include a social security system and severance payment. As of September 1999, the beneficiaries of the social security system were 5.5 million workers (only about 15 percent of the total labor force). It has been observed that the Thai case study's review of safety nets, particularly the existing programs prior to the crisis, was not exhaustive. There were, in fact, many more forms of safety nets provided both formally and informally. For example, for the public sector at least, there was a pension system for civil servants. The Ministry of Labor and Social Welfare also provided a number of welfare programs for the disadvantaged, such as the elderly, the disabled and the unemployed. However, the study identified a number of rescue programs which included the following: the Asian Development Bank's Social Sector Program Loan (SSPL) of US$500 million aimed at supporting social projects via the Ministries of Education, Public Health, Labor and Social Welfare, and Agriculture; and World Bank loans of US$300 million, disbursed through the Social Investment Program (SIP), aimed at creating employment and capacity-building in communities and local governments.

Ford Foundation Study

A recent study on social safety nets in Southeast Asia was undertaken in 2000 under the Ford Foundation's regional offices in Asia. The preliminary report was discussed in Bangkok in February 2001 and the revised report was published in 2003. In spite of the high quality of the study, because of time and space constraints, this study is not reviewed here. It can be said, however, that the study emphasizes social protection as a development issue and not as a welfare or safety net issue and the focus is on 'demand-led' provision of social protection. The study covers China, South Asia and Southeast Asia. For Southeast Asia, the study included Indonesia, the Philippines, Thailand and Vietnam. The Southeast Asia study provides greater coverage of safety nets than do other studies mentioned earlier in this paper, particularly in terms of informal safety nets.

Thailand's Social Safety Nets

Formal Safety Nets

This section provides a detailed examination of social safety nets (SSNs), both formal and informal, in Thailand. Formal SSNs are based on a narrow definition of the social service programs provided by the government and are enforced by law. Informal SSNs can be classified into public SSNs and private (including community, family as well as individual's) SSNs.

With reference to the ILO definition of social security, existing social safety net programs in Thailand may be divided into five categories: social insurance (formal or statutory contributory social insurance); voluntary or self (social) insurance;[15] social assistance; universal benefits welfare programs or general social welfare programs (financed by general or tax revenue); and informal private social safety nets.

Formal or Statutory Social Insurance

There are three programs under this category: social insurance under the 1990 Social Security Act, Workmen Compensation Fund and insurance for car accidents.

The 1990 Social Security Act stipulates that establishments employing at least 10 employees must register their employees in the social security system administered by the Social Security Office. The benefits specified by law include sickness benefits, maternity benefits, disability benefits, death benefits, pension, family benefits and unemployment benefits. In 2000, only the first four benefits were implemented. As of April 2000, about 5.86 million employees were registered; this is an increase from about 5.6 million in 1996 (before the crisis). The number of registered employees increased to 6.82 million in August 2002 (NESDB 2002a, 46).

Under this scheme, the insured person will receive health care treatment at the contracted hospital or clinic free of charge. For the maternity benefit, the insured person or wife of the insured is given a lump sum of 4,000 baht per delivery. The maternity benefit is limited to two deliveries only, and the qualifying period is after at least seven months of contribution.

For sickness benefits, the scheme provides income compensation during sickness at the rate of 50 percent of normal income for no longer than 90 days per episode and not exceeding 180 days per year. An income compensation of 90 days is also given for maternity leave. For chronic illness, which is approved as being disabled, the insured is entitled to 50 percent of normal income for life and 2,000 baht for health care cost per month. For death benefits, survivors receive 20,000 baht for funeral costs and the amount of the cash benefit depends on the length of contribution.

Since December 1998, benefits have been extended to cover old age security and family benefits (TDRI 1998, 35). Beginning April 1 2002, enterprises having one or more employees are required to be registered under the Social Security Act as well.

The Workmen Compensation Fund, enforced by the 1994 Workmen Compensation Act, provides protection for employees in the event of illness or accident related to work. The benefits include payment for treatment of any illness or accident related to work on a fee-for-service basis, and in case of death, survivals will receive a lump-sum amount for funeral costs (100 times the minimum wage) and 60 percent of normal income for eight years. If the illness/accident results in disability, the employee will receive 60 percent of normal income for 15 years. Rehabilitation expenses will also be covered by the Fund. The Fund covers the same group of workers as the Social Security program, but is limited to illness and accident from work, and employers are the sole contributors to the Fund. It is anticipated that, like the social insurance, the Fund will extend its coverage to enterprises employing one or more employees.

Insurance for car accidents is compulsory for every car owner to ensure initial access to medical care for a car accident victim regardless of the victim's financial condition. The 1990 Car Accident Act requires owners of all cars to buy insurance to cover car victims. In 1995, there were approximately 7.85 million policies issued under this Act.

Occupational and/or Private Social Insurance

This category includes three schemes: the Provident Fund, aimed at providing old-age security; private insurance which is insurance arranged with private companies and can be health or old-age security insurance, or both depending on the nature of the contract; and an occupational pension or security scheme. ILO classifies these programs under separate categories outside social insurance and social assistance (ILO 1984, 3–10, 14).

A provident fund is a means of compulsory saving. Workers and their employers pay regular contributions into a central fund and the contributions are credited to a separate account, to which interest is added periodically for each worker. When specified events occur—such as old age, invalidity or death—the total outstanding credit on the account is paid out to the worker or to survivors. The provident fund scheme thus provides a safety net to employees and their family in case of death, retirement or unemployment. An employee can contribute between 3–15 percent of their earnings to the fund while the employer must contribute at a rate not lower than that of the employee. As of August 1997, 951 provident funds with an amount of 124,973 million baht had been registered covering 1.04 million employees and 4,410 employers (TDRI 1998). In September 2002, there were 620 voluntary provident funds, covering 1.22 million employees (NESDB 2002a, 46).

Occupational security schemes include civil servant pension schemes[16] and private or state enterprise occupational pension schemes (ILO 1984, 14). The scheme is available to government officials and employees of state enterprises as well as large private enterprises. One scheme is the health care benefit based on the 1990 Health Care Act for Civil Servants. Another major scheme is the old-age security system, which is in transition from the old system to the new system—Central Provident Fund (CPF).

Social Assistance and General Welfare Programs
In principle, social assistance and welfare programs provide support to those who do not earn an income sufficient to provide for minimum consumption needs (ADB 2000, 220). They are generally financed from general revenue rather than individual contributions. The characteristics of social assistance as well as universal benefits (or general welfare programs) were discussed earlier in the chapter. It should be noted that, in fact, social assistance and general welfare schemes are very different in terms of legal right and nature of eligibility. An example of these programs is the 'health-for-all insurance program' or health card, aimed at guaranteeing access to health care for cardholders. The purpose of the health card scheme is to provide a health safety net for those not covered by any other scheme. A family can apply for a health card by paying a 500 baht registration fee with an additional subsidy of 500 baht by the government. One card covers the cardholder and the person's family (not exceeding five persons). The benefits include free medical care, necessary preventive care and rehabilitation services at the registered provider. As of June 1997, approximately 2,425 million cards had been issued. Assuming an average family size of four persons, the health insurance card covers approximately 9.7 million persons.

In 2002, a health program called '30 baht for any sickness' was established. The success of the implementation of the program is still under review (Siamwalla 2003).

General welfare programs are provided mainly by the Ministry of Public Health (MPH), the Ministry of Labor (MOL) and the Ministry of Social Development and Human Security.[17] The welfare schemes under this category include:[18]
• free health care programs provided by MPH;
• living allowance by MOL;
• employment services by the Department of Employment (DOE), MOL; occupational promotion funds by DOE consisting of Public Economic Welfare Fund, Women's Occupational Promotion Fund, and Rehabilitation the Disable Fund;
• Laborers' Fund by the Department of Labor Protection and Welfare, MOL;

- Industrial Rehabilitation Centers for workers who become disabled due to work accidents, administered by the Social Security Office with technical assistance from the Japanese government;
- Welfare for the Disabled, consisting of nine Rehabilitation Centers for the Disabled, Human Clinic and Allowance for the Disabled. The scheme has been transferred from the administration of the Department of Social Welfare, MOL, to the newly established Ministry of Social Development and Human Security (MSDS);
- Children and Youth Welfare by MSDS;
- Women's Welfare and Protection Centers and Women's Rehabilitation Home by MSDS;
- Welfare for the Elderly Scheme consisting of 19 Nursing Homes, 18 Centers for Social Welfare Services for the Elderly, Allowance for the Elderly and 200 Centers for the Elderly Residing in Temples. The Scheme is under the responsibility of MSDS;
- Regional Disaster Relief Centers by the MSDS;
- Self-Settlement Project under MSDS;
- Hill-tribe Welfare and Development Centers by MSDS;
- Government's Pawn Shops by DPW;
- Teachers' Loan by the Ministry of Education; and
- Students' Loan by the Ministry of Education.

Informal Social Safety Nets

For the sake of convenience, an informal social safety net is used to refer to any form of social welfare service or assistance that is not provided by the government. In particular, informal safety nets include social assistance from relatives, friends, religious and voluntary organizations. In Thailand, where more than one-half of the workforce and population are in agriculture and in rural areas, formal social safety nets have limited coverage. Only a small proportion of the population is covered by any pension plan, and a large number of the people do not receive income compensation during sickness. Many still rely on the informal system.

A study by Ogawa (2002) shows an example of how the elderly in Thailand are dependent upon informal social safety nets. In 1996, 52.9 percent of the elderly relied on their children. Public pensions and private pensions accounted for only 7.3 percent and 2.1 percent of the elderly, respectively. The dependency on children is comparable to the elderly in the Republic of Korea, but contrary to the case of Japan, the U.S. or Germany. Public assistance is almost negligible not only for Thailand but in the other four countries as well (Table 8-1). Japan used to be like this. However, as the Japanese economy grew, the so-called nuclear family emerged as a social phenomenon and the services sector for the aged expanded beyond the nursing home.

Table 8-1   Sources of Income for the Elderly (60 years and older) in Thailand and Selected Countries 1996[a] (%)

Source of main income from:	Japan	U.S.A.	Thailand	Korea	Germany
Work	21.6	15.5	26.9	26.6	4.6
Public pensions	57.1	55.5	7.3	2.9	77.0
Private pensions	1.7	13.3	2.1	0.5	10.1
Savings	2.4	1.5	1.9	4.9	1.6
Assets	2.5	8.5	4.8	4.5	2.0
Children	4.2	0.0	52.9	56.3	0.2
Public assistance	0.3	0.3	0.3	3.7	0.6
Other	2.4	1.6	3.6	0.3	1.7
No answer	7.9	3.7	0.2	0.4	2.2

Note: a. The results are based on self-reporting. The distinction between savings and assets is not clear-cut, but most Japanese view savings as money in their savings account.
Source: Ogawa (2002), Table 11.

In Thailand, where increased trust, reciprocity and functioning of social networks are possible, there are reports documenting many cases of familial breakdown and the erosion of traditional Thai values (World Bank 1999b, 13). In recent years, communities especially in rural areas have witnessed a rapid shift from mutual help and reciprocal labor exchange to a cash economy where rural laborers work primarily for a wage. When younger generations migrate for jobs to urban areas, they often leave small children in the hands of the elderly; as such, the new generation of workers has become detached from the extended family and village life and thus is more individualistic. It has been maintained that the cultural and social norms that were essential to the institutions and relationships of an earlier agrarian era have been eroding. There is also a greater tendency for open confrontation among individuals and groups (World Bank 1999b, 24).

The weakening of so-called social capital can be caused by a number of factors: a breakdown in community trust; increased competition for employment among members who once cooperated; increased incidence of theft, violence, crime and drug dealing; and higher dropout rates among school children. Frustration and psychological stress can lead to heightened household and community tension. Crime rates are rising and the crisis has reinforced the drug trade as an easy way to earn money. This is consistent with the survey by the Social Research Institute (1999), which indicated that problems of drugs, robbery and gambling have increased in communities, especially in Bangkok and other urban areas. In many communities, unemployment is the main problem and has contributed to increased frustration among fresh graduates with no previous work experience.

However, there is the possibility, particularly during the crisis, of rising opportunities to increase informal social connection and assistance through the relationship of trust and cooperation within a society or community. If networks of individuals in society can be strengthened, this would imply an increase in cooperative behavior. The crisis may force a number of families to become more disciplined and resilient. Many Thai communities have been stimulated to increase cooperation and mutual support during the crisis. The TDRI study (2000, 37) indicates some revival of social capital that had been eroded prior to the crisis (for example, the practice of labor exchange in agriculture).

In rural areas, there are at least three major types of village networks: production networks, saving networks and environment networks. In the former two instances, the networks are formed to achieve certain scale economies, such as to secure sufficient inputs for production and to benefit from information exchange. The last type of network is mainly formed for regulating environmental externalities.

Another source of informal safety nets is related to religion and temples. The TDRI study (2000) revealed that during the time of the crisis, temples were an important source of food and shelter for some villagers. Indeed, village people relied heavily on assistance from temples not only for food and shelter but also for consultations in dealing with problems and/or psychological stress. Temples also provide a forum for social gathering in many communities. In 2000, there were 31,111 Buddhist temples, 3,181 mosques (Muslim temples), 2,200 Christian churches and 40 Hindu temples in Thailand.

Nongovernmental organizations (NGOs) are also sources of informal safety nets for many. NGOs have a long history in Thailand. The first was the Red Cross Organization founded during King Rama V's regime followed by a few Chinese public service NGOs. In 1967, Puay Ungpakorn founded a development-oriented NGO, called the Rural Reconstruction Foundation, in Chainart.

Legally or by registration, there are five types of NGOs at present: associations, foundations, chambers of commerce, funeral service associations and labor unions (TDRI 2000, 6). Each of these organizations was established for a specific purpose or activities. For example, chambers of commerce are based on the 1966 Chamber of Commerce Act and funeral service associations are based on the 1974 Funeral Service Fund Act. However, there are many NGOs that are not registered. In practice, voluntary organizations consist of various forms such as groups, societies, centers, institutes, offices, organizations, projects and clubs. It is believed that there are more than 17,000 associations and foundations in Thailand (TDRI 2000, 7).[19]

NGOs in Thailand can also be classified by areas, field of work or interest as follows: children/youth NGOs; women NGOs; workers or labor NGOs; hill-tribe and minority group NGOs; human rights NGOs; slum dwellers NGOs; public Health NGOs; agriculture NGOs; natural resources and environment NGOs; and development coordination and promotion NGOs.

In 1997, there were about 550 organized or active NGOs in Thailand (not counting labor unions and small or unregistered foundations and associations).

About 40 percent of them were in the Bangkok area, followed by those in the North and Northeast. The majority of NGOs (147) were involved in development promotion, followed by those engaging in environment and natural resources (87) (Table 8-2). Unfortunately, the extent of services of these NGOs is not known, although it can be expected that the service-rendering NGOs are providers of informal safety nets.

Strengthening Safety Nets in Thailand[20]

To review briefly, after the burst of the bubble economy in early July 1997, the government applied for IMF rescue. The IMF's board approved the rescue package on August 11 in the same year. Under the umbrella of the IMF, a US$17.2 billion standby credit facility was made available for balance-of-payment support, with disbursement made quarterly over almost three years and contingent on Thailand meeting IMF performance requirements. The total sum included $2.7 billion from the World Bank and the Asian Development Bank to be used to enhance industrial competitiveness, improve capital markets and mitigate social problems arising from the crisis and the austerity program (Lauridsen 149). It should also be noted that there was a change of government during this period. The Chuan Government took office on November 15, 1997.

As reviewed in the previous section, social safety nets seem to have covered a wide range of activities. Nevertheless, the safety nets and the larger social protection framework in Thailand contained many gaps in instruments and coverage. Before the crisis, several appropriate safety net instruments were not available—in particular, unemployment insurance, a pension scheme for the private sector and large-scale transfer programs for the poor, such as food stamps, transfer entitlements for the indigent and so forth.

The activities taken during the earlier stage of the crisis (prior to the Chuan government) include the following:

- The National Social Policy Committee (NSPC) established in July 1998[21] provided funding of 40 million baht for a pilot project to create more space for civic groups at the local level, both formal and informal, to participate in local policy formulation.
- The Ministry of Finance established the Community Organization Development Institute (CODI) to oversee funding and activities concerning income generation for, and strengthening of, community groups.
- The NESDB set up a Subcommittee on Civil Society to provide input and monitor implementation of the 8th Plan.
- The Bank-for-the-Poor Network was developed among eight networks of savings groups and micro credit organizations to try to coordinate their efforts and know-how to help strengthen local community finance.

Table 8-2   NGOs by Field of Service and Region

	Region					
	Bangkok and Vicinity	Lower North and Central Region	Upper North	North-east	South	Total
Agriculture	6	7	10	16	5	44
Children and youth	20	2	15	13	2	52
Labor	5	-	-	1	-	6
Hill tribes	20	-	19	-	-	39
Coordination and development support works	51	9	28	48	11	147
Women	12	-	12	4	1	29
Religion and development	10	-	2	5	-	17
Slums	15	-	-	1	2	18
Primary health care and consumers'protection	37	1	25	9	2	74
Community development	1	4	3	3	1	12
Natural resources and the environment	25	4	18	17	23	87
Human rights	9	-	1	2	1	13
Media	10	1	-	1	-	12
Total	221	28	133	120	48	550

Source: TDRI (2000), Table 1.

• The Social Investment Project was initiated. Subsequently, a major step undertaken by the Chuan government to strengthen the social safety net was to endorse the revision of the 8th National Economic and Social Development Plan to respond better to the crisis along the three major guidelines: alleviation of unemployment problems in urban areas and promoting employment in the rural areas to absorb returning migration; assisting underprivileged groups; preventing and alleviating social problems, especially drug use and crimes, as well as promoting commendable social values. Other major improvements of the safety nets were identified in the Fifth Letter of Intent from the Royal Thai Government to the IMF (see Box 8-1).

The onset of the crisis was a period of intense scrutiny of existing gaps in the social protection framework and debate over how to address them. As will be seen in the following sections, the government strengthened some aspects of the public sector safety nets, such as the severance pay requirements and the

Box 8-1   Thailand: Strengthening the Social Safety Net

With the deepening recession, the government made improvements in the targeting of social safety net programs a priority in the 1998/99 budget. Principal activities in the central government budget for 1998/99 include:

- The extension of the student loan program to maintain attendance in schools and universities to an additional 100,000 students, whose families can no longer afford tuition payments (an increase in spending from B18.3 billion to B20 billion);
- The maintenance of employment-generating public works programs in water supply, irrigation and infrastructure;
- Free medical treatment and improvement of rural health care facilities for an additional three million people;
- The expansion of the micro credit program (10,000 baht per loan) to the unemployed who wish to become self-employed (additional spending of 300 million baht).

These activities are supplemented as follows:

- The expenditure program of state enterprises were redesigned and augmented to focus on infrastructure projects in rural and urban areas (50 billion baht or 1 percent of GDP).
- Coverage under health, disability, death and maternity benefits for the unemployed insured in the Social Security Fund will be extended from six to twelve months effective October 1, 1998. This measure would extend coverage to an estimated additional 100,000 unemployed at an expenditure of 1 billion baht.
- A new Labor Protection Act became effective on August 19, increasing severance payments to long-serving employees (more than six years of tenure) from six to ten months. A subsistence fund would also be created to cover those unemployed whose former employers were forced to declare bankruptcy and were unable to fulfill their severance pay obligations.
- The social investment program was accelerated, within existing programs financed by the World Bank and OECF (SIP) and the ADB (Social Sector Loan), involving a total disbursement of 26 billion baht over three years. Projects to be implemented as soon as possible include:
  - Job training for 120,000 individuals,
  - Small-scale rural employment projects,
  - Up to 200,000 scholarships for primary and secondary education,
  - An expansion of the health care program for those not covered under the Social Security Fund.

Continued on the next page.

Box 8-1   Thailand: Strengthening the Social Safety Net (Continued)

A total disbursement of B12 billion was expected in the remaining
months of fiscal year 1997/98 and fiscal year 1998/99.
- The government would finalize by the end of December 1998 a
detailed plan and implementation timetable for the introduction of a
comprehensive old-age pension system.

Source: Bank of Thailand (1998).

social security scheme, and it vigorously pursued employment generation and
training as ways to assist those with job and income losses. The government did
not, however, launch an unemployment insurance scheme or expand its small-
scale transfer programs for the indigent. There were concerns about permanent
entitlements, fiscal burdens and untimely taxes on labor and fiscal burdens,
and untimely taxes on labor and employers. In addition, there were strong and
deeply felt views on how best to restore the damaged social fabric and strengthen
self-reliance. The Prime Minister and his cabinet, leading civil society thinkers,
and, of course, the views of H.M. the King, shared a determination to restore
traditional Thai values of self-reliance and self-help and an equally strong desire
not to undermine such values in society.

This view has helped precipitate long-pending reforms and initiatives to build
the capacity of communities and families to help themselves and each other.
Thus, in addition to vital improvements to official safety net programs in the
public domain, the Chuan Government with its civil society partners pursued an
innovative second track designed to build an unofficial social protection network,
through empowerment of communities and the development of social capital.

During the first few months of the crisis in 1997, the government became
increasingly concerned with layoffs, not only in the financial sector, but also
in construction and services. The government approached international donor
agencies (the Asian Development Bank, the World Bank and the Overseas
Economic Cooperation Fund of Japan) for financing in two areas: job creation
and budget support for vital services benefiting the poor and unemployed.
The first loan came from the ADB in the form of an emergency Social Sector
Program Loan, which provided balance-of-payments and budget support
aimed at improving health, education and employment services. The second
loan package was the Social Investment Project, financed by the World Bank,
the Overseas Economic Cooperation Fund of Japan (OECF, now JBIC), the
Australian Agency for International Development (AusAID) and the United

Nations Development Program (UNDP). This second loan package financed expansions of selected government programs to create jobs and provide services to the poor and unemployed.

The Project also financed a new Social Investment Fund to support community capacity building and a Regional Urban Development Fund to provide infrastructure loans to municipalities. International donors were to consider follow-up loans to further support the government's efforts in employment generation and the establishment of a more comprehensive social protection system.

The government took other steps to address the unemployment problem as it became clear from various sources that the incomes of the poor and near-poor were declining. The then Ministry of Labor and Social Welfare, for example, in cooperation with relevant ministries formulated an Action Plan for the Alleviation of Unemployment Problems. It set forth seven measures to address the impacts of the crisis including: repatriation of immigrant workers, promotion of Thai workers abroad, employment generation in rural areas, training for the unemployed and employment preservation through support to labor-intensive and export industries.

Financed through a combination of budget allocations and loans from the World Bank, the OECF of Japan and the Asian Development Bank, the government initiated temporary, labor-intensive civil works programs in both rural and urban areas consistent with regional unemployment and poverty patterns. These works included school repair; road, small dam and weir construction; rural industrial promotion; rehabilitation and expansion of small-scale irrigation projects; improvements of basic infrastructure benefiting the tourist industry; and a village center development project which would employ new labor market entrant volunteers.

In addition to civil works projects, employment-generation initiatives also focused on the expansion of vocational and skills-training programs for the unemployed and new labor market entrants; occupational and income-generating promotion; foreign worker supervision; promotion of overseas employment; loans for employment promotion; and the establishment of an employment information system. With assistance under the Asian Development Bank's Social Sector Program Loan, the Ministry of Labor and Social Welfare launched Centers for Assistance to Laid-off Workers, a one-stop service center to help laid-off workers in the areas of severance pay, social security, placement and counseling services, training and low-interest loans. The subsidy for urban bus and rail fares was maintained to protect urban low-income workers.

A second pillar of the government's social protection efforts was the protection of social sector expenditures during the period of fiscal restraint and the targeting of public-financed programs to those least able to pay. With the adoption more recently of a fiscal stimulus package under the Letter of Intent with the International Monetary Fund, the majority of new investment will be allocated to social protection.

Although in the year following the crisis, overall budget appropriations for social welfare services declined, allocations to key programs targeted to the most vulnerable groups were maintained or increased. Scholarship and loan programs to minimize student dropouts were, in fact, expanded and, combined with the commitment of Thai families to education, has helped explain the relatively low rise in dropout rates. In addition, the number of children receiving school meals increased, while operational budgets for teacher training and instructional materials were protected.

Financing for the Public Assistance Scheme (low-income health card) was increased and coverage expanded in response to the substantial increase in enrollment in the program. Maternal and child health activities were also protected. Immunization and prevention programs were extended. Health staff were redeployed to rural areas. Responsibility for resource management was decentralized to universities and vocational schools with increased powers to provinces and municipalities.

The 1999 budget was allocated heavily towards social expenditures. In addition to job training and labor-intensive projects, the budgetary allocation to the secondary education loan program was increased which helped supplement the ADB-financed primary education projects. The school lunch program was expanded significantly. Opportunities for the unemployed to become entrepreneurs though expanded small loan facilities and training programs were strengthened.

With the expectation of traditional family and community-level coping mechanisms becoming strained by the crisis and people's incomes sharply reduced, much discussion centered on the adequacy of existing unemployment assistance benefits and pension schemes. Such savings or tax-based social insurance programs pose a dilemma for policymakers due to the contractionary impact of new taxes or additional savings in the midst of substantial economic downturn.

Thai workers rely on unemployment assistance benefits, notably severance pay requirements, as opposed to an unemployment insurance scheme. Prior to August 1998, employers were required to pay laid-off workers with a minimum of three years service a severance equal to six months of wages. As of August 1998 and coinciding with the crisis,[22] the maximum severance pay requirement for employees with more than 10 years of service was increased from six to ten months. The extent to which severance requirements were being implemented during the crisis is open to question. Government has thus initiated a public compensation fund to ensure that workers dismissed from firms facing bankruptcy receive adequate cash severance support. Fines imposed for violation of the Labor Protection Act finance this fund. In addition, a Workman's Compensation Fund reduces risks of income loss for workers in the formal sector. Employers alone contribute to the Fund. In 1996, the Fund's total contributions exceeded total claims payments (TDRI 1998).

Formerly, Thailand's pension benefits were available only to civil servants, while some larger firms offered provident funds. Other benefits (medical, maternity, invalidity and funeral), but not pensions, were extended to firms and their employees (for firms with at least 10 employees). In the crisis, the government extended social security benefits for the unemployed from 6 to 12 months and reduced the tripartite contribution rate for such benefits by one-third.

In late 1998, a more far-reaching change to the social security system was implemented, establishing pension and child allowance schemes for private sector employees. Due to the crisis and hardships on employers and workers, the implementation plan was scheduled to be phased in with full contribution rates occurring over several years so as to minimize the contractionary impact of the new system. Questions remain about the long-term financial viability of the scheme, given the mandated benefits and contribution rates. A child allowance scheme was financed from general government revenues for children of only enrolled families, a relatively well-off group (according to IMF and World Bank estimates). A further step was undertaken to extend the coverage of social security to all establishments employing one or more persons, expected to start on April 1 2001.

A critical and innovative element of Thailand's response to the social impacts of the crisis is support for decentralization and community development as articulated in the 8th Plan. At the policy and program levels, the government has viewed the crisis as an opportunity to advance reforms towards decentralization, better governance, community empowerment and the forging of broad development partnerships with civil society. The innovative approach is aimed at rebuilding and consolidating the social capital that had been eroded by economic growth and to strengthen the informal, community-based 'safety nets.'

In addition to their successful advocacy efforts, civil society organizations have played an increasingly important role in providing social protection at the community level. The Thai government, as well as donors, has allocated an increasing proportion of their budgets to civil society organizations to implement programs including HIV/AIDs prevention and treatment, care of the elderly, small and medium enterprise development, and environmental protection.

In response to the crisis, many new community-level initiatives have been supported by the government as well as by donors. The Social Policy Committee (SPC) created the Pattana Thai Foundation to channel over 40 million baht in government funds to: conduct pilot projects to support local communities to established civic forums in every province; set up community learning centers for social welfare services and sustainable development; as well as planning, monitoring and evaluation. The SPC has contracted the local Development Institute, a Thai NGO, to coordinate the implementation of these activities by a large number of partners in civil society. In September 1998, the government (with the assistance of the World Bank, UNDP, and AusAID) launched a new initiative in this area—the Social Investment Fund, which provides grants to community-based organizations to undertake investments designed and implemented by the community.

International agencies also played an important role in safety net improvement. Under the Thailand–United Nations Collaborative Action Plan (Thai–UNCAP), many UN agencies—including the UNDP, UNICEF, and the Food and Agriculture Organization—have undertaken community-led activities in pilot areas with special attention to crisis impacts. Several bilateral donors have grant programs that fund community-based activities, such as AusAid's Small Activities Scheme, the Canadian International Development Agency's Canada Fund and New Zealand's Small Projects Fund.

For the purpose of mitigating the social impact of the crisis, the government has obtained loans from the Asian Development Bank and the World Bank for a Social Sector Program and Social Investment Project, respectively. The program was to be implemented over a four-year period and the government has been committed to three social policy areas: labor market and social welfare, education and health. The Social Investment Project loan from the World Bank also requires the establishment of a Social Investment Fund to provide grants to community-based organizations to undertake activities designed and implemented by them (Ammar and Orapin 1998, 23–24).

Since February 2001, the new government under Prime Minister Taksin Chinawatr has come to power. A more radical approach to strengthening social safety nets has been initiated. In June 2001, the cabinet approved a program on urgent stimulation of the economy with a contingent or emergency budget of 58,000 million baht. A major reason for this program is to provide a financial resource for urgent and short-term economic projects that can bypass the time-consuming approval of Parliament. The basic nature of the projects under this program is it must be new or supplementary to an existing public project, the duration must be not more than one year with no extension, and it must focus

Table 8-3   Budget for Grassroots Economic Policy and Social Safety Nets Programs
2001–03

Program	2001	2002	2003	Total	%
Debt Suspension for Small-scale Farmers	2,370.9	9,325.1	6,717.9	18,413.9	9.0
One Tambon One Product (OTOP)	-	-	800.0	800.0	0.4
Village Fund	66,071.0	8,218.0	-	74,286.0	36.3
Thirty Baht for Any Sickness	1,909.9	53,093.8	55,709.0	110,712.7	54.2
New Entrepreneur Promotion	-	181.9	-	181.9	0.1

Source: NESDB (2003), Table 1 and Table 2-2.

on employment creation and using local products. The program consists of five categories of projects: agriculture projects, industry and SME projects, tourism projects, community projects and training projects.[23]

A more direct safety net program on 'Grassroots Economic Policy and Safety Nets' has been launched consisting of six major programs as follows:

• Debt Suspension for Small-scale Farmers Program
• Village Fund Program
• One Tambon One Product (OTOP) Program
• People's Bank Program
• New Entrepreneur Promotion Program
• Thirty Baht for Any Sickness Program.[24]

The allocation of budget for these programs is shown in Table 8-3.

In addition, a number of credit-based programs aimed at helping the poor have been introduced. These programs include a low-cost housing (Ban Uer-artorn or Kind-hearted Housing) project; a low-cost computer (Uer-artorn Computer or Kind-hearted computer) project; and a low-cost taxi purchase (Uer-Artorn taxi) project. Recently, a project on low-cost life insurance (Uer-Artorn life insurance) is being developed.

So far, these programs and projects have gained popularity especially among the poor and lower to middle income people. But the real or long-term achievement of the projects remains a subject for assessment. Some say that these programs are pulling the poor into more long-term debt; some doubt how the poor spent their 'soft loan' credit, etc. Recently, a somewhat internal evaluation[25] has been undertaken by NESDB (June 2003). By and large, as may be expected, the programs were found to be successful.[26] Further efforts in strengthening social safety nets have been made. Most recently, the government has announced an ambitious goal of ending poverty and reaching a welfare state within six years (*The Nation* 2003).

Notes

1 Wickramasekara (1999, 3) also noted that the concept has received increasing recognition since the Asian economic crisis. For example, the Association of Southeast Asian Nations (ASEAN) adopted an Action Plan on Social Safety Nets and established an ASEAN Task Force on Social Safety Nets in 1998; the ICFTU/APRO convened a regional workshop on social safety nets during July 28–August 1, 1998 in Manila, Philippines and made submissions on the issue to governments and international agencies. To be sure, prior to the crisis, in the 1980s, the World Bank and the IMF had made structural adjustment a condition for developing countries to receive or continue receiving loans on concessional terms. The adjustment included the reduction of the social component of the national budget, including subsidized items for mass consumption. This adversely impacted the vulnerable groups and social safety nets were established to compensate for the impacts (ESCAP 2001, 2–3).

2 For example, the Fifth Letter of Intent submitted to the IMF in 1998 (Bank of Thailand 1998).

3 The book was first published in 1958.

4 This definition, in the context of retirement income, includes means-tested and income-tested benefits for low-income elderly and universal flat-rate benefits that are primarily designed as anti-poverty benefits.

5 See also (World Bank 2001) for an elaborate discussion on various safety net programs.

6 The World Bank has, however, used the term social safety nets and social protection interchangeably.

7 See (ILO 1984) for more detail on social insurance and social assistance.

8 Worker's compensation or employment insurance, a subset of social insurance, is usually financed wholly by employers, with the possibility of state help from general revenue.

9 As such, the ILO definition of social security includes anti-poverty programs.

10 In the United States, for example, social security refers only to social insurance retirement, survivors' and disability benefits.

11 Regional Seminar on Strengthening Policies and Programs on Social Safety Nets in Bangkok May 22–24, 2001.

12 Individual country studies were published in ESCAP/ESDI (2001).

13 It is interesting to note that the problems encountered in program administration in four countries included: administrative apathy and lethargy

or lack of enthusiasm, lack of support from program beneficiaries, lack of technical guidelines for successful conduct of program activities, delays in implementation, inappropriate locations and inadequate decentralization.

14 Here, it is difficult to draw a line between regular public services or safety net programs. This, however, shows that 'social safety nets' is, in fact, loosely defined.

15 See World Bank 2001, 143.

16 Depending on the definition of social safety nets, some studies (for example, the Philippines' under the TDRI project) include government social insurance program in social safety net. See also (Charndoevit 2001, 9–10) for more detail on the civil servant pension fund.

17 Since 2002, there has been administrative reform, and names and structure of government agencies have changed. Assignments of program administration and agencies may be in transition and records may be confusing.

18 Details of these social welfare services are given in Ministry of Labor and Social Welfare (2000) and TDRI (1998).

19 Generally, NGOs can be classified, by the nature of their activities, into three major types: service-rendering NGOs, advocating NGOs, and those in between. Another classification divides NGOs into four types: service provider NGOs; empowerment NGOs; support NGOs; and umbrella or network NGOs (TDRI 2000, 8–9).

20 The review in this section is drawn from (World Bank 1999a).

21 The National Social Policy Committee (NSPC) was set up in response to public demand for increased coordination of social policy and attention to the social reform agenda. Chaired by the Prime Minister, the widely representative NPSC is comprised of those ministers responsible for social issues, NGO representatives, members of people's organization, business persons, academicians and a religious leader. A partnership among the public, nongovernmental and private sectors to formulate and monitor social policies is believed to be key to solving the country's social problems. The monitoring efforts at the national level also include: National Committee on the Alleviation of Unemployment Problems; Program Coordination and Monitoring Committee responsible for the Social Sector Program Loan; Prosperity Decentralization Policy responsible for rural economic and social rehabilitation to alleviate rural poverty and unemployment problems; Committee on Social Investment Fund responsible for executing the Social Investment Fund; and Committee on Monitoring Program Loan to Stimulate Domestic Economy.

22 The adjustment was worked out before the crisis.

23 The implementation of the projects is still under way. At the beginning, in

the first year, there were not many 'new' projects submitted for consideration. One factor is that during the post-crisis period, government agencies were busy with project creation. With staff and resource constraints, it was difficult for them to come up with project ideas. A number of 'dropped out' projects, some with new names, have been resubmitted for consideration. See also NESDB (2002b).

24 The names of programs are not official translations.

25 This evaluation was conducted by outside consultants with close supervision of NESDB.

26 Detailed results of the assessment are not presented here. Interested readers can refer to the NESDB (2003).

References

Asian Development Bank. ADB. 2000. As the Century Turns: The Social Challenge in Asia. In *Asian Development Outlook 2000*. Manila: ADB.

Bank of Thailand. 1998. *Memorandum on Economic Policies of the Royal Thai Government*, August 25, Box E. Bangkok: Bank of Thailand.

Charndoeyvit, Worawan. 2001. Social Protection, TDRI Report No. 31 (December). Thailand Development Research Institute. [in Thai]

Cook, Sarah, Naila Kabeer and Gary Suwannarat. 2003. *Social Protection in Asia*. Har-Anand Publication PVT Ltd., India: Ford Foundation.

Economic and Social Commission for Asia and the Pacific, Emerging Social Issues Division (ESCAP/ESID). 2001. *Strengthening Policies and Programs on Social Safety Nets: Issues, Recommendations and Selected Studies*. Bangkok: UN.

Gillion, Colin, J. Turner, C. Bailey and D. Latulippe. 2000. *Social Security Pensions: Development and Reform*. Geneva: ILO.

International Labor Office (ILO). 1984. *Introduction to Social Security*. Geneva: ILO.

International Labor Office (ILO). 1996. *The Cost of Social Security: Fourteenth International Inquiry, 1987–1989, Comparative Tables*. Geneva: ILO.

International Labor Office (ILO). 1999. *Social Security Programs Throughout the World, 1999*. Geneva: ILO.

International Labor Office (ILO). 2000. *World Labor Report 2000: Income Security and Social Protection in a Changing World*. Geneva: ILO.

International Labor Office (ILO). 2002. *Report of Proceedings, ILO/ASEAN Trade Union Council (ATUC) Seminar on Employment Dimension of ASEAN's Economic Integration, Bangkok, 1–3 October 2002*. Geneva: ILO.

Jimanez, Emmanuel 1999. Issues in Modernizing Social Safety Nets. Paper presented at the *Manila Social Forum: the New Social Agenda for East and Southeast.*

Jurado, Gonzales M. 2001. An Integrated Study of Selected Social Safety Net Policies and Programs in Asia and the Pacific. Paper presented at the *Regional Seminar on Strengthening Policies and Programs on Social Safety Nets.* ESCAP, Bangkok: May 1–3.

Knowles, James C., Ernesto M. Pernia, and Mary Racelis. 1999. *Social Consequences of the Financial Crisis in Asia.* Staff Paper No. 60, Economics and Development Resource Center: Asian Development Bank.

Lee, Eddy. 1998. *The Asian Financial Crisis: The Challenge for Social Policy.* Geneva: ILO.

Mingsarn Kaosa-ard. 1999. *Synthesis Report: Social Impact Assessment of Economic Crisis in Thailand.* Bangkok: Thailand Development Research Institute.

The Nation. 2003. June 21.

National Economic and Social Development Board (NESDB). 2002a. *Thailand in Brief.* Bangkok: NESDB.

National Economic and Social Development Board (NESDB). 2002b. *Projects on Economic Stimulation Approved by the Cabinet,* August. [in Thai]

National Economic and Social Development Board (NESDB). 2003. *Report on An Assessment of Grass-root Economic Policy and Social Safety Nets.* Bangkok: NESDB (in Thai).

Nattapong Thongpakde and Srawooth Paitoonpong. 1999. Thailand Country Paper. Paper presented at *Regional Conference on the Impact of the Asian Financial Crisis on the Southeast Asian Transitional Economies.* Phnom Penh: January 21–22.

Navamukundan, Achuthan N. 1999. Social Security. In *Towards an Integrated Market in Southeast Asia: The ASEAN Experience—The Trade Union Agenda,* Labor Education 1999/4, No. 117. Geneva: ILO.

Ogawa, Naohiro. 1989. *Population Change and Welfare of the Aged.* NUPRI Reprint Series No. 32, Nihon University Population Research Institute, Tokyo.

Ogawa, Naohiro. 2002. Aging Trends and Policy Response in the ESCAP Region. Paper presented at the *Fifth Asia and Pacific Population Conference.* Bangkok: December 11–17.

Paitoonpong, Srawooth. 2000. Social Impacts of the Asian Economic Crisis in Thailand, Indonesia, Malaysia and the Philippines: A Synthesis. In *Social Impacts of the Asian Economic Crisis in Thailand, Indonesia, Malaysia and the Philippines,* submitted to the Ford Foundation. Bangkok: TDRI.

Paitoonpong, Srawooth and Chirapun Gullaprawit. 1999. An Inventory of Research, Monitoring and Government Safety Nets with Reference to the Social Impacts of the Economic Crisis: Thailand. Paper presented at the *East Asia Partnership for Poverty Reduction Network Meeting.* World Bank Institute and Institute of Strategic and International Studies (ISIS), Malaysia: May 13.

Petprasert, Narong, V. Chareonlert, K. Kaewtep, J. Boonyaratanasoontorn and B. Thanachaisethawooth. 1999. *A Literature Survey on Theory, Role and Social Impact of Social Safety Nets.* Thai Research Fund. [in Thai]

Reddy, Sanjay. 1998. *Social Funds in Developing Countries: Recent Experiences and Lessons.* UNICEF Staff Working Papers, Evaluation, Policy and Planning Series, Number EPP-EV98-002, New York.

Siamwalla, Ammar. 2001. *Health-for-all Social Security: Policy Targeting.* TDRI Report No. 30 July 2001. [in Thai]

Siamwalla, Ammar. 2003. *Poor Men, Rich Men, and the 30 Baht for Any Sickness Project.* TDRI Report No. 34, June 2003. [in Thai]

Subbarao, K., A.U. Ahmed and T. Teklu. 1996. Selected Social Safety Net Programs in the Philippines: Targeting, Cost-Effectiveness, and Options for Reform. *World Bank Discussion Papers,* No. 317, January.

Thailand Development Research Institute (TDRI). 1998. *A Study on the Extension of Social Security to the Self-employed,* submitted to the Social Security Office, December.

Thailand Development Research Institute (TDRI). 2000. *Social Impacts of the Asian Economic Crisis in Thailand, Indonesia, Malaysia and the Philippines,* submitted to the Ford Foundation. Bangkok: TDRI.

Wickramasekara, Piyasiri. 1999. Responding to the Asian Economic Crisis: Social Investments and Social Safety Nets. Paper prepared for the *23rd ACAES International Conference on Asian Economics, The Post-Financial Crisis: Challenges for Progressive Industrialization of Asian Economics.* Seoul (Korea): December 15–17.

World Bank. 1990. *World Development Report 1990: Poverty, World Development Indicators.* Washington, D.C.: World Bank.

World Bank. 1993. *Poverty Reduction Handbook.* Washington, D.C.: World Bank.

World Bank. 1999a. *Thailand: Social Structural Review, Beyond the Crisis: Structural Reform for Stable Growth,* Report No. 19732-TH. Poverty Reduction and Economic Management Unit, East Asia and Pacific Region.

World Bank. 1999b. *Thailand Social Monitor: Challenge for Social Reform.* Thailand Representative Office, January.

World Bank. 1999c. *Thailand Social Monitor: Coping with the Crisis in Education and Health*. Thailand Representative Office, July.

World Bank. 1999d. *Thailand Economic Monitor*. Thailand Representative Office, October.

World Bank. 2000a. *Economic Monitor*. Thailand Representative Office, January.

World Bank. 2000b. *Economic Monitor*. Thailand Representative Office, June.

World Bank. 2000c. *Thailand Social Monitor: Social Capital and the Crisis*. Thailand Representative Office, January.

World Bank. 2000d. *Thailand Social Monitor: Thai Workers and the Crisis*. Thailand Representative Office, July.

World Bank. 2000e. Poverty in Thailand. In *Thailand's Poverty Reduction Strategy*. Mimeograph.

World Bank. 2000f. *Thailand: Secondary Education for Employment*, Volumes I and II. Washington, D.C.: World Bank.

World Bank. 2001. *World Development Report 2000/2001: Attacking Poverty*. Oxford University Press: World Bank.

World Bank. 2002a. *Globalization, Growth and Poverty: Building an Inclusive World Economy*, A World Bank Policy Research Report. Washington, D.C.: World Bank.

World Bank. 2002b. *Social Funds: Assessing Effectiveness*, World Bank Operations Evaluation Department. Washington, D.C.: World Bank.

World Bank. 2003a. http://www.worldbank.org/poverty/safety/basic.htm. Accessed June.

World Bank. 2003b. http://www.worldbank.org/poverty/safety/types.htm. Accessed July.

9
Credit Crunch in East Asia:
A Retrospective

Masahiro Enya, Akira Kohsaka and Mervin Pobre

In this chapter, we explore the issue of the credit crunch from a comparative perspective. Utilizing longer time series data, we investigate the existence of a credit crunch in selected *crisis-hit* economies in East Asia over the period 1980–2002. We detected some episodes of a credit crunch both before and after the Asian economic crisis. These episodes after the Asian Crisis are somewhat different from those detected by previous studies on the issue. We then review the credit crunch episodes in the broad macroeconomic context in order to assess our results in the longer-run perspective. We are well aware that financial liberalization has changed the financial environments of these countries more or less in due course. Even so, the mixed results we obtained on the existence of a credit crunch do not suggest that the impact of the austerity programs on financial intermediation after the Asian Crisis was ambiguous. On the contrary, they implied that the impact of the programs was so severe that the credit crunch, or supply retrenchment, was overwhelmed by a sharp fall in credit demand because of real and expected persistent overall economic depression.

Introduction

Financial intermediation plays a significant role in economic development. In fact, *the East Asian Miracle* has been supported by financial intermediation rather than by capital markets. The degree of financial intermediation, e.g. measured by broad money as a ratio to GDP, has been distinguishable from those in the other developing economies and regions. In the rapidly growing East Asian economies, the corporate sector depends heavily on external sources of funds, especially from financial intermediaries given their limited internal funds to finance their vigorous investment needs. We should note that this high debt-dependency of the corporate sector is the result of rapid economic growth and stable macroeconomic environment and not vice versa.

In the aftermath of the 1997 crisis, however, the economic recovery in East Asia has not been supported by recoveries of domestic investment as well as bank credits. Credit slowdown was apparent across all the Asian economies. Triggered by the IMF-prescribed monetary tightening policy, it is believed that reduced credit supply further contributed to the already weakening economic activities in these countries. This mechanism is consistent with the pattern of causality between credit and real economic activity as proposed by the *credit view* (Bernanke and Gertler 1995).

The basic tenet of this view is that banks' supply of credit plays a significant role in the transmission of monetary policy to the real sector of the economy. This is based on the assumption that assets in the form of loans are equally relevant as bank liabilities in the transmission of monetary shocks to the real sector of the economy. With a tighter monetary policy, banks respond by curtailing their supply of loans. This arises from information asymmetries in the financial market as well as the imperfect substitutability between financial assets. Thus, according to this mechanism, the leftward shift of the supply of loans explains the observed credit slowdown in the crisis period. Put differently, the credit slowdown can be the manifestation of a *credit crunch* that may come from monetary tightening.

Whether the high-interest rate policy led to a credit crunch in the 1997 crisis period has attracted interest among policy makers and researchers. A number of empirical studies have examined whether and to what extent East Asian countries have been suffering from a credit crunch in the 1997 crisis period. The basic approach is to model a demand and supply for loans and identify whether the observed data on loans is demand or supply determined. A brief review of these studies is presented in the following section.

In this chapter, we analyze the issue on credit crunch from a comparative perspective. To do this, we cover a longer time period to investigate different periods of credit crunch in East Asia. In this study, we cover the period from 1980 to 2002. We detected some episodes of credit crunch both before and after the Asian economic crisis. These episodes after the Crisis are somewhat different from those detected by previous studies on the issue. We then review the credit crunch episodes in a broad macroeconomic context in order to assess our results in the longer-run view.

This approach has the following merits. Studies on the credit crunch in East Asia focused on the most recent experience when financial liberalization was at its peak. We are well aware that financial liberalization has changed the financial environments of these countries in the last two decades. Covering longer periods, we will be able to compare the similarities and/or differences in the nature and causes of the most recent credit crunch with previous experiences. Then, we may be able to understand the differential impacts of a credit crunch in different financial environments.

The rest of the chapter is organized as follows. The next section (Review of Literature) briefly reviews the literature on credit crunch in the East Asian countries after the Asian economic crisis. The third section (Framework) explains the analytical framework that we adopt in the course of the analysis. The fourth section (Estimation Results) presents the estimation results of the study. The fifth section (Discussion) discusses the findings comparing recent credit crunches with previous experiences. The last section concludes the chapter.

Review of the Literature

Several studies investigated whether a credit crunch occurred in the East Asian countries in the 1997 crisis period as a result of the high interest rate policy. Ding, Domac and Ferri (1998) examined whether and to what extent East Asian countries have been suffering from a credit crunch. They examined the evolution of several macroeconomic variables including monetary and credit aggregates as well as the spread between bank lending rates and rates on risk-free assets in identifying whether demand or supply is the binding constraint in the observed credit slowdown. This framework has been applied to Indonesia, Korea, Malaysia, the Philippines and Thailand.

The main finding is that these East Asian countries suffered from an overall credit crunch, although the situation differs considerably across the countries. In Korea and Malaysia, the credit squeeze has been rendered more through a wider wedge between lending rates and risk-free asset yields. They also found evidence in all countries of a flight to quality, a situation where banks shift towards less risky assets (government securities).

Meanwhile, Ghosh and Ghosh (1999) used a disequilibrium framework to investigate a possible credit crunch in Indonesia, Korea and Thailand during 1997–1998. They used macroeconomic variables in their analysis with monthly observations from 1992:1 to 1998:6. Their main finding is that there is little evidence of quantity rationing at the aggregate level in all three countries. Credit slowdown was mainly due to lower demand for credit and that the rising real interest rates and weakening economic activity were the main factors that lowered credit demand.

In Thailand, although both credit supply and credit demand fell in real terms, estimated credit demand has generally fallen faster. Only in January 1998 did they find evidence of a credit crunch. In Korea, excess credit demand in the first half of 1997 became very small at the onset of the crisis, then finally contracted sharply in late 1997 and early 1998. In Indonesia, there is evidence of a credit crunch only in November–December 1997. Thereafter, there is no evidence of credit rationing.

In the study of single country cases, Kim (1999) also estimated a disequilibrium model of the bank loan market to identify the characteristics of the credit crunch and its intensity during the crisis in Korea. The results of his study reveal that the loan market is characterized by a state of predominantly excess demand for loans. Additionally, he found that there has occurred a credit crunch right after the financial crisis in December 1997. This finding is based on monthly data from January 1993 through May 1998. His findings support the idea that the marked decline in the aggregate bank credit is driven by a sharp decline in loan supply attributable to pervasive and stringent regulation on bank capital.

Baek (2002) expanded Kim's (1999) data set to cover from January 1992 to May 2001. Using the same disequilibrium framework, he found evidence of three periods of credit crunch prior to the crisis and two periods of credit crunch after the crisis period. The three credit crunch periods prior to the crisis are 1992:2–1995:4, 1996:1–1996:2 and 1997:1–1997:2, while the two credit crunch periods after the crisis are 1997:12–1998:3 and 2001:2–2001:4. Higher credit risk and remaining uncertainty in the loan market were cited as the main causes of the recent credit crunch in his study.

In the case of Malaysia, Beng and Ying (2001) estimated the extent of excess demand for loans during the recent currency crisis using the Johansen co-integration technique. Their empirical results identify the period from July 1997 to March 1998 as the credit crunch period with the tight monetary policy and erosion of banking institutions' capital base as the main factors responsible for the retrenchment of loan supply. Finally, Ito and Da Silva (1999) looked for empirical evidence of a credit crunch in Thailand using a specially designed survey for commercial banks with their results confirming the existence of a credit crunch. Their study analyzed the developments in Thailand's credit market during the 1997–1998 currency and financial crisis.

Framework

In this chapter, we define credit crunch as a situation where banks curtail their supply of loans at prevailing interest rates, resulting in a decline in the level of actual lending and an excess demand for loans. Bernanke and Lown (1991) define a bank credit crunch as a significant leftward shift in the supply curve for bank loans, holding constant both the safe real interest rate and the quality of potential borrowers. Similarly, the Council of Economic Advisors (1991) defines a credit crunch as a situation in which the supply of credit is restricted below the range usually identified with prevailing market interest rates and the profitability of investment projects (quoted from Ding, Domac and Ferri 1998). Two points can be inferred from the above definitions. First, a credit crunch is primarily a supply phenomenon. Second, it may be understood as a disequilibrium situation. An abrupt change in the lending behavior of banks alters the relationship between credit availability and interest rates.

A change in the lending behavior of banks may be generally due to factors affecting their **ability** to make loans and their **willingness** to supply loans. In the former, regulations from the government play a significant role. Such regulations may come in the form of a higher cost of borrowing, higher reserve requirement ratio and/or capital adequacy requirements. In the latter, expectations of the overall economy and perceived credit risk of borrowers may significantly affect the reluctance of banks to supply loans. Banks may then adjust their lending rates more rapidly and a significant widening of the wedge between the lending rate and a risk-free asset such as the government securities occurs. Furthermore, their preference for more liquid assets may cause them to shift towards these less risky assets resulting in a further decline in the availability of loans. In any of these cases, the relationship between the lending rate and the supply of loans is altered.

Based on the preceding perspectives, we will employ a disequilibrium framework to analyze the behavior of the demand and supply of loans. We characterize the credit market by the following equations:

$$LD_t = \alpha_1 + \alpha_2 i_t + \alpha_3 X_t^D + \varepsilon_t^D \tag{1}$$

$$LS_t = \beta_1 + \beta_2 i_t + \beta_3 X_t^S + \varepsilon_t^S \tag{2}$$

$$Q_t = \min (LD_t, LS_t) \tag{3}$$

where LD_t is the real loan demand in period t, LS_t is the real loan supply in period t, i_t is the real lending rate in period t, X^D_t and X^S_t are sets of explanatory variables affecting the loan demand and supply respectively, α_i and β_i are the parameters to be estimated and ε^D_t and ε^S_t are the error terms of the loan demand and supply functions, respectively. Using this framework, we proceed to develop the model by incorporating the different factors that affect the demand and supply of loans. In this study, we specify the loan demand and supply functions as follows,

$$LD_t = \alpha_1 + \alpha_2 i_t + \alpha_3 P_{t-1} + \alpha_4 IPGAP_{t-1} + \alpha_5 \pi_t + \alpha_6 L_{t-1} + \alpha_7 D_t + \varepsilon_t^D \tag{6}$$

$$LS_t = \beta_1 + \beta_2 i_t + \beta_3 R_t + \beta_4 P_{t-1} + \beta_5 LC_t + \beta_6 \pi_t + \beta_7 GSEC_{t-1} + \beta_8 L_{t-1} + \beta_9 D_t + \varepsilon_t^S \tag{7}$$

where *IP* is the industrial production index, *IPGAP* is the deviation of current *IP* from its long-run trend, π is inflation rate defined as the percentage change in the consumer price index (*CPI*) over the previous year, R is the spread between the lending rate and a risk free asset (government securities), *LC* is the real lending capacity defined as total assets minus statutory reserves, *GSEC* is the real holdings of risk free assets and *D* is a dummy variable that takes account of possible structural changes brought about by financial liberalization.[1] Finally, in the following we also include an interaction term between the dummy variable and the real interest rate in the estimated model, and some additional period dummies to cope with discontinuous changes in actual loans, which were the result of the fact that non-negligible amounts of Non Performing Loans were transferred to asset management corporations in the crisis period after 1997. All real variables are deflated by the CPI. Further details on the variables used in this study are provided in the data appendix (see Table 9-1 and Appendix 9-A1).

A number of points with regard to the above specification of the demand and supply functions merit some explanations. First, in the demand function we include the *IPGAP* variable to capture the borrowers' need for additional working capital in times of adverse shocks in their production. That is, when production temporarily falls relative to its long-run trend, the demand for credit may increase (Ghosh and Ghosh 1998). We measured the long-run trend of production using the Hodrick-Prescott filter method. *IPGAP* is therefore computed as current *IP* less its long-run trend. Second, we specify the production index and the *IPGAP* variables with one period lag to account for the simultaneity problem in the model.[2] Third, we include a risk variable (*R*) in the supply function to account for the bank's perceived credit risk of borrowers. Even with high lending rates, lenders may still be reluctant to lend because of high risk.

Fourth, since both the borrowers and lenders make decisions simultaneously with other financial and portfolio decisions, a list of other stock variables that plays as an alternative to bank loans should also be included (Ito and Ueda 1981). In the supply function, we include government securities held by banks (*GSEC*) to account for their preference for risk-free assets as a major alternative asset in their portfolio decisions. This variable is also specified with one period lag to account for simultaneity problems. However, in the demand function, data availability does not permit us to do the same. Finally, we include the observed level of loans for the preceding period (L_{t-1}) as a predetermined variable. This is consistent with the short-run optimal level in the presence of adjustment. The variables are specified in log-levels except for the interest rates and the *IPGAP*.

We estimate the parameters of the model using the likelihood function and the maximum likelihood methods proposed by Maddala and Nelson (1974).[3]

Table 9-1   Parameter Estimates of the Loan Demand and Supply Functions

Supply function

Variable	Korea			Variable	Malaysia			Variable	Thailand		
	Coefficient	T-stat	P-value		Coefficient	T-stat	P-value		Coefficient	T-stat	P-value
Constant	-0.521	-2.037	0.042	Constant	0.448	6.199	0.000	Constant	0.241	1.146	0.252
i	0.003	2.093	0.036	i	0.005	4.851	0.000	i	0.009	1.632	0.103
R	-0.003	-2.606	0.009	R	-0.004	-5.920	0.000	R	-0.005	-1.493	0.135
IP [-1]	-0.013	-0.689	0.491	IP [-1]	0.035	3.572	0.000	IP [-1]	0.101	1.532	0.125
LC	0.058	2.098	0.036	LC	0.071	3.706	0.000	LC	0.141	3.164	0.002
p	0.002	1.588	0.112	p	0.002	2.692	0.007	p	0.008	2.842	0.004
GSEC[-1]	-0.017	-1.501	0.133	GSEC[-1]	-0.015	-3.268	0.001	GSEC[-1]	-0.009	-1.601	0.109
LOAN[-1]	1.001	28.285	0.000	LOAN[-1]	0.883	44.573	0.000	LOAN[-1]	0.754	20.787	0.000
D	0.010	0.504	0.614	D	0.028	3.236	0.001	D	0.012	0.207	0.836
D*i	0.001	0.193	0.847	D*i	-0.001	-1.120	0.263	D*i	0.005	0.810	0.418

Demand function

Variable	Korea			Variable	Malaysia			Variable	Thailand		
	Coefficient	T-stat	P-value		Coefficient	T-stat	P-value		Coefficient	T-stat	P-value
Constant	0.907	3.906	0.000	Constant	-0.629	-2.120	0.034	Constant	-0.331	-5.650	0.000
i	-0.004	-2.372	0.018	i	-0.010	-2.423	0.015	i	-0.004	-7.004	0.000
IP [-1]	0.111	2.624	0.009	IP [-1]	-0.083	-1.834	0.067	IP [-1]	0.145	9.866	0.000
IPGAP[-1]	-0.001	-2.660	0.008	IPGAP[-1]	0.000	0.567	0.571	IPGAP[-1]	-0.004	-7.531	0.000
p	-0.003	-3.924	0.000	p	-0.009	-2.478	0.013	p	-0.006	-5.421	0.000
LOAN[-1]	0.887	25.760	0.000	LOAN[-1]	1.098	24.554	0.000	LOAN[-1]	0.976	157.936	0.000
D	0.013	1.031	0.302	D	-0.073	-2.081	0.037	D	-0.067	-3.551	0.000
D*i	0.002	1.146	0.252	D*i	0.002	0.451	0.652	D*i	0.002	1.142	0.253

We then use the parameters derived from this estimation technique to estimate the loan supply and demand and compare it with the observed level of credit. By doing so, we will be able to determine whether the loan demand or supply is the binding constraint in the observed credit slowdown and identify whether credit crunch has occurred. We apply the above analysis to Korea, Malaysia and Thailand using monthly data over the sample period 1980 to 2002 (1983–2002 for Thailand).

Estimation Results

Table 9-1 reports the parameter estimates of the loan demand and supply functions for each of the three countries. In the credit supply function, the coefficients of almost all the variables have their expected signs. The real interest rate (i) has the expected positive sign, with an elasticity of 0.007 for Thailand, 0.005 for Malaysia but only 0.003 for Korea. In all countries, the coefficient of the real interest rate is significant.[4] The lending capacity (LC) is also robust across the three countries. It is positive and has an elasticity of as large as 0.79 in Thailand, compared with 0.07 in Malaysia and 0.07 in Korea. The interest rate spread (R), which stands for the banks' credit risk perception of borrowers, has its expected negative sign. However, it is statistically significant in Korea and Malaysia, while not necessarily so in Thailand. The government security variable ($GSEC$) is statistically significant in all three cases.

For the other variables, we obtained some mixed results. The industrial production index (IP) has the expected and statistically significant positive sign in Malaysia and Thailand, while in Korea it has a negative but statistically insignificant sign. The inflation rate is positive and statistically significant in all cases. Finally, the dummy variables for financial liberalization have significant effects in the loan supply functions in Malaysia and Thailand. For these two countries, the interaction term between the dummy variable and the real interest rate does yield significant effects. This suggests that with smaller semi-elasticities of interest rates the loan supply has become less sensitive to interest rate changes. Finally we detected a few significant discontinuous changes in loan supply in Thailand over the post-crisis period, which appears to reflect the above-mentioned asset transfers.[5]

In the loan demand function, we obtained very robust results on the real interest rate and the inflation rate across the three countries. The estimated coefficients of the real interest rate (i) are negative and statistically significant. They are 0.007 in Korea, and 0.008 in Malaysia and 0.005 in Thailand. The inflation rate

(π), which stands for macroeconomic stability, also has a statistically significant negative coefficient. The elasticity is 0.006 for Korea, 0.007 for Malaysia and 0.004 for Thailand.

The industrial production (*IP*), though statistically significant across the three economies, has a positive coefficient in Korea and Thailand but a negative one in Malaysia. This may reflect two opposing effects. A higher production level may reflect good economic conditions and therefore greater need for credit to meet expansion in business enterprises. On the other hand, when production is higher, companies may have better cash flow and therefore may curtail their demand for credit. The output gap (*IPGAP*) has a significantly negative sign in Korea and Thailand and positive but statistically insignificant in Malaysia. The dummy variable for financial liberalization is significant in all three cases. Only in Thailand is the interaction term between the dummy variable and the real interest rate significantly positive, which suggests that the loan demand has also become less interest-rate sensitive.

Overall, in comparison with the previous studies using the disequilibrium framework, our estimates yield more significant and theoretically correct signs in the variables of the loan demand and supply functions. In Ghosh and Ghosh (1999), their estimates for the interest rate in the loan supply function yield a negative and significant coefficient in Thailand and positive but insignificant coefficient in Korea. In the loan demand function, their estimates for the interest rate in Thailand yield a negative but insignificant coefficient. Similarly, Kim (1999) obtained a negative and significant sign for the interest rate in his loan supply function for the case of Korea. Beng and Ying (2001) also obtained a negative and insignificant coefficient for the interest rate in their loan supply function for the case of Malaysia.

Figure 9-1 plots the estimated loan supply and loan demand as well as the actual loan to the private sector. Generally, our estimates yield a good correspondence between the actual loan to the private sector and the minimum of the contemporaneous loan supply and demand. According to our estimates, Korea was mostly in excess demand for loans in the 1980s, and then mostly in excess supply since the mid-1990s onward. Malaysia was generally in excess demand for loans except for the period 1991–95. Thailand was mostly in excess supply of loans in the years of 1994–97 and then persistently in excess demand after the Crisis.

Now we are going to identify periods of credit crunch. As said in the beginning of section three (Framework), to identify credit crunch the following three conditions must be met simultaneously: a decline in an *estimated* supply of loans, a decline in the level of *actual* lending, and an existence of an *estimated* excess demand for loans. Therefore, by definition, there would be no credit

Figure 9-1-1   Actual Loan and Estimated Loan Demand and Supply: Korea

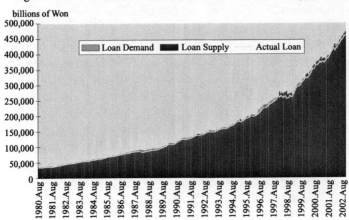

Figure 9-1-2   Actual Loan and Estimated Loan Demand and Supply: Malaysia

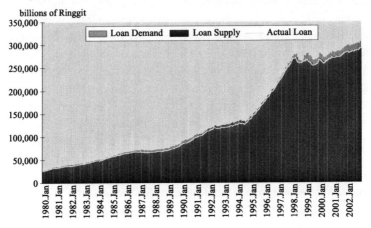

crunch in Korea after the Crisis and in Thailand in the 1980s where we detected an excess supply of loans. With this criterion, we can identify several months of credit crunch in each country as shown in Table 9-2.

In Korea, we can identify two credit-crunch periods in the 1980s and four in the early 1990s, but none after 1997. In Malaysia, two credit-crunch periods are identified in the latter half of the 1980s and several periods after the Crisis, while in Thailand a few credit crunch periods can be identified in the 1980s and the early 1990s, and several after the Crisis. Finally, Table 9-3 summarizes the results of the different surveys on the existence of credit crunch in East Asia after the Asian Crisis.

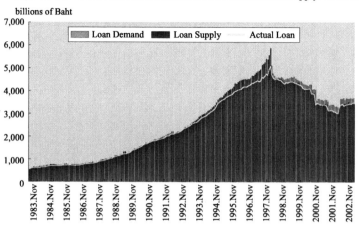

Figure 9-1-3   Actual Loan and Estimated Loan Demand and Supply: Thailand

Discussion

In this section we will discuss the episodes of our identified credit crunch in a broader macroeconomic context. Figure 9-2 provides macroeconomic and monetary developments in Korea, Malaysia and Thailand to facilitate mapping our estimated results onto the actual macroeconomic situations. It is worth noting that according to some criterions in previous studies, Malaysia and Thailand experienced banking crises in 1986 and 1983, respectively, but Korea barely escaped from it in the 1980s.[6] Naturally, these banking crises have much to do with credit crunch, because banks would become more cautious in providing loans in the crises, part of which can be seen in our crunch episodes both before and after the Asian Crisis.

As shown in Figure 9-2-1, in Korea, the first episode of a credit crunch in the early 1980s corresponds to the harsh adjustment in the aftermath of the negative growth of 1979 when the economy transitioned from rapid, inflationary growth to mild, stable growth. Nominal credit growth showed a persistent decline along with lowering interest rates in this period. The second episode of credit crunch in the early 1990s also witnessed a persistent decline in nominal credit growth with decreasing interest rates, reflecting the macroeconomic downturn, while the third episode occurred during the relative stalemate of credit and real economic growth in 1993. Immediately after the Asian Crisis, we can see a sharper decline in credit growth, particularly in 1998, than these credit-crunch episodes. Note, however, that this decline in credit growth was accompanied by a severe fall of real economic growth, which has never been the case in the previous episodes.

Table 9-2   Credit crunch periods

	Crunch period
Korea	
1980s	1981:6-1981:7
	1988:1-1988:3
1990s	1990:3
	1991:3
	1993:3
	1994:1
Malaysia	
1980s	1986:11
	1987:5-1987:6
1990s	1998:2-1998:4
	1998:6
	1998:12-
	1999:4
	1999:11-
	2000:1
	2001:2
Thailand	
1990s	1998:3-1998:4
	1998:9-
	1998:11
	1999:6-2000:2
	2000:5-2000:6
	2000:8-2000:9
	2000:12-
	2001:2
	2001:4-2001:6
	2001:9-2002:1
	2002:10

Table 9-3   Summary of Results on Credit Crunch in East Asia in the 1997 Crisis Period

	Korea	Malaysia	Thailand	Data Frequency	Coverage Period	Methodology
Ding, Domac and Ferri (1998)	Yes	Yes	none	monthly	1997-1998	Observation on Macro variables
Beng and Ying (2001)	-	Yes	-	monthly	1993-1999	Cointegration
Ito and Da Silva (1999)	-	-	Yes	-	1997-1998	Survey
Ghosh and Ghosh (1999)	none	-	none	monthly	1992-1998	Disequilibrium framework
Kim (1999)	Yes	-	-	monthly	1993-1998	Disequilibrium framework
Baek (2002)	Yes	-	-	monthly	1992-2001	Disequilibrium framework
Enya, Kohsaka and Pobre (2003)	none	Yes	Yes	monthly	1980-2002	Disequilibrium framework

Figure 9-2-1   Macroeconomic Indicators: Korea

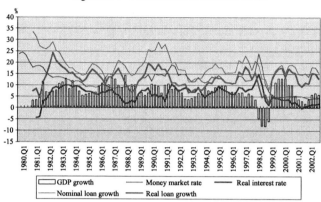

Figure 9-2-2   Macroeconomic Indicators: Malaysia

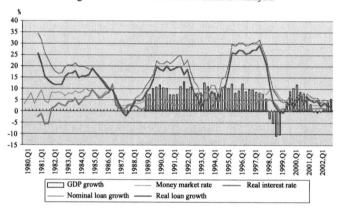

Figure 9-2-3   Macroeconomic Indicators: Thailand

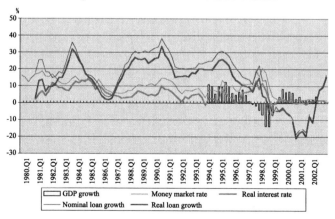

The first episode of credit crunch in Malaysia was in the late 1980s, which roughly corresponds to the period of their banking crisis. We can see persistent slowdowns of credit growth and a sharp fall of interest rates with economic slowdown (Figure 9-2-2). We also see an acute fall of credit growth in the early 1990s, but without decreases in interest rates and economic activity, when we did not detect credit crunch. Then comes the credit crunch after the Asian Crisis with a persistent and sharp fall and then a stalemate of credit growth, along with lowering interest rates and negative economic growth.

If we presume that credit crunch is likely to occur together with a persistent and/or sharp decline of credit growth and falling interest rates, Thailand appears to have had potential credit crunch: after their banking crisis in 1983, in the early 1990s, and even before the Asian Crisis (Figure 9-2-3). Actually, we detected credit crunch in those periods except for the pre-crisis period, when we identified an excess supply of loans. In fact, while we see some falls of interest rates but little slowdown of economic activity in the three cases before the Crisis, the fall of interest rates and real economic activity was, in contrast, unprecedented after 1997.

Conclusion

Even within the framework of a disequilibrium analysis of credit markets, we appear to have witnessed mixed results in the literature as to the existence of credit crunch across economies in East Asia in the recent decades (see Table 9-3).[7] Our result suggests that during the crisis period of 1997 through 1999, credit crunch appeared to exist in Malaysia and Thailand, but not in the case in Korea. How can we reconcile with these apparent contradictory results? Recognizing the important role of financial intermediation, as emphasized at the beginning of this paper, we suggest the following interpretations of our fact-finding.

First of all, by the time of the Asian Crisis it is obvious that Thailand was the hardest hit of the financial intermediations, followed by Malaysia among the three economies under our study. The financial intermediary shrank on both the asset side and liability side in the two economies, which is in contrast to the Korean case after 1997 as well as to their own experiences of credit crunch or near-crunch before the Crisis. The impact of the Crisis on the financial intermediation in Korea appears to be at least relatively mild compared to the other two economies and its own experiences in the recent past. Therefore, we conclude that it is no surprise for us to detect credit crunch in Malaysia and Thailand, but none in Korea after the Crisis.

Second, and more importantly, our results point to the overwhelming role of aggregate demand depression in generating significant declines of credits in East

Asia. In fact, we should note that so-called *V-shaped* recoveries of East Asian economies since the Crisis were not achieved by the resurgence of endogenous private demands (i.e., consumption and investment), and barely supported by that of exogenous demands (i.e., world exports and fiscal stimulus). Even as late as in 2002, we cannot see a significant resurgence of domestic credits to the private sector in Malaysia and Thailand.

Thus, the mixed results on the existence of credit crunch do not necessarily suggest that the impact of the austerity programs on financial intermediation was ambiguous. On the contrary, they implied the impact of the programs might be so severe that even enormous supply retrenchment could be overwhelmed by an even sharper fall in credit demand because of real and expected persistent overall economic depression, as in the case of post-crisis Korea. Because credit crunch is, by definition, a mere difference between retrenchments of both loan supply and demand in the financial crisis.

Lastly, as a caveat, we must be aware that there is a basic difficulty in identifying credit crunch within an aggregate macroeconomic framework, because we cannot distinguish between good and bad borrowers and/or loans. We cannot tell whether observed retrenchments in credit supplies were due to credit rationing against good borrowers or bad ones. One way to amend this difficulty is to take a microeconomic approach such as a questionnaire survey of individual borrowers/creditors as in Ito and da Silva (1999). Even with microeconomic surveys, however, without reliable market risk premiums, we would not be able to have objective judgments on the existence of credit crunch.

Appendix

See Data Appendix following.

Notes

1 The dummy variable takes on the value of unity from June 1996 in Korea, from February 1991 in Malaysia and from June 1992 in Thailand. These periods account for changes in the interest rate policy in each country.
2 We experimented with including longer lags of the *IP* and *IPGAP* variables in the model. However, results from this experiment do not significantly improve the findings when only one period lag is included.
3 While we recognize that the presence of unit root in the variables that we consider in this study may pose some problems in the estimates,

Data Appendix

Data are monthly and cover the period 1980:1 to 2002:8 for Korea, 1980:1 to 2002:9 for Malaysia and 1983:10 to 2002:12 for Thailand.

i	Real lending rate. Lending rate deflated by CPI inflation (computed as year on year percentage change in CPI)	Nominal lending rate CPI	60p, IFS 64, IFS
IP	Industrial Production, logarithm.	Industrial Production For Thailand, IP indices before Jan 1987 are calculated using production unit data.[a]	66, IFS For Thailand, Bank of Thailand Monthly Bulletin, various issues
$IPGAP$	Current Industrial Production less its long-run trend (estimated by the Hodrick-Prescott filter method)	Industrial Production	66, IFS
π	Consumer price inflation rate (computed as year on year change in CPI)	CPI	64, IFS
L	Actual real loans (Loans on Private Sector by DMB deflated by CPI)	Loans on Private Sector CPI	22d, IFS 64, IFS
R	Lending rate minus interest rate on risk-free asset (government security)	Nominal lending rate Treasury Bill Rate	60p, IFS 60c, IFS
LC	Real lending Capacity, logarithm (Total Assets minus statutory reserves, deflated by CPI)	Total Assets (Commercial Banks) Statutory Reserves (Commercial Banks)	Bank Negara Malaysia, *Monthly* Statistics Bulletin, various issues The Bank of Korea, Monthly Bulletin, various issues Bank of Thailand, Monthly Bulletin, various issues
$GSEC$	Real holdings of Goverment securities, logarithm. (deflated by CPI)	Treasury bills holdings (Commercial Banks) Government Securities holdings (DMB) for Korea	Bank Negara Malaysia, *Monthly Statistics Bulletin*, various issues. The Bank of Korea, *Monthly Bulletin*, various issues. Bank of Thailand, *Monthly Bulletin*, various issues.

Note: a.Weights computed as a proportion of the commodity to total unit of production were used to estimate IP indices before January 1987.

unavailability of an appropriate technique at this point in time to handle non-stationary variables in disequilibrium analysis limit us to follow the conventional practice in the literature of specifying the variables in levels.

4 The coefficient is statistically significant at the 1 percent and 5 percent level of significance in Malaysia and Korea, respectively. In the case of Thailand, the coefficient is barely significant at the 10 percent level.

5 Our estimated coefficients of lagged dependent variables almost as large as one suggest very slow adjustment in both loan demand and supply. Accordingly, while our independent variables are statistically significant, a large part of variations in loan demand and supply are explained by their own lagged variables.

6 A 'banking crisis' is defined as a period in which significant segments of the banking system become illiquid or insolvent (Kaminsky and Reinhalt 1999, Caprio and Klingebiel 1997 and 2003). Large scale bank failures, enactment of emergency measures by the government (deposit freezes, nationalizations, deposit guarantees, bank recapitalization plans), reports of significant depositor runs, the level of non-performing loans and the costs of the bailout are among the evidence for a banking crisis.

7 One might point out the limits of the analytical framework of disequilibrium analysis of credit markets here. It is well known that these economies in East Asia have had a long history of financial repression, or at least financial restraint, where the price mechanism did not play a due role in fund allocation because of government regulations and other institutional rigidities until the early 1990s. Partly, for example, coefficients of market interest rates are not necessarily stable in prior studies referred in this paper.

References

Baek, Ehung 2002. A Disequilibrium Model of the Korean Credit Crunch. *ICSEAD Working Paper* No. 2002–22.

Bernanke, Ben and Cara Lown. 1991. The Credit Crunch. *Brookings Papers on Economic Activity*, 2: pp. 205–247.

Bernanke, Ben and Mark Gertler. 1995. Inside the Black Box: The Credit Channel of Monetary Policy Transmission. *Journal of Economic Perspectives*, 9(3): pp. 27–28.

Beng, Gan Wee and Soon Lee Ying. 2001. Credit Crunch during a Currency Crisis. *ASEAN Economic Bulletin*, 18(2): pp. 176–192.

Caprio, Gerard Jr., and Daniela Klingebiel. 1997. Bank Insolvency: Bad Luck, Bad Policy, or Bad Banking? *Annual World Bank Conference on Development Economics 1996.*

—————2003. Episodes of Systemic and Borderline Financial Crises. *World Bank Finance Research Reports* (http://econ.worldbank.org/programs/finance/datasets/data?id=23456).

Ding, Wei, Ilker Domac and Giovanni Ferri. 1998. Is There a Credit Crunch in East Asia? *World Bank Working Paper,* No. 1959.

Enya, Masahiro and Akira Kohsaka. 2002. Monetary Transmissions Immediately After the Crisis in East Asia. Paper Presented at the *8th International Convention of the East Asian Economic Association*: Kuala Lumpur, Malaysia November 4–5, 2002.

Ghosh, Swati and Atish Ghosh. 1999. East Asia in the Aftermath: Was There a Crunch? *IMF Working Paper.* No. WP/99/38.

Ito, Takatoshi and Kazuo Ueda. 1981. Tests of the Equilibrium Hypothesis in Disequilibrium Econometrics: An International Comparison of Credit Rationing. *International Economic Review,* 22(3): pp. 691–708.

Ito, Takatoshi and Luiz Pereira da Silva. 1999. The Credit Crunch in Thailand During the 1997–1998 Crisis: Theoretical and Operational Issues with the JEXIM Survey. *EXIM Review,* 19(2): pp. 1–40.

Kaminsky, Graciela L. and Carmen M. Reinhart. 1999. The Twin Crises: The Causes of Banking and Balance-of-Payments Problems. *American Economic Review* (June), 80(3): pp. 473–500.

Kim, Hyun. 1999. Was Credit Channel a Key Monetary Transmission Mechanism Following the Recent Financial Crisis in the Republic of Korea. *World Bank Policy Research Working Paper,* No. 3003.

Maddala, G.S. and Forrest D. Nelson. Maximum Likelihood Methods for Models of Markets in Disequilibrium. *Econometrica,* 42: pp. 1013–1030.

10
Contractionary Devaluation Revisited:
Can Appreciation be Expansionary?

Bhanupong Nidhiprabha

This chapter presents a simple model that explains how a country may experience a severe contraction after devaluation, particularly in an economy where bank credit is an important source of funds for investment. If firms and banks accumulate large amounts of unhedged foreign debt, a high rate of depreciation that exceeds the threshold level can trigger technical bank failure, and thereby reduce bank lending. Shortages of loanable funds may arise from the redistributive effects of bank deposits and withdrawals from aggressive to conservative banks. A sharp decline in investment and durable consumption would follow. On the other hand, it is equally possible that currency appreciation can stimulate growth despite its negative impact on net exports. The crucial factor is the impact of the currency changes on bank credit.

Introduction

Exchange rate overvaluation is considered to be one cause of the Asian economic meltdown. In particular, countries that tied their exchange rates closely to the U.S. dollar and could not control inflation would experience widening current account deficits. The contagion effect of the Asian financial turmoil led to a contraction in output levels and generated high unemployment. Currency collapses and bank failures were intertwined in this episode of the Asian economic crisis. This paper argues that for countries with accumulated excessive dollar-denominated external debts, the collapse of firms and financial institutions was triggered by massive currency depreciation that, in turn, led to bank panics, financial disintermediation and severe contraction in output.

Some Southeast Asian countries experienced both recession and currency crisis in 1998. Currency realignments lead to changes in profitability of firms and commercial banks. Table 10-1 depicts key macroeconomic variables that are interrelated with exchange rate movements. Rates of change in the nominal exchange rate, real GDP, real investment and domestic credit of five Southeast Asian countries are presented in the table. Output contraction in these countries, and to a lesser extent the Philippines, occurred simultaneously with massive currency depreciation in 1997 and 1998. Obviously the causation runs both ways. Appreciation of the Singaporean dollar in 1994 and 1995 was associated with the country's strong economic growth. In addition, other factors such as the collapse in aggregate demand and domestic credit contributed to output contraction. In the high-inflation countries such as Indonesia and the Philippines, exchange rate depreciation is not unusual since they serve the purpose of maintaining international competitiveness. However, depreciation of the rupiah at a rate of 244 percent and the peso at a rate of 40 percent were totally unexpected in 1998. For low-inflation countries, two-digit currency depreciation is extremely unusual, particularly for Malaysia, Singapore and Thailand.

During this period, investment and domestic credit slowed down or contracted simultaneously. Bank credit and investment slowed after 1998 in all five countries. Except for Singapore and Malaysia where price deflation was evident in 1998, the remaining countries in Table 10-1 experienced high inflation after the large devaluation, but the impact of the contraction in GDP caused inflation to decline in subsequent years.

The unprecedented rate of currency depreciation is shown in Table 10-2, where the data shows the difference between the rates of change of five important variables during the crisis year of 1998 from the average rate of change between the normal years 1994–2001. Indonesia experienced and suffered most from the currency depreciation in terms of output loss and inflation. As shown in Table 10-3, there is a negative correlation between currency depreciation and GDP growth (-0.6) and between the depreciation rate and domestic investment growth (-0.67). On the other hand, currency depreciation is positively related to domestic credit expansion and inflation. High correlations among these five variables give us casual observations of the existing important relationship between currency depreciation and other key macro variables.

The relationship between exchange rate depreciation and output growth can be nonlinear. At a low level of depreciation, output can be stimulated through export growth. However, as the currency depreciates to an unexpected level, the depreciation can lead to adverse consequences since bank balance sheets and the domestic price level would be affected. It is the purpose of this chapter to demonstrate that if the exchange rate depreciates beyond a threshold level that triggers bankruptcies in the banking sector, real output will contract.

The chapter is organized as follows. The next section (Contractionary Effects of Devaluation) investigates theoretical issues surrounding deflationary devaluation. A simple model is constructed to illustrate the possibility of contractionary devaluation. The third section (Thailand's Experience with Contractionary Devaluation) discusses Thailand's experience of contractionary devaluation after July 1997, which was the onset of the Asian turmoil. This is followed by a discussion (The VAR Model) of a Vector Auto Regressive model (VAR) that is applied to Thailand's monthly data after the float in July 1997 to July 2003. The empirical result from the VAR model is used to support the hypothesis of contractionary devaluation. Next (Asian Currency Appreciation), the chapter explores whether the recent Asian currency appreciation can exert a positive impact on output. The last section of the chapter contains concluding remarks and policy implications from the study.

Contractionary Effects of Devaluation

How can devaluation possibly be deflationary? If devaluation can improve the trade balance, other things being equal, then devaluation should be expansionary. Nevertheless, other things do change after devaluation. For example, government stability and its policy credibility can be eroded. Moreover, the absorption level can change due to changes in consumers' expectations, while the real quantity of money and credit can be affected by changes in the price level. Consequently, consumption expenditure can be reduced, private investment can decline and public savings may be enhanced. These scenarios prevent devaluation from being expansionary.

Theoretical Issues
In the short run, when quantities of exports and imports have not yet responded to the devaluation, the existing trade deficit, in terms of the domestic currency, becomes larger because the value of the trade balance is measured in higher domestic prices. The larger the initial trade deficit, the greater the contraction in national income. Hirschman (1949) was the first person to raise this plausible source of income contraction after devaluation. Furthermore, Diaz-Alejandro (1963) cited an example of Argentine contractionary devaluation in 1959 where the devaluation redistributed income from workers to landowners. Since workers' propensity to spend was higher than that of landowners, aggregate consumption expenditure and output declined because of the distributive effect of the devaluation. Krugman and Taylor (1978) argued that the contractionary effect of devaluation would stem from an enlarged budget surplus, because the public sector has a lower propensity to spend than does the private sector. Devaluation would raise trade tax revenues, but the government may have

Table 10-1   Key Macroeconomic Variables 1994–2001
(percentage change)

Indonesia

Year	Exchange rate	GDP	Domestic investment	Domestic credit	CPI (inflation)
1994	3.55	7.54	16.68	20.54	8.48
1995	4.07	8.22	13.06	21.56	9.47
1996	4.14	7.82	4.94	23.01	7.89
1997	24.21	4.70	6.31	42.05	-42.87
1998	244.24	-13.13	-39.04	28.71	58.47
1999	-21.56	0.79	-23.24	23.96	20.44
2000	7.22	4.90	-1.23	25.45	3.75
2001	21.84	3.32	-0.67	5.35	11.51
Average[a]	6.21	5.33	2.26	23.13	2.67

Malaysia

Year	Exchange rate	GDP	Domestic investment	Domestic credit	CPI (inflation)
1994	1.95	9.21	17.79	11.65	3.73
1995	-4.57	9.83	20.29	28.21	3.40
1996	0.46	10.00	5.78	23.43	3.48
1997	11.82	7.32	11.24	34.66	2.71
1998	39.50	-7.36	-43.04	0.41	-12.83
1999	-3.17	6.08	-5.15	1.41	2.82
2000	0.00	8.30	27.86	8.78	1.52
2001	0.00	0.39	-7.95	2.72	1.40
Average[a]	0.93	7.30	9.98	15.84	2.72

Philippines

Year	Exchange rate	GDP	Domestic investment	Domestic credit	CPI (inflation)
1994	-2.59	4.39	8.65	20.45	8.34
1995	-2.66	4.68	3.50	31.99	8.00
1996	1.95	5.85	12.46	39.04	9.07
1997	12.41	5.19	11.70	27.53	5.86
1998	38.76	-0.58	-16.28	-2.73	9.70
1999	-4.41	3.40	-1.98	2.83	6.65
2000	13.06	4.38	5.54	8.55	4.39
2001	15.39	3.22	1.33	0.00	6.11
Average[a]	4.74	4.44	5.89	18.63	6.92

Continued on next page.

difficulty spending this increased revenue.[1] Furthermore, as pointed out by Cooper (1971), the possibility of a decline in business activity after devaluation arises because of the rise in the domestic cost of servicing external debt that is denominated in a foreign currency.

Singapore

Year	Exchange rate	GDP	Domestic investment	Domestic credit	CPI (inflation)
1994	-5.47	11.42	1.27	12.96	3.15
1995	-7.20	8.01	15.06	17.41	1.68
1996	-0.52	7.65	17.08	17.25	1.34
1997	5.30	8.54	13.08	19.49	2.04
1998	12.72	-0.09	-13.27	18.15	-0.30
1999	1.28	6.93	2.47	-0.26	0.10
2000	1.71	10.25	10.99	3.95	1.30
2001	3.93	-2.04	-21.87	14.20	0.99
Average[a]	-0.14	7.25	5.44	12.14	1.51

Thailand

Year	Exchange rate	GDP	Domestic investment	Domestic credit	CPI (inflation)
1994	-0.67	8.99	10.66	29.41	5.08
1995	-0.91	9.24	14.25	22.88	6.07
1996	1.69	5.90	5.20	13.93	5.59
1997	23.76	-1.37	-21.93	34.47	5.57
1998	31.89	-10.51	-50.88	-1.19	8.08
1999	-8.58	4.43	8.70	-4.19	0.31
2000	6.08	4.64	10.91	-7.43	1.58
2001	10.77	1.81	0.42	-6.06	1.59
Average[a]	1.40	5.84	8.36	8.09	3.37

Note: a. excludes years of large devaluation.
Source: ADB (2003).

Since macroeconomic disequilibria became larger if a country postponed devaluation, it would require a larger degree of demand contraction to correct the balance-of-payments deficit (Edwards and Montiel 1989). The long battle between Asian central banks, speculators and hedge funds was tantamount to disequilibria deepening, which thereby raised future adjustment costs. Nonetheless, output contraction may have stemmed from the restrictive monetary policy that had been applied prior to the currency depreciation, since monetary policy has a long lag effect. We therefore cannot attribute the contraction in output to only one factor.

In a simulated global CGE model, Noland et al. (1998) found that devaluation in Asian countries increased net exports. Furthermore, these troubled Asian countries would suffer from a large fall in domestic absorption. However, the deflationary impact of the crisis in this model does not arise from the monetary sector, which was absent in their model. The macro closure of the model forces a proportional adjustment in each component of absorption and allows domestic savings to adjust endogenously. In other words, the contraction in

Table 10-2   Deviation During the Crisis from Normal Episodes
            (percentage change)

Country	Exchange rate	GDP	Domestic investment	Domestic credit	CPI (inflation)
Indonesia	238.03	-18.46	-41.30	5.58	55.80
Malaysia	38.57	-14.66	-53.02	-15.43	-15.55
Philippines	34.02	-5.02	-22.17	-21.36	2.78
Singapore	12.86	-7.34	-18.71	6.01	-1.81
Thailand[a]	26.43	-11.78	-44.77	8.55	3.46

Note: a. For all countries, 1998 was the crisis year, except for Thailand where both 1997 and 1998 are included.

Table 10-3   Correlation Coefficients among Key Macroeconomic
            Variables (five countries)

Variables	Exchange rate	GDP	Domestic Investment	Domestic credit	CPI (inflation)
Exchange rate	1.00	-0.62	-0.67	0.91	0.83
GDP		1.00	0.81	-0.34	-0.79
Domestic investment			1.00	-0.30	-0.56
Domestic credit				1.00	0.76
CPI (inflation)					1.00

domestic absorption is a natural consequence of the improvement in the current account.

There is a distinct possibility that a large depreciation can result in contraction of output rather than spurring the economy out of recession. If a country has accumulated large unhedged foreign debts, a small rate of currency depreciation can push an economy into recession, because the aggressive behavior of banks and financial liberalization combined with inadequate bank supervision can reduce the threshold level of depreciation.

With over-borrowing in foreign currency, a complete halt in intermediary functioning of the financial sector can take place. The net worth of banks can easily be negative if their foreign borrowing is high relative to their total equity. The balance sheet effect would discourage banks from continuing its lending to customers and banks may recall their loans and stop rolling over existing credit lines. In addition, incentives and profitability of bank lending would be reduced. Moreover, large corporations that previously issued dollar-denominated convertible debentures will suffer from rising debt burden when the currency plunges further. In light of the rising level of debt accumulated by these firms, commercial banks would be unwilling to extend more loans. Moreover, with the falling value of collateral, banks would have no choice but to curtail their outstanding loans. It is unrealistic to expect banks to increase their lending activity during such a downturn.

According to Irving Fisher (1933), financial factors were major sources and propagators of the economic decline during the Great Depression. Debt and price disturbances are two major causes of booms and depressions. Over-indebtedness is responsible for over-investment and over-speculation. Financial collapse in developing countries following a currency crisis has led to recessions in troubled Asian countries, which is followed by price deflation. Devaluation triggers over-indebtedness in foreign debt in terms of the local currency and sets up serious disturbances in all other economic variables.

Debt overhang in the private sector also reduces its willingness to borrow and expand their businesses. The private sector will have difficulty servicing its debt due to rising interest costs. As price declines during a recession, the reverse Pigou effect on liability or negative wealth effect, would further reduce private consumption and firms' capital spending. While the literature on contractionary devaluation ignores the financial sector's foreign debt problem, debt deflation literature also disregards the impact of devaluation on debt in terms of local currencies.

Bank credit or money supply can be regarded as an inseparable input in the production function. With a dysfunctional financial system, lack of credit and a reduction in money supply, industrial output can be adversely affected. In particular, small and medium-sized firms that are labor-intensive and depend more on bank credit than do large industrial firms would be more severely affected by not being able to access credit markets.

There is another possibility that aggregate bank credit can be reduced after a massive depreciation. Some banks that are more aggressive than others would tend to source their funds through foreign borrowing. These aggressive banks also have a higher marginal propensity to lend from their disposable deposits than do conservative banks. As the value of the domestic currency declines further, these aggressive banks become vulnerable because the value of their net worth also declines in line with the rate of currency depreciation. When these aggressive banks are nearly technically bankrupt, they would also experience bank runs. A reallocation of deposits will take place, thereby shifting loanable funds from aggressive banks to conservative banks that have a lower marginal propensity to lend. In the end, the total volume of bank credit would decline because of the reallocation of deposits. Moreover, conservative banks themselves would become more cautious in lending and would retain higher excess reserves in anticipation of unexpected withdrawals during a financial crisis.

Because of the credit contraction, interest rates rise after devaluation. In addition, the rising price level caused by the depreciation of the exchange rate reduces the real quantity of money. Both the increase in the cost of capital and the reduction in credit availability translate into a slowdown in investment expenditures.

The relationship between the depreciation of the exchange rate and the growth rate of output can be nonlinear. At a small rate of currency depreciation, domestic demand and exports can be stimulated, as long as the depreciation has not reached the threshold level that triggers financial disintermediation. As the exchange rate depreciates further below the critical level, the contraction in output would be inevitable.

A Model of Bank Failure

In this section, a simple model is developed to illustrate that devaluation may be deflationary. The source of deflation comes from the destruction of the role of commercial banks as financial intermediaries. Instead of relying on differences in propensity to consume of different classes of consumers, the redistributive effect of devaluation can arise from different propensities to lend by different types of commercial banks. To relate the impact of changes in credit to domestic absorption, a standard stock adjustment model of investment with a variable speed of adjustment can be employed.

The Redistributive Effect of Bank Deposit Withdrawals

Assume that there are two types of commercial banks: conservative banks which depend less on foreign borrowing and tend to rely more on deposits as a source of loanable funds, and aggressive banks which have a higher ratio of foreign liabilities to equity than do conservative banks. Suppose further that both banks do not engage in raising capital funds in the short run. Then, the supply of loanable funds of aggressive banks can be represented by:

$$\Delta L^a = (1 - \alpha) \Delta D^a + (1 - \omega)\Delta F \qquad (1)$$

where α is the total reserve (required + excess) ratio of aggressive banks, L^a and D^a are loans and deposits of aggressive banks, and ω is the reserve ratio imposed on foreign borrowing (ΔF). Note that ω can be zero if the capital account is fully liberalized.

For conservative banks, sources of funds are assumed to come from deposits only. Note that $\alpha < \chi$.

The net worth of commercial banks is the difference between their assets (i.e., loans net of bad debts) and liabilities, which are deposits and foreign borrowings in domestic currency. For simplicity in exposition, bonds and other investment assets are assumed to be small relative to loans (L) in total assets of banks. That is:

$$NW = L - D - e^*F^\$ \tag{2}$$

where NW represents net worth, e is the foreign exchange rate and $F^\$$ represents the stock of foreign borrowing. If banks are bankrupt, their net worth is zero or negative.

Let us define the threshold level of the exchange rate (e^*) that causes technical bankruptcy as follows:

$$e^* = \gamma (1 - \varphi)(1 - \theta) (E/F^\$) \tag{3}$$

Let v be the ratio of net foreign liability to equity:

$$v = eF^\$/E, v < 1 \tag{4}$$

Banks cannot sustain the rate of currency depreciation if it exceeds the threshold level of depreciation. That is:

$$d^* = (e^* - e)/e = (1 - \theta) (1 - \varphi)(\gamma/v) - 1 \tag{5}$$

The above equation shows that a banking crisis and a currency crisis are interrelated. The higher the threshold level of the exchange rate depreciation the lower the degree of vulnerability of commercial banks to bankruptcy caused by exchange rate changes. The degree of vulnerability of banks increases as banks become more aggressive in lending (i.e., a higher value of θ), as they depend more on foreign borrowing (i.e., a higher value of γ), and as they become reckless in lending (i.e., a higher value of nonperforming loans, ϕ).

The banking system becomes more vulnerable to exchange rate depreciation if it cannot generate high-quality earning assets relative to its deposits and capital funds. A high level of bad debt will weaken the ability of banks to withstand a fall in currency value. The loan–foreign borrowing ratio (γ/v) indicates the efficiency of banks, since it implies the ability of banks to create earning assets from a given level of foreign borrowing. Moreover, the maximum value of this parameter is determined by the capital adequacy ratio that is imposed by law. Relaxation of capital controls permits an increase in the net foreign liability to equity, thereby making the banking system more vulnerable to exchange rate shocks.

Premature capital control relaxation through the raising of the net foreign liability positions of banks would lower the critical rate of currency depreciation that undermines the banks' net worth. On the other hand, inadequate supervision would lead to poor quality of lending, and thereby increase the vulnerability of banks to a currency crisis. In the medium term, aggressive lending would not pay off if it leads to substandard loans and doubtful debts after currency depreciation.

If the rate of currency depreciation approaches the critical rate, the probability of bankruptcy for aggressive banks will rise. The larger is the rate of currency depreciation, the higher is the probability of bankruptcy of aggressive banks. The expected return from deposits at aggressive banks would be negative, because of the high probability that depositors would lose both principal and interest. Deposit runs take place from aggressive banks to conservative banks, some of which are branches of foreign banks. For ease of exposition, we assume that conservative banks do not borrow in foreign currencies.

If we assume further that all withdrawals from aggressive banks run to conservative banks, then

$\Delta D^c = -\Delta D^a$ and:

$$\Delta L = \Delta L^a + \Delta L^c = (\alpha - \chi) \, \Delta \, D^c + (1 - \omega)\Delta F \tag{6}$$

The total amount of loanable funds for the whole economy would decline since the marginal propensity to lend of conservative banks is lower than that of aggressive banks; that is, $\alpha < \chi$.

The impact of currency devaluation on the level of loanable funds can be evaluated from the following expression:

$$\Delta L \, / \, \Delta e = (\alpha - \chi) \, \Delta D^c / \, \Delta e + (1 - \omega) \, \Delta F / \Delta e \tag{7}$$

The first term on the right hand side of the above equation is negative since $(\alpha - \chi) < 0$, while $\Delta D^c/\Delta e$ is positive. The second term, $\Delta F/\Delta e$, can be negative in the event of capital flight after massive devaluation.[2] It is thus possible for $\Delta L/\Delta e$ to be negative, i.e., devaluation can indirectly lead to a reduction in loanable funds.

The supply of loanable funds can be reduced after a large depreciation, even without capital flight, as long as there are bank runs from domestic (aggressive) to foreign (conservative) banks. Thus, after large currency depreciation, there is the possibility that a contraction in credit will occur because of the redistributive effects of loanable funds from aggressive banks to conservative banks.

The Balance Sheet Channel

One of the monetary policy transmission mechanisms, aside from the interest rate channel, is the balance sheet channel (Mishkin 1995). Bank credit expansion depends on the size of disposable or loanable funds and the rate of return from lending. The lending interest rate net of expected credit risks determines the share of banks' lending in their total assets. For simplicity, we rule out bank runs and concentrate on the amount of loanable funds that arise from changes in foreign borrowing and net worth:

$$\Delta B = \beta \Delta L = \beta \left[(1 - \omega) \Delta F^{\$} + \Delta NW \right] \qquad (8)$$

where B is bank loans and β represents a positive lending coefficient, which is not constant, but varies according to lending profitability.

In effect, we are assuming that lending volume is homogeneous of one degree in the size of total assets or loanable funds. The share of total assets allocated to loans depends on the lending interest rate (r) and the default risks (ϕ), which can be proxied by the foreign leverage ratio of banks' customers to the ratio of foreign borrowing to firms' equity $(F/E)^c$:

$$\beta = \beta_1 r + \beta_2 \varphi = \beta_1 r + \beta_2 e \ (F^{\$}/E)^c; \ \beta_2 < 0 \qquad (9)$$

where ϕ indicates default risks proxied by the foreign leverage ratio of banks' customers.

Moreover:

$$\beta = \beta_1 r + \beta_2 e * l \text{ where } l = (F^{\$}/E)^c \qquad (10)$$

An increase in bank lending is represented by:

$$b = \Delta B = (\beta_1 r + \beta_2 e * l) \left[(1 - \omega)(e \Delta F^{\$} + F^{\$} \Delta e) + \Delta NW \right] \qquad (11)$$

At a small rate of depreciation below the threshold level, banks are induced to borrow from abroad, while the marginal burden of outstanding foreign liabilities can be fully offset by a reduction in net worth. Thus, the impact of a change in the exchange rate can be examined from the following:

$$\delta b / \delta e = (1 - \omega) \Delta F^{\$} (\beta_1 r + 2\beta_2 e * l) \qquad (12)$$

Let us define $J \equiv (1 - \omega) \Delta F^{\$} > 0$, which can be thought of as positive due to capital injection through foreign borrowing or government bailout. Whether devaluation leads to contraction in bank lending depends not only on the available loanable funds (J) but also on the term in the parenthesis, which involves the interest rate, the exchange rate and the firms' foreign leverage ratio:

$$\delta b / \delta e = J (\beta_1 r + 2\beta_2 e * l) \qquad (12')$$

Since J is positive, the sign of the above equation can be either positive or negative depending on the magnitude of the two terms in the parenthesis. Hence, depreciation can lead to expansion or contraction of bank credit. That is, bank credit, despite a fresh injection of capital funds, can expand or contract after a currency depreciation. The determining parameters are the reserve requirement ratio imposed on foreign borrowing or the capital control variable (ω), the lending interest rate (r) and the foreign leverage level of banks' customers (l). If a country liberalizes its capital account and maintains higher interest rates, it is likely that in the initial period of currency depreciation, the impact on bank credit would be expansionary. Unless the foreign leverage ratio of corporations is very high or banks have a strong degree of credit risk aversion, bank credit can expand as long as business firms are not adversely affected by the depreciation.

From equation (12'), we can obtain the level of the exchange rate that can trigger bank credit contraction:

$$\tilde{e} = (r\beta_1) / (2\beta_2\, l) \tag{13}$$

where $\tilde{e}$ is the threshold exchange rate.

The threshold exchange rate is an increasing function of the domestic lending interest rate and is decreasing in foreign borrowing leverage. The higher a firms' foreign lending leverage, the higher the degree of vulnerability of banks to currency depreciation. On the contrary, when the lending interest rate is following a rising trend (i.e., when banks are willing to lend) and when foreign borrowings have been reduced substantially, the threshold exchange rate will be high. Consequently, in this situation, risks of financial and currency crisis remain low.

As the value of the domestic currency plunges further, bank credit can actually contract, because:

$$\delta^2 b / \delta e^2 = 2J\beta_2 l < 0 \tag{14}$$

From the view of bank lending, the reduction in the supply of bank credit forces investors to reduce real spending because alternative means of funding are unavailable or unaffordable, which is particularly the case for investment of small manufacturing firms (Bernanke, Gertler and Gilchrist 1996). We may further hypothesize that, according to the variable stock adjustment model of investment, the availability of bank credit can increase the speed of adjustment between the actual and desired level of capital stocks:

$$\Delta K_t = \mu(K_t^* - K_{t-1}) \tag{15}$$

where μ is the speed of adjustment and

$$K_t^* = \kappa_1 Q_t^e + \kappa_2 r, \kappa_1 > 0, \kappa_2 > 0 \tag{16}$$

where K_t^* is the desired level of capital stock and Q_t^e is expected output.

The speed of adjustment is positively related to the amount of credit expanded relative to the gap between the desired and existing level of capital stock:

$$\mu = \mu_0 + \mu_1 [b / (K_t^* - K_{t-1})] \tag{17}$$

If depreciation is a fraction δ of the existing capital stock, then with some manipulation, we can obtain the expression for gross investment:

$$I_t = \mu_0 \kappa_1 Q_t^e + \mu_0 \kappa_2 r + \mu_1 b + (\delta - 1) K_{t-1} \tag{18}$$

The above equation notes that the level of expected output, the rate of interest, the new volume of bank credit and the existing level of capital stock determine gross investment.

The impact of exchange rate depreciation on investment depends on its impact on expected output, the interest rate level and expansion in bank credit. Currency depreciation that is greater than the threshold level can lead to a contraction in private investment if it leads to a downward revision in output expectations, a rising interest rate and a collapse in banks' lending:

$$\delta I / \delta e = \mu_0 \kappa_1 [\delta Q^e / \delta e] + \mu_0 \kappa_2 [\delta r / \delta e] + \mu_1 [\delta b / \delta e] \tag{19}$$

If the currency is overshooting above the threshold level, contraction in investment spending can occur. In other words, $\delta I / \delta e < 0$ if the rate of depreciation exceeds the critical level dictated by equation (13) such that $\delta Q^e / \delta e < 0$, $\delta r / \delta e > 0$, and $\delta b / \delta e < 0$. During the recessionary period when pessimism dominates business expectations, a further downward slide in the value of the currency translates into a downward revision in sales expectations. The central bank may then resort to an interest rate hike to prevent further deterioration in the value of the domestic currency, which, in turn, further dampens investment expenditures.

If durable consumer goods can be thought of as capital goods, the ability to purchase these products would be reduced by the credit contraction. In effect, domestic absorption can be dramatically reduced after a large devaluation. If the currency depreciation can reduce the investment-savings gap, the current account deficit can be improved significantly. Moreover, household savings can be raised in response to uncertainties, while durable consumption expenditure can be cut as a means to restore liquidity (Mishkin 1976).

If exporters require bank credit to facilitate the production and shipment of export commodities, the reduction in bank lending can also retard exports despite the fact that the export supply price elasticity is high. The higher prices of exports in terms of the domestic currency would not necessarily translate into higher export earnings if exporters were constrained by a liquidity shortage.

Another implication of equation (19) is that, if the exchange rate appreciates, private investment may increase as a result of the upwardly revised expectations on the strength of the economy. With capital inflows and plenty of excess liquidity, the lending interest rate is still on a declining trend while the exchange rate is appreciating. Furthermore, exchange rate appreciation stimulates bank lending because the domestic value of the foreign debt burden of bank customers has declined. Banks are more willing to lend to low-leverage firms whose foreign exchange risk is minimal. It is therefore possible that under this situation, a currency appreciation will bring about output expansion.

Thailand's Experience with Contractionary Devaluation

The depth of the baht depreciation after the float in 1997 and its contagion impact on other currencies in the region can be seen in Table 10-1. As the Korean won and the Indonesian rupiah were breaking new lows in the beginning of 1998, the baht was also being dragged down. The growing pessimism became widespread and capital outflows continued. Banks became hesitant to lend and were increasingly worried about their nonperforming loans. The aggressive Thai banks as well as their large clients borrowed substantial amounts of unhedged loans from abroad.

A surge in capital inflows to Thailand began in the late 1980s and continued unabated until 1996. These flows brought along rapid economic growth and a balance-of-payments surplus. By 1995, the Bank of Thailand realized the adverse consequences of the short-term capital flows and began tightening monetary policy instruments. The Bank of Thailand attempted to address the problem of the widening current account deficit and the overheating economy through a series of measures. A maximum loan-deposit ratio was set at 1.17, while the maximum rate of credit expansion was set at 24 percent in 1995. This ceiling was subsequently reduced to 21 percent in the following year. In August 1995, commercial banks were required to hold reserves of 7 percent of their short-term nonresident baht deposits. In June 1996, all financial institutions were required to hold reserves of 7 percent from new short-term foreign borrowings. These measures were employed by the Bank of Thailand to discourage short-term flows. The result was that all three measures of monetary aggregates decelerated significantly in 1996. The restrictive monetary policy was able to slow the economic expansion down to 6.4 percent in 1996. In hindsight, these tightening measures were undoubtedly belated and inadequate in dealing with the volatile capital flows.

Notwithstanding the restrictive monetary measures imposed by the Bank of Thailand, bank credit expanded unabated in 1997, despite a sharp decline in both M1 and M2. In 1997, a series of bank runs and the collapse of 56 finance companies seriously damaged the stability of financial institutions in Thailand. By 1998, a severe contraction in the financial sector was evident in the reduction of real bank credit and M1. The growth rate of real M2 was positive in 1998 in response to high interest rates and rising demand for precautionary savings during the period of uncertainty. The sharp fall in the velocity of money indicates a severe degree of economic recession.

As interest rates rise together with anticipation of an economic recession, the SET index fell from 1,360 points in 1994 to its lowest level of 207 points in early September 1998. Consequently, the value of Thailand's capital market in 1997 had vanished by 70 percent of GDP since 1995. The massive devaluation of the baht resulted in poor performance of firms listed in the stock market, since a large number of them also borrowed from overseas and imported capital goods through foreign trade credit.

In 1997, an unprecedented capital flight from nonresident baht accounts amounted to $5.7 billion. These accounts include deposits at local banks, which are counterpart funds from foreign portfolio investment. From January to July 1998, capital flight through nonresident baht accounts reached $6 billion. The evidence suggests that far from inducing capital inflows, the overshooting depreciation encouraged capital flight. As mentioned earlier, the depressed stock market led to a substitution effect of assets in the portfolio of the private sector with flows of new savings being allocated to lower-risk assets such as bank deposits. Thus, we observe a rise in deposits at banks in order to secure a larger nominal return from fixed deposit rates as high as 16 percent. The portfolio reshuffle from shares in the stock market to bank deposits occurred after the government announced its guarantee over deposits of all nationalized commercial banks.

The negative wealth effect from the stock market crash and growing pessimism of the economy led to a continuing decline in consumption expenditure from 1997 to 1998. This trend is also evident from the declining sales of department stores. As expected sales declined, it is not surprising to find a reduction in fixed capital formation of the business sector. Because the largest component of GDP is consumption expenditure, a continued reduction in consumption expenditure has become a major cause of recession. As household savings increase, there is no doubt that the current account deficit can be improved accordingly through a narrowing of the investment-savings gap. As such, we have observed a turnaround in the current account into a surplus as early as the fourth quarter of 1997.

When the baht exchange rate hit its lowest point in January 1998, interest rates had already been rising since the July float. Due to the high lending interest rates, bank credit can still expand rapidly in real terms. In addition, because of some lag adjustments, bank credit continued to expand rapidly during the period in which prospects of recovery were not overwhelmed by pessimism.

However, the deep sinking value of the baht led to a rapid shrinking of bank credit as banks became aware of future large nonperforming loans. The newly imposed financial regulations that required banks to increase capital funds and reserves for doubtful debts also caused banks to scale down their lending activity.

Private investment declined sharply as bank credit growth contracted. One year after the float, the real volume of credit was actually reduced. Firms need working capital for their operation and require additional credit to finance their acquisition of capital goods. This is also true for export companies, which receive overseas orders but cannot produce their commodities due to lack of liquidity. In times of credit crunch, even if export prices are attractive, firms will have difficulty obtaining credit to secure imported raw materials for production. In this sense, devaluation may not help to spur exports. Moreover, the decision to purchase consumer durable goods is affected by credit availability and rising lending interest rates. Liquidity shortage and high repurchase costs have contributed to a sharp decline in durable consumption expenditure.

As consumption expenditure declines, value-added tax revenues also fall short of expectations. Tax revenues were raised temporarily in December 1997, partly due to an increase in the value-added tax rate from 7 to 10 percent, as required by the IMF bailout package. The severity of the recession in Thailand can be gauged from a continued decline in revenues since January 1998. As such, we can rule out the possibility of contractionary devaluation that stems from a fiscal surplus effect as envisaged by Krugman and Taylor (1978). Public spending continued to decline below the previous year's level because of austerity measures imposed by the IMF. The planned 982 billion baht fiscal budget for 1998 was cut three times to produce the surplus level stipulated by the IMF conditionality of one percent of GDP. The actual spending for fiscal year 1998 was 836 billion baht—almost a 15 percent reduction in public spending. In the end, the 1998 actual fiscal deficit was 3 percent of GDP, just under the 117 billion baht set by the IMF in subsequent relaxation of the fiscal austerity program. A larger level of deficit could have prevented severe output contraction in 1998, without producing an adverse impact on the external balance.

The VAR Model

Empirical results on the impact of devaluation on output are inconclusive. Hausmann, Panizza and Stein (2001) found little evidence of an impact of the currency pass-through on output. Furthermore, Upadhyaya and Upadhyaya (1999) produced evidence that devaluation had no effect on output over any length of time in six developing Asian countries. It is possible that output contraction can be due to factors other than devaluation. Employing data between 1970 and 1999, Magendzo (2002) found that when controlling for selection bias from a data set of 155 countries, the contractionary effect disappears. Nevertheless, Ahmed et al. (2002) found the opposite result. Their VAR model showed that real exchange rate devaluations tended to cause output contraction in developing countries. As pointed out by Lizondo and Montiel (1989), the direction of the impact of devaluation on output is ambiguous since some potential effects may be ignored. Eichengreen and Hausmann (1999) provide a framework for analyzing the relationship between the exchange rate regime and financial fragility. In this paper, the VAR model allows for the impact of devaluation on the financial sector through bank credit. The impact of currency depreciation on output and private investment are evaluated together with endogenous changes in credit and the price level. The VAR model can capture the long lagged effect of devaluation.

The model consists of the rates of change of five macro variables: investment, bank credit, exchange rate, output and the price level. Since monthly data is used in the model, indexes of private investment and manufacturing output is used as proxies for private investment expenditures and real output. The data covers the period between July 1997 and July 2003. The same lag length of six months is used to preserve symmetry of the system. The length of the lags is determined by the likelihood ratio test. The unrestricted model is tested against a restricted model with a shorter lag length. The same result is obtained when Akaike Information Criterion is minimized. When the analysis of impulse response function is performed, Choleski decomposition is employed to solve the identification problem of the variance-covariance matrix of the error terms. The ranking of variables is determined by the importance of correlation coefficients of variables and the error terms in other equations. The ranking orders are: private investment, bank credit, exchange rate, output and the price level. Note that these variables are expressed in terms of the rate of change (year-on-year). The ranking order seems sensible since output and prices are supposed to be simultaneously affected by other variables in the model.

Figure 10-1 illustrates the impulse response function of Cholesky one standard innovation ±2 standard error shocks in currency depreciation. We observe that devaluation leads to contraction in output and bank credit. The impact of bank credit has a long lasting impact of more than five years. A contractionary impact on output reached its deepest level at ten months after devaluation had taken place. We can conclude that devaluation has a long and lasting impact on contraction of output in Thailand, particularly if the rate of depreciation is very high.[3] The response of private investment to currency shocks

Figure 10-1   Impulse Response Functions to Change in Exchange Rate Depreciation (ER)

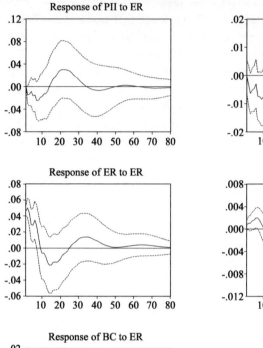

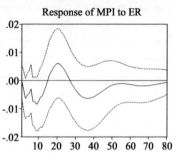

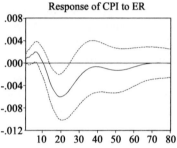

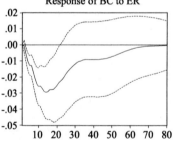

follows a pattern that is similar to the output response. Investment is related to output through expectations of future output. If large devaluation has a negative impact on output, it also discourages private investment through the reduction in expected output.

Analysis of variance decomposition in Table 10-4 confirms that currency depreciation is the most important factor explaining inflation and bank credit expansion. The finding that 66 percent of bank credit variation can be explained by currency shocks within the first two years confirms the earlier theoretical exposition that currency depreciation can have a strong impact on output through its impact on bank credit and investment. About 50 percent of the variation in

Table 10-4   Variance Decomposition of Variables from VAR

PII: private investment growth

Period	GMPI	GPII	GBC	GER	GCPI
Year 1	1.906	85.530	1.069	3.255	8.240
Year 2	2.773	80.401	3.145	6.111	7.569
Year 3	2.922	74.101	3.086	11.772	8.120
Year 4	2.999	73.428	3.054	12.235	8.283

BC: bank credit growth

Period	GMPI	GPII	GBC	GER	GCPI
Year 1	1.215	14.659	54.390	28.213	1.522
Year 2	2.355	5.632	17.437	66.340	8.235
Year 3	2.563	4.555	14.163	68.488	10.231
Year 4	2.283	8.219	14.285	65.610	9.604

ER: exchange rate depreciation

Period	GMPI	GPII	GBC	GER	GCPI
Year 1	5.115	34.723	11.803	45.117	3.243
Year 2	7.020	53.085	6.948	28.316	4.631
Year 3	7.020	51.356	6.869	29.280	5.476
Year 4	6.964	49.820	6.626	30.723	5.867

MPI: manufacturing output growth

Period	GMPI	GPII	GBC	GER	GCPI
Year 1	55.752	28.450	5.667	5.135	4.996
Year 2	27.453	50.631	6.656	8.844	6.416
Year 3	25.380	50.130	6.814	11.074	6.601
Year 4	23.904	47.258	6.624	15.143	7.070

CPI: inflation rate

Period	GMPI	GPII	GBC	GER	GCPI
Year 1	6.583	23.620	8.038	6.947	54.811
Year 2	3.872	36.107	13.745	27.923	18.353
Year 3	4.140	22.987	9.306	46.923	16.643
Year 4	4.017	24.018	9.660	46.230	16.076

manufacturing output can be explained by private investment. The impact of currency depreciation on private investment is even stronger than the impact of bank credit. Nevertheless, private investment exhibits the strongest impact of its own lag effects.

It is argued that the decision to float the baht may not have been the best solution to deal with the crisis. An alternative means would have been to devalue the baht by a certain percentage, the rate that was anticipated by the market. With the benefit of hindsight, if Thailand had chosen to devalue the baht by a moderate level, the adverse consequences and contagion effects that occurred might have been mitigated. Floating the exchange rate deprived the country of a nominal anchor and caused the exchange rate to drift far from its economic fundamentals in the short run. This is not an argument against a flexible exchange rate regime, which has its own merit in cushioning an economy from external shocks. The act of floating the exchange rate itself can be considered as an external shock to the domestic economy. What is needed is a transitional period between the fixed exchange rate and the floating rate. An adjustable peg system of a basket of currencies may be appropriate in preparing the private sector for adjusting to rising foreign exchange risks. Floating a currency during a period of financial crisis can have a devastating effect on output.

Asian Currency Appreciation

The recovery period of five ASEAN economies between 2002 and 2006 is shown in Figure 10-2. Growth was still below the pre-crisis level in 1997. These countries experienced currency appreciation against the dollar by a small percentage. Singapore experienced the highest rates of currency appreciation and economic growth among the five countries. Just like South Korea, income per capita in Malaysia rebounded back to the pre-1997 level by 2000. Because of the larger level of non-performing loans, income levels in Thailand and Indonesia recovered in 2003 and 2004, respectively.

During the recovery, banks in ASEAN countries have worked out their bad debts and disposed on distressed assets, resulting in declining non-performing loans. Countries that had suffered from large non-performing loans found it difficult to resume their normal lending pattern. These economies were not able to regain the pre-shock growth rates because of the low percentage of investment in GDP. In 2006, domestic credits of Malaysia, Indonesia and the Philippines grew in the range of 7–8%, while Thailand domestic credit expanded by only 0.3%. As a result, Thailand's output growth in 2007 was seriously affected.

Investment and bank credit expansion are related to economic recovery between 2002 and 2006 (Figure 10-3). Since investment is determined by factors other than bank credit, differences in consumer confidence, investment climate, cost of financing lead to different speed of capital formation.

Asian economies are facing different problems than those during the pre-1997 period, when many of them suffered from current account deficits and declining international reserves. In 2007, these countries are now experiencing currency appreciation and current account surplus (Figure 10-4). The similarity is that they still have to fend off speculative attack on their currencies. This time around

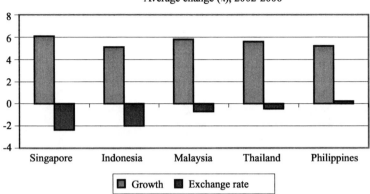

Figure 10-2   Currency Appreciation and Growth
Average change (%), 2002-2006

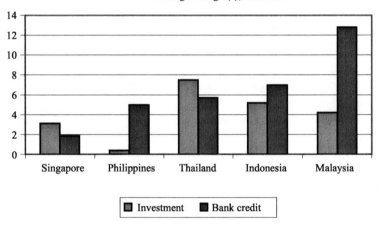

Figure 10-3   Domestic Credit and Investment
Average change (%), 2002-2006

it is in an opposite direction. The speculators are betting that Asian currencies would be appreciating (rather than depreciating) against the dollar. Nevertheless, their currencies were not fixed as they were in the past. The short-term foreign debts are also low. Their banking regulatory systems have been substantially strengthened. The new crisis, if any, would not stem from excessive foreign borrowing and fragile banking system.

The substantial appreciation of Asian currencies against the dollar in 2007 can adversely affect their exports and economic growth. Monetary authorities in ASEAN countries cannot resist the trend of appreciating exchange rates, which is dictated by the movement of the dollar against other currencies. The massive current account deficit in the U.S. requires either major realignment of the dollar value or output contraction in the U.S. economy.

ASEAN's current account surpluses and accumulated foreign reserves in 2007 were in sharp contrast to massive current account deficits and dwindling international reserves in the pre-crisis episode. From Figure 10-4, similar to China and South Korea, the Philippines, Malaysia, Singapore and Thailand experienced current account surplus and large currency appreciation in 2007.

The problem is akin to the pre-1997 crisis: how to deal with capital inflows without allowing exports to be adversely affected by appreciating currency. Sterilization is costly and will not be effective in the long run. Countries with large accumulated international reserves must use interest rate policy to cool down the economy and to prevent asset price bubbles. A property boom has fuelled strong economic growth in some Asian countries. Inflation is a main concern in China, India, Indonesia and Singapore.

Malaysia abandoned the ringgit peg to the dollar in July 2005 and adopted the managed float system, while prohibiting offshore ringgit trading to fend off speculative attack. The Monetary Authority of Singapore (MAS) tightened the monetary policy in 2007 to curb inflationary pressure and intervened in the foreign exchange markets to allow a gradual appreciation in the exchange rate. The currency's secret trading band of the MAS has been widened.

On December 18, 2006, the Bank of Thailand imposed a 30 percent unremunerated reserve-requirement on short-term capital inflows. The measures were later on relaxed as they seriously depressed capital flows into the stock and bond markets. Since March 2007, non-resident investments in debt instruments and unit trusts covered by hedging contracts of at least three months were exempt from the reserve rule of capital controls. The abandonment of stringent capital controls bodes well for a desperate attempt to stem the fast appreciation of the baht.

The dollar continued depreciating by the market anticipation that some Asian central banks would invest their huge reserves in other currencies. As a result of portfolio reallocation from the dollar assets, the gold and oil prices touched their highest level in 2007. In consequences, the resulted cost-push inflation will further lead to a real appreciation of the Asian exchange rates against the dollar.

Despite facing high rates of currency appreciation and export slowdown in 2007, other ASEAN countries, with output growth above 6 percent, performed better than Thailand. The Thai economy grew only 4 percent because of the shrinkage of both domestic consumption and investment. Unlike the Philippines where political problems do not hinder growth, Thailand's political turmoil

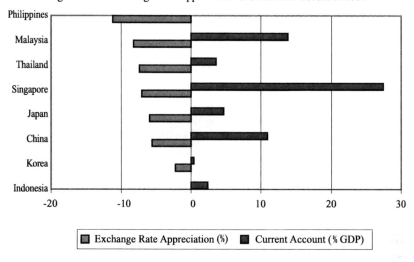

Figure 10-4   Exchange Rate Appreciation and Current Account in 2007

destroyed consumer confidence and investment climate caused by the September 2006 military coup. Other ASEAN countries are able to mitigate the problem of currency appreciation, thanks to their strong domestic demand. It is difficult to cushion the adverse impact of currency appreciation without stimulating bank lending and domestic consumption.

There is no doubt that monetary authorities wish to maintain orderly movement of the currency. But when the export growth engine cannot be relied upon because of the slowdown in world trade and currency appreciation, a growing economy must rely heavily on the domestic growth engine. Increasing foreign exchange rate flexibility by allowing currency appreciation can mitigate the inflationary impact of oil price rises. Stimulating domestic demand is a way to avoid potentially devastating effects of any slump caused by the credit problems in the U.S.

Concluding Remarks

This paper shows that output contraction can follow a massive devaluation, particularly if the banking system has relied heavily on foreign borrowing to excessively finance domestic investment. Furthermore, the existence of a large volume of domestic debt would prolong the recovery, as the real value of private sector debt would be rising after asset price deflation. The so-called debt-deflation process took place in 1997 and 1998. In the aftermath of the currency shock, commercial banks were not willing to lend since the values of the collateral had declined sharply, resulting in the contraction of firms' working capital. Large corporations with high leverage—in particular, firms that had issued debt instruments in foreign currencies—were not able to service their debt after the unprecedented fall of the baht. Banks became more cautious and reduced their credit risk exposure and attempted to rebuild their equity capital. Small and medium-sized firms had difficulty finding alternative sources of funds. The resulting disintermediation had an adverse impact on output.

The policy implication of this chapter reinforces the argument made earlier by Krugman and Taylor (1978) that when devaluation is combined with tax increases, it will aggravate deflation. In the situation described earlier, devaluation should be accompanied by policy measures to increase aggregate demand. The chapter also provides an argument for strong support of the pre-crisis bailout program of the IMF, as opposed to a post-crisis bailout, that prevents a sharp fall in the exchange rate of a troubled economy facing speculative attacks.

Relaxation of capital controls without prudential rules and strengthened bank supervision can prove to be disastrous; the experience in Thailand attests to this. Similarly, floating the exchange rate during capital flight in the absence of policy credibility can push the exchange rate below the threshold level that would trigger financial instability. The higher the level of uncovered foreign debts, the lower will be the level of the threshold exchange rate. Thus floating the baht in July 1997 could easily have triggered both the financial panic and the exchange rate crisis that resulted in a deep recession.

The preceding analysis has showed that whether devaluation or large depreciation can lead to output contraction or not depends to a large extent on the financial structure of the economy. In light of random currency shocks, the degree of vulnerability, which is inversely related to the threshold rate of exchange rate depreciation, will be small when firms have low foreign leverage. As long as depreciating countries have different threshold levels, they are likely to encounter different impacts on output after currency depreciation. Furthermore, whether the same country experiences either output expansion or contraction also depends on the magnitude of the currency changes.

Mild currency depreciation can stimulate growth through export expansion. However, currency depreciation can be contractionary when the exchange rate depreciates substantially above the threshold level, causing bank credit crunch. On the other hand, a country can experience currency appreciation and economic growth as long as domestic credit increases at normal phase. Similarly, if the rate of currency appreciation is excessive, it can thwart economic growth through export slowdown.

Notes

1 This situation seems unlikely when import compression leads to a shortfall in customs duties and when the government has to bail out weak financial institutions.

2 A large amount of capital outflow in the form of withdrawals from nonresident baht accounts occurred during the 1997 financial crisis.

3 In 1998, the rate of depreciation of the baht was around 30 percent, which is larger than the average of 1.4 percent in typical years (Table 10-1).

References

Agenor, Pierre-Richard. 1991. Output, Devaluation and the Real Exchange Rate in Developing Countries. *Welwirtschaftliches Archive*, 127: pp. 16–41.

Ahmed, Shaghil, Christopher J. Gust, Steven B. Kamin and Jonathan Huntly. 2002. Are Depreciations as Contractionary as Devaluation? A Comparison of Selected Emerging and Industrial Economies. *International Finance Discussion Paper*, no. 737 (Sept.), Board of Governors of the Federal Reserve System.

Asian Development Bank. 2003. http://www.adb.org

Bernanke, B., M. Gertler and S. Gilchrist. 1996. The Financial Accelerator and the Flight to Quality. *Review of Economics and Statistics*, 78: pp. 1–15.

Berger, Allen N. and Gregory Udell. 1998. The Economics of Small Business Finance: the Role of Private Equity and Debt Markets in the Financial Growth Cycle. *Journal of Banking and Finance*, 22.

Cooper, Richard N. 1971. Currency Devaluation in Developing Countries. In *Essays in International Finance*, no. 86, Princeton University.

Diaz-Alejandro, Carlos. 1963. A Note on the Impact of Devaluation and the Redistributive Effect. *Journal of Political Economy*, 71: pp. 577–580.

Edwards, Sebastian and Peter Montiel. 1989. Devaluation Crises and the Macroeconomic Consequences of Postponed Adjustment in Developing Countries. *IMF Staff Papers* (Dec).

Eichengreen, Barry and Ricardo Hausmann. 1999. Exchange Rates and Financial Fragility. *Issues in Monetary Policy*, Federal Reserve Bank of Kansas.

Fisher, Irving. 1933. The Debt-deflation Theory of Great Depressions. *Econometrica*, 1: pp. 337–357.

Fischer, Stanley. 2001. Exchange Rate Regimes: Is the Bipolar View Correct? *Journal of Economic Perspectives*, 15: pp. 3–24.

Hausmann, Ricardo, Ugo Panizza and Ernesto Stein. 2001. Why do Countries

Float the Way They Float? *Journal of Development Economics*, 66: pp. 387–414.

Hirschman, Albert. 1949. Devaluation and the Trade Balance: a Note. *Review of Economics and Statistics*, 31: pp. 50–53.

King, Mervyn. 1994. Debt Deflation: Theory and Evidence. *European Economic Review*, 38: pp. 419–445.

Krugman, Paul and Lance Taylor. 1978. Contractionary Effects of Devaluation. *Journal of International Economics*, 8: pp. 445–456.

Lizondo, J.S. and P.J. Montiel. 1989. Contractionary Devaluation in Developing Countries: an Analytical Overview. *International Monetary Fund Staff Papers*, 36(1): pp. 182–227.

Magendzo, Igal. 2002. Are Devaluations Really Contractionary? *Central Bank of Chile Working Papers*, no. 182 (Sept.).

Mishkin, Federic S. 1976. Illiquidity, Consumer Durable Expenditure and Monetary Policy. *American Economic Review*, 66(Sept.): pp. 642–654.

Mishkin, Federic S. 1995. Symposium on the Monetary Transmission Mechanism. *Journal of Economic Perspectives*, 9(4): pp. 3–10.

Noland, Marcus, Li-Gang Liu, Sherman Robinson and Zhi Wang. 1998. *Global Economic Effects of the Asian Currency Devaluations*. Washington, D.C.: Institute for International Economics.

Upadhyaya, K.P. and M.P. Upadhyaya. 1999. Output Effects of Devaluation: Evidence from Asia. *The Journal of Development Studies*, 35(6): pp. 89–103.

11
The Role of the Investment Climate in East Asia: What Really Matters?

Shoko Negishi

Developing countries are facing new competitive challenges in attracting sufficient external financing for sustainable growth. This chapter attempts to reexamine the role of the investment climate as a determinant of external finance in East Asia and other developing regions by looking into various risk factors. The preliminary results indicate a significant positive impact of an improved investment climate in directing foreign direct investment (FDI) to the host country. Of the components of investment climate, improvements in political risk are associated with more FDI inflows. Reduced financial risk may have led to substitution of FDI with capital market flows after the East Asian crisis. Finally, economic risk appears to have been the most influential factor in driving FDI.

Overview

With global financial integration steadily progressing, international capital flows have come to play a significant role in the economic growth of developing countries. Aggregate net resource flows to developing countries nearly trebled over the 1990s, with FDI accounting for more than half of the total flows.

Nevertheless, developing-country shares of private capital flows have declined sharply—from a peak of 14 percent in 1997 to around 7 percent in 2000—due primarily to a dramatic fall in capital market flows (i.e., debt and equity flows). FDI, the single largest source of external finance for developing countries that remained relatively resilient in the face of economic crises, appears to have reached its peak and begun to slow. Moreover, global supply of external finance for emerging markets has been significantly hampered in the past few years due to reduced profits and deteriorating balance sheets of multinationals as well as their reduced appetite for high-risk investments.

As total supply of global capital is shrinking, developing countries are facing greater competition in attracting external finance. Private capital tends to be directed towards countries with a large and growing market, whereas countries with limited access to international capital markets suffer from lack of funds to facilitate their development goals. In order to sustain the level of international capital inflows, and thereby economic growth, there is growing pressure on developing countries to demonstrate a commitment to an improved business environment through sound macroeconomic policies, an appropriate regulatory framework, higher political stability, adequate infrastructure and human capital, as well as good governance.

In response to the new challenges that developing countries are facing, this chapter attempts to reexamine the role of the investment climate as a determinant of external finance in East Asia and other developing regions by looking into various risk factors. The preliminary results indicate a significant positive impact of an improved investment climate in directing FDI to the host country. In terms of the components of investment climate, improvements in political risk continue to be associated with more FDI inflows. Reduced financial risk may have led to substitution of FDI with capital market flows after the East Asian crisis. Finally, economic risk appears to be the most influential factor in driving FDI.

Recent Trends and Background

International capital flows to developing countries have risen substantially over the past decade. Total resource flows increased from around $70 billion on average in the 1980s to a peak of $340 billion in 1997. Private capital flows, accounting for about 80 percent of total external finance in developing countries throughout the 1990s, grew by 13 percent annually to reach $300 billion at its the peak. More than half of these flows have taken the form of FDI, which has grown by 22 percent per annum over the 1990s (Figure 11-1).

On the other hand, FDI flows have been highly concentrated toward select countries, with the top 10 recipients of FDI (based on the cumulative volume of flows over the 1990–2000 period) accounting for more than 70 percent of total FDI in developing countries (Figure 11-2-1). These flows were also substantial in terms of their economic size. The ratio of FDI to GDP is 2.8 percent on average over the 1990s, compared with 1.2 percent for other developing countries. In fact, this trend is strengthening over time with the share of FDI going to the top 10 developing countries rising from 68 percent in the first half of the period to 72 percent in the second half of the 1990s. Similarly, the difference in the FDI-

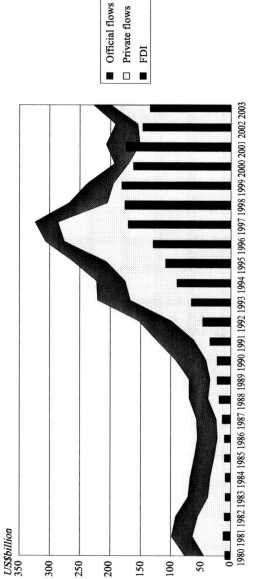

Figure 11-1   Trends in External Finance to Developing Countries

Note: Official flows include both bilateral and multilateral grants and concessional and non-concessional loans, as defined by the World Bank and OECD as official development finance.

Source: World Bank, *Global Development Finance: Country Tables*, various years.

to-GDP ratios between the top 10 FDI recipients and the remaining developing countries has increased from 1.8 percent and 0.8 percent, respectively, in the first half of the decade to 3.6 percent and 1.7 percent in the latter period (Figure 11-2-2).

East Asia received $538 billion of FDI in the past decade, the largest on a cumulative basis among the developing regions, growing by 17 percent per annum. Of those FDI flows in East Asia, China—the largest recipient of FDI in the world—accounted for around 70 percent. FDI flows to East Asian countries began to decline after the peak in 1997; currently, East Asia is in second place next to Latin America and the Caribbean, where FDI increased by 24 percent annually (Figure 11-3). The fall in FDI largely reflects considerable outflows of FDI from Indonesia as well as a decline in FDI inflows to Malaysia, whereas FDI in China remained stable. On the other hand, Korea and Thailand continued to receive significant volumes of FDI, largely in the form of sales of domestic firms (Figure 11-4-1). Recently, however, FDI in East Asian countries has not been sizable relative to their GDP. FDI as ratio to GDP is above the developing-country average only in China and Thailand. In Korea, the ratio has been rising steadily, though it still remains low (Figure 11-4-2). The large exchange rate depreciations and declines in asset prices following the crisis reduced values of domestic assets. Meanwhile various measures were introduced to accelerate business consolidation in both countries, including legislative frameworks to encourage corporate mergers and acquisitions (M&A) transactions as well as FDI inflows.[1] As a result, cross-border M&A sales in Korea and Thailand surged in 1998 to reach $4 billion and $3 billion, respectively, from less than $1 billion in 1997 (Figure 11-5).

The boom in private capital flows during the 1990s led to the reassessment of their benefits and costs. Many studies tested, and generally confirmed, the positive relationship between private capital flows and economic performance of developing countries. FDI, in particular, appears to be associated with an increase in domestic investment and productivity growth in the host country.[2] The negative effect of capital flow volatility on growth does not appear to be long lasting, as many countries increasingly diversify their production patterns and flexibility of exchange rate regimes.

The positive impact of external private capital flows on the recipient economy can be amplified if a country possesses sufficient absorptive capacity, consisting of the robust macroeconomic policy framework, the health of the financial system, the quality of physical infrastructure and human capital, administrative efficiency, the low level of corruption as well as long-running political stability (World Bank 2001). The positive relationship between FDI and domestic investment depends heavily on the recipient's investment climate. A

Figure 11-2   Concentration of FDI

(1) Volume

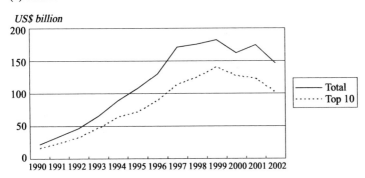

Source: World Bank, *Global Development Finance: Country Tables*, various years.

(2) As share of GDP

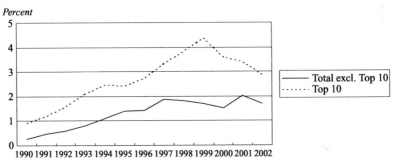

Source: World Bank, *Global Development Finance: Country Tables*, various years;
World Bank, *World Development Indicators*, various years.

Figure 11-3   Regional Trends in FDI

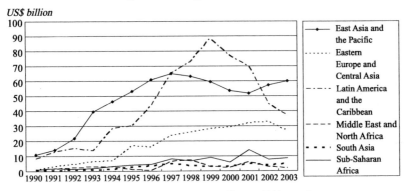

Source: World Bank, *Global Development Finance: Country Tables*, various years.

Figure 11-4   FDI flows in East Asia

(1) Volumes

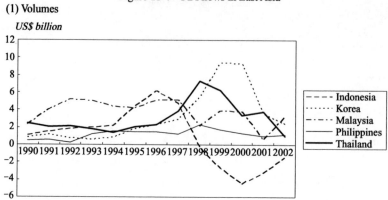

Source: World Bank, *Global Development Finance: Country Tables*, various years.

(2) As share of GDP

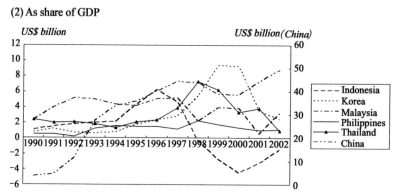

Source: World Bank, *Global Development Finance: Country Tables*, various years; World
Bank, *World Development Indicators*, various years.

number of studies have generated empirical evidence on the role of policy and
institutions in extracting benefits from FDI. Borensztein, De Gregorio and Lee
(1998), and World Bank (2001) conclude that FDI is positively associated with
domestic investment only when the recipient is endowed with a high level of
human capital.

Moreover, a large volume of literature has found that a positive effect of
FDI on productivity may diminish when a recipient's capacity is too low to
absorb technology spillovers from foreign firms (Djankov and Hoekman 2000;
Kokko, Tansini and Zejan 1996). On the other hand, FDI can bring about a
positive impact on productivity when absorptive capacity is high. This has
been confirmed for the case of East Asia in various studies, some of which

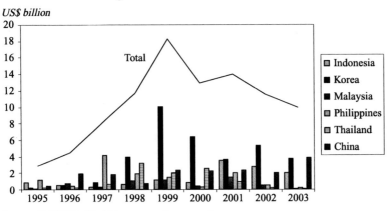

Figure 11-5   M&A Sales in East Asia

Source: UNCTAD, *World Investment Report*, various years.
Note: Involves acquisitions of more than a 10% equity.

are summarized by World Bank (1993, 1997). Among other studies, FDI in Taiwan has been associated with higher productivity in foreign-owned firms resulting in positive spillovers to domestically owned firms (Chuang and Lin 1999; Schive and Majumder 1990). According to Chuang and Lin (1999), a one percent increase in FDI in an industrial sector is associated with an increase of up to two percent in the productivity of domestic firms in the same sector. The benefits of FDI can also be greater in a country where physical and human infrastructure is superior (Mody and Wang 1997).

Some studies have tried to associate the surge in FDI with an improved investment climate in the developing host countries. The argument attributes the concentration of FDI flows partly to investors' sensitivity towards the business environment of the host country. The number of bilateral and regional investment treaties increased significantly, which served to protect the interests of both the investors and the recipients by improving institutional transparency. Higher credibility of macroeconomic and investment policies, as well as political stability in the host countries reduced risks for multinational enterprises to make long-term investments (World Bank 2001, 2002). A simple picture based on a series of surveys of more than 20 developing countries by the European Round Table of Industrialists indicates a strong positive correlation between growth rates of FDI flows and improvements in the investment climate (i.e., building of a regulatory framework governing FDI, liberalizing various restrictions that limit foreign entry and ownership as well as foreign exchange transactions, and improving institutional protection of intellectual property rights) through the 1980–90s (Figure 11-6).

Figure 11-6   FDI and Investment Climate in
              Developing Countries

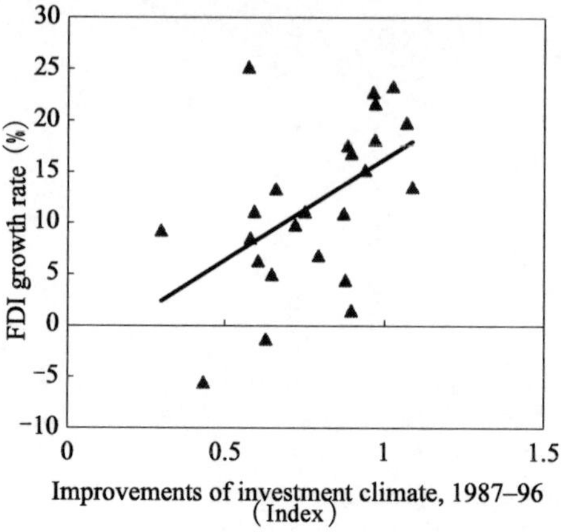

Improvements of investment climate, 1987–96
                   (Index)

Note: Investment climate index is on a scale of 1–6, based on the
   improvements of policies and overall business environment during the
   1987–96 period. FDI growth rates are annual estimates between period
   averages of 1981–96 and 1997–99. Sample countries are selected to
   provide adequate representation of major recipients of FDI flows in all
   regions.
Source: European Round Table of Industrialists 2000; World Bank, *Global
   Development Finance: Country Tables*, various years; World Bank,
   World Development Indicators, various years.

Empirical Analysis

Description of the Model

This section examines empirically the role of the investment climate in
determining patterns of FDI flows. A significant volume of literature has been
dedicated to discussions of determinants of FDI. Measures of FDI vary, but a
large number of studies have applied the ratio of FDI to developing countries'
GDP (UNCTAD 1992, 1998). An econometric model to explain the pattern of
FDI usually takes into account overall economic performance of the recipient
countries as well as their relative attractiveness as an investment location.

Economic and institutional characteristics of recipient countries that
are considered to significantly affect investment decisions by multinational
enterprises include the following.[3]

Market size: the current and future size of the recipient country's internal
market has been considered to be one of the crucial factors in past research
on determinants of FDI.[4] Large and growing markets can accommodate more

suppliers and help them achieve scale and scope economies (UNCTAD 1992, 1998). A higher GDP growth rate, as a proxy for future market size, has been found to be associated with larger FDI inflows to the recipient economy (Root and Ahmed 1979; Nigh 1985). In this model, the average growth rate of GDP over the three years prior to the current period (GGDP) is used as a proxy for investors' view of future economic performance of the recipient country.

Openness: openness to trade of the host country, represented by the level of export orientation, should increase a country's attractiveness to multinationals by providing greater access to export markets (a third of world trade is accounted for by intrafirm transactions by multinationals, who also provide the bulk of FDI flows) (Caves, Porter and Spence 1980; Saunders 1982). This model applies the ratio of exports to GDP in the recipient countries to measure export orientation (EX).

Industrial country performance: the volume of FDI flows in developing countries is determined by not only the availability of resources in the industrial world, but also their investment profitability relative to industrial markets. The overall economic performance of industrial countries, measured by the growth rate of the Group of Seven countries' GDP ($G7$), will capture changes in the potential rate of return from investments in emerging markets relative to industrial countries.

Investment climate: a good investment climate—in terms of sound macro-economic policies, open regimes towards foreign investment and nondiscriminatory frameworks for business facilitation—is likely to induce FDI inflows to the recipient economy (World Bank 2002; UNCTAD 1998). Risk factors—political, economic or financial—in developing countries could have negative impacts on the cash flows associated with FDI projects (Moosa 2002). Measures such as establishing a regulatory framework to protect the property rights of investors and institutional transparency to reduce corruption can increase locational attraction of host developing countries for foreign investment (Drabek and Payne 1999; Hoekman and Saggi 1999; Wei 2000). In this chapter, we modified the Country Policy and Institutional Assessment (CPIA) index compiled by the World Bank as a variable to represent investment climate of recipient countries. The CPIA assesses the quality of a country's present policy and institutional framework in four categories: economic management, structural policies, policies for social inclusion/equity and public sector management, and institutions. There are 20 items for assessment to be grouped into the above four categories, and each item carries a 5 percent weight in the overall rating (Table 11-A1, see Appendix).[5] The scale for the ratings ranges from 1 (low) through 6 (high).

Although the CPIA is conducted annually, the original indices (ic) are not directly comparable over time since the country coverage has changed. To overcome this problem, we computed a mean value as a benchmark for each year and created a new series, IC, corresponding to each country in the sample to indicate their position relative to the benchmark, thereby making the time-series indices roughly consistent:

$$IC_j = \frac{ic_j}{ic} = \frac{ic_j}{1/n \sum_j^n ic_j} \quad (j = 1, ..., 30),$$

A critical problem with the CPIA index is associated with disaggregation by components. Not only has the country coverage changed over time, but so have the components of each category. In addition, there is a code of disclosure involved in using the categorical indices. Therefore we instead used the International Country Risk Guide (ICRG) rating system. The ICRG system comprises 22 variables in three subcategories of risk: political, financial and economic. Political risk is comprised of 12 components, and the financial and economic risks are each comprised of five components (Table 11-A2, see Appendix). Each component is assigned a maximum numerical value (risk points), with the highest number of points indicating the lowest potential risk for that component and the lowest number (0) indicating the highest potential risk. In calculating the composite rating, the political risk rating contributes to 50 percent of the composite rating, while the financial and economic ratings each contribute 25 percent (International Country Risk Guide).[6]

With the set of variables described above, the following equation is estimated for panel data from 1981–2000, which covers 30 developing countries that account for more than 80 percent of FDI flows to developing countries:[7]

$$FDI_i = \alpha_i + \beta_1(GGDP_i) + \beta_2(EX_i) + \beta_3(G7_i) + \beta_4(IC_i) + \beta_5(T) \quad (i = 1, ..., 30)$$

GDP growth rates and exports are lagged to avoid endogeneity, under the assumption that FDI is determined largely on the basis of long-term commitments by multinationals (World Bank 1999). The model is estimated by the general least squares method with cross-section weighting to correct for possible heteroscedasticity. Meanwhile the fixed effects estimation was used to allow a variation of constant variables across countries.

Results
The set of variables and results are summarized in Tables 11-1-1 and 11-1-2, with the indices based on the CPIA and the ICRG, respectively. Column (1) of each table presents the impact of policy as well as other economic determinants on the level of inward FDI to the recipient countries for the entire sample period. As predicted, GDP growth rates are positively correlated to FDI flows in both cases. Similarly, greater openness of the economies brings more FDI. On the

Table 11-1   FDI and the Investment Climate[a]
(1) Country Policy and Institutional Assessment

FI	(1) 1981-2000	(2) 1981-96	(3) 1997-2000
$\hat{Y}$	0.048*	0.033*	-0.001
	(3.60)	(3.21)	(-0.03)
X	0.043*	0.035*	-0.056***
	(4.15)	(2.98)	(-1.84)
$\hat{G7}$	-0.047**	-0.029**	0.051
	(-2.23)	(-2.08)	(0.30)
IC	1.086*	0.869*	1.204
	(4.49)	(4.69)	(0.83)
T	0.078*	0.064*	-0.010
	(10.05)	(9.07)	(-0.13)
Adjusted R^2	0.65	0.52	0.85

(2) International Country Risk Guide

FI	(1) 1981-2000	(2) 1981-96	(3) 1997-2000
$\hat{Y}$	0.059*	0.036*	0.014
	(4.58)	(3.47)	(0.44)
X	0.043*	0.036*	-0.072**
	(4.12)	(3.07)	(-2.26)
$\hat{G7}$	-0.036***	-0.012	0.108
	(-1.71)	(-0.82)	(0.71)
IC	0.020*	0.017*	0.044*
	(4.01)	(3.90)	(2.63)
T	0.060*	0.044*	0.074
	(6.39)	(4.69)	(0.86)
Adjusted R^2	0.50	0.54	0.89

Note: a. FI refers to the ratio of FDI inflows to developing countries' GDP; $\hat{Y}$ is the average growth rate of developing countries' GDP over three years prior to the current period; X is the ratio of developing countries' exports to their GDP; $\hat{G7}$ is the GDP growth rate of the Group of Seven countries; IC refers to the investment climate index (CPIA or ICRG); and T refers to a time trend. *, **, *** denotes significance at the 1% level, at the 5% level and at the 10% level, respectively. T-values are shown in parentheses.

other hand, GDP growth rates of the G7 countries have negative effects on FDI inflows. This suggests that a rise in the industrial countries' GDP should reduce the relative rate of return from investment in developing countries, which offsets the positive effect from the increase in total supply of resources.

The impact of the investment climate of recipients on FDI, using both indices, is positive and statistically significant. An improvement in investment climate will increase FDI inflows at approximately the same degree. By applying the forecast values of each economic variable published in World Bank (2002) to the model, we can predict that an increase in the investment climate indices by 0.01

(or one percentage point) across countries every year could result in a cumulative increase of FDI flows of around $9 billion in the case of CPIA, compared with the scenario where the investment climate is assumed to remain constant over the same period. When the actual value of the ICRG index is applied through 2002, FDI is expected to increase to $330 million on a cumulative basis for the period of 2003–05.

The next exercise is to examine possible structural changes in the relationships before and after the East Asian crisis. Columns (2) and (3) in each table show the results for the pre- and post-crisis periods, respectively. Results from the pre-crisis sample indicate the same patterns as for the whole sample period in both regressions. The impact of the investment climate is positive and significant, although the coefficient value is slightly smaller. While the results of the post-crisis period using the CPIA index lose statistical significance (except for the export variable, which is now negatively correlated with FDI), the coefficient of the ICRG index remains positive and statistically significant. The overall instability of the post crisis results may not only be due to the considerably reduced sample size, but may also be a reflection of a time lag in the slowdown of FDI flows and a much slower recovery of the real economy in developing countries (World Bank 2001).

The second step is to break down the investment climate index into its components and examine their impacts on FDI separately. The results of this exercise are presented in Table 11-2. The political element of the investment climate appears to play a positive role in attracting FDI into the recipient economy throughout the observation period. The coefficient becomes greater in the latter part of the period, though the results become less stable, indicating that the importance of policy performance may have increased after the crisis. The financial factor was a positive and statistically significant determinant of FDI before the crisis. The coefficient, however, becomes negative in the post-crisis period. This result may imply that reduced financial risk perceived by international investors is likely to increase financial resources through capital markets, i.e., debt and equity, rather than FDI.[8] The economic risk element shows a similar pattern, though the coefficient loses statistical significance in the post-crisis regression. The coefficient of the economic factor is the largest of the three components of the investment climate, indicating the utmost importance of economic risk in an investment climate.

Estimated impacts of improvements in the investment climate on FDI could also vary by components. Table 11-3 presents estimated changes in FDI flows to the East Asian countries during the 2003–05 period, assuming that the investment climate index as measured by the ICRG continues to increase by one percent annually. Benefits from improved political risk would be greatest

Table 11-2 FDI and Investment Climate by Components[a]

(1) Political factor

FI	(1) 1981-2000	(2) 1981-96	(3) 1997-2000
$\hat{Y}$	0.060*	0.037*	-0.005
	(4.56)	(3.53)	(-0.16)
X	0.042*	0.038*	-0.072**
	(4.02)	(3.19)	(-2.62)
$\hat{G7}$	-0.037***	-0.011	-0.171
	(-1.72)	(-0.75)	(-1.60)
IC^P	0.014*	0.012*	0.047*
	(2.78)	(3.05)	(4.55)
T	0.069*	0.051*	-0.023
	(7.29)	(5.69)	(-0.38)
Adjusted R^2	0.50	0.53	0.93

(2) Financial factor

FI	(1) 1981-2000	(2) 1981-96	(3) 1997-2000
$\hat{Y}$	0.061*	0.036*	-0.003
	(4.57)	(3.47)	(-0.09)
X	0.043*	0.029**	-0.044
	(4.00)	(2.46)	(-1.42)
$\hat{G7}$	-0.042***	-0.016	0.043
	(-1.95)	(-1.03)	(0.26)
IC^F	0.014***	0.026*	-0.047***
	(1.80)	(3.89)	(-1.70)
T	0.072*	0.042*	-0.022
	(7.06)	(4.07)	(-0.28)
Adjusted R^2	0.49	0.53	0.88

(3) Economic factor

FI	(1) 1981-2000	(2) 1981-96	(3) 1997-2000
$\hat{Y}$	0.052*	0.036*	0.001
	(4.03)	(3.43)	(0.04)
X	0.042*	0.035*	-0.049c
	(4.04)	(2.93)	(-1.63)
$\hat{G7}$	-0.047**	-0.023	0.062
	(-2.27)	(-1.59)	(0.33)
IC^E	0.038*	0.024*	-0.009
	(4.30)	(3.06)	(0.24)
T	0.068*	0.057*	-0.008
	(8.15)	(7.16)	(-0.09)
Adjusted R^2	0.50	0.53	0.89

Note: a. FI refers to the ratio of FDI inflows to developing countries' GDP; $\hat{Y}$ is the average growth rate of developing countries' GDP over three years prior to the current period; X is the ratio of developing countries' exports to their GDP; $\hat{G7}$ is the GDP growth rate of the Group of Seven countries; IC refers to the investment climate index (CPIA or ICRG); and T refers to a time trend. *, **, *** denotes significance at the 1% level, at the 5% level and at the 10% level, respectively. T-values are shown in parentheses.

Table 11-3   Estimated Cumulative FDI Changes from Increases
in ICRG Indexes by 1%, 2003–05 (US$ million)

	Political	Financial	Economic
China	148.5	83.0	56.0
Indonesia	508.8	9.3	7.2
Korea	-51.3	27.0	22.9
Malaysia	109.6	4.6	3.5
Philippines	-137.1	4.4	3.3
Thailand	-88.6	8.6	6.7

in Indonesia, with $500 million, followed by China and Malaysia. For Korea, the Philippines and Thailand, on the other hand, the one percent increase appears insufficient to compensate for possible deterioration in macroeconomic variables. Improvements in financial and economic risks would bring by far the largest increases in FDI to China, followed by Korea. The remaining countries could also enjoy modest gains.

Conclusions and Policy Implications

This study found new evidence on the role of the investment climate in attracting foreign investment. A good business environment, as measured by the CPIA and ICRG indices, turned out to be an effective determinant of FDI. Economic risk appears to be the most influential factor of the investment climate. Reduced financial risk may have led to substitution of FDI with capital market flows after the East Asian crisis. Improvements in political risk continued to be associated with more FDI inflows.

International investors, after the series of financial crises, have become more risk averse in selecting the locations and the types of investment projects, and the investment climate appears to have become increasingly more important for developing countries in securing a sizable injection of private external finance. The simulation exercise indicates that an improvement in the investment climate indices by one percent per annum could lead to a sizable increase in FDI for some economies of East Asia, though for others investment climate improvements may not be sufficient to maintain the level of inflows.

Further examination needs to be done in order to verify the role of the investment climate. This analysis has been conducted on an aggregate basis with panel data, and as a result, it does not analyze differentiation across sectors as well as by origin of FDI. In addition, further breakdown by risk components, particularly for the political factor, could explain some results that are contradictory to our conventional perception, such as the cases for Korea and the

Philippines. It would be useful to look at the sectoral and/or bilateral patterns of flows to study other potential determinants of foreign investment, e.g., the impact of clusters and microeconomic factors. Moreover, further breakdown of the investment climate would be desirable to evaluate the role of human capital and technological innovation, as well as governance and institutional flexibility.

As liquidity constraints are being tightened in both private and public sectors of industrial economies, developing countries are facing a serious challenge in attracting external funds to finance their development goals. There is strong pressure on developing economies to improve their business environment by increasing their economic and political stability, and by adopting adequate investment policies and sound governance. Moreover, FDI can be more beneficial in increasing domestic investment and productivity in countries with good policy and institutions.

The competitive pressure could be particularly strong in some of the East Asian countries, as China has become the world's largest recipient of FDI flows. So far, international investors appear to have responded favorably to China's accession to the World Trade Organization, reflecting prospects for greater opportunities and further liberalization. This study, however, suggests that other East Asian countries may be able to attract FDI, if necessary, to assist sustainable growth, by focusing on improving their business environment, including political, economic and financial risks. Continued reduction in such risk factors should be able to boost not only FDI, but other forms of capital flows into the East Asian countries as well. According to the simulation exercise, additional FDI flows obtained by an improved investment climate may be greatest in China, yet insignificant relative to the current level of FDI, at far less than one percent. On the other hand, other East Asian economies could potentially benefit from reduced political risk through institutional reforms, if they are at the sufficient level, as the FDI gains may account for one to eight percent of the current level of inflows.

In order to achieve the most desirable results, the East Asian economies are advised to not only focus on reducing political risk, but to strengthen their monitoring systems to accompany financial openness, thereby helping to restore health and stability to the domestic financial system. Additional infrastructure, e.g., in utility and transportation systems, should reduce operating costs for foreign affiliates. Educational reforms may increase the stock of human capital, thereby fostering spillovers from FDI. Many East Asian countries, with their institutional flexibility, should be capable of these reforms. The surge in M&A sales in the post-crisis economies, following the various liberalization measures, suggests that international investors will be responsive to new opportunities once they are made available.

Appendix

See Tables 11-A1, 11-A2, 11-A3.

Notes

1 See World Bank (2000) for a detailed discussion of policy measures introduced after the East Asian crisis.
2 A summary and some new evidence are provided in World Bank (2001, ch. 3) and IMF (2001, ch. 3).
3 Other economic variables that may affect the pattern of FDI include relative interest rates, exchange rates and wages of the recipient economies. The author tested the model with the first two variables, but the coefficients were neither statistically significant nor did they change the final results.
4 The literature includes Root and Ahmed (1979), Schneider and Frey (1985), Papanastassiou and Pearce (1990), and Wheeler and Mody (1992). See also UNCTAD (1998) for a detailed discussion.

Table 11-A1   Categories of Country Policy and Institutional Assessment

A. Economic management
       Management of inflation and macroeconomic imbalances
       Fiscal policy
       Management of external debt
       Management and sustainability of the development program
B. Structural policies
       Trade policy and foreign exchange regime
       Financial stability and depth
       Banking sector efficiency and resource mobilization
       Competitive environment for the private sector
       Factor and product markets
       Policies and institutions for environmental sustainability
C. Policies for social inclusion/equity
       Gender
       Equity of public resource use
       Building human resources
       Social protection and labor
       Monitoring and analysis of poverty outcomes and impacts
D. Public sector management and institutions
       Property rights and rule-based governance
       Quality of budgetary and financial management
       Efficiency of revenue mobilization
       Quality of public administration
       Transparency, accountability and corruption in the public sector

Source: World Bank (2003).

Table 11-A2   Categories of International Country Risk Guide

A. Political risk components
   Government stability
   Socioeconomic conditions
   Investment profile
   Internal conflict
   External conflict
   Corruption
   Military in politics
   Religious tensions
   Law and order
   Ethnic tensions
   Democratic accountability
   Bureaucracy quality

B. Financial risk components
   Foreign debt as a percentage of GDP
   Foreign debt service as a percentage of XGS
   Current account as a percentage of XGS
   Net liquidity as months of import cover
   Exchange rate stability

C. Economic risk components
   GDP per head of population
   Real annual GDP growth
   Annual inflation rate
   Budget balance as a percentage of GDP
   Current account balance as a percentage of GDP

Source: International Country Risk Guide (2003).

5 For a reference to further guidelines, see http://www.worldbank.org/ida/ cpiaq2001.pdf, for example.
6 For a reference to further guidelines, see http://www.icrgonline.com/.
7 The 30 countries used in the study are given in Table 11-A3 (see Appendix). The value of large-scale privatization transactions has been deducted from the volume of FDI for some countries where a small number of such transactions account for a large share of total FDI inflows.
8 See Hausmann and Fernandez-Arias (2000) for the detailed argument.

References

Borensztein, E., J. De Gregorio and J.W. Lee. 1998. How Does Foreign Direct Investment Affect Growth? *Journal of International Economics*, 45(1): pp. 115–135.

Table 11-A3   List of countries

Sub-Saharan Africa	Cameroon	CAM	57.54
	Côte d'Ivoire	COT	51.63
	Nigeria	NIG	48.40
	South Africa	SOU	66.58
East Asia and the Pacific	China	CHA	66.04
	Indonesia	IND	48.73
	Korea	KOR	77.00
	Malaysia	MAL	69.90
	Papua New Guinea	PAP	62.13
	Philippines	PHI	64.19
	Thailand	THA	72.75
Eastern Europe and	Hungary	HUN	76.85
Central Asia	Poland	POL	74.94
	Turkey	TUR	58.77
Latin America and	Argentina	ARG	71.65
the Caribbean	Brazil	BRA	63.73
	Chile	CHI	73.02
	Colombia	COL	52.06
	Ecuador	ECU	53.65
	Honduras	HON	61.21
	Jamaica	JAM	72.13
	Mexico	MEX	70.13
	Peru	PER	63.23
	Venezuela	VEN	58.96
Middle East and	Egypt	EGY	66.90
North Africa	Jordan	JOR	69.88
	Morocco	MOR	69.52
	Tunisia	TUN	74.50
South Asia	India	IDI	57.54
	Pakistan	PAK	47.63

Note: The numbers in the fourth column indicate the ICRG composite index in 2000.

Caves, R.E., M.E. Porter and A.M. Spence. 1980. *Competition in the Open Economy*. Cambridge: Harvard University Press.

Chuang, Y.C. and C.M. Lin. 1999. Foreign Direct Investment, R&D and Spillover Efficiency: Evidence from Taiwan's Manufacturing Firms. *Journal of Development Studies*, 35(4): pp. 117–137.

Djankov, S. and B. Hoekman. 2000. Foreign Investment and Productivity Growth in Czech Enterprises. *World Bank Economic Review*, 14(1): pp. 49–64.

Drabek, Z. and W. Payne. 1999. The Impact of Transparency on Foreign Direct Investment. *World Trade Organization Staff Working Paper*, ERAD-99-02, revised 2001, Geneva.

European Round Table of Industrialists. 2000. *Improved Investment Conditions:*

Third Survey on Improvements in Conditions for Investment in the Developing World. Brussels: The Round Table.

Hausmann, R., and E. Fernandez-Arias. 2000. Foreign Direct Investment: Good Cholesterol? *Inter-American Development Bank Research Department Working Paper*, 417: Washington, D.C.

Hoekman, B. and K. Saggi. 1999. Multinational Disciplines for Investment-Related Policies. In P. Guerrieri and H. E. Sharer. eds. *Global Regionalism and Economic Convergence in Europe and East Asia: The Need for Global Governance Regimes*. Rome: Institute of International Affairs.

International Country Risk Guide. 2003. http://www.ICRGOnline.com/

International Monetary Fund (IMF). 2001. The Information Technology Revolution. In *World Economic Outlook*, Ch. 3, Washington, D.C.: IMF.

Kokko, A., R. Tansini and M.C. Zejan. 1996. Local Technological Capability and Productivity Spillovers from FDI in the Uruguayan Manufacturing Sector. *Journal of Development Studies*, 32: pp. 602–611.

Mody, A. and F.Y. Wang. 1997. Explaining Industrial Growth in Coastal China: Economic Reforms ... and What Else? *World Bank Economic Review*, 11(2): pp. 293–325.

Moosa, I.A. 2002. *Foreign Direct Investment: Theory, Evidence and Practice.* United Kingdom: Palgrave.

Nigh, D. 1985. The Effect of Political Events on U.S. Direct Investment: A Pooled Time-Series Cross-Sectional Analysis. *Journal of International Business Studies*, 16: pp. 1–17.

Organization for Economic Cooperation and Development (OECD). 2001. *Geographic Distribution of Flows.* Paris: OECD.

Papanastassiou, M. and R.D. Pearce. 1990. Host Country Characteristics and the Sourcing Behaviour of U.K. Manufacturing Industry. *Discussion Papers in International Investment and Business Studies.* Series B, 2(140). Department of Economics, University of Reading: United Kingdom.

Root, F.R. and A.A. Ahmed. 1979. Empirical Determinants of Manufacturing Direct Foreign Investment in Developing Countries. *Economic Development and Cultural Change*, 27: pp. 751–767.

Saunders, R.S. 1982. The Determinants of Inter-Industry Variation of Foreign Ownership in Canadian Manufacturing. *Canadian Journal of Economics*, 15: pp. 77–84.

Schive, C. and B.A. Majumder. 1990. Direct Foreign Investment and Linkage Effects: the Experience of Taiwan. *Canadian Journal of Development Studies*, 11(2): pp. 325–342.

Schneider, F. and B.S. Frey. 1985. Economic and Political Determinants of Foreign Direct Investment. *World Development*, 13(2): pp. 191–275.

United Nations Conference on Trade and Development (UNCTAD). 1998. *World Investment Report: Trends and Determinants*. Geneva: UNCTAD.

United Nations Conference on Trade and Development (UNCTAD). 1992. *The Determinants of Foreign Direct Investment: A Survey of the Evidence*. Geneva: UNCTAD.

Wei, S. 2000. Local Corruption and Global Capital Flows. In W.C. Brainard and G.L. Perry. eds. *Brookings Papers on Economic Activity* Washington, D.C: Brookings Institution Press.

Wheeler, D. and A. Mody. 1992. International Investment Location Decisions: the Case of U.S. Firms. *Journal of International Economics*, 33: pp. 57–76.

World Bank. 1993. *The East Asian Miracle: Economic Growth and Public Policy*. New York: Oxford University Press.

World Bank. 1997. *Global Development Finance, Volume 1*. Washington, D.C.: World Bank.

World Bank. 1999. *Global Development Finance, Analysis and Summary Tables*. Washington, D.C.: World Bank.

World Bank. 2000. *Global Economic Prospects and the Developing Countries*. Washington, D.C.: World Bank.

World Bank. 2001. *Global Development Finance: Building Coalitions for Effective Development Finance*. Washington, D.C.: World Bank.

World Bank. 2002. *Global Development Finance: Financing the Poorest Countries*. Washington, D.C.: World Bank.

World Bank. 2003. http://www.worldbank.org/ida/cpiaq2001.pdf

Index

8th National Economic and Social Development Plan 217
1966 Chamber of Commerce Act 215
1990 Car Accident Act 211
1990 Social Security Act 210

Abe 1, 7–8, 10, 13, 95, 126, 136, 193
Action Plan on Social Safety Nets 225
aging 126, 136
agricultural product specialization 9
agro-based economy 141
Ahmed 265, 283, 290
Akaike Information Criterion 265
Amanah Ikhtier Malaysia (AIM) 208
Ambatkar 109
Ammar 223
Amsden 16
analysis of variance decomposition 266
Annual Survey of Manufacturing Industries 144
APEC 46, 54, 95
appreciation 249, 251, 262, 268–272
Ariff 94
Article XXIV 64
Ascher 92
Asian bond 30–31
Asian Bond Market Initiative (ABMI) 31
Asian (financial) crisis 1, 11, 14, 19, 28, 30, 32, 40, 112, 152, 202, 231, 240–241, 244, 275–276, 286, 288, 290
Asian Development Bank (ADB) 9, 17, 25, 180, 190, 193, 202–206, 208–209, 212, 216, 218–221, 223, 253
Asian NIEs 54, see also NIEs
Asian Tigers 15
assets utilization 146
Association of Southeast Asian Nations (ASEAN) 2–4, 6–7, 11, 15, 17, 19, 26, 30–32, 41, 43, 45, 47–49, 54–58, 60, 81–95, 98–99, 101–105, 109–124, 192, 225, 268–271
ASEAN Economic Community (AEC) 6, 81–82, 86, 88–90, 105
ASEAN Framework Agreement on Services (AFAS) 81, 86–87
ASEAN Free Trade Area (AFTA) 1, 5, 30, 32, 45, 47–50, 54–55, 57, 81–82, 84–89, 93–95
ASEAN Investment Area (AIA) 45, 81
ASEAN Secretariat 2, 85, 89–90, 101, 104
ASEAN Vision 2020 81
ASEAN+3 2–3, 11, 30, 56, 82, 89, 95, 98, 105
ASEAN-4 43
ASEAN-6 84
ASEAN-10 47–48
ASEAN-China Free Trade Agreements (FTAs) 99, 109, 118, see also Free Trade Agreements (FTAs)
ASEAN–Japan CEP 95

Athukorala and Menon 88
austerity programs 10–11, 231, 245
Australian Agency for International
    Development (AusAID) 219, 223
Ayeyarwaddy delta 166

Baek 234
baht exchange rate 263
Balassa 124
Bali Summit 90
bank failure 12, 247, 249, 256
Bank of Thailand 225, 262, 270
Bank-for-the-Poor Network 216
BAPPENAS 207
Bartel 126
Becker 127
Beng 180, 234, 239
Bernanke 232, 234, 260
Bhagwati 100
Bhanupong 1, 11–13, 249
Bogor declaration 45
Borensztein 280
Borrus 64
Breusch-Godfrey LM test 152
BRICs 110
broad money 231

Canadian International Development
    Agency 223
capital control 11, 21, 257, 270, 272
capital flight 11, 258, 263, 272
capital intensity 143, 147,153
capital intensity growth 156
capital market 10, 27, 33, 216, 231,
    263, 275–276, 286, 288
capital productivity 8, 142, 146, 155
capital-augmenting technical progress
    152–153, 156
capital-labor ratio 143, 147
Caprio 247

Cash-for-Work scheme 204
Caves 283
Central Provident Fund (CPF) 212
CEPA 56
CEPT 104
CES production function 8, 142–144,
    157
CGE (general computable
    equilibrium) model 6, 60–61, 253
Charndoevit 226
Chen 16
Chiang-Mai Initiative 2, 11, 30, 57
Chinloy 127–128
Chirathivat 94, 99
Chow's breakpoint test 152
Chow's forecast test 152
Chuan Government 216, 219
Chuang 281
Chulalongkorn and Monash General
    Equilibrium (CAMGEM) Project
    98
Clark 126
CMLV 81, 85–86
Cobb-Douglas production 152
Cobb-Douglas-type of production
    function 143
Cold War 83
Community Organization
    Development Institute (CODI)
    216
community-level initiative 223
comparative advantage 161
complementary effects 8, 128
Comprehensive Economic
    Cooperation Agreement (CECA)
    92
Comprehensive Economic
    Partnerships (CEPs) 6, 82, 88–89,
    100–101, 105
constant returns to scale 129, 143

consumer price index 236
Contractionary Effects of
Devaluation 250
Cook 193, 202
Cooper 12, 54, 92, 105, 157, 219, 252
cost-push inflation 270
Council of Economic Advisors 234
Country Policy and Institutional
Assessment (CPIA) index
283–284, 286, 288
credit crunch 232, 244
Credit Market 180
credit view 232
cross-border M&A 278
currency depreciation 10, 20, 23, 34,
249–250, 253–261, 265–267, 272

da Silva 234, 245
de Gregorio 280
Debt Suspension for Small–scale
Farmers Program 224
debt-deflation process 272
debt-dependency 231
decomposition 126, 131–133, 136,
265
depreciation 166
devaluation 12, 249–251, 253,
255–256, 258–259, 261, 263–266,
271–272
Diaz-Alejandro 251
Ding 233, 235
Djankov 280
Dobson 64
Doi Moi policy 160
Domac 233, 235
domestic absorption 253–254, 256,
261
double cropping of rice 161, 166–167,
171, 173, 175, 186
Drabek 283

dual track economic development
strategy 14, 29

East Asian Free Trade Area (EAFTA)
82, 93, 95
East Asian Miracle 15, 34, 231
Economic Business Group Fund 208
economic integration 1–2, 5–6, 30,
39–40, 54, 62, 81–82, 88–89,
201–202
Economic Partnership Agreements
(EPAs) 2–3, 5, 7, 57–58, 61, 91,
105
Edwards 253
EE sector 151
efficiency-seeking type 53
Eichengreen 265
elasticity of substitution 153
electrical and electronics (sector) 141,
145, 155
electronic components industries 145
Elek 100
Engle-Granger procedure 151
Enterprise Stabilization Guarantee
Fund (ESGF) 208
environmental protection 222
Enya 11, 231
ESCAP 10, 194, 197–198, 202, 205,
225
EU 1, 5, 42–43, 47–50, 57–58, 60,
62–63, 81, 93–94, 101, 105, 119
European Economic Community
(EEC) 62
Euro Zone 31
excess capacity 8, 23, 25, 146,
148–149, 155
exchange rate overvaluation 249
export competitiveness 28, 34, 141
export-oriented manufacturing sector
141

factor substitution 142–144, 151–152, 156
Fernandez-Arias 291
Ferri 233, 235
Fifth Letter of Intent 217
financial intermediation 231
fiscal balance 35, 165
fiscal deficit 165
Fisher 255
Food and Agriculture Organization (FAO) 223
food safety standard 5
Food-for-Work scheme 204
Ford Foundation 209
foreign affiliate 44, 53, 289
foreign borrowing 1, 10, 254–257, 259–260, 262, 269, 271
foreign borrowing ratio 257
foreign direct investment (FDI) 1–3, 12, 17, 19–20, 24, 26, 29, 31–32, 40, 42–47, 49–50, 52, 54–61, 64, 79, 83–84, 87–88, 99, 102–104, 109, 111–112, 119, 124, 148, 162, 201, 275–276, 278–291
FDI flow 40
FDI liberalization 59–60
Fosgerau 131
Frankel 46, 92
Free Trade Agreements (FTAs) 2–6, 15, 30, 32, 34, 39–40, 54–63, 77, 85, 91–92, 95, 98–100, 105
bilateral FTAs 3–4, 30, 32, 55, 92, 95, 99
Frey 290
Fujita 9, 160, 190

garden (*uyin hcan*) 170
GATS 87
GATS-plus 86
GATT commitment 59

GATT/WTO 39, 46, 56–57, 62, 64, 80, *see also* World Trade Organization (WTO)
General Agreement on Trade in Services (GATS) 86
Gertler 232, 260
Ghosh 233, 236, 239
Gilchrist 260
Gillion 194
globalization 39
Government Service Insurance System 204
Government Service System (GSIS) 208
Grassroots Economic Policy and Safety Nets 224
Great Depression 169
Green Revolution 161
Group of Seven countries (G7) 283, 285
GTAP 98
Guarantee Fund for Small and Medium Enterprises (GFSME) 208

Hanoi Action Plan 104
Hardcore-Poverty Development Program 208
Hashimoto 128
Hausmann 264–265, 291
Hiemenz 110
high performance economies (HPEs) 15
High Yielding Varieties (HYVs) 166, 168
high-interest rate policy 232
Hirschman 251
HIV/AIDs prevention and treatment 222
Ho 128

Hobday 154
Hoekman 280, 283
Hoffman 152, 157
human capital 150, 156
human capital model 127

ICRG index 286
ILO 194, 198–200, 210–212, 225
ILO Social Security Standard
    (Minimum Standards)
    Convention 199
Imamura 128
International Monetary Fund (IMF)
    9–11, 21, 84, 193, 207, 216–217,
    221–222, 225, 232, 264, 272, 290
IMF bailout package 264
IMF conditionality 264
IMF-3 21
IMF-3 countries 21
IMF-3 economies 24
industrial integration 3
industrial production index 236, 238
industrialization 15–17, 19, 26, 31, 49,
    83, 141
informal credit 181
informal credit market 180
Initiative for ASEAN Integration
    (IAI) 81
Institute of Strategic and
    International Studies (ISIS) 5
institution-driven 39–40
inter-industry relationship 50–52
inter-industry specialization 7, 110,
    114, 118
inter-industry trade 110
International Country Risk Guide
    (ICRG) 12, 284, 286, 288, 291
international division of labor 3
international input–output table 50
intra-ASEAN trade 84, 94, 104

intra-industry specialization 7, 116,
    118, 121
intra-industry trade 110, 114
intra-regional dependence 46, 50–52
intra-regional trade 9, 18, 20, 27, 30,
    46–50, 52, 83, 87, 94
intra-regional trade interdependence
    54
Investment Incentives Act 1968 141
investment-savings gap 261, 263
Ito 234, 236, 245

Japanese multinationals 53
Jarque-Bera statistics 151
JBIC 219
Jimanez 194
Jorgenson 128, 142–143
JSEPA 55
Jurado 198, 202, 205

Kabeer 193, 202
Kaminsky 247
Kawai 64, 148
Khor 152, 157
Kim 234, 239
Kiyota 60–61
Klingebiel 247
Knowles 202–203
Kohsaka 11, 231
Koike 128
Kokko 280
Krueger 100
Krugman 7, 116, 142, 251, 264, 272

labor cost-output ratio 146
labor productivity 8, 127–128,
    130–131, 134, 136–138, 142,
    145–146, 155
labor productivity growth 128
Labor Protection Act 218

Laborers' Fund 212
labor-intensive method 153
labor-saving production technology
    154
Lai 8, 141, 154, 220
land tenure system 161
Langhammer 92, 110
Lazear 128
LDCs 83
Lee 280
lender of last resort 11
liberalization 201
liberalized capital account 14, 25
Lichtenberg 126
life-cycle 195
Lin 281
linear homogeneity 143
liquidity constraint 289
Lizondo 265
Lloyd 95, 98
Look-East Policy 91
low cost labor 27
low–wage labor 53

M1 208, 262–263
M2 22, 208, 262–263
Magendzo 265
Mahani 4, 14
Maisom 152, 157
Majumder 281
Malaysia Industrial Code 144
Mallikamas 98
Manila framework 30
Market Share Analysis 119
market size 282
market-driven 1, 30, 39–40, 81
market-seeking type 53
Mercosur 47, 93
mergers and acquisitions (M&A) 43,
    278, 289

Ministry of Labor (MOL) 212
Ministry of Labor and Social Welfare
    209, 220, 226
Ministry of Public Health (MPH) 212
Mishkin 258, 261
Mody 281, 290
Monetary Authority of Singapore
    (MAS) 270
monopoly 22, 161
Montiel 253, 265
Moosa 283
Most Favored Nation (MFN) tariff
    rate 116
multinational company (MNC)
    26–27, 29, 46, 118–119, 121, 147,
    156
multinationals 43–44, 48, 52–54, 275,
    283–284
Myanmar Agricultural Development
    Bank (MADB) 180, 190
Myanmar Agricultural Produce
    Trading (MAPT) 174, 187–188,
    190
Myanmar Agricultural Service
    (MAS) 170
Myanmar Rice Trading Leading
    Committee (MRTLC) 181, 185,
    188

Narayanan 154
National Economic Summit (NES)
    209
National Productivity Corporation
    148
National Social Policy Committee
    (NSPC) 216, 226
Negishi 12, 275
neo-classical production function 143
NESDB 210–211, 216, 224, 227
new development paradigm 15, 33

new economic development paradigm
14, 29
New Entrepreneur Promotion
Program 224
new regionalism 1–3, 5–6, 15, 30, 32,
95, 98–99
Newey-West procedure 152, 157
Newin regime 162
Ng 16
NGOs 215, 217
NIE-4 41, 47–48
NIEs 15, 49, 57–58, 64, 83, 87
Nikhomborirak 87
Noland 253
Non Performing Loan (NPL) 20, 236
North American Free Trade Area
(NAFTA) 1, 5, 47–50, 57, 93

ODA 167
OECF 218–220
Ogawa 213–214
Oguchi 149
Ohno 16
One Tambon One Product (OTOP)
Program 224
Okamoto 6–7, 95, 109, 116, 124, 149,
189
openness 201, 283
Orapin 223
Overseas Economic Cooperation
Fund of Japan 219

paddy field (le) 169–170, 181, 185,
187–188
Paitoonpong 10, 193, 207
palm land (dani hcan) 170
Panagariya 100
Panizza 264
Pattana Thai Foundation 223
Payne 283

Pearce 290
PECC 44
pegged exchange rate 1
People's Bank Program 224
perfect competition 143, 157
Pernia 202–203
Petri 46, 49, 92
physical and human infrastructure
281
picking winners 16
planned (compulsory) cropping 162,
169, 181, 185, 187–188
Pobre 11, 231
Porter 283
preferential trade arrangements
(PTAs) 82, 84, 94–95, 98, 101
productivity 3, 7–9, 12, 26–27, 31,
116, 126–128, 133, 136–138,
141–142, 146–147, 154–155, 157,
201, 209, 278, 280–281, 289
productivity growth 201
Puay Ungpakorn 215
Public Economic Welfare Fund 212
Public Employment Service Office
(PESO) 208

quality contribution 126–127, 131,
133, 137
quality decomposition by age and
education 136

Racelis 202–203
Raisan 128
Rajan 92, 95
Ravenhill 97, 99
Reddy 195–197
regional integration 4, 8–9, 27–28, 30,
34, 52, 64, 87, 89, 94–95, 110
regional trade agreements (RTAs) 39,
54, 64, 80, 98–100

regional trade integration 8
Regional Urban Development Fund
    220
Rehabilitation the Disable Fund 212
Reinhalt 247
research and development (R&D) 156
Research Institute of Economy, Trade
    and Industry (RIETI) 6
reserve–requirement 270
revealed comparative advantage
    (RCA) 110, 113–115, 118, 124
Rice Double Cropping 171
Rodrik 16
Root 290
rules-of-origin 3, 5
Rutngamlug 88

Sachs 35
safety nets 195, 201, *see also* social
    safety nets (SSNs)
  formal safety nets 210
  informal (social) safety nets 197,
    209, 213
Saggi 283
saving rate 163
Schive 281
Schneider 290
Scollay 100
self-sufficiency 187
semiconductor 141, 145–146, 149
semiconductor and components
    industries 146
serial correlation 152
Shandre 7–8, 126
short-term capital inflow 270
silver worker 7
skilled human resource 156
skilled labor 8, 18, 101, 109, 143, 147,
    153, 156

skilled worker 19, 53
skin-deep industrialization 26
SLORC/SPDC 161–162, 167
small and medium enterprise
    development 222
small and medium-scale enterprise
    (SME) 28–29, 63, 224
Small Projects Fund 223
Small–Scale Entrepreneur Fund 208
Social Investment Fund 204, 220,
    223, 226
Social Investment Project 217
Social Policy Committee (SPC) 223
Social Research Institute 214
social safety nets (SSNs) 9–10, 193–
    198, 200–203, 205–207, 209–210,
    213, 216, 223–226
Social Sector Loan 218
Social Sector Program Loan (SSPL)
    209, 219–220
Social Security Fund 218
Social Security System (SSS) 208
Sothitorn 114, 124
sources of growth 155
Spearman's Rank Correlation
    Coefficient 118, 120, 122–123
Special Scheme for Low Cost
    Housing 208
speculation 20, 255
Spence 283
Spengler 126
state control 162
state economic enterprises (SEEs)
    162, 165
state intervention 14, 16
statutory reserve-requirement (SRR)
    22, 35
statutory social insurance 210
Stein 264

Stephenson 87
sterilization 270
stock market 20, 25, 27, 33, 263
substitution elasticity 154, 156
Summer Paddy Program 161, 166–167,
    173, 181, 186–187
sustainable economic development 162
Suthiphand 6, 81, 114, 124
Suwannarat 193, 202
swap arrangement 30, 57

Tan 152, 157
Tansini 280
Taylor 251, 264, 272
technical progress, 141, 153, *see also*
    technological progress
technological progress 152
tertiary education 133–134
total factor productivity (TFP) 129,
    137, 142–143, 148–151, 155
TFP growth 149–150, 155–156
Thailand Development Research
    Institute (TDRI) 10, 202, 206,
    211, 215, 217, 222, 226
Thailand-United Nations
    Collaborative Action Plan
    (Thai–UNCAP) 223
Tham 148–149
Thangavelu 8, 136
The Nation 224
Thirty Baht for Any Sickness Program
    224
Thomas 148
trade deficit 163
trade liberalization 39, 63
trade-oriented policy 9
treasury bills (TB) 165

Ueda 236

UNICEF 223
Unit Labor Cost 143, 146
United Nations 43
United Nations Conference on Trade
    and Development (UNCTAD) 87,
    103, 105, 112–113, 195, 282–283,
    290
United Nations Development
    Program (UNDP) 154, 219, 223
Upadhyaya 264
Urata 6, 39, 45, 60–61, 64, 92
US multinationals 54

Vector Auto Regressive (VAR) model
    12, 251, 264–265
Village Fund Program 224
Viner 98
Vision Group 56
Vivian 194

Wade 16
Wang 109–110, 148, 192, 281
Washington Consensus model 15
Wei 192, 283
well-educated human resources 27
Wheeler 290
Whole Township Special Rice
    Production Program 167
Wickramasekara 194, 200, 225
Women's Occupational Promotion
    Fund 212
Wong 16, 150
Wonnacott 99
working capital 180
Workmen Compensation Fund 210
World Bank 9, 12, 15–16, 34, 43, 111,
    148, 193–197, 200–201, 203, 207,
    209, 214, 216, 218–220, 222–223,
    225–226, 278–281, 283–286, 290

World Trade Organization(WTO) 2,
    5–7, 30, 32, 39, 46, 55–58, 62–64,
    80, 82, 91, 93, 95, 101, 116, 121,
    289
  WTO membership 32
  WTO process 82
  WTO-plus 93, 101

Yamazawa 45, 93
Ying 234, 239
Yong 89
Yusuf 95

Zejan 280